Making Peace in Drug Wars

Over the past thirty years, a new form of conflict has ravaged Latin America's largest countries, with well-armed drug cartels fighting not only one another but the state itself. In Colombia, Mexico, and Brazil, leaders cracked down on cartels in hopes of restoring the rule of law and the state's monopoly on force. Instead, cartels fought back—with bullets and bribes—driving spirals of violence and corruption that make mockeries of leaders' state-building aims. Fortunately, some policy reforms quickly curtailed cartel–state conflict, but they proved tragically difficult to sustain.

Why do cartels fight states, if not to topple or secede from them? Why do some state crackdowns trigger and exacerbate cartel–state conflict, while others curb it? This study argues that brute-force repression generates incentives for cartels to fight back, while policies that condition repression on cartel violence can effectively deter cartel–state conflict. The politics of drug war, however, make conditional policies all too fragile.

Benjamin Lessing studies criminal conflict—organized armed violence involving non-state actors who do not seek formal state power. Prior to his graduate work at UC Berkeley, Lessing lived in Rio de Janeiro for four years, conducting field research on arms trafficking in Latin America and the Caribbean for non-governmental organizations including Amnesty International, Oxfam, and Viva Rio, Brazil's largest NGO.

Cambridge Studies in Comparative Politics

General Editor

Kathleen Thelen *Massachusetts Institute of Technology*
Erik Wibbels *Duke University*

Associate Editors

Catherine Boone *London School of Economics*
Thad Dunning *University of California, Berkeley*
Anna Grzymala-Busse *Stanford University*
Torben Iversen *Harvard University*
Stathis Kalyvas *Yale University*
Margaret Levi *Stanford University*
Helen Milner *Princeton University*
Frances Rosenbluth *Yale University*
Susan Stokes *Yale University*
Tariq Thachil *Vanderbilt University*

Series Founder

Peter Lange *Duke University*

Other Books in the Series

Christopher Adolph, *Bankers, Bureaucrats, and Central Bank Politics: The Myth of Neutrality*
Michael Albertus, *Autocracy and Redistribution: The Politics of Land Reform*
Ben W. Ansell, *From the Ballot to the Blackboard: The Redistributive Political Economy of Education*
Ben W. Ansell, David J. Samuels, *Inequality and Democratization: An Elite-Competition Approach*
Leonardo R. Arriola, *Multi-Ethnic Coalitions in Africa: Business Financing of Opposition Election Campaigns*
David Austen-Smith, Jeffry A. Frieden, Miriam A. Golden, Karl Ove Moene, and Adam Przeworski, eds., *Selected Works of Michael Wallerstein: The Political Economy of Inequality, Unions, and Social Democracy*
Andy Baker, *The Market and the Masses in Latin America: Policy Reform and Consumption in Liberalizing Economies*

[continued after Index]

Making Peace in Drug Wars

Crackdowns and Cartels in Latin America

BENJAMIN LESSING

University of Chicago

CAMBRIDGE
UNIVERSITY PRESS

CAMBRIDGE
UNIVERSITY PRESS

University Printing House, Cambridge CB2 8BS, United Kingdom

One Liberty Plaza, 20th Floor, New York, NY 10006, USA

477 Williamstown Road, Port Melbourne, VIC 3207, Australia

314-321, 3rd Floor, Plot 3, Splendor Forum, Jasola District Centre, New Delhi - 110025, India

79 Anson Road, #06-04/06, Singapore 079906

Cambridge University Press is part of the University of Cambridge.

It furthers the University's mission by disseminating knowledge in the pursuit of education, learning and research at the highest international levels of excellence.

www.cambridge.org
Information on this title: www.cambridge.org/9781107199637
DOI: 10.1017/9781108185837

© Benjamin Lessing 2018

First published 2018

A catalogue record for this publication is available from the British Library

Library of Congress Cataloging in Publication data
Names: Lessing, Benjamin, author.
Title: Making peace in drug wars : crackdowns and cartels in
Latin America / Benjamin Lessing, University of Chicago.
Description: Cambridge, United Kingdom ; New York, NY : Cambridge University Press, 2017. |
Includes bibliographical references and index.
Identifiers: LCCN 2017033487 | ISBN 9781107199637 (hardback : alk. paper)
Subjects: LCSH: Drug control–Latin America. | Drug traffic–Latin America. |
Insurgency–Latin America. | Violence–Latin America.
Classification: LCC HV5840.L3 L47 2017 | DDC 364.1/3365098–dc23
LC record available at https://lccn.loc.gov/2017033487

ISBN 978-1-107-19963-7 Hardback
ISBN 978-1-316-64896-4 Paperback

To my parents, for this life.

To Andy Kotowicz, for the music.

Contents

Figures

Tables

Preface

Complexo da Maré, Rio de Janeiro, August 17, 2016

The first pages of a book like this are usually the last ones written, so it feels right to start (and end) it here in Maré. My earliest visits to this sprawling collection of *favelas* (slums) in 2003 opened my eyes to the absurdity of Rio's drug war, with its home-grown drug syndicates locked in a decades-long militarized conflict with brutal and corrupt police. It was here, talking with locals, that I began to understand the intertwined dynamics of violence and bribery driving and sustaining this conflict. It was here that I saw first-hand the capacity of enlightened state policy to radically transform those dynamics, mostly for the better. And it is here that I now see the tragic fragility of such policies and the terrifying resilience of this conflict.

Rio's residents have been cynically predicting for years that the "Pacification" strategy—a novel approach to policing that, since its rollout in 2008, vastly curtailed violence while re-establishing state control in some 200 favelas—would be dismantled once the 2016 Olympics ended. As I write, the Olympic flame is still burning, and many of the city's largest favelas are still Pacified, but here in Maré, the end of Pacification is in plain view. As we turn off Avenida Brasil at the entrance to the Nova Holanda neighborhood, gone is the army soldier who stood guard on my previous visit in 2015; in his place stands a teenager holding an AR-15 automatic rifle almost as long as he is tall, next to a makeshift barrier made from scrap I-beams. He looks us over through the windows we perfunctorily roll down, then waves us on with the barrel of his weapon. When our car cannot fit between the I-beams, he shouts and some nearby kids come and clear a path for us. A few blocks down the bustling street, on a busy corner, more armed youths stand around a large table stacked with small packages labeled "Crack Nova Holanda, $2."

Except for the crack—drug syndicates used to prohibit its sale but eventually gave up—and the nifty new printed labels, the scene is indistinguishable from my earliest visits to Maré. The lines demarcating gang turf might be invisible and the codes of behavior unspoken, but the openly armed presence of the traffickers leaves no doubt as to who holds the local monopoly on the use of force. Indeed, more shocking than the age of the traffickers or the sophistication of their operation is the fact that their presence is—for residents—unremarkable. Open-air drug markets are simply part of the landscape; nearby street stalls sell produce and cell phone accessories, while patrons of neighboring bars and beauty salons shoot the breeze. True, a house has collapsed from gunfire during a shootout with police the night before, and the cleanup efforts are creating a hopeless traffic jam on the narrow street. But this too echoes the dynamics of the past: the favela is at its most dangerous when the police enter it.

The same could have been said of most of Rio's nearly 1,000 favelas, from the mid-1980s until as recently as 2007. Then, Pacification changed everything. Surprise police incursions aimed at arresting or killing as many traffickers as possible were replaced with pre-announced occupations and, eventually, a permanent "Pacifying Police Unit" (UPP) trained to respect residents' rights. Traffickers learned to give up their turf peacefully, some fleeing to other favelas, some staying to carry on the drug trade on new terms imposed by the state: no public selling and no use of firearms. To even the skeptics' surprise, the largest and most heavily armed favelas in Rio—places dominated by drug syndicates for more than a generation—were quickly and often bloodlessly Pacified within a few years.

Maré's turn came late: occupation by army troops—the first step of the Pacification process—was finally announced in March 2013. I visited a few days before the occupation, at the urging of a friend who runs an NGO here: "You are not going to believe it." The traffickers were all gone. The street-corner tables were abandoned, the checkpoints too. "The traffickers were running around yesterday, loading up kombis with arms and whatnot. Then they all split," one resident told me. Such was the reputation of the Pacification program that Maré was Pacified without firing a shot, without, incredibly, even being occupied. That evening, as we drove through the usually heavily armed dividing line between two syndicates' turf, we turned off our headlights and rolled down our windows as always, but nobody was there to scope us out and wave us through. It was eerie.

Soon the army took up its posts, but the promised UPP unit never materialized to relieve them. For the next year and a half, Maré was in limbo, occupied by troops that the army had grudgingly agreed would stay at least until the 2014 World Cup. On a visit in 2015, the strategic points of entry and exit were still guarded by uniformed soldiers, looking understandably bewildered. These young men from across Brazil, many from the rural interior, had shown up for mandatory military service and inexplicably been sent to conduct something akin to counterinsurgency in a dense mega-slum on the periphery of their country's most famous city. They were neither eager nor equipped to actively fight the drug trade, and a strange cohabitational arrangement coalesced, with traffickers moving off into the narrow streets where army vehicles could not go. A filmmaker friend who shot a documentary in Maré during this period told me that every day, her team would first get approval from the local army commander, then from the local drug boss.

The army announced its impending departure from Maré in 2015. The state government, facing severe resource constraints and rising crime in middle-class, non-favela neighborhoods, canceled the Maré UPP. Instead, policing practice reverted to its old ways: occasional incursions by heavily armed patrols, based outside the favela. Before long, the traffickers were back in control.

Life in Maré goes on, and not all for the worse: new schools have opened; my friend's NGO has expanded, inaugurating a branch in the rival gang's turf; citizen groups have continued to become more vocal about police abuses and politicians' broken promises, to some real effect. But as we drive out of Maré tonight, past the new generation of heavily armed teenagers in flip-flops patrolling both sides of the turf line, it is hard not to fear for the post-Olympic future of this city.

"Maré" means "tide" in Portuguese, fitting for a place that stands as Pacification's high water mark. Pacification came this far and no farther; how far it will now recede remains unclear. Traffickers have returned to attacking state forces in the larger favelas, making a mockery of the very term "Pacification"; public support has dwindled; and the strategy's formulator is retiring. Amidst Brazil's political crises and Rio's post-Olympics budget shortfalls, it is easy to imagine the entire program collapsing. Skeptics had long predicted this; to them, Pacification epitomized the old Portuguese expression *para inglês ver*—"for the English to see"[1]—creating Potemkin favelas for the media, NGOs, and most of all international visitors, that would inevitably crumble once the eyes of the world were off Rio.

The skeptics are wrong; Pacification was and remains more than a façade. The policy significantly curtailed a costly and murderous urban drug war, and has gone further than any predecessor in bringing some semblance of normalcy and rule of law to the city's more than one million slum residents. Pacification's advances are real, not least because they have shown what is possible. Its current malaise flows from the profoundly vexed politics of drug war, offering an opportunity to learn and, one hopes, help make the next reform more resilient.

To explain why Pacification initially succeeded where thirty years of crackdowns failed, yet soon stalled and now faces potential rollback, this book delves into the interplay among policymakers, police, and cartels. It takes a comparative approach, looking beyond Maré and Rio to other cities, countries,

---

[1]   The expression apparently dates back to England's imposition of anti-slavery laws on the Portuguese empire in the early nineteenth century. In 1831, Brazil signed a law freeing its slaves, but it was just "for the English to see," and slavery continued in practice until 1888.

and time periods. While Rio's conflict was abating, cartel violence in Mexico escalated almost beyond belief, eclipsing even Colombia's harrowing drug war throughout the 1980s. These conflicts have all proven incredibly destructive and impossible to solve through force alone. Policies like Pacification, however imperfect and hard to sustain, offer real hope.

In the pages to come, I analyze these conflicts using the tools and language of contemporary political science; I develop concepts, defend claims, and draw conclusions. But readers should not let the image of life in Maré, and the fundamental perversity of this conflict, out of sight. Millions of citizens, often the most vulnerable among us, live in the crossfire of an endless war whose original purpose—protecting people from the effects of certain drugs—seems lost in the ashes. We can, we must, do better.

Acknowledgments

No part of this book has seemed more daunting to write than this section. There is simply no way to fully express my gratitude for the support, guidance, and friendship I have received from so many brilliant and brave people, over such great spans of time and space. Singling out a few of them is a deeply imperfect but inevitable solution. Here goes:

First and foremost, my family and loved ones, who have stood by with patience and encouragement.

Second but equally foremost, my teachers, commentators, colleagues, and peers. This book began as a doctoral dissertation, and I owe a very special debt of gratitude to my advisors at UC Berkeley, David Collier, Robert Powell, Ruth Berins Collier, and Peter Evans, four titans of scholarship who taught me—by example—not only how to do great research but how to remain human while doing it. To their great credit, they swallowed whatever reservations they had about a "dissertation on gangs" and helped me find the path forward. At Berkeley, I also had the privilege to work with and learn from Paul Pierson, Sean Gailmard, Henry Brady, Jas Sekhon, Ted Miguel, Harley Shaiken, and many others. In addition, I benefited enormously from a postdoctoral fellowship at Stanford University's Center for International Security and Cooperation and Center on Democracy, Development, and the Rule of Law, where I had the shockingly good fortune to be assigned both Jim Fearon and David Laitin as mentors, and many fruitful interactions with Larry Diamond, Frank Fukuyama, Beatriz Magaloni, Martha Crenshaw, and Anne Clunan, among many others.

To my surprise, my education did not end with my appointment at the University of Chicago; on the contrary, my colleagues' dogged intellectual energy has made my time here as important to my development as a scholar and a writer as my years at Berkeley. I especially thank Lisa Wedeen, Dan Slater, Paul Staniland, John Meirscheimer, Bob Pape, Mike Albertus, Monika Nalepa, Dali Yang, Gary Herrigel, Alberto Simpser, John Patty, Maggie Penn, and Tianna Paschel. Beyond my home department, Brodwyn Fischer, Ethan Bueno de Mesquita, Mauricio Tenorio, Jim Robinson, Emilio Kourí, Chris Blattman, and Oeindrila Dube have all been critical interlocutors. I benefited enormously from a book conference, generously supported by the political science department, the Center for Latin American Studies, and the Urban Institute, with the central participation of Deborah Yashar, Will Reno, Ana Arjona, Jim Fearon, Beatriz Magaloni, and Brodwyn Fischer, as well as many other faculty and graduate students. Sana Jaffrey and Yuna Blajer de la Garza provided critical research assistance and support.

I am equally grateful to a host of scholars and writers who have offered me invaluable feedback and encouragement along the way. A short list includes: Alba Zaluar, Alma Guillermoprieto, Andreas Schedler, Angelica Durán-Martínez, Claudio Ferraz, Daniel Hidalgo, Daniel Mejía, Desmond Arias, Eli Berman, Ernesto Dal Bó, Guillermo Trejo, Gustavo Duncan, Jake Shapiro, Jorge Giraldo, Justin McCrary, Liz Leeds, Luis Astorga, Marcelo Bergman, Mark Kleiman, Michel Misse, Paul Gootenberg, Peter Andreas, Peter Reuter, Phillip Cook, Rafael Di Tella, Rich Snyder, Sebastián Mazzuca, Shannon O'Neil, Simeon Nichter, Stathis Kalyvas, Stergios Skaperdas, Steve Levitsky, Steven Dudley, Suresh Naidu, Vanda Felbab-Brown, and Viridiana Rios.

The manuscript was vastly improved thanks to the careful editing and thoughtful suggestions of Maria Gould and Zoe Mendelson, and graphic design advice from Michael Yap. Douglas Engle (douglasengle@gmail.com), veteran chronicler of Rio's drug war, provided the cover photo. Some material is drawn from Lessing, Benjamin. 2015, "Logics of Violence in Criminal War." *Journal of Conflict Resolution* 59 (8): 1486–1516, DOI: 10.1177/0022002715587100.

I also want to acknowledge the generous institutional support I have received from the Open Society Institute (special thanks to David Holiday), Centro Andino de Fomento-CAF (special thanks to Daniel Ortega), the National Science Foundation, the Social Science Research Council, the Harry Frank Guggenheim Foundation, the Smith Richardson Foundation, the UC MEXUS foundation, and, at Chicago, the Neubauer Collegium, the Division of Social Sciences and the Department of Political Science. It simply would have been impossible to complete this study without support from so many generous sources.

This book is, in part, the fruit of many months and years spent living in Brazil, Colombia, and Mexico. There are a host of dear friends and gracious souls without whom my life would have been miserable and quite possibly brutish. I mention a few here, and apologize to the many I have left out.

In Colombia: Alejandro López, the late Álvaro Camacho, Ana María Ibáñez Londoño, Andres Zambrano, Angelica Quintero, Anita Hoyos, Daniel Coronel, Diana Hoyos, Francisco Leal Buitrago, Jorge Restrepo, and Manuel Hoyos. In Mexico: Alejandro Poiré, Andrea Gamero, Beatriz Llamusí, Carlos

Vilalta, Esther Grynberg, Guy Cheney, <Gyborg>, Lisa María Sanchez, Malgorzata Polanska, Miguelito Hennessey and Alejandra Díaz, Pablo Garcia, Raul Benítez, Sandra Ley, Sofía Ramírez, and–quite unexpectedly–Zoe Mendelson.

In Brazil: Luke Dowdney, Adriana Perusin, André Rodrigues, Bete and Lucas Formaggini, Brígida Renoldi, Bruno Paes Manso, Chris Vital, Def Yuri, Flora Charner, Gueddes, Ilona Svabo de Carvalho and Rob Muggah, Ignacio Cano, Ivan Figueira, Kelly Hayes, Jessica Rich, the late Jim Shyne, Joana Monteiro, João Trajano Santo-Sé, José Júnior, Luciana Costa, Ludmilla Curi, Maga Bo, Esther and the late Moisés Kestenberg, Patricia Motta, Paula Miraglia, Pedro Strozenberg, Rangel Antônio Bandeira, Rodrigo Duarte, Rubem César Fernandes, Tatiana Amoretty, Tatiana Guinle, Tom Phillips, and Thays Martins.

The same goes for my friends and family in the United States: Aaron Lessing; Alex Theodoridis; the late Andy Kotowicz; At and Bonnie Lessing; Avi, Bindi, Raiva, and Rafi Desai Lessing; David Klagsbrun; Eric Rosenblum; Jay Desai; Jocelyn Boyea, Joshua Lessing; Lee Traband; Mike, Emily, and the late Judy Chiariello; Natasha Manley; Neil Shah; Paul Campbell; Rebecca Feldman and Jay Reiss; and Yunus Dogan Telliel.

I've dedicated this book to my parents, but I owe almost as much to my brilliant sister, Shana Lessing. She has stood by me, challenged me, made me a better person, and helped keep me sane all these years. Bringing my nephew Kadir into the world is, as one of her students might put it, the cherry on top that ties it all together.

Abbreviations and Acronyms

ADA	Amigos dos Amigos [Friends of Friends drug syndicate] (Rio de Janeiro)
AR	Auto de resistência ["Act of resistance", term for police killings of civilians] (Rio de Janeiro)
AUC	Autodefensas Unidas de Colombia [United Self-Defense Forces of Colombia, paramilitary group] (Colombia)
BOPE	Batalhão de Operações Policiais Especiais [Police Special Operations Battalion] (Rio de Janeiro)
CIA	Central Intelligence Agency (United States)
CISEN	Centro de Investigación y Seguridad Nacional [Center for Research and National Security] (Mexico)
CV	Comando Vermelho, *alias* Falange Vermelha [Red Command drug syndicate] (Rio de Janeiro)
DAS	Departamento Administrativo de Seguridad [Administrative Department of Security] (Colombia)
DEA	Drug Enforcement Agency (United States)
DFS	Dirección Federal de Seguridad [Federal Security Directorate] (Mexico)
DTO	Drug trafficking organization
La Familia	La Familia Michoacana [The Michoacán Family Cartel] (Mexico)
FARC	Fuerzas Armadas Revolucionarias de Colombia [Revolutionary Armed Forces of Colombia, rebel group] (Colombia)
FBI	Federal Bureau of Investigation (United States)
GAFES	Grupo Aeromóvil de Fuerzas Especiales [Special-Forces Airmobile Group] (Mexico)

GPAE	Grupamento de Policiamento em Áreas Especiais [Policing in Special Areas Unit] (Rio de Janeiro)
LSN	Lei de Segurança Nacional [National Security Law] (Rio. de Janeiro)
M-19	Movimiento 19 de Abril [19th of April Movement, rebel group] (Colombia)
MAS	Muerte a Secuestradores [Death to Kidnappers, militant group] (Colombia)
NSA	Non-state actor
NRI/OBIVAN	Observatorio Internacional de Violencia Asociada a Narcotráfico [Narcoviolence Research International]
PAN	Partido Acción Nacional [National Action Party] (Mexico)
PC	Policía Civil [Civil Police] (Rio de Janeiro)
PCC	Primeiro Comando da Capital [First Command of the Capital prison gang] (Rio de Janeiro)
PDT	Partido Democrático Trabalhista [Democratic Labor Party] (Rio de Janeiro)
Los Pepes	Personas Perseguidos por Pablo Escobar [Persons Persecuted by Pablo Escobar, armed group] (Colombia)
PF	Polícia Federal [Federal Police] (Rio de Janeiro)
PGJ	Procuraduría General de Justicia de la Ciudad de México [Office of the Attorney General of Mexico City] (Mexico)
PGR	Procuraduría General de la República [Office of the Attorney General] (Mexico)
PM	Polícia Militar [Military Police] (Rio de Janeiro)
PMDB	Partido do Movimento Democrático Brasileiro [Party of the Brazilian Democratic Movement] (Rio de Janeiro)
PRD	Partido de la Revolución Democrático [Party of the Democratic Revolution] (Mexico)
PSDB	Partido da Social Democracia Brasileira [Brazilian Social Democratic Party] (Rio de Janeiro)
PRI	Partido Revolucionario Institutional [Institutional Revolutionary Party] (Mexico)
PT	Partido dos Trabalhadores [Workers' Party] (Rio de Janeiro)
Sometimiento	Sometimiento a la justicia [Voluntary submission to justice, government policy] (Colombia)
SSP	Secretaría de Seguridad Pública [Public Security Secretariat] (Mexico)
UPP	Unidade de Polícia Pacificadora [Pacifying Police Unit] (Rio de Janeiro)

1

Introduction

1.1 THE PUZZLE OF CARTEL–STATE CONFLICT

In December 2006, just ten days after his inauguration, Mexican President Felipe
Calderón launched a "battle with no quarter" against his country's drug cartels,
involving the largest non-humanitarian deployment of Mexico's army in modern
times. Calderón's crackdown did not start Mexico's drug war—cartel-related
killings had doubled under the previous administration—but it would, he hoped,
end it. Whatever political calculations informed his decision, and there were
many, Calderón clearly believed that a militarized crackdown would *work*: that it
would reverse rising drug violence, cripple the cartels, exorcise the thoroughgoing
corruption that had reigned for decades, and restore public order and the rule of
law. It did none of these things.

If trafficking and corruption continued predictably apace over Calderón's
six-year term, violence exploded unimaginably. Not even the most vocal critics
of his strategy anticipated that the conflict would *escalate* by an order of
magnitude, claiming a staggering 70,000 lives by 2012. Moreover, though the
lion's share of these killings were among traffickers, Calderón's tenure saw
an equally sharp and unexpected eruption of cartel–state violence. Traffickers
invaded police stations, assassinated mayors, blockaded cities, and publicly
called on Calderón to withdraw federal troops. Cartel attacks on army troops,
once unheard of, became everyday occurrences. Such brazen armed defiance
undermined government claims that traffickers were merely exterminating
one another, and deepened the sense of crisis and loss of state control that
Calderón's crackdown was meant to allay. More than a decade later, cartels'
armed resistance continues.

Mexico is not the only place where militarized crackdowns[1] on cartels led to
unexpected anti-state violence. In 1984, Colombian Justice Minister Rodrigo

---

[1] Throughout, I define "crackdowns" to mean increases in the degree of state repression on cartels.
See Section 1.2 for further discussion.

Lara Bonilla launched the first serious offensive against his country's cocaine traffickers, not to curb violence—cartels were then peacefully dividing a wildly lucrative boom in global demand—but to fight corruption. The crackdown triggered not only Lara Bonilla's own assassination but a decade of withering, anti-state "narco-terrorism" and some of the most severe urban violence on record anywhere. Drug lord Pablo Escobar led Colombia's cartels into an overt war on the state—and eventually among each other—that convulsed a nation and, for a time, overshadowed an ongoing civil war.

In Rio de Janeiro, the same 1980s' cocaine boom fed the takeover of the city's retail drug trade by a sophisticated criminal syndicate born in the dungeons of Brazil's military dictatorship. Its willingness to fight back against state repression led authoritarian officials to erroneously categorize it as a left-wing insurgency, christening it the "Comando Vermelho" ("Red Command," CV). From the 1990s on, increasingly repressive crackdowns on the CV and its rivals produced acute escalation, while curbing neither rampant police corruption nor traffickers' armed dominion over the city's nearly one thousand *favelas* (slums). Violence peaked in 2007, with police alone killing 1,330 alleged criminals in armed confrontations, including a lethal but failed attempt to retake Complexo do Alemão, the CV's principal favela stronghold.

What sets these cases apart from drug violence in general, and from turf wars among traffickers in particular, is the phenomenon I call *cartel–state conflict*—sustained armed confrontation between sophisticated and well-armed drug trafficking organizations (DTOs) and state forces.[2] Once unique to Colombia, cartel–state conflict has now ravaged Latin America's three largest countries, producing casualties and social disruption on par with many civil

2   The term "cartel" is controversial; I use it for the following reasons: (1) "DTO" is unwieldy and imprecise: only a very small and specific subset of DTOs ever attack states, namely, those with sufficient division of labor to maintain a dedicated capacity for armed violence. (2) "cartel" is the local nomenclature for such DTOs in two of my three cases: the Mexican and Colombian DTOs I discuss are *named* "cartels" and referred to collectively as such by authorities, the groups themselves, and local journalists and scholars. (3) Similarly, "drug cartel" is widely used in US and international media, and some scholarship, to refer to such groups. (4) The main argument against using "cartel"—that these groups rarely if ever meet the technical definition of an economic cartel by engaging in collusive price-fixing—is correct as far as it goes, but seems outweighed by common usage. (5) Moreover, the cartels under study are in fact made up of semi-autonomous actors, among whom real cooperation does sometimes occur. That said, the term remains problematic; as Grillo (2011) points out, it has been politically useful to both journalists and drug warriors for reifying and making into a tangible enemy a rather diffuse group of actors. A further drawback is that Rio de Janeiro's DTOs are neither named nor commonly referred to as "cartels," making the term awkward in this case. Yet Rio's DTOs share the key characteristic of interest: the organizational capacity to engage the state in sustained armed confrontation. There is also no perfect term for them even when considered in isolation (they are known locally as *facções* (factions), which is a misnomer even in Portuguese). I use "syndicate" when discussing Rio's DTOs in isolation, and "cartel" when considering them together with the Mexican and Colombian cases.

wars.[3] Even where cartel–state violence is numerically overshadowed by inter-cartel killings (as in Mexico), systematic armed defiance of state authority is uniquely damaging to social and political life. Civilians, especially vulnerable populations living in peripheral areas often better served by cartels than the state, find themselves caught in the lethal crossfire of a shooting war whose stakes seem alien to the local economic and political development it violently disrupts.

Why did cartels respond to these crackdowns with sustained anti-state violence? Why do cartels fight states at all, if not to topple or secede from them? The answer may seem obvious: "To keep the state off their back." Yet this answer is clearly insufficient: all organized crime groups—including major drug cartels—would like less state repression; precisely for this reason, they usually adopt evasive strategies, eschewing anti-state violence that could attract attention. Indeed, this is why leaders were surprised when cartels responded to initial crackdowns by attacking the state. Leaders then intensified crackdowns, declaring "war" with strategic, state-building objectives borrowed largely from civil-war contexts: crushing armed opposition, restoring the rule of law, and establishing a monopoly on the use of force. Yet these objectives proved unattainable, despite unprecedented deployments of state forces. Instead, leaders found themselves caught in escalatory spirals of armed violence, social disruption, and erosion of public confidence in the state as its enforcement agents proved both brutal and corrupt. Cartels, for their part, suffered immense losses in merchandise and personnel, yet fought on.

Fortunately, not all of the surprises have been unpleasant; some repressive approaches heralded rapid abatements of cartel violence far beyond policymakers' expectations. These "pleasant surprises" suggest that, whereas initial state crackdowns seem to trigger and exacerbate cartel–state conflict, enlightened state policy can curtail it. Together, these episodes point to this book's core insights: there is nothing inevitable about cartel–state conflict. Cartels use violence, especially anti-state violence, when it is in their interest. Incentives matter, and few things shape cartels' incentives as thoroughly as state policy. The implications go well beyond the cases studied here: using repressive force wisely against criminal and armed groups is a struggle for states everywhere. If cartel–state conflict represents an extremely bad unintended consequence of initial crackdowns, what sorts of policies produced abatement?

In August 1990, as Pablo Escobar's campaign of terror was reaching its peak, incoming Colombian president César Gaviria introduced a policy facilitating voluntary surrender (*Sometimiento*) and plea bargaining for wanted criminals. The policy's formulators had modest hopes: "We expected the possible surrender of some paramilitaries ... and maybe a few mid-level *narcos*, but the big fish, the capos, it was unlikely they would turn themselves in" (Pardo

---

[3] In both Mexico and Brazil, armed clashes between traffickers and state forces regularly produce more than 1,000 "combatant" deaths per year, a common criterion for civil war.

Rueda 1996, 267).[4] Instead, within a few months, three of the country's top drug lords had surrendered under the new policy. By July 1991, Escobar himself had followed suit, bringing an abrupt respite from the violence.

Rio too witnessed an unexpected turnaround. After record violence in 2007, authorities began experimenting with a new policy approach inspired in part by "focused deterrence" experiments in the United States and Rio. Pacification, as it came to be known, involved pre-announced militarized occupations of individual favelas, permanent installation of "Pacifying Police Units (UPPs)"[5] and an explicit shift in priorities away from eradicating drug traffic toward minimizing violence and the armed presence of traffickers. Pacification proved successful in the smaller favelas where it debuted, but many traffickers fled to Alemão, the Comando Vermelho's massive favela stronghold. Recalling the 2007 botched invasion, police and military forces preparing to Pacify Alemão in 2010 publicly warned of a potential second bloodbath. To their surprise, most traffickers fled or peacefully surrendered. More surprising still, over the next three years traffickers continued to eschew violence, allowing the state to recapture enormous swathes of territory while barely firing a shot. By 2013, some 200 favelas were under Pacification, and deaths from cartel–state clashes had fallen by almost 70 percent.

The varied responses of cartels to different repressive approaches constitute a central puzzle: *if some militarized anti-cartel interventions trigger or exacerbate intense cartel–state conflict, why do others drastically curb it?* What characteristics of *Sometimiento* and Pacification made them effective? The answer is not that the state backed off: overall state repression *expanded* with the implementation of these reform policies, and Pacification in particular involved unprecedented increases in police manpower and deployment of federal armed forces. Rather, I argue, it is the fact that much of this increased repressive capacity was held in reserve, as a deterrent. By conditioning repression on cartel behavior, reform policies created counter-incentives that led cartels to eschew anti-state violence. Backed into a corner, cartels fight; given an attractive alternative to conduct their business in less violent ways, most do.

This raises a second aspect of this book's central puzzle: *if state policy shapes cartel–state conflict, what shapes state policy?* Initial crackdowns and the ensuing cycles of escalation have stretched on for decades, outliving any realistic hope of definitively destroying cartels; violence-reducing strategies, meanwhile, seem tragically difficult to implement and to sustain despite their apparent efficacy. The *Sometimiento* and Pacification policies only came about

---

4   Author's translation.
5   UPP stands for Unidades de Polícia Pacificadora. The term "UPP" has become a synecdoche for the larger Pacification strategy, and the terms are often used interchangeably. This is a mistake, because Pacification involves occupation by non-UPP special forces prior to implantation of a UPP unit in a community. Moreover, due to the program's success, "UPP" became a kind of brand name; for example, a raft of favela social programs was named "UPP Social," although it had nothing to do with policing and was implemented by the city, not state, government.

after numerous failed attempts at reform, and both proved all too fragile once implemented. *Sometimiento* collapsed when Escobar fled prison, and intense cartel–state conflict raged for nearly two years until his death at the hands of state forces. In Rio, Pacification's initial success and rapid expansion soon produced severe growing pains. From 2013 onward, policing practice in the larger Pacified favelas partially reverted to the *status quo ante*, and cartels began to re-engage the state militarily. Although cartel–state violence and homicide in general remain well below pre-Pacification levels, the increasingly non-pacific reality of Pacified Rio has severely undercut public support. The economic and political crises that rocked Brazil in 2016 further darken Pacification's future.

In Mexico, policy reform efforts never succeeded in the first place. As violence accelerated through 2010 and 2011, Calderón doubled down on his "no quarter" strategy. He flatly rejected public calls for violence-reducing approaches, equating them with the highly corrupt (though peaceful) state management of cartels practiced up until the 1990s. Yet once Calderón left office, it became clear that some of his own top security officials had sought to reform policy in a more conditional direction. This effort largely failed, especially in terms of the administration's public stance, though it probably influenced operations within some security agencies. Calderón's successor, Enrique Peña Nieto, came into office promising violence-reducing policy reforms, but these were never specified or clearly implemented; instead, he largely copied Calderón's approach (Hope 2015). No official measures have been released since 2011, but media and other sources suggest that cartel-related violence (including anti-state violence), while down from its 2011 peak, continues at alarmingly high levels.

The similarities and differences among the cases' trajectories raise a host of questions. Are initial crackdowns *ex ante* mistakes? Once cartel–state conflict has set in, why do reform efforts so often fail? Are leaders myopic? Stubborn? Uninterested in reducing violence? Or are they (also) fundamentally constrained by weak institutions and the fraught politics of drug wars? If so, what factors mitigate these constraints and facilitate implementation of violence-reducing policies? And, once implemented, what self-undermining dynamics make violence-reducing policies difficult to sustain in the long run?

The answers this book develops to its two central questions stand at the intersection of strategy and politics, with implications for both policy and theory. As with all types of war, any satisfying theory of cartel–state conflict must account for both sides' interests, and explain how sustained and costly violence can be an equilibrium of the strategic interaction between them (Fearon 1995a). Cartels may operate in illegal markets that lack legal property rights and governance, but their overall strategic environment is fundamentally structured by the state: by its formal laws and policies, and by its capacity and will (or lack thereof) to enforce them. State leaders in turn must formulate repressive policy in contexts of limited resources, complex and often inefficient institutional structures, and rampant police corruption.

Equally important are the distinctive politics of drug war. State policy is not simply a strategic response to cartel behavior. Leaders are severely constrained in their policy decisions and public stances, and not only by the international treaties and acute pressure from the United States that undergird the global drug-prohibition regime. Domestic factors can be equally or more important: resistant, often corrupt police corps; opportunistic political rivals; and widespread public perceptions of traffickers as venal, demonic figures with whom negotiation and detente are taboo. Cartels are not immune to politics either. Global prohibition surely informs their lack of interest in seizing formal state power, while domestic political considerations shape their efforts to influence and penetrate the state at different levels. Cartels are, in this view, a unique type of interest group: illegal and armed to be sure, and with preferred policies that lie beyond the political pale, but nonetheless keenly engaged in honing their public image and political voice.

This study—the first extended cross-national comparison of cartel–state conflict to my knowledge—tilts unabashedly toward the theoretical, drawing on, and hopefully contributing to, several rich traditions in comparative politics. Most obviously, it speaks to long-noted connections between state formation, war-making, and organized crime (Tilly 1985). Indeed, leaders often frame cartel crackdowns as state-building exercises, explicitly aiming to (re)claim the monopoly on the use of force, consolidate the rule of law, eliminate armed non-state actors, and protect citizens. While these crackdowns led to expansions in state coercive capacity, they largely failed to deliver on overarching, state-building goals; in some places, state presence and rule of law probably receded. Reform policies that prioritized violence reduction over drug eradication, in contrast, have had tangible success in extending state presence and restoring order. If unreformed drug war is ineffective at making states, it is likely because the very act of prohibiting and repressing large illicit economies like the drug trade creates lucrative black markets. These are, by nature, state-less areas, power vacuums that often produce violent competition for primacy among criminal groups (Gambetta 1993; Skaperdas 2001) and generate the illicit profits used to corrupt state officials. Drug war, if made naively, can *unmake* states.

The literature on civil war—particularly the "rationalist explanations of war" (e.g., Fearon 1995a) and "logics of violence" (e.g., Kalyvas 2006) approaches—provides critical theoretical and methodological foundations, but understandably sidelines issues of corruption within state forces. I develop formal models and logics of violence that adapt these approaches to the distinct contours of cartel–state conflict; the results may in turn illuminate civil wars whose belligerents depend on criminal profits (e.g., Keen 1998) and "wartime political orders" that lie in the gray zone between war and peace (e.g., Staniland 2012). I draw on another tradition that sees corruption as a form of political influence (Huntington 1968; Scott 1972), while rectifying the view that corruption and violence are substitutes; as we will see, they are all too often complementary. An eclectic literature on policymaking (e.g., Kingdon 1984; Schickler 2001) informs my analysis of the politics and optics of drug war, and may in turn be enriched by it. Finally, the qualitative and quantitative data presented here both flesh out my theory and provide a rich empirical basis for further research into this novel and increasingly destructive form of conflict.

1.2   THE ARGUMENTS

1.2.1   Conditionality of Repression as Explanation

Cartels, presumably, get no inherent pleasure from attacking the state;[6] they do so when the benefits outweigh the costs. State policy has an overwhelming effect on this calculus. On the one hand, the very act of repressing the drug trade creates incentives for cartels to fight back. On the other, if attacking the state will bring down additional state repression, then cartels have incentives to eschew such violence. To disentangle these opposing sets of incentives, I distinguish the overall level or *degree* of repression directed at the drug trade from the extent to which that repression is *conditioned* on cartels' use of violence. Much of the variation in cartel–state conflict can be explained by changes in these two dimensions of state anti-narcotics policy.

Increases in the degree of repression, I argue, create incentives for anti-state violence, while increases in the conditionality of repression create disincentives; the respective mechanisms are quite distinct. In the following section, I introduce several key logics of violence by which increases in the degree of repression create "positive" incentives for cartels to fight back. Explaining the benefits cartels reap from attacking the state—and how those benefits can grow when the state cracks down—is one of this book's central theoretical contributions. Nevertheless, these positive incentives cannot by themselves explain the dynamics of cartel–state conflict, since overall degrees of repression generally increased not only with the blanket crackdowns that initially triggered and exacerbated anti-state violence, but also with the reform policies that—where implemented—curbed it. These reform policies, it seems, must have created countervailing *dis*incentives to anti-state violence.

Repressive policies create these disincentives, I argue, by conditioning the amount of repression a cartel faces on its choice to use violence. The extra repression (if any) that traffickers incur by attacking the state is likely to constitute the primary cost of anti-state violence. To be sure, guns (and the physical means of violence more generally) are not free, but neither are they restrictively costly. US traffickers, for example, avoid killing police not because

---

[6]   Individual cartel members who carry out violence against state forces may very well act on strong emotional impulses; honor, vindication, and revenge may be important motivations for individual soldiers, as they surely are in many contexts of armed conflict. For the cartel itself, though, violence is presumably instrumental and strategic; any bloodlust among its rank-and-file amounts to a felicitous source of morale and motivation.

bullets are expensive, but to avoid the additional repression that cop-killing will engender, over and above whatever "baseline" they face just for trafficking.

I call this aspect of anti-narcotics policy the *conditionality of repression*, in the same sense that "conditional cash transfers" are conditional on recipient behavior, or the International Monetary Fund's practice of "Conditionality" ties loans to recipient countries' economic policies. In policy circles, conditional approaches are often referred to as "selective repression" or "focused deterrence" (or given proper names like Rio's "Pacification," Boston's "Ceasefire," or the eponymous "High Point Strategy"). Analytically, though, it is not the targeting of specific cartels per se that deters anti-state violence, but rather the fact that *how much repression cartels face depends on how much (or how little) anti-state violence they employ*; "conditionality" is meant to capture precisely this quality. Repression *can* be made conditional on other types of violence or bad behavior, but states are likely to condition first and foremost on anti-state violence. Moreover, my goal is to explain anti-state violence, so I focus on this form of conditionality throughout.

Figure 1.1 represents the *degree* and *conditionality* of repression as two dimensions of state policy, producing four state-policy ideal types; overlaying my theoretical claims about the incentives for or against anti-state violence created along each dimension yields predictions about cartel behavior under

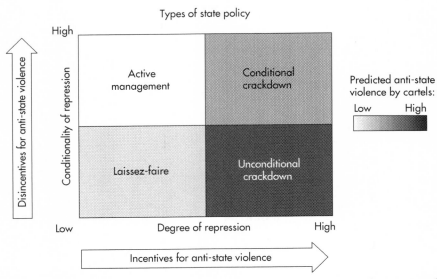

FIGURE 1.1. **Degree vs. Conditionality of Repression: Policy Types and Incentives for Violence**. *Degree of repression* measures the overall amount of force directed at cartels; *conditionality of repression* measures how much additional repression a cartel incurs by engaging in anti-state violence.

each policy type. Under "Laissez-Faire," the state makes little effort to rein in the activities of traffickers, and also does not try to dissuade them from specific forms of violence. In "Active Management," the state is more concerned with making cartels follow rules than in eliminating them; this requires enough repressive force to punish rule-breakers,[7] but in practice such punishment can be quite rare. Though active management does not logically require corruption, in my cases, it has taken the form of systematic extraction of illicit rents from traffickers by police. In "Unconditional Crackdowns," repression is high but conditionality low—the state simply maximizes its efforts to destroy or hurt cartels regardless of their use of violence. Finally, in "Conditional Crackdowns," the degree of repression remains high—the state is still on a war footing, as it were—but cartels can earn a reprieve from repression if they eschew anti-state violence.

These two dimensions of repressive policy constitute the independent or explanatory variables of my argument, with inverse predicted effects on anti-state violence by cartels. High degrees of repression produce incentives for anti-state violence, and so are a necessary condition for sustained cartel–state conflict; they are not, however, a sufficient condition. High conditionality of repression dissuades anti-state violence, and can at least partially overcome the strong incentives to fight back created by high degrees of repression. This framework thus predicts that anti-state violence is most acute under unconditional crackdowns, low to moderate under laissez-faire and conditional crackdowns, and very low or nonexistent under active management.

The book's central empirical finding is that unconditional crackdowns indeed led to an increase in anti-state violence, while shifts to more conditional approaches produced abrupt reduction in such violence. Moreover, where conditionality was high and overall repression low, states have been able to effectively (if corruptly) manage cartels and other criminal groups, leading to very low levels of anti-state violence. Table 1.1 summarizes the evidence: pooling case-episodes from all three conflicts and coding them by policy type, I find that cartel–state violence consistently took on its predicted values. In that sense, *conditionality of repression* is the "master variable" of this book. To reiterate, though, conditionality of repression does *not* explain cartels' incentives to fight back in the first place. These vary directly with the degree of repression, operating through logics of violence I elaborate. Rather, conditionality explains why some crackdowns lead to reduction in violence: by creating enough disincentives to outweigh the positive incentives.

In Rio, for example, early crackdowns (1980s–1990s) were unconditional: heavily armed police made tactical incursions aiming to arrest, or more likely kill, as many traffickers as possible. Traffickers, responding to the positive incentives for violence these crackdowns created, fought back. For decades

---

[7] For this reason, these two dimensions are not fully independent. This fact emerges algebraically in the formal models of Chapter 4.

TABLE 1.1. *Predicted Effects of Policy Types on Anti-State Violence and Observed Outcomes.*

	Laissez-Faire	Active Management	Unconditional Crackdown	Conditional Crackdown
IVs — Degree of Repression	Low	Low/Moderate	High	High
Conditionality of Repression	Low	High	Low	High
DV — Anti-State Violence	Low/Moderate	Low	High	Moderate
Case-Episodes Colombia	Cocaine Bonanza 1970s–1983	–	Crackdown: 1983–1991 Manhunt: 1992–1993	*Sometimiento:* 1991–1992 ["Lawn-mowing": 1995–]
Rio de Janeiro	–	Rent Extraction (Numbers Racket): –1970s	Crackdown: 1980s–2007 [Pacification Eroded: 2013–]	GPAE (localized): 2001–2003 Pacification: 2008–2012
Mexico	Interregnum: 1990s–2003	State-Sponsored Protection Racket: –1990s	Limited Crackdown: 2003–2006 Full Crackdown: 2006–	[Focus on Zetas (navy only): 2011–2013]

The case-episodes represent policy regimes, and are coded into types by the independent variables (IVs): degree and conditionality of repression. Evidence for this coding is presented in the case studies; square brackets indicate episodes whose coding is more conjectural. The episodes all saw levels of anti-state violence consistent with the predicted values for the dependent variable (DV).

(1990s–2007), the state periodically increased the *degree* of repression, but continued to offer little or no reprieve to traffickers who eschewed violence. In perhaps the ultimate example of unconditional repression, the elite BOPE Special Operations Battalion,[8] already highly trained and essentially licensed to kill, stopped allowing traffickers to surrender in the mid-1990s (Soares 2011); this gave traffickers every incentive to literally fight to the death. Cartels responded by expanding their own military capacity, and cartel–state conflict steadily intensified. The Pacification strategy (2008–2013) further raised the overall degree of repression, involving the armed forces and a serious expansion of police manpower. However, it also deliberately increased the conditionality of repression. By pre-announcing favela occupations, and by explicitly targeting traffickers' armed presence rather than the drug trade per se, the policy guaranteed that cartels would only face the full brunt of state repression if they fought back. This sharp increase in conditionality, I argue, pushed cartels toward non-violent, evasive strategies.

I now briefly elaborate the concept of conditionality and explore a few of its characteristics. I then return to the question of how state repression gives cartels "positive" incentives to fight back.

1.2.1.1 Conceptualizing Conditionality

"Conditionality" is, at bottom, a measure of how much harder the state goes after traffickers who employ a given type of violence than traffickers who do not. If the state goes after both types equally hard, then repression is entirely unconditional. Presumably, though, certain kinds of violence will get a drug dealer into trouble, more trouble than he or she is already in just for dealing drugs. Conditionality is a measure of how *much* more. High conditionality implies a larger "wedge" between the amounts of repression directed at non-violent versus violent traffickers, and it is this wedge that creates incentives for traffickers to avoid violence. Conditionality can also be viewed conversely, as the relative reprieve a trafficker earns for eschewing violence.

Throughout this book, I use "conditionality" to mean conditionality with respect to anti-state violence. Since states are likely to punish anti-state violence at least as much as any other forms of violence, this form of conditionality is likely to be the most salient. In US contexts, for example, traffickers face a fair amount of repression just for trafficking, and perhaps not much more for engaging in inter-gang violence;[9] killing a cop, however, triggers a major increase in police repression. Conditionality (with respect to anti-state violence) is high, and as a result, killings of US police are rare. Indeed, and ironically, the US Drug Enforcement Agency (DEA) is known to respond so severely to

---

[8] BOPE stands for Batalhão de Operações Policiais Especiais.
[9] Focused-deterrence efforts like Boston's Ceasefire program sought to fight gang violence precisely by directing additional repression at traffickers who engaged in it; such programs are conditional with respect to inter-cartel (or -gang) violence.

violence against its agents that cartels almost always avoid it, even in the midst
of full-blown domestic cartel–state conflict.[10]

Because it measures the difference between two values, conditionality alone
does not tell us all we need to know. Compare the scenario I call "laissez-faire,"
where neither non-violent nor violent traffickers are pursued much, with
unconditional crackdowns, in which both are pursued maximally. In both
scenarios conditionality is low—creating little deterrence—because traffickers
do not incur any *additional* repression for using violence. These two scenarios
differ in their degree of repression, which affects their "positive" incentives for
violence. Under laissez-faire, these incentives are weak, because the degree of
repression is low. Higher degrees of repression create more incentives to fight
back, which is why unconditional crackdowns are prone to anti-state violence.

Conditional repression aims to deter traffickers from fighting back by
countering these positive incentives, and deterrence, as Thomas Schelling
famously put it, "requires that you keep something in reserve" (1966, 173).
An implication is that if the state is *already* directing most of its repressive
capacity at cartels in general, repression will be highly *un*conditional. To see
this numerically, say the state devotes 95 percent of its repressive force toward
fighting cartels irrespective of their use of violence. Then traffickers who kill
cops will incur, at most, an increase in repression of about 5 percent.

Conversely, *highly conditional repression requires directing significantly less
than the maximum possible repression at non-violent drug traffickers.* Indeed,
a maximally conditional policy would set the baseline degree of repression to
zero, essentially decriminalizing non-violent trafficking, and put most or all of
the state's repressive capacity into deterring traffickers from becoming violent.
Decriminalization, however, is politically unviable, at least for international
cocaine smuggling. To avoid international and possibly domestic opprobrium,
states must continue to actively repress non-violent trafficking to some degree.
Yet if that baseline level of repression is too high, there will not be enough
in reserve to deter cartels from fighting back. In the cases I study, conditional
reforms came in the wake of unconditional crackdowns and the escalation they
engendered; that is, they occurred in settings where the degree of repression
was already high, possibly close to maximum capacity. As a result, increases in
conditionality were often achieved by *lowering* the amount of repression aimed
at non-violent traffickers.

Simplistic though this arithmetic may seem, it causes no end of problems.
One is political: as Schelling (1966, 173) noted, "coercive warfare ... is likely
to look restrained. The object is to exact good behavior ... not to destroy the
subject altogether." Since the "subjects" here are drug cartels, which political
leaders have often demonized and sworn to destroy, the optics of restraint can
be devastating. Under Rio's Pacification strategy, for example, police often

---

10 The case of Enrique "Kiki" Camarena, killed in Mexico in 1985, is the exception that proves
the rule; I discuss the incident in Chapter 7.

walk right by traffickers clearly identifiable by their walkie-talkies, or fail to patrol alleys known to contain points of sale; to its many critics, this restraint is evidence that Pacification is a "farce." Yet this restraint is precisely the source of Pacification's deterrent force, and the more effective the deterrent—i.e., the more that cartels avoid using anti-state violence—the less repression is actually applied in practice. Another problem is logistical: repressive force must not only be held in reserve, but also credibly unleashed if and when cartels *do* engage in violence. This involves, at a minimum, subjugating anti-cartel operations to a centralized, impartial, and effective state intelligence-gathering mechanism.

Much of the analysis in this book focuses on the effects of *changes* in the degree and conditionality of repression. In particular, I explore the effects of "crackdowns," which I define as any increase in the degree of repression. Crackdowns can have varying effects on conditionality, depending on how they are structured. In practice, many initial state crackdowns are unconditional: governments simply try to arrest or kill as many traffickers as possible, without regard to their use (or not) of violence. Such crackdowns create no additional disincentives to violence, while increasing cartels' positive incentives through the logics of violence I analyze. This is why cartels often respond to initial unconditional crackdowns by switching from evasive strategies to one of violent confrontation. Conversely, a crackdown that is structured so that the brunt of the increase in repression falls only on cartels that opt for violence simultaneously increases the conditionality of repression. Such crackdowns, I find, can very effectively induce cartels to switch (back) to non-violent strategies.

1.2.1.2 Types of Conditionality

"Conditionality" does not refer to a specific policy; there is no single "conditional approach." Rather, conditionality is a variable on which policies can be scored. The policies identified as conditional in this study differ in many respects; the key quality they share, I argue, is that they deliberately direct more repressive force at traffickers who opt for violence than those that do not. There are many ways to achieve this effect in practice. Thus, Pacification's pre-announcing of police occupations contributes to its conditional nature (by giving traffickers a chance to peacefully flee), but is certainly not a necessary component for any given policy to be conditional. Just as there are countless ways to write a contract, each generating its own unique set of incentives, there are many ways to structure state repression so that it is conditional, and we must think through the incentives produced by each on a case-by-case basis.[11]

One important distinction is whether a violent cartel, once targeted for additional repression under a conditional policy, can still earn a reprieve by reverting to peaceful strategies. For example, a conditional approached proposed by Mark Kleiman (2011) called on the Mexican government to first

---

[11] I thank Ethan Bueno de Mesquita for suggesting this comparison.

publicly identify the most violent cartel, destroy it (with help from the United States), then move on to the next-most violent cartel, and so on. I call such a policy, for lack of a better phrase, conditional *across* cartels, since it creates incentives for all cartels to avoid being named "most violent cartel," but for the cartel so named creates no further disincentives to violence. Rio's Pacification policy, in contrast, does not condition the decision to occupy a specific favela on the incumbent cartel's use of violence; once a favela is occupied, though, traffickers face significantly less repression if they eschew violence. I call such a scheme conditional *within* cartels.

Conditionality across cartels is preemptive but not reforming: it deters as-yet untargeted cartels from adopting violence, but gives the targeted cartel every reason to fight for its life. Only conditionality *within* cartels creates incentives for a targeted cartel to switch from violent to non-violent strategies. To do this, conditionality within cartels requires some form of retroactive "forgiveness," so that a once-violent cartel can earn a reprieve going forward if it gives up its violent ways. This distinction is critical in the Colombian case, where a period of conditionality across cartels failed to curb anti-state violence by the targeted cartel (Medellín), but a shift to conditionality within cartels induced a sharp abatement. In this case, the element of "forgiveness" was literal: a plea bargain deal for Escobar that forgave past violent acts conditional on his surrender. In Rio, Pacification is also conditional within cartels, but forgiveness is collective: with the occasional exception of known criminals with outstanding warrants, the traffickers in a Pacified community are not punished for past violence, conditional on non-violence under Pacification. Elsewhere, the across/within distinction is less salient, and for simplicity I characterize an overall level of conditionality.

I focus on conditionality of repression with respect to anti-state violence, but of course state repression *can* be made conditional on any type of violence, or any other identifiable cartel action for that matter.[12] In general, the starkest conditionality is with respect to violence against state actors—think again of the overwhelming response in US police corps when officers are killed. Other likely triggers for additional repression include "terror tactics" such as bombings and bus-burnings, which I argue are often directed at state leaders even when the victims are primarily civilian. Nonetheless, it is possible for repression to be conditioned on inter-cartel violence, especially high-visibility actions like torture, mutilation, and public slayings.

This means that conditionality might play a role in diminishing forms of violence beyond cartel–state conflict. For example, in pre-1990s' Mexico, repression was highly conditional: cartels faced little repression as long as they followed the rules of the game. While those rules certainly prohibited

---

12   In theory, repressive policy can be conditional on anything. Broadly speaking, we might define a criminal justice policy as conditional to the extent that it creates incentives for those who have committed crime *A* to avoid committing a second, presumably worse, crime *B*.

and effectively deterred anti-state violence, they also likely dissuaded extreme and highly visible inter-cartel violence, as Angelica Durán-Martínez's work suggests (2015, 12). When repression became more unconditional in Mexico, and thus eroded disincentives for anti-state violence (the argument I make in Chapter 7), it may have also reduced cartels' incentives to conceal or minimize inter-cartel violence. Conversely, in Colombia, conditionality across cartels left the Cali cartel virtually unexposed to state repression, whose leaders may have concluded (correctly, as it turned out) that they would not incur additional repression for attacking their rival, Medellín. In these ways, my argument *may* account for some of the variation in forms of violence beyond anti-state violence. However, explaining inter-cartel turf war and strictly anti-civilian violence lies beyond the scope of this study.

1.2.2 Why Fight the State? Cartels as Violent Interest Groups and the Centrality of Corruption

I turn now to cartels' "positive" incentives for anti-state violence: why does unconditional repression induce cartels to fight back? To put it another way, what do cartels get out of attacking the state?

The most straightforward logic is one of pure defense: for cartels, fighting back during busts, raids, and other instances of law enforcement may be more effective at minimizing losses than non-violent "hiding" tactics. This logic, however, cannot account for many common forms of cartel violence, including death threats, targeted assassinations of officials, and terrorist attacks, which often occur well before or after enforcement. Useful here is Schelling's distinction between brute force and coercion, "between," as he put it, "holding what people are trying to take and making them afraid to take it" (Schelling 1966, 2). Much cartel violence seems intended not to "hold what state agents try to take" during acts of repression, but at making state agents afraid to repress cartels in the first place.

Perhaps the clearest example of coercive violence is Pablo Escobar's terrorist campaign, aimed quite explicitly (and successfully) at compelling Colombian lawmakers to nullify extradition. The underlying logic—using high-profile violence to pressure leaders for de jure policy change—helps explain cartel bombings and attacks on public infrastructure. However, a great deal of anti-state violence is directed at the enforcers of the law, not its authors. To what end? Again, brute-force defense during enforcement may play some role, but cannot explain threats, assassinations, and other forms of violence that seem punitive.

A central claim of this book is that anti-enforcer violence also has a coercive impetus, intimately linked to the possibility of corruption. In this third logic, cartels negotiate a bribe with enforcers, while simultaneously threatening violence if no bribe agreement is reached—offering, in Pablo Escobar's infamous phrase, *"plata o plomo"* ("the bribe or the bullet," literally "silver or lead"). As Escobar understood, fear of "the bullet" gives corrupt enforcers incentives to accept smaller bribes than they otherwise would; it might even induce normally honest enforcers to turn a blind eye.[13]

In these coercive logics, violence is used to influence the end-result behavior of states. This recalls James C. Scott's classic argument (1969a, 1972) that interest groups' ultimate goal is to influence not de jure policy per se but *policy outcomes*, whether through lobbying at the de jure level, through corruption at the de facto level of policy enforcement, or both; in this, cartels are no different. What sets cartels apart from licit interest groups—and even traditional mafias—is their (occasional) armed opposition to state forces; in this, they resemble insurgencies. Yet this resort to armed violence is, I argue, best understood as part of an interest-group-like strategy of influence. Following Scott, I distinguish *violent corruption*, aimed at weakening enforcement, from *violent lobbying*, aimed at weakening de jure policy.

This view of cartels as violent interest groups contrasts with popular characterizations of cartels as "criminal insurgencies" (e.g., Sullivan and Elkus 2008) and drug war as a subtype of civil war (e.g., Castañeda 2013; Schedler 2013) by emphasizing a central fact: cartels are simply uninterested in seizing formal state power. Unlike classic insurgencies, cartels fight not to conquer the state or part of its territory, but to constrain and influence the state's behavior in ways that benefit their (principally economic) interests (Table 1.2). Similar aims have been attributed to groups like Mexico's Zapatistas, initially dubbed "postmodern insurgencies" (Fuentes 1994; Munck and De Silva 2000) but perhaps better described as "armed pressure groups" (Guillermoprieto, 1994). Such groups fight the state not to topple or secede from it, but to force it to make policy concessions.[14] For such non-revolutionary insurgencies, the desired concessions are generally at the de jure level: legislation, demarcation, and other formal policies. Cartels sometimes operate at this level too, particularly when their de jure demands resonate with the public, as banning extradition did in 1980s' Colombia. Yet cartels differ from non-revolutionary insurgency in that their overriding concern is with enforcement; this makes corruption, as per Scott's argument, a highly attractive and nearly universal strategy.

In this way, cartels are like traditional organized crime groups (and some licit but unsavory interest groups), regularly bribing law enforcement, judges, and where possible, high-level officials. Indeed, corruption may be even more important to cartels: whereas the defining business activity of mafias is

13 Throughout, I treat the case of "pure" intimidation without actual bribery as a subtype of violent corruption in which cartels coerce enforcers to take a bribe of zero. While society may rightly draw legal and normative distinctions between bribe-taking and "pure" intimidation, from cartels' perspective the primary difference is simply the "price" of the bribe.
14 Fearon and Laitin (2007) argue that in theory, most or all insurgencies *could* be satisfied by sufficient policy concessions, but that, in practice, commitment problems lead them to fight "all or nothing" wars for formal state power. The question then is why armed groups are ever willing to settle for concessions. In Part I, I explore this question with respect to cartels.

TABLE 1.2. *Cartels, Insurgencies, Mafias, and Licit Interest Groups.*

Aims Vis-à-Vis the State:

		Constraint/Influence	Conquest/Secession
Tactics Employed	**Anti-State Violence**	Drug cartels (sometimes) Armed pressure groups/ "Postmodern insurgencies"	Classic insurgencies
	Corruption	Drug cartels Mafias Licit interest groups (sometimes)	–
	Traditional Politics	Licit interest groups Drug cartels (sometimes) Mafias (sometimes) Armed pressure groups/ "Postmodern insurgencies" (sometimes)	Non-violent protest

often understood as selling protection (Gambetta 1993), cartels are first and foremost drug trafficking organizations, and frequently buy their protection directly from state agents (Snyder and Durán-Martínez 2009b).[15] Corruption, in this sense of bribery in exchange for weakened enforcement, represents a principal–agent problem *within* the state. For leaders intent on fighting the drug trade, this problem is acute: they must equip law enforcement with enough repressive capacity to deter and incapacitate traffickers, but this very capacity can be used by enforcers to extort traffickers for larger bribes.[16]

The centrality of corruption in cartels' strategies requires moving beyond a unidimensional account of state capacity and the unitary-actor view of the state common in conflict studies. Like civil war, cartel–state conflict seems to be associated with states that are, in some sense, low-capacity; yet Mexico, Brazil, and Colombia are at best "weakish" states, certainly not the failed

[15] Cartels also resemble mafias in practicing state-like activities such as public-goods provision to win the loyalty of citizens, with the ultimate aim of making law enforcement less effective.

[16] This principal–agent problem is only as acute as the divergence between the preferences of leaders (principals) and enforcers (agents). For leaders more interested in managing and taxing the drug trade than in reducing drug flows, having police extract bribes in exchange for non-enforcement may be the desired outcome; Mexico under the Partido Revolucionario Institucional (PRI) seems to fit this description.

states often seen in civil-war settings.[17] The civil-war literature often treats the decisive aspect of state capacity as the ability to physically penetrate territory and eliminate armed opponents (e.g., Fearon and Laitin 2003). Cartel–state conflict has thus far occurred in places where states' key weakness lay not so much in amassing and deploying repressive force, or even identifying and locating traffickers, but rather preventing state agents from taking bribes in exchange for weakened enforcement.[18] Bribery of state troops by insurgents is rare enough that civil-war scholars rarely discuss it; in the world of cartel–state conflict, it is a first-order problem. At a minimum, then, state capacity must be analyzed both in terms of the size of the state's coercive apparatus *and* leaders' ability to direct that apparatus to their desired ends.[19]

The prevalence of corruption brings us back to the puzzle of cartels' use of anti-state violence: if the state repression can be partially nullified through bribery, then why confront the state militarily? As Table 1.2 illustrates, cartels differ most starkly from licit interest groups and even traditional mafias[20] not in their resort to both corruption and "lobbying" efforts, but in their resort to violent versions of these strategies.[21] Violent lobbying—essentially a domestic form of coercive diplomacy—was devastating in Colombia but rarer elsewhere. Violent corruption, it turns out, is both more common across cases and more puzzling: to paraphrase the leaders of Colombia's Cali cartel, why kill cops when you can buy them? The formal model developed in Chapter 4 provides a counterintuitive answer: killing some cops makes buying the rest cheaper. Credible threats of violence can help pressure enforcement agents into taking (smaller) bribes, or simply intimidate them into non-enforcement altogether. Since bribe negotiations can still fail sometimes, cartels must occasionally carry out their threats lest they become non-credible in the future.

This enforcer-targeted violence has its costs, first among which is any additional repression it draws from authorities. If police are highly incorruptible, so that cartels have to regularly carry out their threats, these costs of

---

17 I thank Will Reno for suggesting this point.
18 I include in this formulation the leaking of intelligence by state agents, allowing traffickers to avoid capture, and corruption among prison officials, allowing for escapes or the running of cartel business from behind bars.
19 Note that this latter dimension does not always map onto our standard notion of "corruption." As Darden (2008) notes, systematic graft does not always weaken the state administrative apparatus, and can even *strengthen* it, if it gives leaders greater control over their inferiors. I discuss Mexico's state-sponsored protection racket under the PRI as an example of such "state-strengthening corruption" in the concluding chapter.
20 Few mafias possess the military capacity and willingness to engage in sustained anti-state violence; one possible exception, the Sicilian mafia's "war" on state agents in the early 1990s, was quite short-lived.
21 Violent corruption and violent lobbying are not mutually exclusive strategies; indeed, cartels often engage in both simultaneously. In this they differ from Kalyvas' logics of discriminate and indiscriminate violence, which insurgents presumably choose between in any given locale, though they may employ both globally.

violence probably outweigh the benefits. But where corruption is rampant, with enforcers systematically extracting a share of cartels' profits (as occurred in all three of my cases), cartels have enormous incentives to lower the price of bribes through *plata o plomo* threats. Moreover, as the model makes clear, the more repressive force directed at anti-narcotics operations, the stronger are cartels' incentives to make *plata o plomo* threats, and the more likely they are to act on those threats. The implication for state capacity is troubling: if two states crack down with equal physical repressive capacity but different degrees of corruption in the ranks, cartels should have greater incentives to fight back against the state with more rampant corruption. Sending well-armed but corrupt forces to combat cartels, this analysis suggests, is a recipe for cartel–state conflict.

Astute readers will perceive the idea of conditionality lurking in the preceding paragraph: cartels, I claim, weigh the added leverage that violence provides against the additional repression it is likely to bring down. The key is "additional": for licit interest groups, repression is *entirely* conditional, because they face no repression at all when not engaged in violence. It is hard to imagine a K Street lobbyist physically threatening legislators, or a restauranteur threatening a health inspector, precisely because it would transform them into criminals. Because cartels are already subject to significant repression, the added influence gained through violence can easily outweigh the cost of any additional repression.

1.2.3 Conditionality of Repression as Outcome

If repressive policy drives the onset and abatement of cartel–state conflict, what explains repressive policy? If conditional crackdowns can curtail cartel–state conflict, why are they not implemented more universally? And why, in the cases where they were implemented, has conditionality proven difficult to sustain?

To answer these questions, I turn from the pooled comparison of within-case episodes above to cross-case variation in the trajectories of cartel–state conflict. The stylized template presented in Figure 1.2 provides a structure for analyzing this variation, dividing trajectories into phases based on the policy types and corresponding outcomes discussed above. The theory introduced in the foregoing sections concerns the vertical arrows within each phase, which map cartels' embrace or eschewal of anti-state violence in response to state policy. In contrast, this section outlines how and why states shift from one policy type to another, shown as horizontal arrows. Of particular interest are shifts toward and away from conditional approaches, represented by the two rightmost arrows.

The initial phases of cartel–state conflict look broadly similar across cases. In an early, peaceful period, cartels were either largely left alone or, in Mexico, effectively managed by the state. At some point, this status quo became untenable and states decided to crack down on the drug trade. While the

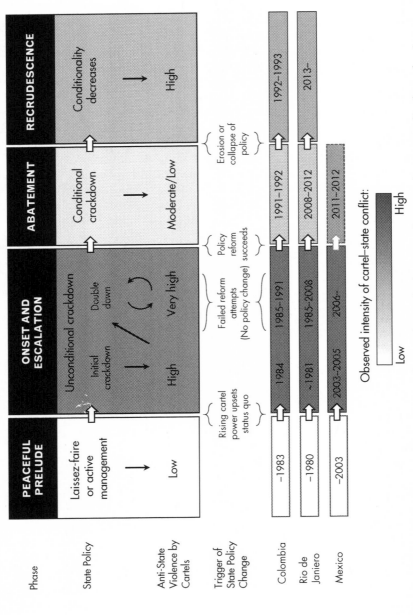

FIGURE 1.2. **Stylized Trajectory of Cartel–State Conflict.** Within each phase, cartels respond to state policy by eschewing or employing anti-state violence, as shown by the vertical arrows; Part I of the book seeks to explain these responses. Movement from one phase to another occurs when state policy changes. The proximate causes (triggers) of policy change are shown as horizontal arrows; these are discussed in Part III.

specific problems that crackdowns were intended to fix differed across cases (inter-cartel violence in Mexico vs. state penetration in Colombia), the common underlying cause of those motivating problems was an increase in cartel power, due largely to exogenous changes in drug-market structure and conditions. These initial unconditional crackdowns led to the onset of cartel–state conflict. (Crackdowns also seem to exacerbate inter-cartel violence, though this pattern is less clear across cases.) States then doubled down, expanding the degree of repression without increasing conditionality, and cartels responded with further escalation.

Across cases, as violence reached extreme levels, policy reformers within the state security apparatus began to seek alternative strategies explicitly aimed at reducing violence. The most effective conditional-repression policies identified, Rio's Pacification and Colombia's *Sometimiento*, resulted from successful reform efforts. To my surprise, I discovered that *a very similar but unsuccessful reform effort* occurred in Mexico, with some of Calderón's own security staff developing and advocating for conditional policy alternatives. This effort, though it probably influenced navy operations, was largely a failure, and Calderón stuck to his at least nominally unconditional approach. Meanwhile, successful reform in Rio and Colombia came only after numerous failed attempts, some abortive, some partially successful at a small scale or for a limited duration. Thus, failure of reform efforts seems to leave states in an escalatory spiral of unconditional crackdowns, until (and if) a successful policy reform leads to increases in the conditionality of repression, and consequently an abatement of cartel–state conflict. Sadly, a "recrudescence" phase has generally followed, in which conditional policies have suffered growing pains, mission creep, or abrupt cancelation; as the effective conditionality of repression falls, cartels turn again to anti-state violence.[22]

What explains these shifts? That initial crackdowns were unconditional is, perhaps, not terribly puzzling: leaders may not have been particularly interested in minimizing cartel–state conflict, either because it was not salient at the time (as in Colombia), or because they anticipated a rally-around-the-flag effect (as seems to have occurred in Mexico (Romero et al. 2014)). Alternatively, they may have believed that cartels *could* be definitively destroyed or neutralized through a brute-force, generalized crackdown. The real puzzles come after cartel–state conflict has escalated and proven resilient—giving leaders ample motives to curb it. Why did some conditional-repression policy reforms succeed while others failed? And why have conditional policies, once implemented, been difficult to sustain, despite their apparent efficacy?

My answer is that implementing conditional repression is difficult and costly, for both logistical and political reasons; unconditional repression is easier and politically safer, and therefore tends to be the default option. The

---

22 The term "recrudescence," is clunky but precise and apt: Merriam-Webster defines it as "a new outbreak after a period of abatement."

central challenge of conditional repression is that "coming down harder" on cartels that act violently requires, logically, "going easier" on those that do not. This requires, first, overcoming *logistical constraints* to effectively identifying and targeting more violent cartels, often aggravated by low capacity and institutional fragmentation of the state's coercive apparatus. Second, and ultimately more decisive, are the *acceptability constraints* specific to the politics of drug war, in which any retreat from a maximal effort to eradicate the drug trade can be politically toxic. Only when both sets of constraints are sufficiently mitigated are conditional approaches implemented. Tragically, implementation can set in motion dynamics that exacerbate these constraints, leading to erosion or collapse in the "recrudescence" phase.

Logistical constraints are linked to institutional factors. Fragmentation of security agencies makes it difficult for central governments to coordinate enforcement and intelligence gathering, and hence to effectively condition repression on cartel behavior. Colombia's police institutions are highly centralized, Brazil's somewhat less so, and Mexico's incredibly fragmented both vertically (local, state, and federal police forces) and horizontally (army, navy, and federal police forces). However, fragmentation can be mitigated (or exacerbated) by political cohesion (or competition) across levels of governance. Under the dominance of Mexico's Partido Revolucionario Institucional (PRI), institutional fragmentation was vastly mitigated, but has come to the fore since the end of PRI hegemony in the late 1990s (Davis 2006). In Rio de Janeiro, conversely, a political coalition spanning municipal, state, and federal levels of government since 2008 allowed for an unprecedented level of policy coordination and operational cooperation, mitigating logistical constraints.

Beyond logistics, the politics of conditional repression are fraught. Acceptability constraints derive from strong normative concerns about going soft on crime, selectively enforcing the law, and above all pacting or even negotiating with criminal groups, who are generally put in a different moral category than "political" armed groups like insurgencies. While normative concerns may sometimes amount to smokescreens for underlying material incentives (such as the economic and diplomatic consequences of US decertification), I find that they have real constraining power. For example, leaders in Colombia refused to negotiate openly with Pablo Escobar on precisely such moral grounds, tragically prolonging his campaign of violent lobbying—even as the selfsame officials successfully and publicly negotiated the demobilization of the M-19 guerrilla insurgency. In Brazil, a predecessor of the Pacification strategy successfully reduced cartel–state conflict, but fell prey to political accusations of pacting with the drug trade.

Successful implementation of conditional-repression policies requires overcoming or minimizing these obstacles. Comparing successful and failed reform efforts across cases, I find that three factors were most decisive. First, reframing the problem to be solved—from combating the drug trade writ large to reducing the violence associated with it—greatly eased acceptability constraints. Second, the amelioration (or not) of institutional fragmentation through political cohesion played an important role in overcoming logistical constraints. Finally, the ability to "layer" (Schickler 2001) conditional policy over existing repressive activity and conduct localized policy experimentation eased both types of constraint, allowing reformers to hone conditional policies and build effective capacity, while amassing enough public support to neutralize political opposition.

Given the efficacy of conditional crackdowns once implemented, their eventual erosion or collapse—and the resulting resurgence of cartel–state conflict—are tragic outcomes whose causes merit explanation. Drawing on an admittedly small and heterodox set of observations (two cases in Rio and one in Colombia), I argue that implementation itself can set in motion self-undermining dynamics by aggravating acceptability and logistical constraints. First, reframing the problem as violence reduction, though it facilitates implementation, worsens the political optics of subsequent developments. Under unconditional crackdowns, cartel violence may be interpreted by leaders as a sign of cartel desperation, and hence an indicator that repression is "working." Once leaders have made violence reduction the explicit goal of repressive policy, even sporadic violence becomes an indicator of failure. A related problem is corruption. Conditional repression, as the model of violent corruption in Chapter 4 shows, does not necessarily reduce bribery. Even when bribery is rampant prior to implementation, it can be particularly damaging to the optics of conditional approaches, which are often attacked by critics as corrupt pacts with cartels. Finally, the very efficacy of conditional crackdowns when implemented can lead to their rapid replication and expansion, straining institutional and logistical capacity to the breaking point. In Rio, for example, as leaders made up for shortfalls in UPP recruiting with traditional police and military forces, the effective conditionality in Pacified areas likely fell, leading cartels to re-engage militarily.

1.3 INFERENTIAL STRATEGY AND ALTERNATIVE EXPLANATIONS

This book has modest aims, seeking less to rigorously test hypotheses or accurately measure a treatment effect than to build clear and compelling concepts and theory that improve on existing explanations. Also, as noted, I restrict attention to cartel–state conflict; though I treat inter-cartel turf war as a relevant factor, I am not offering a theory of its dynamics nor a complete accounting of its interactions with cartel–state conflict. I also do not seek to explain cartels' relation to civilian populations.

My central claim is that state anti-narcotics policy is a key driver of cartel–state conflict. This contrasts with explanations that treat state policy as merely palliative or reactive, and drug violence itself as the unsurprising result of underlying market, geographical, or institutional conditions. Common explanatory factors invoked by analysts include growing/shrinking profit margins;[23] the presence of large, hegemonic cartels; rivalry among cartels; the US war on drugs; the US supply of firearms; widespread police corruption, weak institutions and low state capacity; and scarcity of legitimate economic opportunities that might keep youth from entering the drug trade. A related alternative explanation is that cartels attack the state when they have the capacity to do so, not because of anything the state does. All of these factors are important, and some constitute necessary conditions for cartel–state conflict; alone, though, they cannot explain observed variation as well as my state-policy approach.

Some alternative explanations can be ruled out through cross-case comparison. The claim that drug-market fragmentation—breaking up large, oligopolistic cartels—curtails cartel–state conflict was a plausible inference for Mexican officials circa 2006 to draw from the Colombian experience, but has since proven incorrect: freshly splintered cartels continue to attack state forces in Mexico. Conversely, the claim that cartel–state conflict is simply a by-product of inter-cartel turf war, a plausible inference from the Mexican case, is disproved by the Colombian and Brazilian cases, where cartel–state conflict began prior to, and contributed to the onset of, turf war. US influence on drug policy in Colombia and Mexico is undeniable, but its near total absence in Rio suggests that its role is easily exaggerated; a close reading of the other two cases supports this. Similarly, while US-supplied weapons contributed to violence in Mexico (Dube et al. 2013), this is not a relevant factor in Brazil, and probably not Colombia either.

Most inferential leverage, though, comes from within-case variation over time: the onset, and in some cases abatement, of cartel–state conflict. The complexity of these conflicts—with large and shifting casts of state, societal, and criminal actors—combined with the unavailability of systematic micro-data on key variables like enforcement operations, and the fundamental non-observability of others like bribery, cartel profits and drug flows, makes hypothesis-testing a challenge. However, critical inferential leverage comes from a central feature of this within-case variation: large and rapid shifts in the intensity of cartel–state conflict. This recalls a principle from medicine and epidemiology: strong or anomalous variation relative to baseline, temporal proximity, and a plausible mechanism for a causal effect can constitute a

---

23 One indication of the puzzling nature of cartel–state conflict is that it has been attributed to both an increase in the profits flowing to Mexican cartels in the wake of the closure of Caribbean trafficking routes in the late 1980s and early 1990s, and a shrinking of profits due to increases first in border patrols after 2001 and then Calderón's crackdown after 2006. This parallels a long-standing debate in civil war scholarship over whether increases in GDP are likely to increase or decrease the likelihood of civil war onset (Blattman and Miguel 2010, 10–12): in both cases, the larger the pie, the more there is to fight over. However, in civil war, the issue is that poorer states may be less able to deter rebels from fighting, while in drug war, the notion is that lower profits make for more vicious competition and less pacting among cartels.

sufficient basis for causal inference in the absence of randomization (Bradford Hill 1965; Glasziou et al. 2007).

Thus, in my cases, abrupt shifts in cartels' use of anti-state violence cast doubt on slow-moving or invariant institutional or environmental factors, and point to more temporally and spatially proximate explanations. In Mexico for example, while large profit margins, a surfeit of unemployed youth, easy access to guns, and weak state institutions might seem like a recipe for violence, these have all been present for years if not decades. The explosion of anti-state violence, on the other hand, represents an abrupt break with the past: attacks by criminal groups on state forces—unheard of prior to Calderón's policy "treatment" in 2006—reached an average of two per day in 2011, and still ran in the hundreds per year in 2014. Conversely, the relatively bloodless recapturing of Rio's largest and most heavily guarded favelas, and the related drop in the rate of police killings in armed confrontations, are welcome but highly unexpected outcomes precisely because nothing like that occurred in the more than two decades of cartel–state conflict preceding the Pacification strategy. In both cases, this points to the *explicit and substantial shifts in state policy* that immediately preceded sharp variation in cartel–state conflict as key causal factors (Figure 1.3).

To bolster this central claim, I take a multimethod approach. Part I elaborates several logics of violence, modeling key mechanisms that link state policy and background characteristics to cartels' decisions to employ (or not) various modalities violence. The case studies combine process tracing—the careful piecing together of qualitative "causal process observations" made during fieldwork, including dozens of semi-structured interviews with poli-cymakers and enforcers in each country[24]—with secondary source material and the available quantitative data, including the results of a large-scale data collection project I undertook in all three countries. This project, named "NRI/OBIVAN,"[25] employed native-speaker coders in each country to produce event-level data based on media reports of cartel-related violence. Unfortunately, resource constraints limited the temporal scope of these datasets, but the data provide insight into the variation in modalities of violence within and across cases.

Explaining conditionality as an outcome takes us out of the austere realm of strategic interactions between armed actors and into a messier world of policymaking processes (Figure 1.2). Some policy changes—like doubling down on unconditional repression in the face of violent blowback, or expanding

---

[24] See Appendix B for a list.
[25] The project is hosted by think-tank NGOs in each country, and staffed by university student coders. Its name in Spanish and Portuguese is Observatorio Internacional de Violencia Asociada a Narcotrafico (OBIVAN); I have given it the English name Narcoviolence Research International (NRI). The project owes its existence to generous funding from the Open Society Institute and the Centro Andino de Fomento.

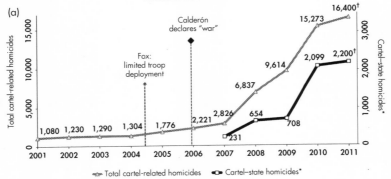

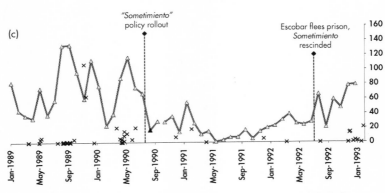

FIGURE 1.3. **Cartel–State Conflict and Key Policy Changes in Mexico, Brazil, and Colombia.**

Sources: Mexico: (SNSP 2011); *See Chapter 7 for details. †Estimates from partial-year data. Rio: ISP-RJ (2016); SSP-RJ (2003). Colombia: Author's coding of media reports (NRI).

and consolidating conditional policies once they prove effective—amount to extensions of a policy type in response to cartel actions. But shifts among policy types—and hence from one phase of cartel–state conflict to the next—have a wider range of triggers. Some are fairly exogenous to the local dynamics of cartel–state conflict, such as the shifts in international drug flows that drove cartel expansion, or the breakdown of single-party rule in Mexico; others are more endogenous, such as the success of policy reform efforts in Brazil and Colombia. Critically, leaders' decisions at these moments depend not only on "hard" pragmatic considerations, but on the often toxic politics of drug war.

To grapple with these concerns, I draw on theories of policymaking that emphasize "extra-strategic" factors such as norms and shared understandings of appropriateness (e.g., March and Olsen 1984, 2004); the way problems are (re-)framed, the pool of policy ideas, and the appearance of political opportunities (Kingdon 1984); and the mechanics of reform itself (Hacker 2004; Schickler 2001). In the framework I develop, logistical and acceptability constraints can be mitigated or exacerbated by various factors, which in turn influence the success and sustainability of conditional reforms. I consider a series of potential factors that were suggested by reformers themselves as causally important. The abundance of these candidate factors and the small number of observed policy shifts makes strong causal inference impossible. Still, cross-case comparison of the processes by which state policy evolved over time provides evidence that some factors were more decisive than others.

1.4 SCOPE AND CASES

1.4.1 Scope Conditions

Cartel–state conflict falls between the analytical cracks of better-studied phenomena: civil war, drug-related violence in general, organized crime, and interest group politics. To see this, consider this book's working definition of *cartel–state conflict* as "sustained episodes of armed conflict between state forces and at least one drug-trafficking organization (DTO)." Its scope depends on how two key terms are specified: (1) DTO and (2) conflict. This book focuses narrowly on "pure" DTOs whose primary activity is drug trafficking and who have no intention of seizing de jure political power over the national territory or any portion thereof. Thus Pablo Escobar's Medellín cartel is included, while the Fuerzas Armadas Revolucionarias de Colombia (FARC), who have been involved in the drug trade since at least the early 1990s (Labrousse 2005), are not. I also focus on episodes with durations greater than one year, in which trafficking organizations clearly adopt a consistently confrontational strategy toward state forces. Thus Rio de Janeiro's drug syndicates, who regularly fire on police during favela incursions, are included, whereas drug retailing groups in other Brazilian cities that generally avoid anti-state violence are not, even if there are isolated incidents of confrontation.

If we broaden the definition of "DTO" to include all armed groups that traffic drugs, the scope expands to encompass many civil wars, insurgencies, and terrorist groups. Conversely, widening the focus to criminal activity writ large leads to the broader study of organized crime groups (which rarely adopt sustained armed opposition to state forces). Likewise, if we expand "conflict" to include sporadic anti-state violence by traffickers, or unilateral violence by state forces against passive, non-violent traffickers, the concept of cartel–state conflict stretches to include a significant portion of drug-related violence in general. If, alternatively, we define "anti-state violence" to include hard-ball political pressure, the scope would encompass many legal interest groups.

Empirically, "conflict" and "crime" are sometimes portrayed as a spectrum, along which armed groups can move with increasing fluidity (Cornell 2005). This has produced a profusion of contested analytic subtypes, like "narco-guerrillas" and "narco-terrorists," further muddled by largely unresolved "greed vs. grievance" debate over the true motives of rebels (Blattman and Miguel 2010, 18). My narrow focus on "pure" drug trafficking organizations highlights the central and unexamined puzzle of why cartels attack the state if not to overthrow or secede from it. This puzzle evaporates if we include armed groups that, however nominally or unrealistically, strive to topple the state or establish regional autonomy. Similarly, it becomes trivial if we include cases of anti-state "attacks" that cannot reasonably be considered strategic—such as one-off, unplanned, accidental, or sporadic incidents—and irrelevant if we examine cases where police use unilateral violence against traffickers who do not fight back.

Ideally, the insights produced by studying "pure" cartels resonate for scholars of these related phenomena. Still, the scope conditions for the findings of this study are relatively restrictive: if the claims made here travel, they will do so most convincingly to contexts where groups (1) have or can easily acquire significant firepower and/or coercive capacity; (2) engage in a profitable but illegal activity which the state seeks to repress *but whose rents it cannot directly expropriate for itself*; and (3) possess plausible avenues of state penetration, especially bribery. It is worth pointing out that countless criminal groups meet these criteria; they thus represent negative cases, groups that could potentially engage in anti-state violence, but choose not to.

A second key scope condition is within-case: the theory developed here is not meant to explain inter-cartel turf war or strictly anti-civilian violence, two substantively and normatively important phenomena that have generated rich and sophisticated research agendas (e.g., Calderón et al. 2015; Dell 2015; Mejía et al. 2013). This book mostly brackets these other forms of violence, addressing them only to the extent that they play into the dynamics of cartel–state conflict. Obviously, turf war can be causally related to cartel–state violence—indeed, the former triggered the latter in Mexico. Yet cartel–state conflict and inter-cartel turf have each occurred in the absence of the other. As I argue in Chapter 2, these are logically distinct types of violence, with different causal mechanisms at play, and requiring different conceptual approaches. Thus, I do not develop a theory of crackdowns' direct effect on inter-cartel turf war, though I do discuss interactions between inter-cartel turf war and cartel–state conflict. Similarly, I do not try to explain cartels' behavior toward civilians, though I do show how some anti-civilian attacks are part of a cartel strategy to pressure leaders for changes to de jure policy.

1.4.2 Case Selection

The restricted scope of cartel–state conflict laid out above leaves us with a phenomenon that is, in a global sense, quite rare: most DTOs at most times avoid anti-state violence, even in the countries studied here. Indeed, the periods selected, Colombia (1983–1993), Rio de Janeiro (1981–) and Mexico (2003–), may encompass the entire universe of positive cases; they are certainly the most salient. Yet while rare, cartel–state violence has proven to be both intense and resilient once it arises, lasting roughly a decade in Colombia and still ongoing after more than ten years in Mexico and thirty in Rio de Janeiro.

Four issues of case selection merit discussion. First, the three conflicts I study constitute positive cases, selected on the book's primary dependent variable of cartel–state conflict. However, there is crucial within-case variation over time, which is the key to my inferential strategy. These case-episodes, some positive and some negative, are pooled to support my claims about the effects of policy on anti-state violence by cartels. Analyzing additional contexts where cartel–state conflict *might have* occurred but did not, like Bolivia or São Paulo, Brazil, is a potential next step; however, within-case variation offers a more controlled environment for building and initial testing of theory. When I turn to state policy as outcome, I focus on the overall trajectory of cartel–state conflict in each country case. I treat these trajectories as "reactive sequences" (Mahoney 2006),[26] exploring the factors that trigger movement from one phase to another. As Figure 1.2 illustrates, trajectories vary significantly across country-cases, providing analytic leverage.

Given this approach, the temporal scope of the study includes preceding "peaceful preludes" and, where applicable, posterior "aftermath" periods. Cartel–state conflict in Mexico and Rio de Janeiro is ongoing, and any line in the sands of time must be arbitrary. Since 2012, Mexico has become marginally less violent and Rio significantly more so; obviously these developments call for explanation, but offering one cannot be the main focus of this book, which is based on field research mostly carried out in 2008–2011. Nonetheless, the theory developed here helps specify possible explanations for recent developments, and how they might be tested.

---

[26] That is, these episodes constitute "chains of temporally ordered and causally connected events" in which "each event within the sequence is in part a reaction to temporally antecedent events" (Mahoney 2006, 509). Mahoney makes no assumption of path dependence.

The Colombia case study focuses on the Escobar years (roughly 1976–1993). This paradigmatic example of criminal war simply must be accounted for by any theory of cartel–state conflict. Moreover, during this period, the dynamics of the drug war were relatively distinct from those of Colombia's ongoing armed insurgencies, who largely avoided contact with the drug trade for ideological reasons.[27] By contrast, the post-Escobar period saw a severe blurring of the line between criminal and civil war: a gruesome three-way conflict erupted among the state, trafficker-linked paramilitary groups, and left-wing guerrillas increasingly involved in coca cultivation as Cold-War funding dried up. Explaining this hybrid civil war is beyond this study's scope, but the period is of interest because the many smaller "pure" drug cartels that succeeded the Medellín and Cali duopoly largely eschewed anti-state violence. I conjecture that the critical factor was not cartel fragmentation (as Calderón would later infer, leading him to adopt a "decapitation" strategy in Mexico) but increased conditionality. The strength of this argument is limited by the blurred analytic lines of this period: an alternative reading is that cartel–state conflict in Colombia never ceased, but was simply subsumed into the broader civil war.

This points to a third issue, comparing different time periods across cases. Studies of conflict processes frequently compare episodes that occurred in different historical time periods (e.g., Fearon and Laitin 2005; Weinstein 2006; Wood 2001), while comparative historical analyses in general (e.g., Collier and Collier 1991; Mahoney 2001) rely on the notion that key events within each case play out at similar points in "analytic time" (Collier 1993), even if at different points in historic time. These considerations justify the temporal focus of this study.

Nonetheless, historical time cannot be ignored. It is important, first and foremost, in terms of the international political context in which sub-national conflicts occur (Reno 1998). Cold War concerns, for example, certainly played a more significant role in 1980s' Colombia than in contemporary Brazil and Mexico. At the same time, US pressure on and aid to Latin American countries to curb drug production and trafficking steadily increased from Nixon onward.[28] Whereas extradition was an open political question in Colombia throughout the Escobar period, in contemporary Mexico it is firmly in place.[29] On the other hand, attitudes toward global prohibition have softened, with former leaders of Mexico, Colombia, and Brazil now

---

27 Just how distinct is open to debate: the first paramilitary groups were founded in the mid-1980s by Escobar associates, some of whom went on to become his mortal enemies and lead the paramilitary movement in the 1990s and 2000s. The first paramilitary clashes with guerrillas and massacres of civilians occurred during the 1980s. However, paramilitary activity in this period paled in comparison to what it would become, and is not central to the dynamics of conflict surrounding the Medellín cartel.

28 I am indebted to Francisco Leal Buitrago for pointing this, and much else, out to me.

29 Extradition is not at issue in the Brazilian case.

openly calling for decriminalization of some drugs (Cardoso et al. 2009). Second, the cases are causally inter-related: Colombia's cocaine boom drove the contemporaneous rise of Rio's CV; the dismantling of the Medellín and Cali cartels in the early 1990s contributed directly to the growth of Mexican cartels over the following 15 years; and as just noted, Colombia's "victory" over Escobar influenced Calderón's decision to launch his war. These considerations do not invalidate cross-temporal comparison, but they should be borne in mind.

A final question is whether it is valid to compare Rio de Janeiro's drug war, largely circumscribed within urban favela communities, with the national-level conflicts of Colombia and Mexico. I argue that it is, for three reasons. First, in Brazil, policing policy is determined primarily by state governors, not presidents or mayors; this makes individual states, rather than Brazil as a whole, the proper level of analysis for questions of crime and security policy. In particular, the Pacification approach was formulated by and attributed to Governor Sérgio Cabral and his security secretary José Beltrame, not Brazil's president. Second, the phenomenon of sustained cartel–state violence observed in Rio is highly anomalous with respect to the rest of Brazil (Lessing 2008), but similar in many respects to Colombia and Mexico. Although Rio is an urban, retail drug market, the *sui generis* nature of its drug trafficking organizations—resilient, prison-based syndicates with significant organizational and military capacity—has given the conflict characteristics more common to producer-transshipment countries. Finally, the scale of the conflict is comparable: although precise figures for total cartel-related deaths are lacking, we know that police alone have killed more than 10,000 people in armed confrontations since 2003.[30]

Including Rio has the great benefit of expanding this study's leverage beyond the now familiar Mexico–Colombia paired comparison (e.g., Durán-Martínez 2015; Felbab-Brown 2009). While this comparison has provided many useful insights, there are crucial questions on which it sheds little light. Above all, why did the splintering of the drug trade into small cartels essentially end cartel–state violence in Colombia in the early 1990s, and wildly exacerbate violence in Mexico since 2008? Including the case of Rio, where splintered prison-based drug syndicates have for decades engaged in frequent clashes with state forces despite (or because of?) lethal militarized police repression, can help answer this question.

Indeed, in comparative perspective, Colombia proves the true outlier in many respects. Nowhere else were the dynamics of violence so driven by the actions of a single actor (Pablo Escobar), and consequently, nowhere else did conditionality take such an individualized, juridical form (essentially, a plea-bargain agreement). As such, coding repressive policy in terms of conditionality is more challenging in the Colombian case. In addition, as I

---

[30] Dowdney (2003) uses firearm mortality statistics to argue that Rio's drug war has produced more fatalities than many civil wars and armed conflicts.

discuss in Chapter 3, the empirical pattern of violence in Colombia was distinct, with particularly high concentration of bombings and other tactics. This is the result, I argue, of the uniquely propitious conditions for violent lobbying that prevailed when cartel–state conflict first broke out there.

1.5 SUMMING UP AND LOOKING AHEAD

States, or rather the leaders who determine policy, face a triple deterrence problem. First, they seek to deter drug traffickers from engaging in what is by any measure a spectacularly lucrative economic activity. Second, they seek to deter their own enforcers—police, investigators, judges, and sometimes the armed forces—from accepting bribes from traffickers in exchange for lax enforcement. Finally, they seek to deter traffickers from resorting to violence, particularly violence against the state itself. The latter challenge, Chapter 2 shows, cannot be taken for granted: cartel–state conflict is no mere by-product of inter-cartel turf war; rather, it can occur independently of turf war, driven by logics of violence all its own.

The goals of reducing drug trafficking, corruption, and anti-state violence form a kind of "unholy trinity": pursuing one goal can undermine the others. This claim flows from the analysis in Part I, which lays out the core logics of anti-state violence by cartels, both informally (Chapters 2 and 3) and formally (Chapter 4). Giving enforcers enough interdiction capacity to deter trafficking necessarily gives them extortionary power over traffickers, potentially increasing corruption. Rampant corruption, in turn, gives cartels additional incentives to use violence, in the form of *plata o plomo* threats. Effective anti-corruption efforts, or more realistically, deploying supposedly "cleaner" forces (such as the army in the Mexican case), may reduce bribery in the short run. However, it does not necessarily reduce, and may even increase, traffickers' incentives for anti-state violence—both as physical defense against augmented enforcement, and as coercive pressure on initially non-corrupt forces to start taking bribes. Moreover, if state leaders overplay their hand with unsustainable policies, traffickers may directly pressure them to back off through terror campaigns. Conditional repression can deter cartels from engaging in anti-state violence, but requires applying less than maximum repression against non-violent traffickers; this may increase the flow of drugs.

Part II illustrates my theory in action through case studies of Colombia, Rio, and Mexico (Chapters 5, 6, and 7), which share a common structure. First, I summarize each case's trajectory, filling in the stylized template of Figure 1.2 with proper nouns and specifying my claims that changes in the degree and conditionality of repressive policy drove the onset, escalation, abatement, and recrudescence of cartel–state conflict. After considering alternative explanations and analytic approaches, I present the details of each case, offering evidence for my core claims as they arise in chronological order. Along the way, I focus descriptive attention on the policy reform processes that, in some cases but not others, led to the implementation of conditional policies (and abatement of cartel–state conflict), and discuss the political fates of these policies once implemented. Part III then puts these accounts in comparative perspective to elaborate a theory of why some reform attempts succeeded and others failed (Chapters 8 and 9), and explore the challenges of sustaining conditional policies over time and the factors that have led, in practice, to their erosion (Chapter 10).

I conclude (Chapter 11) with the implications of my findings for policy and for theory, particularly state-formation theory. Do drug wars make states? Unconditional crackdowns are often launched with explicit state-building objectives, but have largely failed to deliver on them. My findings suggest several possible reasons. Unlike traditional war, drug war creates market opportunities for new entrants with every enemy it eliminates or cripples. Prohibition and repression create massive illicit profits, which fuel the further corruption of state forces. Cartel–state conflict further darkens the prospects for state-building, directly challenging the monopoly on the use of force and, as I argue, worsening corruption through coercive violence. The complementarity of corruption and coercion has implications for literatures on political development and armed conflict as well.

In terms of policy, the infeasibility of simultaneously reducing trafficking, corruption, and violence means that states must make difficult trade-offs; yet as my cases sadly show, it is possible to fail on all three counts. The tragedy of militarized drug war is not just the amount of violence visited on Colombia, Brazil, and Mexico, but how little seems to have been gained in return: drugs continue to flow, and corruption remains rampant. Conditional repression is hard to implement and sustain, but has proven effective when done right. Given an international context in which large-scale cocaine trafficking remains illegal, and consumer-country demand remains strong, building the logistical capacity and political support to sustain conditional approaches is the best path forward.

PART I

A THEORY OF CARTEL–STATE CONFLICT

2

What Is Cartel–State Conflict?

This chapter delineates the concept of "cartel–state conflict" and its relationship to other conflict types and the theories scholars have advanced to explain them. The militarized drug wars of Colombia, Mexico, and Rio de Janeiro have caused destruction on par with some of the most violent civil wars; the peaks of violence involved both intense fighting among cartels for turf and sustained armed confrontation between cartels and state forces. Nonetheless, cartel–state conflict and inter-cartel turf war are logically and causally distinct conflict types: each can exacerbate the other, but each can also occur in the absence of the other, or in widely differing proportions. Cartel–state conflict is also distinct from civil war, a fact which the popular "criminal insurgency" concept has obfuscated. I present a framework for analysis that distinguishes conflict types by central goals and battle aims; introduces the key logics of violence that operate within each conflict type; and discusses the (imperfect) mapping between conflict types, logics, and observed patterns of violent events, i.e., the "microdynamics of conflict."

2.1 A FRAMEWORK FOR THE STUDY OF CONFLICT AND CRIMINAL VIOLENCE

This chapter delineates the concept of cartel–state conflict: what it is, what it is not, and where it stands in relation to other conflict types and the theories scholars have advanced to explain them. The study of drug war and criminal conflict in general is relatively new and under-theorized, and a dearth of clear concepts has led some scholars to conflate cartel–state conflict with other conflict types, or treat it as a mere by-product. The conceptual brush-clearing undertaken here clarifies the similarities, differences, and potential causal linkages among conflict types, setting the stage for the theory of cartel–state conflict I develop in Chapters 3 and 4 (see also Lessing 2015). In the process, I explain my analytic approach and place it within a framework for the broader study of conflict and criminal violence.

The drug trade is a violent business. Though well-known, this fact is quite puzzling: trafficking is based on voluntary economic transactions, and so does not logically require violence. Extant scholarship on drug violence, focused on consumer markets in first-world settings, generally attributes such "systemic violence" to a lack of enforceable contracts and property rights (Goldstein 1985; Skaperdas 2001). Yet the sheer intensity of drug violence in Latin America raises questions that this approach is poorly equipped to answer. In Mexico, Colombia, and Rio de Janeiro, drug wars are not just matters of sporadic, score-settling and reputation-building violence, but sustained militarized conflicts in which states and powerful DTOs alike mobilize well-equipped armies, producing casualties and social disruption on a scale that is really only comparable with civil war. Indeed, at the height of the Escobar period in Colombia, cartel–state conflict overtook a long-standing civil war as the nation's primary security threat (Pardo Rueda 1996).

Obviously, these levels of violence could not have occurred in the absence of large and powerful DTOs with the capacity to amass and field significant firepower. These "cartels," in turn, are the product of the acute profitability and barriers to entry that characterize markets for cocaine transshipment. (Rio de Janeiro is an exceptional case of a once-competitive retail market "oligopolized" by sophisticated syndicates with cartel-like profits and firepower, an outcome I have argued is due to their unique, prison-gang structure (Lessing 2008).) Yet profits and oligopoly alone are not enough to produce militarized drug war. Cartels, like all oligopolistic firms, have incentives to collude with one another, and frequently do. They also, like all criminal groups, have incentives to avoid drawing the attention of authorities through violence, which many do as well. The oligopolistic nature of some markets may guarantee that when violence breaks out, it will be intense, but we must dig deeper to understand the onset and resilience of militarized drug war.

In all three cases of militarized drug war studied here, the peaks of overall violence were composed of both cartel–state conflict and inter-cartel turf war, in varying proportions. This book offers an explanation of the former, bucking the trend in recent research on Mexico—where turf war has been so extreme that most research focuses exclusively on it of treating anti-state violence by cartels as an afterthought both causally and substantively. To be sure, turf war and cartel–state conflict are causally related, but a critical empirical finding of this study is that each has occurred independently of the other, and causal arrows appear to run in both directions. Meanwhile, security analysts who (correctly) highlight the importance of cartel–state conflict in Mexico, have misleadingly dubbed it "criminal insurgency," leaving unexamined crucial differences in the battle aims of cartels versus insurgents. While the rich literature on civil war provides critical theoretical foundations, many of its basic assumptions simply do not carry over to the strategic and political realities of drug wars.

To grapple with these issues, I advance a framework for thinking about varieties of conflict, presented briefly here and fleshed out in the sections below. I begin by distinguishing conflict types by the overarching strategic goals of the actors involved. In Kalyvas' seminal analysis of civil war, "[competitive] state building is the insurgents' central goal and renders organized and sustained rebellion of the kind that takes place in civil wars fundamentally distinct from phenomena such as banditry, mafias, or social movements" (2006, 218). Building on this insight, I conceive of *civil war*, *cartel–state conflict*, *inter-cartel turf war*, and *protection* as broad, purposive efforts or activities characterized by different overarching goals, which in turn orient multiple, specific logics of violence (Table 2.1). Whereas the central goal of inter-cartel turf war is competitive market share, that of cartel–state conflict is, I argue, quite distinct: the weakening of de facto state repression. Moreover, both goals clearly differ from those posited by Diego Gambetta in his canonical analysis of mafias as providers of protection (1993), which has largely oriented the study of violence in organized crime.

These differing central goals have implications for actors' proximate aims in fighting, and hence in the predominant functions that violence plays. In some conflicts, actors' aim in fighting is essentially *conquest*—seizing territory or resources from opponents (or possibly eliminating them altogether); in others, the aim is *constraint*—altering opponents' behavior. These "battle aims" echo Thomas Schelling's seminal distinction between two primordial functions of violence, brute force and coercion:

> There is a difference between taking what you want and making someone give it to you, between fending off assault and making someone afraid to assault you, between holding what people are trying to take and making them afraid to take it ... It is the difference between defense and deterrence.

> (Schelling 1966, 2–3)

Critically, this distinction is not monolithic; violence can play different functions at different levels of analysis. Schelling offers an example from inter-state war, whose overarching aim is clearly conquest:

> What is pure pain, or the threat of it, at one level of decision can be equivalent to brute force at another ... tactics that frighten soldiers so that they ... surrender represent coercion based on the power to hurt; to the top command, which is frustrated but not coerced, such tactics are part of the contest in military discipline and strength.

> (Schelling 1966, 8–9)

Conversely, conflicts aimed at constraint, including cartel–state conflict, may certainly involve violence that is brute force at the "local," tactical level, but the larger purpose of that violence remains fundamentally coercive.

My framework then extends Kalyvas' core methodological insight that there is variation in the types and intensity of violence *within* any given conflict,

TABLE 2.1. *Varieties of Conflict: Central Goals, Logics of Violence, and Observed Outcomes.*

Varieties of Conflict

	Civil War (Kalyvas 2006)	Cartel–State Conflict	Inter-Cartel Turf War	Protection (Gambetta 1993)
			Systemic Drug Violence (Goldstein 1985)	
Central goal	Competitive state-building	Weaken de facto state repression	Acquire market share	Facilitate non-contractible transactions
Proximate battle aims	Conquest	Constraint	Conquest	Constraint
Overarching function of violence	Brute force	Coercion	Brute force	Coercion
Logics of Violence: empirical "footprint" • = Logics discussed in Chapter 3	*Target Informants:* discriminate violence *Instill Terror:* indiscriminate violence	• *Reduce Losses to Enforcement:* defensive violence during busts • *Violent Corruption:* mix of bribery and enforcer-targeted violence • *Violent Lobbying:* terror tactics, overt de jure policy demands	*Expropriate or Eliminate Rivals:* intense clashes until victor prevails • *Signal Strength:* sporadic, highly visible violence • *Draw Repression Onto Rival ("Calentar la Plaza"):* attacks on rival's turf, attribution disputes	*Punish Defectors:* sporadic violence when uncertainty is high
Micro-level outcomes		Cartel–cartel killings		
		Cartel–state killings		
	Anti-civilian killings			

The top section shows the central goals for each form of conflict, as well as the proximate aim of fighting (conquest vs. constraint) and the corresponding function of violence (brute force vs. coercion). The middle section enumerates different logics of violence, and respective empirical "footprints," within each conflict type. The bottom section shows how broad classes of micro-level outcomes can be usefully but imperfectly mapped to conflict types.

and that this variation can be fruitfully explained in terms of different "logics of violence." Each logic shows how a specific strategic situation or set of conditions creates incentives to employ a specific form of violence. Kalyvas' theory of civil war, for example, posits competing logics of discriminate and indiscriminate violence against civilians. These come into play under different tactical conditions and may have both coercive and brute-force effects at the "local" level, but both nonetheless serve the central brute-force goal of competitive state-building.

In parallel fashion, I argue that cartels are motivated to use violence against the state by three principal logics: loss reduction, violent corruption, and violent lobbying. I define and analyze these logics in Chapters 3 and 4; for now, the key point is that they are distinct from the logics that operate in inter-cartel turf war, as well as in markets for protection. One contribution of my approach is to disentangle these logics, which are often conflated under the broad concept of "systemic violence" (Goldstein 1985) in the literatures on drug violence and organized crime.

Each logic predicts a rough empirical "footprint," a spatio-temporal pattern in the types of violence likely to be employed. Identifying the conditions under which different logics become operative can thus help explain observed patterns at the level of individual violent acts, i.e., the "microdynamics of conflict" (Kalyvas 2008). For example, the logic of violent lobbying predicts high-profile, often terrorist violence aimed at imposing political costs on leaders, coupled with overt calls for de jure policy change. One necessary condition for this logic to operate is that the desired policy change be at least plausible, politically and logistically. Thus, my theory predicts that terrorist violence is more likely when states implement de jure policies that are unpopular, unsustainable, or of low public salience such that changes incur low political costs. The chapters to come detail how different aspects of state policy (as well as other factors) impact the strategic conditions cartels face, activating or nullifying different logics of violence and thus driving the resulting patterns of observed violence.

The bottom section of Table 2.1 maps conflict types and their corresponding logics onto empirical outcomes; the mapping is deliberately "fuzzy." Unfortunately, individual observations cannot always be precisely assigned to logics of violence, and hence to conflict types, whether for lack of the often incredibly detailed information needed to do so (Kalyvas 2008), or because they truly straddle conceptual categories. This means that we cannot *define* cartel–state conflict or inter-cartel turf war in terms of the identity of participants and victims, or easily observed modalities of violence like "bombings" and "assassinations"; rather, turf war and cartel–state conflict predict general patterns of violence. To a first approximation, we can treat violence among traffickers as turf-war violence and violence between traffickers and state forces as cartel–state conflict, but this is an approximation. Some anti-state violence could be motivated by turf war, as the logics enumerated in Table 2.1 suggest. Moreover, the same imperfect fit between individual observations and conflict types occurs at a more fine-grained level between observations and the different logics of violence *within* each conflict type. I explore these issues in detail in Chapter 3.

This brisk overview has surely left the reader with questions if not grave doubts. Let us walk more carefully through the arguments underlying the framework presented in Table 2.1, and consider some of its implications for analysis. I start by conceptualizing cartel–state conflict as a variety of drug violence, then focus on its relationship to inter-cartel turf war in particular, and conclude by comparing and contrasting it with civil war.

2.2   VARIETIES OF DRUG VIOLENCE

One way to approach cartel–state conflict is as a type of drug violence, and more broadly as a form of criminal violence. As criminal activities go, drug trafficking is both unusually lucrative and surprisingly violent. While this can be said of all market segments of the drug trade, from production to consumption, it is particularly true of the smuggling/transshipment sector. There, both profits and violence can reach staggering levels. The connection between these two facts runs through market structure: international cocaine smuggling has high barriers to entry, and thus tends to be oligopolistic (Reuter 2013); for *sui generis* reasons, so is Rio's retail market. A few large firms capture enormous profits, and can thus afford to amass significant firepower. This alone does not guarantee violence, which, after all is costly. But when violence breaks out, it takes place at a massive, militarized scale. Extant theories of drug and criminal violence offer some important points of departure for explaining violence, but require further disaggregation to adequately account for militarized drug war.

In terms of profits, though popular estimates of the total size of drug trade flows are likely inflated (Thoumi 2005)—$500 billion a year, the UN claimed at one point—even rigorous conservative estimates find illicit drugs to be "a modest contributor to total world trade" (Reuter and Greenfield 2001, 163). More pertinently, heroin and cocaine trafficking alone account for nearly 80 percent of transnational criminal activity (Figure 2.1). Moreover, while the bulk of drug profits accrue within consumer countries, particularly at the retail level, the percentage markup is highest for transnational smuggling (Reuter and Greenfield 2001, 166–167). This is one reason that this sector tends to be concentrated in a few large and highly profitable firms. Current estimates of Mexican cartels' yearly revenues from trafficking drugs into the United States vary widely, from RAND's conservative $6.6 billion to the US Justice Department's possibly alarmist $39 billion. The cocaine trade was almost certainly *more* lucrative during the heyday of the Colombian cartels in the 1980s, since prices were higher and repression was lower. Pablo Escobar was famously cited by *Forbes* magazine as one of the richest men in the world; Castillo (1987) estimated, based on contemporary spot prices, that he was earning revenues on the order of $8 billion per year.

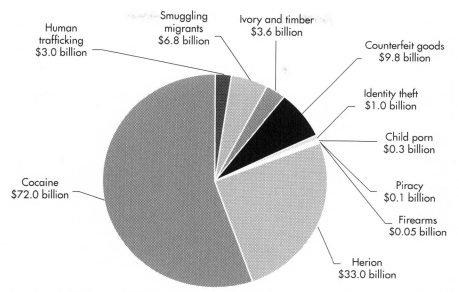

FIGURE 2.1. **Varieties of Transnational Organized Crime, by Estimated Annual Value.**
Author's elaboration with data from UNODC (2010a).

The stunning profitability of drug trafficking is a reminder that, like all black-market and vice forms of crime, it is based on voluntary, positive-sum transactions, and so does not logically require violence; on the contrary, violence is usually bad for business. Indeed, as crime researcher Peter Reuter points out, many consensual markets for illicit goods—like prostitution and bookmaking—are mostly peaceful, concluding that "illegality itself is insufficient to generate high levels of violence in a market" (2009, 275). The drug trade is notoriously, puzzlingly violent, but here too there is great variation within and across market segments. Trafficking of marijuana and psychedelics generates far less violent than that of cocaine and heroin; European retail markets are less violent than those in the United States; and US markets were extremely violent during the 1980s' crack epidemic, but violence abated even while crack use remained rampant. Militarized drug war is essentially limited to markets for the production and transshipment of cocaine and heroin (Rio's retail market is an exception), but many production and transshipment markets never witness militarized drug war.

Goldstein's (1985) canonical three-way typology offers a first cut at these varieties of drug violence. He distinguishes "economic–compulsive violence" (users committing property crimes to obtain funds to purchase drugs) and "psychopharmacological violence" (violence due to the effect of the drugs themselves), from "systemic violence," associated with the machinations of drug firms. Importantly, Goldstein's typology is based on the motives for or logics of violence, not necessarily the observable forms violence takes (e.g., murder, battery, death threats, etc.).

Reflecting a concern with retail settings like the then-violent US crack market, the first two types of violence are exclusive to drug consumers; as motives of individuals in somewhat desperate situations, they are likely to be atomistic, idiosyncratic, and far from perfectly rational. For these reasons, such violence, when widespread, resembles an epidemic rather than a war. Moreover, even if these types of violence were occasionally directed at state forces, it would not constitute a sustained armed challenge to state authority.

Systemic violence is almost by definition instrumental or "rational," presumably undertaken as part of drug firms' larger profit-maximization strategy. This makes it *prima facie* puzzling, because unlike robbery, kidnapping, or extortion, trafficking does not logically require the use of violence; at each stage of the production and supply chain, there are buyers and sellers who stand to make mutually beneficial deals. Nonetheless, from coca and poppy fields to street corners, the drug trade is riddled with systemic, and hence strategic, violence. Even in large consumer markets like the United States, researchers find that most violence is systemic (Friman 2009, 285–286); violence in production and transshipment settings is essentially systemic by definition, since it involves only drug firms, not consumers. Militarized drug war can thus be seen as a form of systemic violence: in oligopolistic market segments featuring organized, large-scale drug firms, systemic violence itself becomes organized, large-scale, and persistent.

Because "systemic violence" includes everything from street-corner tussles to all-out militarized drug war, further distinctions are necessary. Traditionally, systemic violence in the drug trade and other black markets has been attributed to the illegal nature of the economic transactions, which rules out legally enforceable contracts and property rights (Andreas and Wallman 2009; Schelling 1967; Skaperdas 2001). When buyers fail to pay or sellers fail to deliver, physical violence may be the aggrieved party's only recourse. Although such violence is costly in the short run, it can actually be Pareto-improving in the long run if it allows buyers and sellers to credibly commit to deals and leads them to reliably follow through in equilibrium. In Gambetta's seminal analysis of protection, a reputation for violence can be a socially useful stand-in for state enforcement of contracts, ultimately serving as a mutually beneficial "lubricant of economic exchange" (Gambetta 1993, 2).

Another function of violence, though, is to forcibly expropriate turf from or destroy competitors. This type of violence is often bundled conceptually with reputational violence, because both ultimately derive from an inability to sign enforceable contracts, and both are presumably part of a larger profit-maximizing strategy on cartels' part. But expropriation differs in that the value of violence lies in its actual use: the physical seizure of turf or elimination of a rival. In contrast, the value of a reputation for violence—i.e., the capacity to make credible threats—lies precisely in not having to carry out those threats

(Schelling 1966). Reputational violence could occur as part of a larger logic of expropriation, as a way of convincing a rival to cede territory (as opposed to a means of guaranteeing mutually beneficial trades *à la* Gambetta). Even then, though, it serves as a "costly signal" of actors' strength and resolve, and if signals are effective, they do not need to be re-sent. Broadly speaking, then, reputation-building violence is likely to be sporadic, particularly if the structure of drug firms remains stable, while sustained, intense cartel-on-cartel violence is likely to be driven by goals of expropriation. I call conflicts driven by such goals of expropriation *inter-cartel turf war* or simply "turf war."

Inter-cartel turf war is best understood in terms of economic theories of industrial organization, which explore the relationship among the number of firms in a market, the nature of competition, and the equilibrium behavior of firms and resulting outcomes. Both perfect competition and monopoly, it turns out, are fairly easy to analyze; in oligopolistic markets, i.e., those with a few firms, many types of equilibria are possible. In some, firms collude or cooperate to reap mutual gains, approaching a monopoly outcome; in others, they compete away profits, approaching a competitive outcome. Despite licit firms' recourse to contracts and property rights in general, the illegality of collusion means that, like criminal firms, they cannot rely on contracts to support collusion.[1] Collusive pacts—the economic definition of the word "cartel"—allow all firms involved to reap large profits, but since firms have incentives to cheat, these pacts are unstable. Of course, unlike licit oligopoly, drug firms can resort to violence to physically seize turf and eliminate rivals, but from an abstract modeling perspective, the costliness of violence is not so different from inefficient advertising "arms races" in the battle for market share.[2] The upshot is that, just as it is difficult to predict when oligopolistic markets like air travel or automobiles will be characterized by collusion or intense competition, it is difficult to know when concentrated segments of the drug trade will be characterized by peaceful division of territory and when acute turf war will break out. Most recent research on Mexico's drug war focuses on explaining the onset and dynamics of such inter-cartel turf war (e.g., Calderón et al. 2015; Dell 2015; Trejo and Ley 2016).

In most settings, violence among traffickers does not imply violence between traffickers and state forces. In the retail markets of developed countries, for example, small-scale turf wars are common enough (e.g., Hagedorn 1994; Levitt and Venkatesh 2000), but violence against state forces remains exceedingly rare, despite often high levels of anti-narcotics repression. Even

---

[1] This is why both settings are best modeled with non-cooperative game theory; indeed, the origins of game theory are often traced to Cournot's seminal 1838 analysis of duopoly.

[2] As Powell (2002) notes, the modern conflict-as-bargaining-breakdown literature began with Fearon's seminal application of economic theories of bargaining among firms to the context of war, while the notion of war as bargaining goes back at least to Schelling.

in production and transshipment settings, DTOs generally avoid direct confrontation with states. Of course, drug enforcement produces occasional police casualties, but in many cases these constitute, from the perspective of DTOs, accidents: stray bullets or friendly fire; a rogue, hot-headed lieutenant; killing an unidentified undercover agent, and so on. Sometimes, DTOs may decide to kill highly corrupt police officials who have reneged on some deal; however, as a form of reputational violence, this is likely to be quite sporadic. *Cartel–state conflict*, marked by a sustained and deliberate strategy of confrontation on the part of sophisticated and well-armed DTOs (which I shorthand throughout as "cartels"), is globally quite rare; the three cases studied here stand out as prominent, if not unique, anomalies. This alone suggests the importance of distinguishing cartel–state conflict from inter-cartel drug war; in the next section I explore this distinction further.

2.3 CARTEL–STATE CONFLICT VS. INTER-CARTEL TURF WAR

Looking exclusively at Mexico's conflict, one might conclude that militarized drug war is primarily about inter-cartel battles for turf and hegemony, and that cartel–state conflict constitutes unavoidable, but perhaps substantively minor, collateral damage. Even on its own terms, this is an oversimplification; in comparative perspective, it is clearly wrong. As the cases of Rio and Colombia makes clear, cartel–state conflict can occur independently of turf war, follows dynamics of its own, and can be equally if not more destructive than inter-cartel fighting. The two forms of conflict are causally interrelated to be sure, but causal arrows run in both directions: either can trigger or exacerbate the other.

Mexico's ongoing drug war has been characterized by very intense, prolonged, and multilateral fighting among cartels. The vast majority of cartel-related killings there appear to be between traffickers—some 88 percent by the Calderón government's 2011 count—and the most brutal and graphic of these *ejecuciones* (executions) clearly bear the fingerprints of competitive dynamics. Moreover, these killings seem to be structured at the meso-level by well-publicized feuds and battles among Mexico's principal cartels: violence spikes in a city or state when cartels clash over control, and abates when one or another achieves hegemony. For good reason, understanding the deeper causes of inter-cartel turf war has become a critical avenue of ongoing research (e.g., Mejía et al. 2013; Trejo and Ley 2013); even scholars studying the effect of state repression on drug-war violence generally restrict their dependent variable to inter-cartel violence (e.g., Calderón et al. 2015; Dell 2015).

This tendency to treat cartel–state violence as an afterthought, or simply lump it in with inter-cartel violence, reflects an assumption—sometimes tacit or inadvertent—that cartel–state conflict is essentially a by-product of inter-cartel fighting. The timing of the Mexican case lends itself to such a view: it was the intensification of turf war that triggered the state's shift toward unconditional crackdowns, first in 2004, when then-President Vicente Fox deployed army troops to Nuevo Laredo in an attempt to quell acute fighting between the Sinaloa and Gulf-Zetas cartels (Grillo 2011, 102–106). This episode produced the first examples of systematic armed violence by cartels against state forces. Cartel–state violence then surged again in the wake of Felipe Calderón's far more extensive crackdown, itself a response to rising inter-cartel violence throughout 2006. To many, this suggests that cartel–state violence is basically epiphenomenal to inter-cartel turf war; an important proponent of this view is Calderón's former head of intelligence, Guillermo Valdés, who elaborates an explicit causal account in which the mere physical presence of state forces in areas beset by turf war makes anti-state violence "inevitable" (Valdés 2013, 391–392).

This thesis simply does not travel. In Colombia, the opposite scenario prevailed: cartel–state violence preceded and clearly triggered inter-cartel violence. Pablo Escobar's war on the state, launched in the name of and with financing from virtually all of Colombia's cocaine traffickers, overshadowed even the country's ongoing civil war for much of the mid-1980s and early 1990s. The turf war that eventually erupted between the Medellín and Cali cartels, though also very violent, was shorter in duration and largely constrained to those two cities, while anti-state violence importantly had national reach. When Escobar turned himself in under the *Sometimiento* policy, turf war abated almost by necessity; when he escaped, and cartel–state conflict resumed, so did turf war. And while Cali's pursuit of Escobar contributed to his downfall, it was ultimately his death at the hands of state forces that ended both cartel–state conflict and turf war in 1993.

In Rio, the scenario is mixed. Intense turf battles among cartels have been going on since at least the early 1990s, and officials generally (and self-servingly) portray the drug war as primarily an inter-cartel affair, with police-trafficker clashes a kind of trailing indicator. On the other hand, armed confrontation between Rio's primary syndicate and state forces predates the rise of rival syndicates (and ensuing turf war) by several years. In any case, cartel–state conflict has consistently accounted for a significant share of overall drug-related violence. Between 2003 and the 2008 rollout of the Pacification strategy, deaths from armed confrontations between civilians and police (a rough measure of cartel–state conflict) varied from 15 to 25 percent of *all* firearm homicides. Assuming that the vast majority of cartel-related homicides involve firearms, but that not all firearms homicides were cartel-related, this represents an absolute lower-bound estimate of the share of cartel–state homicides among total drug-related homicides in Rio, about twice that of Mexico.

Even in Mexico, though, cartel–state conflict is substantively important. The very intensity of inter-cartel fighting in Mexico obscures what is, on its own terms, a great deal of cartel–state violence. Since 2010, cartels attacks on army troops have occurred at rates of one to three *per day*, while thousands of police and public officials have been killed, in addition to some 8,000 suspected

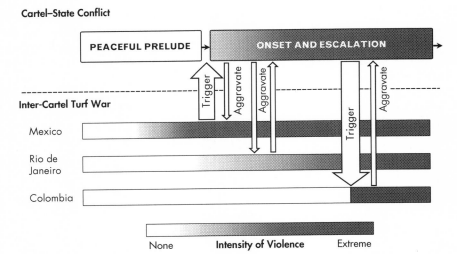

FIGURE 2.2. **Cartel–State Conflict and Inter-Cartel Turf War: Timing and Causal Relations.** Turf war preceded and triggered cartel–state conflict in Mexico; the two conflict types co-evolved in Rio; and in Colombia, cartel–state conflict preceded and triggered turf war. Shading indicates the intensity of each form of conflict. The arrows represent causal relationships between the two forms of conflict; thick arrows indicate triggers and thin arrows indicate aggravating factors.

traffickers killed by state forces. True, this is dwarfed in numerical terms by the more than 70,000 killed in turf war. Yet a naive arithmetical accounting of death tolls risks seriously understating importance of cartel–state conflict. Brazen cartel attacks on state forces and public infrastructure have impact beyond the number of officials killed. Systematic armed confrontation with state forces fundamentally erodes official authority, public order, and the rule of law, doing disproportionate damage to social and political life. To see this, we need only ask ourselves, "Which would have the larger substantive impact, the total cessation of cartel–state conflict in Mexico, or a numerically equivalent reduction in inter-cartel homicides?"

Inter-cartel turf war is thus neither a sufficient nor necessary condition for cartel–state conflict. Figure 2.2 summarizes the timing of cartel–state conflict onset with turf war in my three cases. In Colombia, cartel–state conflict began at a time where cartels were not only at peace, but actively collaborating in mutual defense; turf war did not set in until, and was probably triggered by, the escalation of cartel–state conflict. In Rio, cartel–state conflict co-evolved with turf war, but armed cartel resistance to police actions began when there was a single, hegemonic cartel. In both cases, cartel–state conflict exacerbated turf war by encouraging traffickers to break away from confrontational "market-leader" cartels engaged in the most extreme anti-state violence. In Mexico, turf war preceded cartel–state conflict, and triggered initial state crackdowns on cartels. This, however, does not imply that turf war alone caused cartels to fight back against the state—in the United States, for example, police crackdowns in response to gang wars do not produce anti-state violence, and have even led drug gangs to avoid brazen forms of inter-cartel violence (Rafael 2007, 33–39).

Additional evidence of the causal independence of cartel–state conflict can be found at the micro-level, as I explore in more detail in the case studies. In Rio, of 872 media reports of armed clashes from 2007 to 2010, fully 89 percent were between state forces and cartels. In Mexico, the share is lower but still significant. Moreover, a sub-national analysis of official cartel-related homicide data shows that inter-cartel violence is only very weakly correlated spatio-temporally with cartel–state homicides (Figure 7.2).

Overall, an epiphenomenal account of cartel–state conflict fares poorly. A better approach is to map the multiple causal arrows linking turf war and cartel–state conflict. These, I argue, run in both directions. Turf war can trigger or exacerbate cartel–state conflict by contributing to the conditions that make anti-state violence cartels' best response to government repression; two key examples are increased cartel firepower and expanded state repression. Yet cartel–state conflict can also trigger or exacerbate turf war by upsetting delicate inter-cartel pacts. The final section of Chapter 3 discusses these causal channels in more detail.

Where turf war and cartel–state conflict co-exist, the empirical distinction between them can become fuzzy, as when a cartel attacks state officials that are protecting a rival cartel. In the limit, the distinction may evaporate, such as where a public official is universally understood to be no more than an employee of a given cartel. Generally, though, the "state-ness" of targets matter, however corrupt. After all, they can only be corrupt by virtue of being state agents, endowed with some capacity to direct enforcement against one or another cartel. The analysis of violent corruption to come makes clear how this capacity interacts with state repressive policy to generate unique incentives for cartel violence.

This raises another potential objection: if cartels' use of anti-state violence is, to a first approximation, part of profit-maximizing strategy, one might argue that cartel–state conflict is ultimately aimed at beating one's rivals and coming out on top, and that the concept should be subordinated to turf war. This would be a mistake. As the variation in cases demonstrates, pacting vs. fighting among cartels is logically independent (though not unaffected by) the decision to confront the state. Thus, in Table 2.1, turf war and cartel–state conflict share a conceptual level, both subordinate to the profit-maximizing logic of systemic violence.

2.4 CARTEL–STATE CONFLICT VS. INSURGENCY

A different set of arguments, also developed in response to the Mexican case, puts central emphasis on cartels' willingness to confront the state, but attributes this to their nature as "criminal insurgents."

> Not surprisingly, the cartels have not sat idly by while Calderon [*sic*] cracks down. If the Mexican anti-crime effort succeeds, the state's powers will grow and the cartels will lose their influence—an unacceptable outcome to the *narcos*. In response, the cartels have launched a war of attrition against the government. (Sullivan and Elkus 2008, 6)

The "criminal insurgency" literature has been influential in policy and US military circles, fueling contentious public debate about whether Mexico's drug war constitutes civil war or even state failure (Grillo 2011, 204). It even led to a diplomatic kerfuffle in 2010 when then US Secretary of State Hillary Clinton said that Mexican cartels increasingly resembled insurgents and compared the situation to Colombia's civil war. This conceptual contestation has real-world stakes: on the one hand, "civil war" carries a possibly undeserved stigma of chaos and loss of state control (Grillo 2011, 202–206) and could have consequences for international intervention (Bergal 2011); on the other, it confers a potentially undeserved sense of righteous struggle on drug cartels (Kalyvas 2015).

Analytically, the "criminal insurgency" approach quite helpfully drew attention to cartel–state conflict as a critical phenomenon, and correctly saw state crackdowns as the trigger (though it did not identify conditionality of repression as an important factor). Moreover, its fundamental premise is correct: cartels *do* fight to retain influence. Yet these authors never put forth an explicit theory of how attacking state forces is supposed to accomplish that. Conceptually, "criminal insurgency" lumps where it should split. As its formulators readily admit, it expands the concept of "insurgency" to include not only revolution and secession but intimidation and degradation of state forces for their own sake (Sullivan and Elkus 2008, 6–7). This replaces the canonical understanding of insurgency's central goal as "competitive state-building" (Kalyvas 2006, 218) with the significantly broader notion of "state weakening." By eliding critical differences in rebels' and cartels' battle aims, this conceptual stretching (Sartori 1970) obscures rather than illuminates a fundamental puzzle: why fight the state if not to topple or secede from it?

As noted in Chapter 1, the answer "to keep the state off one's back" is insufficient: criminal groups everywhere would like the state off their back, but rarely resort to violence. In most sectors of the drug trade, including but not limited to US retail drug markets, violence against police is nearly unheard of, for fear of drawing down more heat. Even Prohibition-era gangsters like Al Capone and Detroit's notoriously violent Purple Gang rarely if ever targeted state forces, and never as part of a systematic campaign (Kavieff

2000). Indeed, a search for "out-of-sample" comparison cases of sustained criminal violence against the state for this study yielded only one significant example: the Sicilian Mafia's "war" on the Italian state in the early 1990s. This episode contrasts sharply with Gambetta's (1993) classic account of the Sicilian Mafia, or Cosa Nostra, in which anti-state violence is virtually absent. Moreover, the "war" was quite short-lived: after several spectacular bombings (reminiscent of Escobar's contemporaneous tactics), the violence quickly abated (Stille 1996). It remains unclear why. While Cosa Nostra leaders may have come to see anti-state violence as counter-productive, producing even stronger state repression, an emerging body of journalistic evidence[3] suggests that the attacks produced a new state–Mafia pact with Silvio Berlusconi's ascendant Forza Italia party that effectively weakened such repression. Either way, if sustaining a shooting war with the state in response to crackdowns were generally a winning strategy, more trafficking and organized crime organizations in more varied contexts would do it.

A more fruitful way to think about drug wars is to treat belligerents' proximate aims of fighting as a core dimension along which conflicts vary, and a key outcome to be explained. This approach is well-founded in civil-war scholarship. As noted above, Kalyvas sees insurgents' central goal of "competitive state-building" as a defining and distinguishing characteristic of civil war (2006, 218). The UCDP/PRIO Armed Conflict Dataset includes only conflicts in which armed groups fight "for the replacement of the central government, or the change of its composition," or "control of a certain territory … secession or autonomy" (UCDP 2011, 3; Gleditsch et al. 2002).[4] For Fearon and Laitin, such battle aims may not define insurgency (2003, 76), but characterize it in practice:

> The aim of the rebel side in almost all civil wars is to take over the central government or to take political control of a region of the country. Rebel groups rarely say "we are fighting in order to induce the government to change its policy on X, and once that is accomplished we will disband and leave politics." (2007, 1–2)

Tellingly, this is *precisely* what cartels have said when attacking the state. Consider these communiqués from Colombian drug lord Pablo Escobar, regarding his five-year campaign of public bombings, high-level assassinations, systematic extermination of police, and elite kidnappings:

3 The most accessible source for non-Italian speakers is the 2014 film *La Trattativa*, translated as *The State-Mafia Pact*, by journalist Sabina Guzzanti.
4 For this reason, none of Mexico's cartel violence appears in its Armed Conflict Dataset, and the Americas register as the world region with the least battle deaths (Themnér and Wallensteen 2013, 4).

We solemnly promise … that once extradition is legally prohibited, we will immediately suspend our military actions against the extraditers.

(Quoted in *Semana* 1986)[5]

Recognizing the position of the National Constitutional Assembly [banning extradition], we have decided to disband our entire military organization.

(Quoted in *El Tiempo* 1991)

Similarly, Mexico's Knights Templar cartel greeted incoming president Enrique Peña Nieto with *narcomantas* ("narco-banners") reading, "If you honor your promise [to alter the course of the drug war], we will lay down our arms … otherwise we will continue to defend our territory" (Ezequiel 2012).

Generalizing, then, the proximate aim of fighting in revolutionary insurgency is *conquest*, in which belligerents aim to definitively expropriate from or replace opponents. When rebels fight states, this implies competitive state-building, if only within a portion of the national territory. Importantly, inter-cartel turf war is also a war of conquest: the central goal is to win market share at the expense of competitors. Cartel–state conflict, by contrast, is a war of *constraint*: belligerents aim "merely" to coerce opponents into changing their behavior (i.e., their policies, when fighting states).

Table 2.2 extends this distinction, sorting examples of intra- and inter-state conflict types by their battle aims. This highlights the similarities between cartel–state conflict and coercive diplomacy—such as armed embargoes—and, perhaps, international terrorism: Pape (2003, 343) finds that most suicide terrorists, like Pablo Escobar but *unlike* Fearon and Laitin's rebels, "consistently announce specific political goals and stop suicide attacks when those goals have been fully or partially achieved."[6] In any case, the conquest/constraint distinction is meant to characterize, not define: just as insurgents *could* fight wars of constraint but rarely do, drug cartels *could* seek to seize formal state power, but have not. Thinking about why sheds light on the distinct logics of cartel–state conflict.

What explains variation in battle aims? I suggest three related factors: the nature of the rents being fought over, the function of violence when resorted to, and the politics of negotiation. All three factors play a role in canonical theories of conquest: in weakly institutionalized settings, actors will use violence to physically appropriate mutually prized territory, resources, or political power when they cannot reach stable bargained solutions (Fearon 1995b; Powell 2002; Wagner 1994; Walter 2009). In these theories, the "pie"—whatever is at stake—usually has a transferable, zero-sum quality, so that one side's loss is the other's gain, and one side can "buy off" the other. Second, fighting can usually

---

5   All quotes from foreign sources are the author's translations.
6   It bears emphasizing, however, that terrorism is a flexible tactic; it can and has been used as part of revolutionary insurgency and many other types of conflict.

TABLE 2.2. *Conflict Types by Belligerents' Aims of Fighting: Conquest vs. Constraint.*

		Proximate Aim of Fighting	
		Conquest (Expropriate/replace opponent)	Constraint (Change opponent's behavior)
Belligerent Dyads — Sub-national	State vs. Domestic Non-State Actor (NSA)	Revolutionary insurgency	**Cartel–state conflict**
	Domestic NSA vs. Domestic NSA	**Inter-cartel turf war**	Coercive politics
Belligerent Dyads — International	State(s) vs. States(s)	Interstate war	Coercive diplomacy
	State(s) vs. Foreign NSA	Foreign intervention	International terrorism

Cell contents are examples, not exhaustive descriptors. Real-world cases may straddle cell borders or shift over time: an initially viable revolutionary insurgency could, for example, deteriorate into a criminal war in which jungle-bound rebels subsist on drug profits with no ambition to conquer the center or secede.

distribute the pie in a way that is difficult or costly to reverse, or can otherwise "lock in" a flow of rents, by preventing adverse shifts of relative power. Finally, negotiation is open but anarchic: both sides can freely make, take, or reject offers, but cannot commit themselves to agreements beyond the current period. Since fighting destroys some of the pie, there are always peaceable divisions both sides would prefer to war, making wars of conquest puzzling; commitment problems are a central explanation of why such Pareto-improving deals are not struck (Fearon 1995b). Yet it is no mystery why, once bargaining breaks down, actors turn to fighting: because it can yield decisive control over whatever is being bargained over, resolving the commitment problem. Thus, even if rebels could in theory be bought off with pure policy concessions, they may fight to conquer state power because only this will lock in their preferred policy outcomes (Fearon and Laitin 2007).

All three factors differ in cartel–state conflict. Public negotiating with cartels is taboo, yet tacit agreements may actually be *more* viable because cartels can credibly commit not to disarm. At stake is an enormous "pie" of illicit drug profits, which are neither zero-sum nor fully transferable: the state does not win a dollar for every dollar of cocaine it interdicts, nor can it directly profit from controlling the trade itself. Bargained solutions involving transfers of drug profits generally involve corruption, which implies a principal–agent problem *within* the state, violating the unitary-actor assumption of most models of conflict. Finally, violence, when practiced, generally has a coercive function, making the opponent worse off without directly seizing any benefit for the aggressor.

In particular, violence is unlikely to "lock in" a flow of benefits, for several reasons. First, in these settings, decisive victory is probably either unrealistic or undesirable. Critically, for cartels, *even outright military victory over the state would not lock in their preferred policy or distribution of rents.* Whereas victorious insurgencies can reasonably hope to win international legitimacy and support, an overt narco-state granting itself a domestically legalized monopoly in trafficking is basically unthinkable in the current international system. Conversely, since eliminating one cartel generally opens up market opportunities for its rivals (a dynamic far less likely to hold for insurgencies), even successful fighting by the state cannot lock in its preferred outcome; rather, states must engage in "a struggle to control organized crime [that] is a never-ending process, not a battle or a war that can be completed" (Skaperdas 2001, 174).

Second, adverse shifts in power during peacetime may be smaller or non-existent in cartel–state conflict. Whereas the assumption in civil war is that rebels disarm (or otherwise become weaker) whenever they stop fighting, cartels might be expected to maintain a capacity for violence even when not attacking the state, to guarantee transactions or fight turf wars.[7] Cartels could thus credibly promise not to disarm following policy concessions, allowing states in turn to credibly promise not to renege on those concessions.[8] Another reason cartels may be less subject to adverse shifts in power during "peacetime," going beyond a state-as-unitary-actor framework, is that they can corrupt state enforcers (and hence weaken the state) without fighting. In sum, both the strategic dynamic driving commitment problems and the mechanism by which fighting resolves them may be less relevant in cartel–state conflict.

On the other hand, actual negotiation seems significantly more vexed. First, while negotiating with rebels might be unsavory or unpopular, negotiating with cartels and other criminal organizations is essentially taboo. Indeed, Pablo Escobar repeatedly sought "political status" (i.e., to be treated as an insurgent) precisely to avoid this taboo.

Still, informal and sub rosa negotiations do occur (as they did with Escobar), so what might an agreement look like? An obvious "bargained solution" is bribery for non-enforcement; this is central to cartel–state conflict, as we will see, but it involves a severe principal–agent problem between state leaders and state enforcers, and is hardly anyone's idea of a positive outcome. Focusing on direct negotiations with leaders, cartels might promise to stop trafficking

---

7 Indeed, cartels might well retain more firepower by *not* fighting the state for a period than by fighting. This is the opposite of what happens in costly-process models of civil war.

8 I thank James Fearon for suggesting this possibility in a discussion of an earlier version of this manuscript.

in exchange for amnesty, as Escobar did in 1980s' Colombia; given the profitability of trafficking, though, such promises are unlikely to be credible (Escobar's were not). More importantly, even if states could buy off incumbent cartels, it would produce severe adverse selection: new cartels could fill the unmet demand (or credibly threaten to do so), then seek their own sweetheart deal.

The most realistic "deal" is likely to involve offering incumbent cartels, in exchange for non-violence, greater leeway to profit from trafficking. This is just another way of saying "conditional repression," i.e., cracking down harder on cartels that opt for violence than those that peacefully traffic. The formulation here highlights the political challenge of conditional approaches: in Colombia, ruling out a particularly painful form of state repression—extradition—was for a time politically acceptable, but more often conditionality is construed as "buying off" otherwise violent criminals with profits from a non-violent but illegal activity that states are committed by international treaty (and diplomatic pressure) to combat.

Theories of cartel–state conflict thus need to explain how sustained fighting can be an optimal response for cartels when neither definitive victory nor a sustainable deal are meaningful possibilities, and where forestalling adverse shifts in power—a potential driver of stalemated civil wars—is not a major factor. This points to mechanisms in which anti-state violence maximizes an ongoing flow of rents from illicit activity,[9] with particular attention to the coercive use of violence to punish, and not only protect oneself from, opponents. The next chapter presents two such mechanisms.

---

[9] In many costly-process models of war, the flow payoffs to fighting are exogenously determined.

3

Logics of Violence in Cartel–State Conflict

This chapter introduces the central logics that drive cartels to use violence against the state. Purely defensive violence to physically reduce losses from state repression is one important logic of violence, but cannot explain cartels' use of threats, retribution, and terror tactics, all common and clearly coercive in nature. I distinguish two coercive logics by which anti-state violence can influence policy outcomes. In "violent corruption", cartels use threats of violence against police and other enforcers to induce lax enforcement and more advantageous bribe agreements; in "violent lobbying", cartels use high-profile, terroristic violence to pressure state leaders into making changes to de jure policy. I summarize the factors favoring each and their predicted empirical footprints. Violent lobbying is subject to collective action problems among cartels, and thus unlikely under conditions of turf war; I present quantitative evidence that it was more salient in Colombia (where cartels were united at onset in a mutual-protection organization) than Rio de Janeiro and Mexico. Overall, violent corruption is the more prominent pathway. I then discuss several logics of anti-state violence that could arise from inter-cartel turf war, potential pathways of causal interaction between turf war and cartel–state conflict, and "general equilibrium" effects of repression when criminal markets are fragmented.

3.1 INTRODUCTION

My core argument is that cartels' choices to adopt or eschew strategies of confrontation and anti-state violence are largely shaped by the state's repressive policies. This may seem trivially true—if the state left cartels to their own devices, surely they would have little reason to attack the state. But a little reflection shows that the converse is not true: almost every DTO in the world, from the smallest street-corner crews to the most powerful cartels, faces some degree of state repression—often quite significant repression—whereas systematic anti-state violence by DTOs is quite rare, even among cartels. State repression of the drug trade is a necessary but not sufficient condition for cartel–state conflict.

When police enforce drug laws, most traffickers in most parts of the world do not fight back. Instead, they respond with evasive, "hiding" strategies: maintaining anonymity or a low profile, carrying out drug transactions as discreetly as possible, and during busts, either fleeing or, when flight is impossible, submitting peacefully. Occasionally, though, some DTOs—almost always powerful cartels with significant organizational and military capacity—adopt different, "fighting" strategies: issuing threats of violence against enforcers to deter busts, physically standing their ground or firing upon police when busts occur, and even resorting to terrorist violence to pressure political leaders. Such strategies draw attention to their perpetrators, making this approach incompatible with the "low profile" that hiding strategies aim to cultivate. For this reason, although in practice cartels have a range of options from nonviolence to extreme violence, I treat the distinction between hiding and fighting as a stark one.

Of course, traffickers have a third option: bribery. From individual street-level deals to full-blown "state-sponsored protection rackets," corruption—in the sense of bribes in exchange for lax or non-enforcement—plays a central role in cartel–state interactions. In production and transshipment settings from Afghanistan and Burma to Colombia and Mexico, corruption of and occasional collusion with state agents has been more common over the last forty years than armed confrontation. Moreover, cartels in these settings often do not even *threaten* anti-state violence: even if police were to refuse bribes and enforce the law, traffickers would simply hide. This is quite distinct from a situation in which enforcers accept bribes offers out of fear for their lives should they refuse.

This preponderance of negative cases leaves us with twin puzzles. First, why do crackdowns *ever* induce cartels to adopt fighting strategies? And second, why do some crackdowns appear to trigger or exacerbate anti-state violence, while others induce an abrupt switch to more pacific strategies? This chapter provides answers to these questions by considering the world from the cartels' perspective, and asking under what conditions it would make sense to switch from a hiding to a fighting strategy, and vice versa. To put it another way, what are the potential benefits and costs to anti-state violence, and how does state policy affect the trade-off?

The "logics of violence" approach I employ to answer these questions serves a triple purpose. First, it provides clear statements of the positive incentives actors have to engage in specific forms of violence. Second, it identifies conditions under which each logic operates (or fails to operate), thus providing a theoretical link between explanatory variables and the onset, escalation, or curtailment of cartel–state violence. Third, because logics differ in both their necessary conditions and their predicted pattern of violence, this approach can help explain observed variation in modalities of violence within a larger conflict.

I present three main logics that might drive cartel–state conflict. The most straightforward is *loss reduction*, a form of brute-force, defensive violence: fighting back during raids, busts, and patrols may be more effective at physically minimizing cartels' losses—including incarceration of their members—than "hiding." Explanations of cartel–state conflict as the "inevitable" result of state repression often rely heavily on this mechanism, and it certainly may play an important role. However, it clearly cannot account for many observed modalities of violence in cartel–state conflict, such as unilateral, unprovoked attacks; assassination of uncooperative enforcers *after* enforcement has occurred; and direct threats against government leaders of terrorist attacks if policy demands go unmet. Such violence is clearly coercive, aimed at deterring the state, not defending oneself from it.

To fill this gap, I distinguish two coercive logics of anti-state violence in drug war: *violent corruption* and *violent lobbying*. Violent corruption involves the use of coercive violence—the power to hurt one's opponent—in the negotiation of bribes. The core logic is straightforward: by threatening police or other enforcers with punitive violence if they enforce the law, cartels can obtain cheaper and/or more frequent bribes. However, the interaction of this basic logic with repressive crackdowns set in motion by state policymakers is quite complex, so I develop a formal model to more rigorously analyze its dynamics and map out possible outcomes. One key finding is that, while pure defensive violence can play a role by limiting enforcers' ability to extract bribes, the dynamics of violent corruption change dramatically if violence has a coercive function as well.

In violent lobbying, cartels seek to use their power to hurt state leaders and policymakers—often through high-profile "terror tactics" like bombings—coercively, to induce changes in formal, de jure policy. Escobar's very public terror campaign to knock down Colombia's extradition treaty is the leading example, but cartels in Mexico and Brazil have occasionally engaged in violent lobbying as well. Because it aims to impose costs on leaders, the logic of violent lobbying predicts intense, disruptive violence often directed at or involving civilians; such violence, by nature, is more salient than the often hidden violence associated with bribe negotiation. Nonetheless, violent lobbying is less common across cases than violent corruption; my analysis of these logics offers an explanation: lobbying generally requires collective action among cartels, which is unlikely under conditions of turf war.

This chapter also discusses two logics arising from inter-cartel turf war that nonetheless might account for some anti-state violence by cartels: competitive signaling and what is known in Mexico as *calentar la plaza*, i.e., bringing down heat on rivals. I then delineate possible causal connections between turf war and cartel–state conflict.

The logics discussed are not intended to exhaust the universe of possible motivations; in particular, I do not consider the issue of "expressive" or irrational violence.[1] Nor are these logics mutually exclusive: a single act of violence can achieve multiple ends, intimidating, say, both police and rivals. Consequently, and critically, the mapping between logics and individual empirical observations is not perfect: we cannot always precisely infer the theoretical motivation of a given violent event from the type of violence employed, or other easily observed characteristics. Rather, each logic has a predicted empirical "footprint," such that observed patterns in empirical outcomes can be attributed, probabilistically, to different logics.

Putting the pieces together, the theory yields a number of predictions:

1. Both violent corruption and violent lobbying can be triggered by crackdowns, and are more likely to be triggered when the crackdown is unconditional.
2. Under violent corruption, crackdowns increase the probability of violence when police fear physical confrontation more than getting caught for bribe-taking. This implies that violence is not purely defensive, but intended to hurt enforcers as well.
3. The necessary conditions for violent corruption are the least restrictive, suggesting that it will occur more frequently and consistently than violent lobbying; I conjecture that it is often the genesis of cartel–state conflict, even where violent lobbying or other logics end up overshadowing it.
4. Turf war among cartels can, on its own, provide incentives to attack state forces; however, these seem unlikely to be the primary drivers of cartel–state conflict.
5. An increase in the intensity of inter-cartel turf war has multiple aggravating effects on the corruption channel, making violence more likely. However, it has mixed effects on the lobbying channel; the net effect is probably negative.

To facilitate reading, this chapter introduces the core logics and associated empirical footprints in summary fashion. Chapter 4 delves more deeply into the logics of violent corruption and lobbying, presenting the results of a formal game-theoretic analysis and an extended discussion.

---

[1] One cannot spend time talking with favela youth without feeling that violence has an irrational or senseless quality to it. Yet I follow Fearon (1995a), Kalyvas (1999), and many others in suspecting that even the most gruesome violence frequently serves some instrumental end. The key is, I think, to distinguish the motivations of the individual soldiers and perpetrators—whose behavior may be hard to explain in rational-choice terms—from the organizations that employ them. The sustained nature of cartel–state conflict, and the survival and sometimes expansion of the most violent cartels (witness Los Zetas in Mexico), suggests that for the latter, anti-state violence is largely strategic.

3.2 VIOLENT CORRUPTION AND VIOLENT LOBBYING AS STRATEGIES OF INFLUENCE

As Chapter 2 argues, cartel–state conflict is a war of constraint: cartels' overarching aim in fighting is to induce states to change policies. This was obviously the case with Pablo Escobar's overt war against the Colombian state over the status of extradition. However, it is less clear in Mexico and Brazil, where public demands by cartels for changes in de jure policy have been less common. Directly pressuring leaders and legislators is only one way to achieve influence; as James Scott (1969a) argued, corruption must also be understood as a mode of influence, with *policy outcomes* the true variable of interest.

I argue that Scott's insight extends—indeed is critically relevant—to criminal firms and their use of violence. After all, if "the businessmen who protect their black-market sales by buying protection from a well-placed politician are changing the outcome of policy as effectively as they might by working collectively through chambers of commerce for an end to government price controls" (Scott 1969a, 1142), then the traffickers who offer police and judges a choice between *plata o plomo* ("the bribe or the bullet," literally "silver or lead") are changing the outcome of policy as effectively as they might by working collectively through a group-funded terror campaign to pressure leaders for an end to extradition. Corruption is centrally important for cartels because it is often far easier to weaken the enforcement of laws through bribery than to change the laws themselves, particularly since the laws in question stem from drug prohibition on normative grounds rather than market regulation on technocratic grounds. At the same time, cartels are already subject to state repression, so they often risk little additional sanction by seeking to corrupt officials.

Corruption, at its heart, is a principal–agent problem within the state; to analyze it, we must abandon a view of the state as unitary actor. To this end, I adapt Scott's distinction between "legislation" and "enforcement" phases of the policy process. Since relevant anti-narcotics policy is not limited to legislation, I refer instead to the policy *formulation* phase, yielding de jure policy, which the *enforcement* phase then translates into de facto policy. I call efforts to influence the formulation of de jure policy *lobbying*, an activity normally aimed at *leaders* (policymakers, including chief executives, legislators, and high-level commanders); and efforts to influence enforcement or de facto policy, *corruption*, an activity normally aimed at *enforcers* (police, soldiers, investigators, etc.). This is a restricted definition of "corruption" as "bribery in exchange for lax or non-enforcement"; some activities commonly understood as corruption—unethical or illegal payments to legislators or leaders to change laws or regulations—count here as lobbying.[2] In practice, the distinction is not

---

2 Other common types of corruption, such as embezzling public funds or selling political appointments, lie outside this conceptual framework.

always empirically clear: some officials have influence over both de jure and de facto policy, such as judges handing down specific sentences (enforcement) that simultaneously set precedents (policy formulation). Here, Scott's (1969a) point that corruption's benefits are particularistic while lobbying's are more universal can help distinguish between a corruption effort aimed at reducing one's own sentence and a lobbying effort to ensure a favorable precedent.

Figure 3.1 illustrates my adaptation of Scott's framework, a picture of standard, if shady, interest group politics; so far, violence plays no role, and for good reason. Strategies of state capture—including bribery, corruption, blackmail, vote buying, and (illicit) campaign contributions—are, to use the language of Chapter 2, aimed at constraining the state's actions. Typically, though, the state-capture strategies of licit groups would be undermined by outright violence, which could lead to demonization, increased scrutiny, and a sharp increase (possibly from zero) in state repression. For this reason, even when licit interest groups resort to unethical tactics in their lobbying and corrupting efforts (Dal Bó and Di Tella 2003; Dal Bó et al. 2006), they usually stop short of physical violence.

Cartels, however, already face a significant level of state repression. On the one hand, this may give them incentives to "hide," reducing their losses to law enforcement through anonymity and flight; they may further complement this

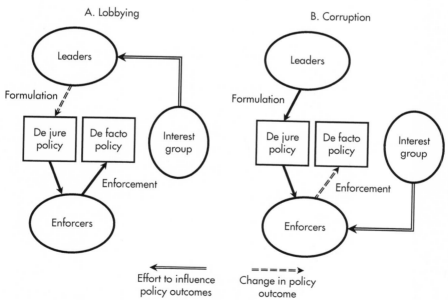

FIGURE 3.1. **Lobbying vs. Corruption.** Following (Scott 1969a), interest groups may seek influence over policy outcomes by (a) lobbying leaders, influencing the formulation of de jure policy, or (b) corrupting enforcers, influencing de facto policy.

with non-violent strategies of policy influence, using money to bribe enforcers and/or influence leaders. On the other hand, state repression against trafficking, if unconditional, can make fighting advantageous by reducing the relative *increase* in repression that anti-state violence incurs: unlike a K Street lobbyist, a trafficker does not risk *becoming* a wanted criminal by resorting to violence because he or she already *is* a wanted criminal. Moreover, the illegal nature of trafficking often gives cartels reasons to acquire some degree of firepower, making violent approaches logistically straightforward.

Figure 3.2 illustrates three potential advantages cartels might get from violence, operating at three different levels. First, when busts and other forms of law enforcement occur, violence might prove more effective than hiding at the level of loss reduction, i.e., physically reducing cartels' losses. If police cannot be corrupted or intimidated, so that they always enforce the law, then the only advantage cartels get from fighting is this defensive, loss-reducing value.

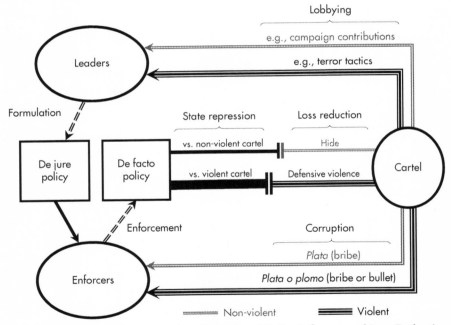

FIGURE 3.2. **Violent and Non-Violent Strategies of Policy Influence and Loss Reduction.** Arrows represent potential cartel strategies for influencing repressive policy outcomes; rectangles represent de facto state repression and cartel actions to physically reduce their losses from it. At each level (Lobbying, Corruption, and Loss Reduction), cartels can engage in violent or non-violent tactics. If repression is conditional, though, violence at *any* level triggers increased state repression (i.e., the thicker line for state repression against violent cartels); for this reason, cartels rarely "hide" at one level and "fight" at another.

If, however, corruption is a realistic possibility, then how cartels *would* respond to enforcement if and when no bribe agreement were reached affects the negotiation of the bribe itself, in two ways. First, if fighting reduces cartels' loss relative to hiding, then it simultaneously reduces enforcers' extortionary power to extract bribes: after all, there is no reason for cartels to pay a bribe larger than loss that enforcers can impose.[3] But whether or not fighting reduces cartels' own losses when enforcement occurs, it almost certainly imposes costs on enforcers in the form of physical harm. The more pain cartels can impose on enforcers, the more incentives enforcers have to *avoid* enforcing by accepting a bribe. This is the logic of *plata o plomo*: threatening to punish enforcers if no bribe agreement is struck makes enforcers willing to accept cheaper bribes.

Finally, violence can operate at a third level, imposing pain not on enforcers who do not agree to a bribe, but on leaders who refuse to make de jure policy concessions. In the logic of violent lobbying, terror tactics and other high-profile violence create acute political costs for non-compliant leaders, creating incentives to cede to cartels' demands for changes to de jure policy.[4]

Cartels may be motivated by any combination of these logics to engage in specific forms of violence; however, the overall choice between violent and non-violent strategies is stark, since the two approaches undermine one another. The advantages of fighting—including increased leverage over state actors—come at the cost of the low profile that hiding affords, and vice versa. To the extent that repression is conditional, choosing violent strategies triggers an increase in enforcement, represented in Figure 3.2 by the thicker "state repression" line.[5]

Crossing cartels' use of violence with the level of intended policy influence yields four distinct strategies of policy influence (Table 3.1). Non-violent, "hiding" strategies correspond to conventional corruption and lobbying.[6] In *violent lobbying*, cartels use violence to pressure leaders for de jure policy change (usually corresponding to reduced repression along a specific policy dimension). In *violent corruption*, cartels use violence to reduce effective enforcement. This usually means a credible threat of violence if a bribe agreement is not struck; possible variants include a threat with a bribe offer of zero (what one might call "pure intimidation"), pressuring enforcers to

[3] In this way, somewhat paradoxically, the defensive value of violence at the loss-reduction level reduces enforcers' coercive power over cartels at the level of corruption.
[4] Just as the dynamics of loss-enforcement ultimately affect the dynamics of corruption, the combined dynamics of these two levels play into the war of attrition between leaders and cartels that takes place at the level of lobbying. In particular, they determine how much damage leaders can really inflict on cartels, and so in part how long cartels will be able to hold out.
[5] This mutually exclusive quality is truer of the strategic level than the tactical: groups engaged in confrontational strategies may find hiding advantageous in specific situations, but they cannot go back to being non-violent groups flying below the state's radar.
[6] Corruption is always illicit, but lobbying is sometimes above-board, hence the "illicit" qualification.

TABLE 3.1. *Violent and Non-Violent Cartel Strategies of Policy Influence.*

		Level of policy influence	
		Formulation (de jure)	Enforcement (de facto)
Type of cartel strategy	**Fighting**	Violent lobbying	Violent corruption
	Medellín cartel	Narco-terrorism	*"Plata o plomo?"* (bribe or bullet?)
	Hiding	(Illicit) lobbying	Corruption
	Cali cartel	Narco-politics	"We don't kill judges, we buy them."

Cartels can (and do) mix between columns, seeking influence at both formulation and enforcement stages. Mixing between rows is less common, since the advantages that fighting brings come at the expense of the low profile hiding provides, and vice versa. Colombia's Medellín and Cali cartels illustrate this, offering empirical examples of all four strategies.

inflict increased repression on rivals, or the elimination of stubbornly honest individual enforcers. The promised violence can theoretically involve only pure defensive violence, i.e., inflicting no pain on enforcers, but in practice is usually at least partially punitive; as the formal model in Chapter 4 shows, the dynamics of violent corruption change considerably depending on how much cartel violence hurts enforcers.

Table 3.1 shows how these four strategies are exemplified by the two principal cartels of Colombia's "narco-violence" period (1984–1993). Pablo Escobar and his Medellín cartel epitomized the fighting approach at both levels of policy influence. Escobar's infamous offers of *plata o plomo* to judges, investigators, and police—backed up by hundreds of killings—captures the essence of violent corruption in a phrase still used throughout Latin America. At the de jure level, his campaign of terrorist violence—bombings, high-level assassinations, kidnappings of members of the political elite—accompanied by overt, and ultimately successful, demands to abolish extradition, is perhaps the most dramatic example of violent lobbying on record.

The Cali cartel, in contrast, deliberately eschewed violence and cultivated an air of low-key respectability. Leader Gilberto Rodríguez Orejuela famously rejected Escobar's violent corruption and characterized his own "hiding" approach with a pithy phrase of his own: "We don't kill judges ... we buy them" (Lee 1994, 205). (Escobar, of course, also "bought" judges; he just found that death threats made it easier and cheaper to do so.) At the de jure level, Rodríguez Orejuela foreswore Escobar's all-out war, ultimately collaborating with state forces to bring him down (Morales and La Rotta 2009) in 1993. He then organized the "Champagne Project," offering huge donations to both major presidential candidates in exchange for a promise of a de jure policy of amnesty. When Ernesto Samper accepted his offer, Rodríguez Orejuela declared, "We've got ourselves a president" (Chepesiuk 2003, 190). Indeed, Samper won the election, and, for a time, kept his promise. Ironically, though, the payments later came to light, and the ensuing "narco-politics" scandal forced Samper to crack down, leading to Orejuela's eventual capture (Serrano Cadena 1999).

Note that while there is a sharp divide between hiding and fighting strategies—since it is hard to maintain a low-profile once one has engaged in anti-state violence—both cartels could and did engage in both corruption and lobbying; there is nothing mutually exclusive about the columns in Table 3.1. Indeed, corruption and lobbying can sometimes be complements, unlike Kalyvas' (2006) logics of discriminate and indiscriminate violence, which are essentially pure substitutes. Indeed, the distinction between lobbying and corruption can become murky even when it is licit groups doing the lobbying. When cartels lobby non-violently, it is almost by definition, illicit, and hence by some accounts, an act of corruption. The Samper affair highlights this: when the Cali cartel's contributions came to light, a massive scandal ensued which ultimately led to the cartel's takedown. That said, the distinction can be operationalized by focusing on the level of policy an action is (principally) intended to act on. Since the stated aim was to change de jure policy, rather than to purchase the non-enforcement of a de jure policy already in effect, the case is better thought of as lobbying.

Similarly, gray cases exist at the frontier between violent forms of corruption and lobbying: when Escobar had the pro-extradition presidential candidate Luis Carlos Galán assassinated in 1989, it was probably aimed more at affecting the future of Colombia's de jure policy on extradition, though it may have also had the effect of intimidating government enforcers, who would presumably be more inclined to accept a bribe in the future. On the other hand, I argue that Escobar's 1984 assassination of Rodrigo Lara Bonilla, then minister of justice, was ultimately driven principally by the logic of violent corruption, the following-through on a *plata o plomo* offer that Lara Bonilla refused to accept.

Recalling that cartels need not choose between the two, I find that violent corruption is the more common mechanism. To be sure, violent lobbying is, by its nature, highly salient and disruptive—generally carried out by means of terror tactics calculated to generate a sense of crisis and attendant political costs for leaders. As such, it dominates headlines and histories, directly touching a broader swath of the population than enforcer-directed violent corruption. But, I argue, the conditions favoring violent lobbying are more restrictive, and as a result, it is far rarer in comparative perspective. Mexico and Brazil have witnessed only intermittent, seemingly tentative, violent lobbying campaigns, and even in Colombia violent lobbying began well after the onset of violent corruption.

3.2.1 Key Factors Favoring Violent Corruption and Lobbying

The real question a cartel faces is not so much which column of Table 3.1 to locate itself in, since it can engage in both corruption and lobbying, but which row. Each logic of violence is about the choice to use violence or not at a given level of influence, not about which level to opt for. Of course, resource constraints theoretically require cartels to trade off between corruption and lobbying; this, however, is likely a second-order problem, for two reasons. First, as I argue below, in many cases lobbying is simply not an advantageous strategy regardless of the resources cartels bring to bear. Second, those resources—basically the ability to hurt state actors—are ones that cartels generally possess in abundance, and so resource constraints may rarely bind. The fact that car bombs and other terror tactics were used, if rarely, in Mexico and Rio shows that cartels there possessed the wherewithal to engage in violent lobbying, but did not find it as advantageous as in Colombia.

The model of bribe negotiation presented in Chapter 4 derives in a formal setting both the drivers and predicted footprint of the logic of violent corruption. At its core, the model combines two insights from the literature on organized crime and corruption. First, Fiorentini and Peltzman's observation that "the greater the effectiveness of [states'] deterrence activities, the more they create incentives [for criminals] to invest in corruption and manipulation of the deterrence agencies themselves" (Fiorentini and Peltzman 1997, 27). Second, Dal Bó et al.'s (2006) argument that the ability to simultaneously make threats and offer bribes should lead to lower bribes in equilibrium. My model formally distinguishes these bribe-reducing benefits from the potential loss-reducing, defensive function of anti-state violence, illustrating how crackdowns in a context of rampant corruption create additional incentives for cartels to use violence coercively, as a complement to bribery.

The model explores the conditions under which corruption is likely to be violent, that is, under which it makes sense for cartels to adopt *plata o plomo* threats as a strategy for reducing total bribe payments. Three conditions stand out. First, conditionality of repression must be sufficiently low, so that cartels do not face a steep increase in repression for making and acting on threats of violence against enforcers. Second, violent corruption is more likely when cartels' capacity to inflict pain on enforcers, the "*plomo* effect" if you will, is strong. This effect only yields a tangible benefit (reducing equilibrium bribe prices) when bribery is a realistic possibility; thus, a third factor favoring equilibrium violence is a general context of corruption, in which enforcers are relatively bribable.

The conditions favoring violent lobbying are more restrictive than violent corruption. While the underlying idea is similar—making refusal to cooperate costly for the relevant state actor—the nature and likelihood of that cooperation differs: violent corruption requires only a realistic chance that enforcers will accept bribes in exchange for non-enforcement, while violent lobbying requires a realistic chance that leaders will change a de jure policy already in place. A necessary condition for violent lobbying, therefore, is some "open question" of de jure policy that could plausibly be changed or revoked, since there is no point in trying to force policymakers to the bargaining table unless there is a viable open question about which to bargain. I call this quality of a given de jure policy its *susceptibility* to violent lobbying—its elasticity with respect to violence, if you like. In a sense, the susceptibility of a de jure policy is the corollary to enforcers' likelihood of accepting a bribe. However, susceptibility depends on a host of political factors that do not arise in the case of corruption: international pressures, domestic sentiment, leaders' own public commitments to a given policy (Fearon 1994), and their vulnerability to electoral or other challenges. These can change over time and in response to violence itself, often in unpredictable ways. Once attacked, leaders may face public humiliation if they give in to cartels' demands; on the other hand, years of extreme violence can push public opinion toward conciliatory positions, as happened in Colombia (Pardo Rueda 1996).

Overall, states' international commitments to drug prohibition and eradication make for few susceptible, open questions of de jure policy. Examples from my cases of policies that inspired violent lobbying include: extradition of traffickers in Colombia; the deployment of army troops to Michoacán, Mexico, to fight the cartels; and isolation of imprisoned drug syndicate leaders in Rio de Janeiro. While all of these policies provoked incidents of violent lobbying, only extradition—in the 1980s, in Colombia—remained an open political question long enough to produce a sustained campaign of violence.

A second, equally restrictive necessary condition for lobbying—violent or not—follows from Scott's (1969a) original analysis. Lobbying presents a collective-action problem, because the benefits of any change in de jure policy are universal—they accrue to all the firms in the industry (Scott 1969a)—while the costs are borne only by those who contribute. Of course, it is always possible to write laws and policies in ways that benefit individuals, but to the extent that the potential benefits of (violent) lobbying are universal and non-excludable, firms will be tempted to free-ride. In the case of violent lobbying, each cartel has an incentive to let other cartels shoulder the costs of all-out armed conflict with the state, while nonetheless sharing in any ultimate benefits achieved (which include not only any eventual changes to de jure policy, but the additional repression that falls on one's violent rivals). As with conventional, non-violent lobbying among licit interest groups, mechanisms for cost-sharing and deterring free-riders (Olson 1965) should help make violent lobbying an efficient pursuit, while turf war among cartels should tend to undermine it.

3.2.2 Predicted Empirical Footprints and Observed Outcomes

With respect to corruption, the model of bribe negotiation presented in Chapter 4 yields a conceptual map of potential outcome scenarios, ranging from a non-corrupt and non-violent ideal to others in which both violence and bribery occur in equilibrium. Real-world episodes can then be located within this conceptual map. I describe these scenarios briefly; Chapter 4 defines them formally, analyzes how policy changes can induce shifts from one to another, and provides empirical examples from my case studies.

Figure 3.3 plots these six scenarios along two dimensions. The horizontal axis indicates whether cartels are playing hiding or fighting strategies; the vertical axis shows the complementary likelihoods of enforcement and bribery in equilibrium, ranging from always to never. Under *peaceful enforcement*—roughly speaking, how policing is supposed to work—bribe agreements are never reached, enforcement is sure to occur, and cartels respond with non-violent, evasive tactics. *Violent enforcement* is equally non-corrupt, but cartels now respond to enforcement by fighting back. Under *state-sponsored protection* and *coerced peace*, enforcement never occurs because bribe agreements are always reached, but cartels differ in what they *would* have done if no

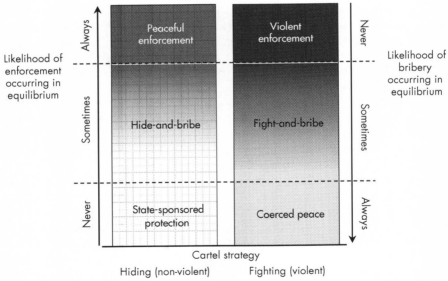

FIGURE 3.3. **Conceptualizing Violent and Non-Violent Corruption.** In the bribe-negotiation model of Chapter 4, six equilibrium outcome scenarios are possible. Darker shading indicates a higher equilibrium probability of enforcement; at the other extreme, bribes are always struck and there is no enforcement. On the left, the cartel responds to enforcement—when it occurs—with non-violent, hiding tactics; on the right, with violence.

bribe agreement were reached—hiding and fighting, respectively. In between are more realistic *hide-and-bribe* and *fight-and-bribe* equilibria; in these scenarios, both bribery and enforcement occur with some probability, and changes in the degree of repression and other variables affect their relative likelihood.

The model predicts distinct empirical footprints for each outcome scenario. Most pertinently, the fight-and-bribe scenario is characterized by intermittent violence, occurring whenever bribe negotiations fail, and targeted at enforcers as punishment. If brute-force, defensive violence is especially effective at minimizing cartels' losses as a result of enforcement, which I suggest is likelier when the drug market in question is territorial, fighting may take the form of open clashes as cartels stand their ground in the face of police action. Where enforcement is more juridical than territorial, and where cartels have more reach, assassination of enforcers, often judges, is the logical modality.

The model also makes predictions about the effect of crackdowns. A key finding is that, from fight-and-bribe and coerced-peace scenarios, unconditional crackdowns provoke additional cartel–state violence when they occur in a context of widespread police corruption.[7] The intuition is that crackdowns give corrupt enforcers more leverage over cartels, pushing up bribe demands. To temper these demands, cartels threaten additional violence if no agreement is reached. The result is more frequent fighting but a smaller bribe when an agreement is reached. This mechanism only works, though, when police are more "afraid" of cartel violence than they are of the expected state sanction for bribe-taking. This, in turn, presumes that cartel violence is not purely defensive, but also imposes significant pain on police, and is more likely when corruption is widespread and hence rarely punished. In sum, unconditional crackdowns, in which cartels are pursued with relatively equal intensity whether or not they employ anti-state violence, can produce violent, anti-state responses from cartels.

Crackdowns can also induce a shift from one scenario to another, and in particular can change cartels' decisions about whether to use fighting or hiding strategies. Such shifts produce more abrupt changes in outcomes. From non-violent scenarios like hide-and-bribe or state-sponsored protection, an unconditional crackdown can induce cartels to switch to a fighting strategy; this generally leads to more frequent bribes (since enforcers are now coerced into making smaller bribe demands), but also to violence when bribe agreements are not struck. Conversely, a conditional crackdown that directs additional repression against cartels if they opt for violence can induce an abrupt switch to non-violent, hiding strategies, producing sharp drops in clashes and enforcer-targeted violence.

---

[7] In this setting, pure intimidation, in which enforcers simply choose not to enforce the law without actually accepting a bribe, is equivalent to a bribe priced at zero. This rests on the assumption that enforcers' expected punishment for corruption is constant with respect to the bribe price. One future avenue of research would be to relax this assumption.

The predicted empirical footprint of violent lobbying differs from violent corruption. Cartels are rarely in a position to physically target leaders; they can, however, inflict indirect, political costs on leaders by using violence to create social and economic disruption. For this reason, violent lobbying is generally effected through terror tactics like car bombs, massacres, and prominent kidnappings, as well as forced closing of businesses and schools, coerced street protests, and open (if unilateral) communication with leaders. Violence is likely to be clustered in time to foment a sense of crisis, so that cartels can offer to call off the attacks in exchange for policy concessions.

In terms of state policy, the key variable is not so much the conditionality of a given repressive policy per se, but its *susceptibility*—i.e., how easily leaders could be coerced into reversing it. This is because a conditional crackdown only creates incentives to avoid violence as long as leaders can sustain it. If cartels believe that a highly repressive policy, conditional or not, is susceptible to violent lobbying, then a cartel campaign of terror today could lead to *less* repression tomorrow. Strategically, violent lobbying resembles a war of attrition, so as soon as both sides know who has more wherewithal, the fighting should stop. Yet susceptibility is fundamentally a *political*, not strategic, characteristic of policies; as such, it is complex and unpredictable. In the formal analysis of violent lobbying in Chapter 4, I show how shifting uncertainty over susceptibility could drive violent lobbying in practice. One implication is that outbursts of violent lobbying might occur after changes in government, as a kind of screening device to test a new leader's commitment to status-quo policies.

Empirically, violent corruption appears to be more prominent across cases. Even in Colombia, where Escobar's violent lobbying against extradition is widely treated as *the* story (Reuter 2009, 277), violent corruption came first—Escobar threatened a judge and murdered two police officers in 1976—and continued to make *plata o plomo* offers throughout the narco-terror period (Bowden 2001). In Mexico, as in Brazil, nothing like Escobar's sustained lobbying campaign has been recorded, while routinized bribe payments in exchange for non-enforcement are common enough to be embedded in the language (Poppa 2010, 42; Soares et al. 2005, 259). In both settings, the vast majority of officials killed are local police (ISP-RJ 2016; *Proceso* 2011), suggesting enforcer-targeted violent corruption. Even violence against relatively high-level state actors in Mexico appears to be more associated with police corruption than official state policy (Bailey and Taylor 2009).

Nonetheless, terror attacks accompanied by overt demands on leaders to change de jure policy, though rare, have occurred in both Mexico and Brazil. In 2009, for example, the Familia Michoacana cartel organized street protests (*Reforma* 2009) and launched a simultaneous attack on twelve federal police stations across the state of Michoacán, Mexico (Grillo 2011). A leader of the cartel then made a televised plea for dialog with President Felipe Calderón and demanded the withdrawal of the federal police from Michoacán, clarifying that

"We have no issue with the Army or the Navy" (*El Universal* 2009). Rio de Janeiro's cartel leaders, who are mostly incarcerated, have launched numerous coordinated terror attacks—usually bus-burnings, roadblocks, and the closing of business districts—over the years to pressure authorities, most often for changes in carceral policies (Penglase 2005).

A quantitative assessment provides additional evidence of the general prominence of violent corruption. Figure 3.4 presents results from a novel cross-national dataset of drug-related violent-event media reports, coded according to criteria developed in 2009, prior to the formulation of the theory presented here. Violent actions were assigned one of a closed list of over sixty types, designed to err on the side of specificity and allow for eventual aggregation of rarer types into more practical categories. Column heights show each category's relative frequency, within the universe of actions identified as cartel–state violence in each country. The bottom row presents categories aggregated at a low and atheoretical level: "bombing," for example, combines two raw action types: "intentional explosion" and "planting of explosives." "Unilateral attack" is the most complex category, combining frontal attacks, ambushes, prison breaks, sabotage, and "attempted" variants,

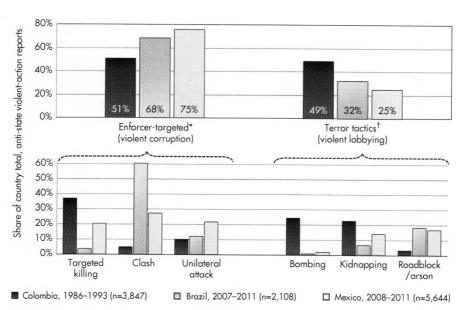

FIGURE 3.4. **Cartel–State Violent Actions by Type.**
*Includes all non-terror violent actions identifiable as cartel–state. †Includes all terror actions regardless of victims.
Source: Author's coding of newspaper reports. See Appendix A for details.

while "clash"—*any* situation in which two or more groups exchange lethal force—is itself a raw type.

The top row draws on the theory presented above to further aggregate action types into two broad categories: enforcer-targeted actions, corresponding to violent corruption, and terror tactics, corresponding to violent lobbying. This correspondence is far from perfect. In the late 1980s, for example, Pablo Escobar made a standing offer of rewards for any police officer killed; many resulting victims were not involved with anti-narcotics, and had received no *plata o plomo* threats.[8] Rather, this enforcer-targeted violence was in fact part of a violent lobbying campaign, aimed at inflicting political costs on leaders. Killing of judges, as mentioned, can serve both logics. Meanwhile, some terror attacks could have been motivated by inter-cartel competition, with little or no lobbying intent. Overall, though, the data reveal an anomalous prominence of terror tactics in Colombia, and a general dominance of violent corruption over lobbying.

The theory laid out above, I argue, offers purchase on explaining these patterns. In Colombia, the conditions for violent lobbying were met at the outset of Escobar's war on the state. In 1984, cartels were peacefully united under Muerte a Secuestradores (MAS) (Chepesiuk 2003, 64), a mutual-protection organization masterminded by Escobar, who had the authority to tax members to finance collective military campaigns. Colombia's extradition treaty was *susceptible*: "Throughout [its] life, from 1982 until its end in 1991, there were really very few voices in the political arena who defended it as an instrument" (Pardo Rueda 1996, 301), and there was significant popular opposition to its implementation as well (López Restrepo 2005, 199). At the same time, ongoing peace negotiations with guerrilla groups—which the Colombian state only engaged in after attempting to destroy the guerrillas outright—convinced Escobar and his colleagues that the government would, eventually, negotiate with them as well (López Restrepo 2005, 203). In other words, fighting now could lead to a reprieve in the future.

By contrast, in Mexico, two factors came together to make lobbying very unpromising: intense competition among cartels undermined potential collective action, while Calderón's political ownership of the crackdown he launched effectively tied his hands against de jure policy change. Thus, Familia Michoacana's flirtation with violent lobbying was an exception that proves the rule: its regional focus and hegemony within Michoacán state mitigated the free-rider problem, while its policy demands seem to have been carefully crafted to increase their palatability. Moreover, its campaign was largely unsuccessful, suggesting that it underestimated Calderón's susceptibility to pressure for policy change; in Chapter 4's formal model, this type of information asymmetry is a necessary condition for violent lobbying to occur in equilibrium. In Rio, violent lobbying frequently focuses on carceral policy, a low-salience issue with small

[8] Interviews, former police officers, Medellín, June 29, 2012.

audience costs for leaders, and demands are often particularistic: transfers of specific leaders or policy changes within units controlled by the dominant cartel. Still, the bulk of Rio's violence derives from violent corruption: the dominant type, by far, is open clashes, the vast majority of which take place within their *favela* (slum) turf in response to police incursions, as detailed in Chapter 6.

3.3 TURF-WAR LOGICS OF ANTI-STATE VIOLENCE

Violent corruption and lobbying, though quite different, are both logics of constraint: the attempt to influence policy outcomes through coercive violence. Cartel–state conflict, however, often co-exists with, and in Mexico was preceded by, inter-cartel turf war: the use of violence by cartels to expropriate territory or market share from one another. As a war of conquest, we would expect turf war to obey different logics than cartel–state conflict; indeed, it is a worthy and challenging research agenda in its own right. Without seeking to explain turf war, I include it in the analysis here, for two key reasons. First, the presence and intensity of turf war may exacerbate or attenuate cartels' incentives to engage in violent lobbying and violent corruption. I consider these interaction effects in a subsequent section.

Second, turf war may itself generate incentives for anti-state violence. In these cases, the *victims* of violence may be state agents, but the violence is ultimately aimed at rival cartels, part of a competitive struggle for turf. Obviously, most violence driven by turf war victimizes members of rival cartels; in this section, I consider less common but still important cases where cartels could find anti-state violence could arise from logics other than violent corruption and lobbying.

3.3.1 Competitive and Internal Signaling

An under-appreciated fact about theories of violence is that they attribute, often implicitly, different functions to violence itself. In many canonical models of "war as bargaining breakdown," violence definitively distributes control over some piece of territory or other asset (e.g., Fearon 1995b), but it may also weaken or incapacitate an opponent (e.g., Powell 2012), or it may do nothing more than inflict pain (e.g., Dal Bó et al. 2006). A fourth primordial function of violence is as a signal. In this view, violence—quite apart from its physical, "battlefield" effects—conveys important information about the perpetrator's operational capacity, internal cohesion, resolve, and so on.

Violence as a costly signal often has an seemingly irrational or wasteful quality. A good example is what was perhaps the first organized armed campaign of drug cartels on record. In 1981, virtually all the top traffickers in Colombia joined forces under the banner MAS to free the sister of drug baron Jorge Luis Ochoa, who had been kidnapped by the M-19 leftist guerrilla for ransom. MAS's first military actions involved capturing M-19 members and leaving them in front of newspaper offices shackled, beaten unconscious, and

wearing notes that read "I am a kidnapper" (Castillo 1987, 115). The fact
that the victims were left alive strongly suggests that the motivation was not
to directly weaken the M-19 per se but to communicate MAS's capacity and
resolve to inflict further damage. Indeed, MAS had distributed leaflets from
airplanes at sporting events announcing its intentions to do just that prior
to the onset of the anti-M-19 violence. But as game theory teaches, talk is
cheap, and signals must be costly to be effective (Spence 2002). If taking the
trouble of identifying M-19 members, kidnapping them, and then releasing
them alive might seem wasteful, that is largely the point: only an organization
with sufficient resources and resolve could afford to send such a costly signal.
The tactic worked: within weeks, Ochoa's sister was released, and the M-19
never targeted the cartels again; in fact, the incident led to a decade of warm
relations between Pablo Escobar and the M-19 leadership.

In this example, neither the victim nor the intended receiver of the violent
signal were state actors. Conversely, many examples of violence against state
actors, such as high-level assassinations of police or judicial officers, may be
understood as signals whose intended recipients are also part of the state. In
these cases, signaling forms part of a larger strategy of violent corruption or
violent lobbying, ultimately aimed at affecting policy at either the de jure or de
facto level.

A third possibility exists, in which violence against state actors serves as a
signal not to the state but to members of the drug trade itself. To the extent that
cartels kill cops, or attack army outposts, or machine-gun public buildings, or
assassinate mayors, so that other traffickers see that they are willing and able to
do so, the motivating logic derives from turf war, not cartel–state conflict: the
aim of such violence is ultimately to acquire rivals' market share or territory,
as opposed to changing state policy.

Reuter (2009) usefully distinguishes two subtypes of violent signaling.
Typically, signaling is part of a *competitive* strategy aimed at rival cartels.
However, larger organizations like Mexico's cartels may be complex enough
to experience significant and problematic internal information asymmetries. In
situations like this, violent signals—think of Al Capone beating an underling
to death in front of his colleagues—may be directed at an organization's own
members.

It seems unlikely that a cartel would risk attacking state forces *solely* to
communicate its strength to rivals or upstarts within its organization. That said,
because anti-state violence is rare, logistically difficult, and almost certainly
more costly than inter-cartel violence, it would make a powerful signal to other
traffickers. Any such positive value a cartel sees in sending such signals would
contribute to the larger decision to take a violent strategy vis-à-vis the state.
This channel could thus play a contributing role in the onset of cartel–state
conflict.

Key Factors and Empirical Footprint: There is no reason to send signals
unless one has private information to convey. As Reuter (2009) notes, we

would not expect internal signaling to occur in market sectors where firms are so small that serious internal information asymmetries are unlikely to arise. Similarly, signaling violence should be sporadic when the industrial organization of drug markets is stable, since informative signals only need to be sent once. Conversely, state crackdowns that weaken or fragment cartels, or that otherwise generate uncertainty about the strength of rivals and upstarts, are likely to feed this type of violence.

As for the type of violence predicted, the costlier the signal, the more strength and resolve is communicated. This could point toward high-profile assassinations and brazen, tactically ambitious attacks targeting state officials or forces. That said, the gruesome mutilation and public display of victims—most of them *not* state agents—as well as credit-claiming tactics like Mexico's ubiquitous *narcomantas* ("narco-banners") left behind at crime scenes, all serve as powerful signals. In the event-level data I collected, such propagandistic actions were most common in Mexico, nearly 17 percent of all violent-action reports, versus about 4 percent in Rio and only 1 percent in Colombia. This could reflect a need to send signals in a strategic environment constantly destabilized by Calderón's strategy of decapitating and fragmenting cartels. It also substantiates the conjecture that cartels can find sufficiently costly signals short of anti-state violence, making the signaling channel unlikely to be solely responsible for the onset of cartel–state conflict.

3.3.2 *Calentar la Plaza*: Bringing Down Heat on Rivals

In Mexico, *la plaza* can mean both a piece of turf and the concession to run local criminal activity there (Poppa 2010, 42). *Calentar la plaza*, literally "to heat up the plaza," is a form of misdirection, in which cartels use violence, particularly anti-state violence, to deliberately attract state repression to a region under the control of a rival, in order to interfere with their rent-producing activities or otherwise weaken them.[9] This logic of violence includes "false flag" attacks in warfare, designed to create the incorrect belief that an attack was carried out by someone else, but extends to cases where it is sufficient to foment doubt or a sense of crisis that will attract government repression.

Naturally, this logic of violence may involve false credit-claiming and public disputes about the true authorship of violent events, as in this comuniqué from Pablo Escobar:

> The purpose of the massacres and terrorist attacks perpetrated in the city of Medellín in the last few days was to sow confusion and damage our sincere desires for peace and rapprochement with the Colombian legal system ... These deeds were led and financed by Mr. Gilberto Rodríguez Orejuela [leader of the Cali cartel].
>
> (Quoted in *El Tiempo* 1990)

---

[9] Interview, CISEN intelligence officer, Mexico City, September 28, 2010.

Escobar's claim was plausible: at the time, he was in the midst of a delicate de facto negotiation with the state over the terms of his voluntary surrender under the *Sometimiento* policy. Moreover, Escobar had transitioned from bombing to elite kidnappings, which he found generated more leverage, and had just released one of his hostages as a sign of goodwill. The Cali cartel had been trying to kill Escobar since 1988, and probably saw his voluntary surrender as a bad outcome; scrambling the negotiations with a false-flag attack would have been a clever tactic.

Another prominent and tragic example of this logic, and the attribution disputes it typically engenders, was the 2008 grenade attack on a crowd of civilians celebrating Mexico's independence in the town square of Morelia, Michoacán, killing eight and wounding more than one hundred. Suspicion immediately fell on the Família Michoacana cartel, then dominant in Michoacán. The cartel adamantly denied responsibility, blaming its rival Los Zetas, and sending text messages to journalists and hanging *narcomantas* with messages such as "Don't let them fool you: La Familia of Michoacán is with you and does not agree with acts of genocide" (Lacey 2008). These claims also seem to have been true: officials soon captured three Zeta hitmen who confessed to the attacks (García 2008). The Zetas had motives to "heat up the plaza": they had been "betrayed" (Grillo 2011, 219) and pushed out of Michoacán by La Familia in 2006.

Key Factors and Empirical Footprint: Clearly, the logic of *calentar la plaza* is driven by turf war among cartels. Moreover, it requires that the target cartel be facing something less than maximum repression, perhaps because it has pacted or is trying to pact with the government, or simply because the government is applying conditional repression and the cartel has previously avoided violence. The attacking cartel must stand to gain by exposing the target cartel to additional repression, yet not be excessively afraid of inadvertently exposing itself. These conditions were met in the example of Escobar negotiating his voluntary surrender: Escobar was strategically withholding terroristic violence as part of a larger strategy of violent lobbying, while the Cali cartel (in Escobar's telling) had the partial complicity of state enforcers, reducing the risk of engaging in terrorist actions. A few months earlier, at the peak of Escobar's car-bombing campaign, such attacks by the Cali cartel would have made little sense, at least in terms this particular logic.

The predicted empirical footprint is well-illustrated by these examples of public bombings in Mexico and Colombia. Since the aim in this logic of violence is to draw attention from the public and the authorities, it makes sense to target civilians with terror tactics. Targeting state forces might also make sense, as long as authorities remain unable to discern the true identity of the perpetrator. Another empirical marker of false-flag violence is a subsequent flurry of propaganda in which responsibility for the violence is disputed. These disputes can help distinguish *calentar la plaza* violence from violent lobbying, in which the perpetrators not only take credit for terror attacks but specifically link them to over de jure policy demands.

Finally, it is worth noting that this logic, unlike most others, could be *strengthened* by conditional crackdowns. If the state's policy is to increase repression against any cartel that engages in anti-state violence, then cartels have incentives to frame their rivals, thus exposing them to additional repression. Indeed, some calls for conditional approaches to cartel repression emphasize the need for better police intelligence precisely to counter any possible incentives for false-flag attacks (e.g., Kleiman 2011).

3.4 INTERACTIONS OF CARTEL–STATE CONFLICT WITH TURF WAR

In Chapter 2, I argue that inter-cartel turf war and cartel–state conflict are fundamentally different types of conflicts; nonetheless, as Figure 2.2 shows, these two conflict types can causally affect, and sometimes even trigger, one another. In this section, I distinguish a number of possible channels of causal interactions. There are many plausible channels and not enough cases to rigorously test them; the analysis is, consequently, conjectural and intended to help guide future research.

3.4.1 Effects of Cartel–State Conflict on Turf War

The effects of cartel–state conflict onset in a context of ongoing turf war would seem to depend on the nature of state repression prior to onset. In one scenario, what I call "punching the referee," the state has not already maxed out repression, and repression is at least somewhat conditional on inter-cartel violence. In situations like this, as Durán-Martínez (2012) has shown, cartels are likely to limit turf war, or at least hide it from view, in order to minimize attention from law enforcement. If, however, cartels make the leap to attacking authorities, such dispute-containment probably becomes moot. Once you have punched the ref, as it were, you might as well play dirty pool with your opponent.

Cartel–state conflict may also induce turf war where none existed. As Chapter 5 discusses in detail, cartel–state conflict began in Colombia under conditions of inter-cartel peace. Repression grew increasingly conditional *among* cartels, eventually pushing the Cali cartel, and later Los Pepes, to break with Medellín and actually align with the state in its war on Escobar. While this alignment was never officially acknowledged, and the degree of active collaboration versus passive coordination is still a topic of debate, there is no question that the state not only directed little or no repression against Cali and Los Pepes, but ultimately "helped" them by taking out their rival. Conversely, without the brutal and extralegal attacks of Cali and Los Pepes, it is not clear that the state would have vanquished Escobar.

Such cartel–state collusion against more-violent cartels in Mexico and Rio is occasionally rumored to exist. When the Mexican Navy began stepping up repression of Los Zetas in 2011, Calderón issued public denials that he was secretly favoring Joaquín "El Chapo" Guzmán and the Sinaloa cartel. In Rio, the Amigos dos Amigos (ADA) cartel is often said to be less violent and more aligned with the police against the highly confrontational Comando Vermelho. Still, such collusion, if it exists, appears to be far less thoroughgoing than in the Colombia case: both ADA and Sinaloa have been subject to a significant amount of repression in their own right.

The stronger parallel is with paramilitary groups. The founders of Los Pepes went on to form the Autodefensas Unidas de Colombia (AUC), a massive paramilitary army that fought Colombia's guerrillas throughout the 1990s, usually in collusion with state forces. Paramilitaries, by positioning themselves as the lesser of two evils, are often able to avoid the brunt of state repression. While we are accustomed to thinking of paramilitaries as foils to revolutionary insurgents, the rise of *autodefensas* in Mexico and *milícias* in Rio—both of which have quickly captured huge swaths of territory from drug cartels with the tacit approval of the state—shows that the "greater evil" need not pose an existential threat to the state.

3.4.2 Effects of Turf War on Cartel–State Conflict

How does the advent of turf war between cartels, or its intensification, affect cartels' choices to adopt fighting strategies, whether at the policy formulation or enforcement levels? I hypothesize three main channels, affecting the logics of violent corruption and lobbying in different ways. On the whole, turf war seems more likely to aggravate violent corruption, and attenuate violent lobbying.

The first channel is the usefulness of anti-state violence as a competitive signal, discussed earlier. More dire inter-cartel competition, and in particular a more unstable industrial organization of the drug trade (perhaps due to crackdowns), should lead a cartel to derive more value from anti-state violence in the form of a signal to its rivals and own members. This extra value should come into play whether anti-state violence is committed in the name of corruption or lobbying; in fact, it might be stronger in the lobbying channel if only because the type of violence needed to effectively lobby is often quite spectacular and brazen. For example, a cartel might get a little competitive signaling value from a shootout with cops, since rivals would learn something about the local crew's strength and resolve by observing the battle, but get far more signaling value from a technically sophisticated or risky terroristic attack on major state or civilian targets.

Nonetheless, it is hard to believe that the need to signal strength to rivals could, on its own, push cartels into fighting strategies vis-à-vis the state; a more plausible pathway is the accumulation of firepower. As the analysis in Chapter 4 shows, one factor in determining the relative payoff to hiding versus fighting is the expense of accumulating enough firepower to effectively intimidate the state. If a cartel already has considerable firepower as a result of its ongoing interaction with rivals, then it may not need to acquire much or any additional firepower to threaten the state, making fighting more appealing on the margin.[10] This pathway to fighting seems particularly apt with respect to the Mexican case. This channel could also make violent lobbying more attractive, if the cost of imposing violence is a constraining factor. It is quite plausible, for example, that the military buildup of MAS that Escobar oversaw contributed to his decision to attack the state at the outset of the narco-violence period.

Finally, a third channel, perhaps the strongest, cuts in opposite directions: turf war exacerbates the collective action problem at the heart of violent lobbying, making it less likely. On the other hand, it could increase the returns to the selective non-enforcement resulting from violent corruption. In particular, if competition for turf is fierce, competition for protection from corrupt officials is also likely to be fierce. As cartels bid up the price of bribes, the incentives for violent corruption increase. In fact, a cartel looking to invade another's turf might find that, short of violence, it is unable to induce police to betray their incumbent benefactors.

On the whole, the free-rider problem seems like it should outweigh these other conditions, meaning that turf war should have an aggravating impact on violent corruption but an attenuating impact on violent lobbying. A suggestion of such attenuation can be seen in a July 2010 car-bomb attack in Ciudad Juárez. In graffiti found near the attack site, the Juárez cartel took responsibility for the attack, and threatened another bombing unless the FBI and DEA investigated corrupt ties between federal agents and the Sinaloa cartel, which at the time was threatening Juárez's turf. The case is notable for fitting the empirical pattern associated with violent lobbying: terroristic violence, targeting civilians but aimed at high-level authorities, However, the change the cartel sought is really one of enforcement, not policy formulation, and the intended audience of this act are enforcers. Ultimately, this example suggests that when turf war is very intense, the public nature of de jure policy makes it so unattractive a goal that even when the tactics of narco-terror are seen as propitious, they are used toward particularistic, de facto ends.

3.5   "DYNAMIC DISPERSION": GENERAL EQUILIBRIUM EFFECTS FROM MARKET FRAGMENTATION

In working through the logics that lead cartels to respond to state repression with anti-state violence, I often employ a so-called partial-equilibrium approach: holding all factors constant save one, and observing how changes in that one variable affect outcomes of interest (what formal theorists call "taking comparative statics"). I use this technique to explore how changes in state repressive policies affect a cartel's choice of strategies. Such partial-equilibrium analysis is an important first step, but because it holds so many factors

---

[10]   In an extension to the violent corruption model of Chapter 4, not included here, I show that a prior endowment of arms makes cartels more likely to play fight-and-bribe strategies.

constant, it runs the risk of overlooking "general equilibrium" effects involving simultaneous changes in multiple variables.

One absolutely critical factor that I hold constant is the question of how many cartels are in the market, and whether and to what degree they are competing with one another. In reality, higher degrees of market fragmentation, with multiple cartels engaging in violent competition, can have important effects on the effective conditionality of repression. The effective maximum the state can apply to any one cartel is a function not only of how willing and able the state is to concentrate on any one cartel (what I have called conditionality *among* cartels) but also how many cartels are operating and how they are behaving. If there are many cartels and *all* are violent, then even if conditionality is high, repressive force must be spread around, reducing the amount of repression that any one faces.

To see how general-equilibrium effects interact with conditionality, consider Kleiman's (2009) notion of "dynamic concentration," one form of conditional repression. The idea is for the state to focus its repressive force on a particular group or region, usually the most violent or crime-ridden, with the (credible) caveat that it will continue to thus focus *until the violence abates*, at which point it will move on to the next most troublesome region. Ideally, this produces a virtuous circle: the first group is now peaceful, and the state can concentrate its force on a second group, which, seeing how the first group now enjoys less repression, will be even quicker to self-pacify.

Kleiman contrasts dynamic concentration with a traditional, static approach that assigns repressive force to districts once, at the founding, and then polices them more or less equally; an unconditional approach, to use the terminology of this book. However, unconditional repression can also drive dynamic changes, particularly on the criminal side of the equation. In the wake of state repression, existing groups can fragment, or expand into new activities, and new criminal groups can form and enter the market. Unconditional repression in the face of market fragmentation and market entry produces the opposite of dynamic concentration's virtuous circle, a kind of *dynamic dispersion*.

In dynamic dispersion, the state's policy of pursuing groups equally means that it must apply $\frac{s}{N}$ to each group. Holding s constant for a moment, if a new group emerges or enters the criminal fold, raising N, the amount of repression each group faces falls. This not only makes life easier for each market participant, but may also make further market entry for other would-be criminal firms more appealing. And with each new market entrant, the deterrent effect of state repression falls even further.

The potential for positive feedback should be obvious: if the state has "maxed out" its degree of repression, so that s cannot increase in the short run, then the effective repression faced by any violent cartel falls with each new cartel that becomes violent. Moreover, there may also be less repression directed at other forms of criminal activity: if only the tiniest fraction of homicides, no matter how brutal, are investigated much less prosecuted, all sorts of violent criminal activities that would normally be risky and ill-advised can suddenly become profitable propositions. This may also be a factor in the diversification of cartels' activities and the rise of armed criminal organizations not primarily dedicated to drug trafficking. And for each new criminal band that emerges and commits a crime, the prospects for other potential entrants to criminal activity only get better. The potential for an escalatory spiral of violence is clear.

A related issue concerns the impact of individual cartel decisions in a concentrated versus fragmented context. In Colombia, there were essentially two cartels, only one of which took a violent stance toward the state. In this way, a single man, Pablo Escobar, could essentially decide the overall level of cartel–state violence. This allowed him to engage in the very precise coercion and bargaining that led up to his voluntary surrender in 1991. In Rio, although all three major cartels have confronted the state, the CV is a kind of "market leader." Traditionally the largest and most confrontational cartel, the CV's apparent switch to non-violent strategies in 2010 presaged a similar switch by the ADA cartel that controlled the Rocinha favela until its Pacification in 2011, while the CV's increasing use of violence within Pacified favelas since 2012 has also been "followed" by ADA. In Mexico, we lack any clear observations of cartels switching from violent to non-violent strategies, but we can conjecture that since even the largest cartels are small relative to the total market, their individual decisions to use violence or not have a smaller effect on the overall equilibrium.

4

Modeling Violent Corruption and Lobbying

To clarify and analyze the central causal logics of my theory, this chapter presents game-theoretic models of violent corruption and violent lobbying. Violent lobbying can be captured by a very simple war-of-attrition framework—a "toy" model of a dispute over de jure policy between cartels and state leaders; adding sufficient incomplete information generates violence in equilibrium. Violent corruption, however, involves a principal-agent problem between leaders and state enforcers, yielding counterintuitive dynamics. Conventional wisdom treats corruption and confrontation as strategic substitutes; this ignores the complementary role that violent threats play during bribe negotiation. In equilibrium, the likelihood and size of bribes depends on what cartels do if no agreement is reached: either "hiding"—taking evasive actions to reduce loss—or "fighting"—employing violence that may physically reduce losses but also inflicts pain on enforcers. For that reason, I develop a more in-depth sequence of models that provide two important contributions. First, baseline models of "hiding" and "fighting" responses by cartels provide a framework for conceptualizing and mapping the set of possible outcome scenarios: ideal-type scenarios where bribery never occurs ("Peaceful" and "Violent Enforcement") or always occurs ("State-Sponsored Protection" and "Coerced Peace"), and more realistic "Hide-and-Bribe" and "Fight-and-Bribe" scenarios. Second, by endogenizing cartels' choice of strategy, a richer version of the model explores how state policy choices interact with parameter conditions to determine which scenario occurs in equilibrium. State crackdowns, I find, can yield both incremental and sudden increases in anti-state violence when (a) corruption is sufficiently rampant, and (b) repression is insufficiently conditional.

4.1 A MODEL OF VIOLENT CORRUPTION

4.1.1 Introduction: Crackdowns in Corrupt Contexts

If you want a quick and dirty measure of police corruption, ask a taxi driver "If a cop pulled you over, would you offer a bribe?" In low-corruption settings like Northern Europe, Japan, and much of the United States, the answer is probably "No way." This is how law enforcement is supposed to work: when police catch an infractor, neither side even considers bribery a real possibility, and the law is always enforced.

In much of the world, however, your taxi driver is more likely to answer, "Obviously." In such settings, bribery in exchange for lax or non-enforcement is not just common, but expected; it is just part of what police, customs officials, health inspectors, and other state enforcers *do*. Just as economists like to point out that the very existence of a middle class is, world-historically, a rare exception to the Malthusian rule of subsistence and occasional mass starvation, it is worth remembering that non-corrupt policing is a precious and hard-won public good. Anyone who has been shaken down by street cops in Mexico City or Rio de Janeiro for minor infractions will not need reminding.

Though everyday extortion of basically law-abiding citizens may be the most pernicious form of police corruption from a normative and sociological viewpoint, the bulk of bribe payments are probably concentrated in the policing of vice and smuggling activities. This is because drug traffickers, prostitutes, casino operators, rum-runners, and the like are engaged in activities that are both illegal and lucrative (so they stand to lose a lot if police enforce the law, and are unlikely to report a cop who demands a bribe) but also "victimless" (so that non-enforcement by police generates little social and moral outrage). In these settings, police have a lot of "power to hurt"—coercive leverage over their marks—while facing little expected sanction from bribe-taking. This allows them, in theory, to extract a significant share of the rents from illicit economic activity.

How large a share police get depends on contextual factors. Thomas Schelling (1967) notes that in 1960s' Miami, the mafia controlled when and where police enforced the law, and could thus effectively extract rents from the direct providers of illicit goods and services. Because the mob held monopoly power in both directions, it successfully extorted half of bookmakers' profits while paying the police relatively small bribes. But, Schelling argues,

> It could have been the other way around, with the police using the syndicate as their agency to negotiate and collect from the bookmakers, and if the police had been organized and disciplined as a monopoly, it would have been the police, not the syndicate, that we should put at the top of our organizational pyramid ... [Instead] the initiative and entrepreneurship came from the syndicate, which had the talent and organization for this kind of business, [while] the police lacked the centralized authority for exploiting to their own benefit the power they had over the bookmakers. (1967, 67–68)

In settings where corruption is rampant, entrenched, and tacitly accepted, police—especially agents in direct contact with illicit businesses—often possess precisely this "talent and organization." In such cases, it is not merely "the other way around"; police may simply cut out the middleman and directly negotiate with criminals. Corrupt enforcement agents take the place of mafiosos as the "licensed collector[s] of the rents associated with the franchise held by the corrupt police department" (Reuter 2009, 277). When bribery for non-enforcement is widespread and regularized, policing becomes a system of illicit rent extraction; even if busts sometimes occur, they ultimately play into the larger dynamic of bribe negotiation, as we will see. In extreme cases, we get what Snyder and Durán-Martínez (2009b) call "state-sponsored protection rackets," with enforcement virtually never occuring[1] and bribe money wending its way upward to the highest levels of government.

Some leaders, however, genuinely seek to curtail drug trafficking (or other black-market activity); for them, rampant corruption presents an acute dilemma, one this model illuminates. Enforcement, from the point of view of cartels and other illicit firms, imposes business costs: interdiction of merchandise and capital (possibly including weapons), and the arrest or even killing of employees.[2] Imposition of these losses is simultaneously the preferred outcome of leaders (who presumably seek to put illicit firms out of business) and the threat that corrupt enforcers use to extract bribes in exchange for non-enforcement. Leaders cannot meaningfully crack down without giving enforcers increased power to interdict and otherwise impose costs; but by doing so they necessarily, if inadvertently, hand enforcers additional extractive leverage over illicit firms during bribe negotiations.

The central finding of this chapter is that crackdowns in corrupt settings, by increasing the bargaining leverage of enforcers, give drug cartels significant incentives to engage in anti-state violence. To see how this might be the case, first note that systems of illicit rent extraction—i.e., regularized bribery—can be quite extortionate in drug-trafficking settings: the kingpin of Rocinha, the largest favela in Rio, said at his 2011 arrest that he had regularly paid 50 percent of his gross receipts in bribes to police, often leaving him without any profits at all (Werneck 2011). One way for cartels to avoid extreme extortion is to "threaten back": if enforcers face armed violence when no agreement is reached, they are more likely to settle for a smaller bribe. This is the driving

---

1 I introduce a formal definition of the term "state-sponsored protection" here, denoting equilibria in which bribes are always struck and enforcement never occurs, but in which cartels have not threatened enforcers with violence (in contrast to equilibria in which bribes are always struck but enforcers would face cartel violence if they enforced the law, which I call *coerced peace*). I use Snyder and Durán-Martínez's (2009b) term because, as my analysis shows, state-sponsored protection equilibria require greater state complicity than occasional or even frequent bribery, and likely involve the kind of information-sharing mechanisms seen in Mexico under the PRI, their leading empirical example.
2 In both this discussion and the model to follow, state repression *only* imposes business losses; I set aside questions of when enforcement might physically destroy an entire cartel, or lead to its fragmentation. Obviously, these are important questions, not least because state leaders sometimes adopt deliberate strategies aimed at fragmenting cartels. However, the history of the drug war provides ample evidence that while individual DTOs can be destroyed or eliminated, doing so generally opens up market share for new DTOs to capture; the drug trade abides, and with it the kind of dilemma I analyze here.

logic behind Escobar's *"plata o plomo"* ("the bribe or the bullet") threats, a phrase still used throughout Colombia and Mexico. Precisely the same logic, I claim, drives Rio's traffickers willingness to occasionally clash with police, despite being severely outgunned. As an upper-level manager of the drug trade in one of Rio's largest favelas explained to me:

> There's no way to pay [the police] everything they demand, because if we did we'd end up just working for them ... If there's no money to pay them with, well then it'll be with bullets.[3]

In another favela, where profits were considerably larger, a senior manager told me that the price of the *arrego*—a slang term for regular bribe payments to police—had remained stable at one million *reais* per week (about US$400,000) for several years. Since this represented only 20 percent of the weekly revenue, I asked why the police didn't try to raise the price of the *arrego*. "Because," I was told, "he knows if he tries to raise it, we'll fight (*enfrentar*)."[4]

Violence, of course, may also play a brute-force, defensive function during busts: standing and fighting, as opposed to evasive "hiding" tactics, may physically reduce the losses that police impose when they enforce the law. Thus, even if corruption were not a factor, crackdowns might exacerbate cartels' incentives for anti-state violence as pure defense. However, traffickers' frequent recourse to violent threats prior to, and violent retribution in the wake of, enforcement suggest that anti-state violence also has a critical coercive impetus, one intimately linked to the possibility of striking a successful bribe agreement. To disentangle these incentives, and the way state policy shapes them, this chapter develops a formal model of bribe negotiation.

4.1.1.1 Contributions and Results

The model sheds new light on the dynamics of violent corruption, clarifying cartels' incentives to resort to *plata o plomo* threats and how state policies affect them. Scholars of drug wars have long recognized a relationship between corruption and violence (e.g., Andreas 1998; Bailey and Taylor 2009; Misse 2003; Reuter 2009; Snyder and Durán-Martínez 2009b), but often treat the two as strategic substitutes, arguing that cartels pay bribes precisely to avoid confrontation. This overlooks a critical complementarity: in equilibrium, threats of violence can make bribery more likely, more affordable, or both. True, the choice between *plata* and *plomo* is dichotomous in each instance. Yet even in if officials *always* choose bribes over bullets and no blood is spilled, a credible threat of cartel violence "off the equilibrium path" still induces them to accept an offer they would otherwise reject; indeed, such inducement is one way to formally define coercion (e.g., Acemoglu and Wolitzky 2011; Chwe 1990).

Dal Bó et al.'s *"Plata o Plomo?"* (2006) model partially formalizes this logic: in their model, threatening to punish bribe-takers lowers the equilibrium

---

[3] Interview, mid-level CV manager, Rio de Janeiro, March 29, 2010.
[4] Interview, high-level Terceiro Comando manager, Rio de Janeiro, August 4, 2014.

bribe price, and increases overall corruption. However, despite invoking Escobar as motivation, their model involves apparently licit groups not targeted for destruction by the state—the power to hurt runs only one way. Moreover, bribe agreements are always reached, so there is no violence in equilibrium.[5] In the model developed here, bribe negotiation sometimes fails—due to cartels' private information about their profits—and the likelihood that it fails is one key outcome of interest. In addition, when negotiation fails and cartels choose to fight, they simultaneously defend themselves against loss from enforcement and inflict pain on enforcers; the amount of pain inflicted turns out to have a critical effect on the dynamics of crackdowns.

In an important contribution, Snyder and Durán-Martínez (2009b) identify unstable bribe agreements as a key driver of cartel violence. However, their non-formal analysis tells us little about why, when bribery proves impossible, cartels "fight" rather than "hide." Indeed, traffickers in other Brazilian cities avoid confrontation even when bribe negotiations break down (Lessing 2008). Similarly, Escobar's Cali-cartel rivals rejected his violent approach, saying, "We don't kill judges, we buy them" (Lee 1994, 205). These groups do not even *threaten* enforcers with violence should bribery fail; rather, they minimize the impact of enforcement through "hiding" tactics like flight, anonymity, and keeping a low, respectable profile. Such "hide-and-bribe" strategies avoid the costs associated with anti-state violence, while foregoing the bribe-reducing leverage, and any advantage in terms of loss reduction, that violence yields. To analyze this trade-off and how state crackdowns affect it, the full specification of my model offers cartels a three-way choice between paying, hiding, and fighting,[6] explicitly accounting for any additional state repression that fighting will incur by formalizing the concept of conditionality.

Three core results bear highlighting. First, the presence of rampant corruption gives cartels strong positive incentives to adopt fighting strategies. In scenarios where corruption is rare or impossible, the only advantage cartels get from fighting is to reduce their losses to enforcement; where corruption is rampant, however, threatening to fight if no bribe agreement is reached can have an additional, coercive effect, inducing enforcers to make smaller bribe demands than they otherwise would. Second, when this coercive effect is sufficiently strong, state crackdowns no longer reduce the frequency of violence, but increase it. "Sufficiently strong," the model reveals, has an intuitive meaning: law enforcers fear cartel reprisals more than official punishment for bribe-taking. In this way, cracking down on cartels that have already adopted fighting strategies, particularly in contexts of rampant corruption, can exacerbate violence. Finally, crackdowns can affect cartels' choice between hiding and fighting in the first place; unconditional repression can push cartels

---

5 Konrad and Skaperdas (1997) derive inefficient equilibrium violence, but coercion is similarly unidirectional.
6 This resembles Bailey and Taylor's (2009) three-way typology of cartel strategies; however, their treatment of the state as a unitary actor is more suited to the study of violent lobbying.

from hiding into fighting strategies, while increases in the conditionality of repression pushes cartels from fighting toward hiding.

Along the way, the model yields a conceptual map of the different scenarios that can prevail between cartels and police in equilibrium. At one logical extreme, police are incorruptible or face steep expected sanctions for bribe-taking, so that bribery never occurs. In these scenarios, crackdowns simply increase the loss that cartels suffer under enforcement (i.e., the size of busts); if cartels fight in response to enforcement, it is solely to reduce their losses, and violence has purely defensive value. At the other extreme, bribery *always* occurs, and crackdowns simply increase the share of cartel profits that enforcers are able to extract. Here, cartels always pay the bribe, but what they *would have done if no bribe agreement were reached*, that is, whether they hide or fight off the equilibrium path, still affects the equilibrium size of bribes. In between these extreme "ideal types," we get more realistic scenarios in which bribe agreements and enforcement both occur with some probability; here, crackdowns affect both the size of bribes and the probability they will be paid. I offer empirical examples of each of these scenarios, and explore the ways that changes in the degree and conditionality of repression can lead to movement from one scenario to another.

4.1.1.2 Technical Caveats

Before turning to the details, three technical points warrant emphasis. First, I analyze the effects of changes in state repressive policy, without solving for leaders' optimal policy. This illuminates the tradeoffs leaders face—no policy simultaneously minimizes drug interdiction, cartel–state violence, and bribery—while avoiding heroic assumptions about their preferences over these outcomes and the political costs of changing policies. As Rodrik (2013) argues, pat political-economy assumptions about leaders' interests can produce spurious or vacuous analyses, particularly if leaders do not fully understand the relevant mechanisms.[7] I do consider the effects of policy shocks on cartels' and enforcers' utility, but eschew a naive social-welfare approach that simply sums the utility of all players for a *political* analysis: policies that raise the welfare of traffickers are likely to be unpopular, while those that reduce police welfare (even by curtailing ill-gotten gains) may produce institutional resistance or even insubordination.

Second, I follow the war-as-bargaining-breakdown literature in assuming that conflict is costly, and hence must be driven by some combination of information asymmetries and commitment problems (Fearon 1995b; Powell 2006). Here, though, there are two separate inefficiencies to be explained. The poorly paid cop and the wealthy capo he is about to arrest clearly have

---

[7] This is why it is standard in macroeconomics to analyze, say, the effects of different monetary policy approaches without explicitly modeling the Fed chairman's preferences over unemployment versus inflation, or her understanding of zero-lower-bound dynamics.

options they both prefer to enforcement, which destroys some of the "pie" through interdiction. That they nonetheless sometimes fail to agree on a bribe constitutes the first inefficiency. Here, it is driven by a "standard" information asymmetry: as in Dal Bó and Powell (2009), the size of the "pie" (here, drug profits) is private information and cannot be credibly communicated; to avoid being exploited, the offer-taker rejects the worst offers. This is one—but certainly not the only—plausibly relevant mechanism; others remain to be explored in future work, especially uncertainty over multiple police "types" of differing corruptibility (though I do consider changes in force corruptibility as a comparative static). The justification for using a standard mechanism is the presence of a second inefficiency to be explored. When bribe negotiations fail, why do cartels sometimes "pay" back police with costly bullets, as the trafficker quoted above put it, instead of hiding? Fighting instead of hiding constitutes the second inefficiency, because ex-post punishment inflicted on police makes fight-and-bribe outcomes Pareto inferior to hide-and-bribe ones.[8] In this model, they can nonetheless occur in equilibrium because enforcers cannot commit to *not* exploiting an unarmed cartel.

Finally, this static approach permits a relatively clear and tractable analysis of the core logic of violent corruption. Understanding the one-shot interaction is an important step toward a dynamic model that can address reputation-building, learning, and related issues. Indeed, the ongoing, non-decisive nature of cartel–state conflict suggests folk-theorem results, with ability to punish in the stage-game determining what outcomes are sustainable in dynamic equilibrium.

4.1.2 Bribe Negotiation With and Without Anti-State Violence: A Basic Framework

In this section, I develop a simple framework for analyzing the interrelationship of repressive policy, law enforcement, bribery, and violence, centered around a negotiation over a potential bribe. In all versions of the model, an enforcer demands a bribe in exchange for non-enforcement, and a cartel either pays the bribe or suffers enforcement. What happens when the cartel does not pay changes in each iteration of the model. I begin with a baseline model of non-violent bribe negotiation where the cartel's only options are to pay or hide. Then, to explore how the dynamics of corruption differ when cartels fight back, I replace the hiding option with fighting. In one iteration, fighting has only defensive value, reducing the cartel's loss if and when enforcement occurs. I then add a punitive "*plomo*" effect, so that fighting also hurts enforcers. Comparing these three versions yields two key insights: first, the "*plomo*" effect constitutes a powerful additional incentive, over and above loss-reduction, for the cartel to adopt a fighting strategy. Second, when this "*plomo*" effect is sufficiently

---

[8] See note 23.

large, crackdowns increase rather than decrease the equilibrium probability of fighting.

This basic framework illustrates the potential benefits to cartels of fighting over hiding strategies, but does not formally account for the costs, and hence can tell us little about cartels' choice between hiding and fighting. In the subsequent section, I develop a richer version of the model that formalizes cartels' costs of adopting fighting strategies: their costs of acquiring firepower, and any additional state repression that fighting incurs—the conditionality of repression, in my terminology. In this specification, the dynamics of crackdowns specific to hiding and fighting carry over from the basic framework, but crackdowns also affect cartels' choice *between* strategies.

4.1.2.1 A Baseline "Hiding" Model

Setup: All versions of the game have two strategic players, a cartel D (he) and a state enforcer P (she), plus non-strategic state leaders S who publicly and exogenously set repressive policy parameters at the outset of the game. In this basic framework, D earns profits from drug trafficking activity, which are modeled as a random variable y. D knows how much he made (i.e., the realized value of y), but P knows only that y is distributed uniformly over $[\underline{y}, \bar{y}]$. P then makes a bribe demand, b, in exchange for non-enforcement; D either pays b or rejects the demand.[9]

If D rejects the bribe demand, P enforces, causing D to lose a fraction of his profits to interdiction.[10] How much D loses depends on what D does in response to enforcement. First, I consider an evasive, "hiding" approach that eschews violence and seeks to minimize D's losses through flight, anonymity, stashing of merchandise, and so on. Define the interdiction rate (i.e., D's loss) under hiding as a function $h(s) \in (0, 1)$, so that D receives $y(1 - h)$. s is the *degree of repression* directed at D, determined publicly and exogenously by policymakers (S) prior to play.[11] The higher the degree of repression (s), the higher the interdiction rate when P enforces: $\frac{\partial h}{\partial s} > 0$. Hiding imposes no pain on P, so she simply earns a fixed wage, which I normalize throughout to zero.[12]

---

[9] How bargaining protocols are modeled can have implications for the results of a model. Generally, allowing one player to make a take-it-or-leave-it offer. Ultimately, D's private information prevents P from retaining all the bargaining power.

[10] To simplify the analysis, I abstract from enforcement outcomes that give D negative utility. Individual traffickers face imprisonment and death, not only interdiction; for the cartel qua firm, though, such outcomes are important only as they affect the bottom line. In any case, allowing P to impose negative utility does not fundamentally change the analysis, but can lead to bribes larger than D's total profits, raising the question of credit constraints and muddling the exposition.

[11] I take up the question of conditionality of repression below.

[12] In reality, police wages may be increasing in the size of the busts they carry out, perhaps through performance-based bonuses or promotions, perhaps through an informal policy of allowing cops to keep a portion of seized cash and property. Moreover, paying cops higher salaries is often touted as a corruption-fighting strategy. Still, police wages are likely to have

If D pays the bribe, P does not enforce; D retains $y - b$, his profits minus the bribe, while P receives the bribe b minus an expected sanction for bribe-taking and non-enforcement, designated by λ. This critical parameter is meant to capture, in a very reduced form, all the negative consequences to P of accepting a bribe. This includes any psychological or moral costs (what Scott (1972, 24) calls "scruples"), so that if P is personally honest, she would have a higher λ, as well as any expected official punishment (i.e., the probability of being caught and punished times the severity of the punishment). In practice, both "scruples" and the probability of being caught probably depend overwhelmingly on how many *other* enforcers are taking bribes, so λ can be thought of as measuring the general culture or prevalence of corruption within a force.

I generally treat λ as a "sticky" parameter rather than a choice variable decided by state leaders. Of course, policymakers can try to raise λ by increasing the legal sanction for bribe-taking, but if the chances of being caught and punished are very low, this may be ineffective. As Rose-Ackerman (2008, 560) notes, "Tough laws are not sufficient. Many highly corrupt countries have exemplary formal statutes that have no real meaning because they are seldom enforced." Theoretical (e.g., Tirole 1996) and empirical (e.g., Fisman and Miguel 2007) work finds that corruption is a tipping-point phenomenon, either rampant (generating a low λ that feeds further corruption) or rare (generating a high λ, keeping cops honest). How to tip a corrupt, low-λ police force to a clean, high-λ one is a research agenda unto itself. In practice, cultures of corruption are persistent, so it is more realistic to think of λ as stably low or high in the short run *for any given agency, corps, battalion, etc.*, and changes in λ as resulting from leaders deploying different corps with differing degrees of endemic corruption. For this reason, rather than examine marginal changes in λ, I compare low-λ (high-corruption) or high-λ (low-corruption) scenarios.[13]

This provides some leverage for addressing the common practice of deploying low-corruption forces, like the army or elite police squads like Rio's BOPE[14] and Colombia's Bloque de Búsqueda. The model shows how the dynamics of bribe negotiations may change dramatically when a corrupt force is replaced with one less corrupt; a more complicated model would be needed to formally investigate the dynamic, general equilibrium effects when multiple police forces

a fixed component, and the total wage paid is likely to be small relative to the size of the loss they can impose on traffickers. Modeling this wage as fixed, and hence normalizable to zero, highlights this issue for the state.

13 Note too that I model λ as lump-sum, independent of the size of the bribe; modeling λ as a loss function, so that larger bribes produce larger expected sanctions, does not substantively change the results, but makes exposition more cumbersome. Future work could test more complex specifications for λ, including a potential discontinuity at $b = 0$, if, say, authorities make a distinction between just not enforcing and actively taking a bribe.

14 *Batalhão de Operações Policiais Especiais*, Special Police Operations Battalion, an elite unit trained in urban warfare and anti-insurgent techniques.

overlap. This is an important avenue for further research, particularly given that in the United States, at least, overlapping federal and local jurisdictions were critical in reducing endemic police corruption in US cities (Reuter 1995, 94–95). Empirically, though, the Latin American cases point to a more depressing possibility: contact with the drug trade can lead to the corruption of previously clean forces; both the BOPE and the Bloque de Búsqueda came to face serious charges of corruption.

Analysis: In the last round, D will pay whenever $y - b \geq y(1 - h)$ and will hide otherwise; this defines a cutpoint $\hat{y} = \frac{b}{h(s)}$:

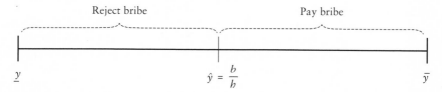

A higher b will be paid with lower ex-ante probability, and vice versa; P, taking this into account, calculates a "naive" optimal bribe demand, call it b_H^*, which comes out to $\frac{h(s)\bar{y}+\lambda}{2}$. If "everyone has their price," then P's is b_H^*. Critically, this price is increasing in the degree of repression, s: the more repressive force that P can bring to bear, the greater the potential interdiction rate, $h(s)$, and hence the more leverage P has in demanding a bribe from D. b_H^* is also increasing in $\bar{y}$: the larger D's potential profits, the larger a bribe P would like to demand.

Corruption is not inevitable, however. Note that b_H^* is also increasing in λ: if P is very honest or very afraid of being punished for bribe-taking (so that λ is large), then her "price" will be quite high.[15] In such situations, the "naive" optimum b_H^* may be more than D would ever be willing to pay (and hence may not be a true optimum). D would never pay a bribe larger than the maximum loss P can impose through enforcement, $h(s)\bar{y}$. Setting $b_H^* \geq h(s)\bar{y}$ yields the following condition:

$$\lambda \geq h(s)\bar{y} \qquad \text{(peaceful-enforcement condition)}$$

When this condition holds, there is no bargaining range—since the smallest bribe P would ever accept (λ) is greater than the largest bribe D would ever pay—so bribes are never paid and P always enforces. The bribe negotiation, bound to fail, becomes a meaningless formality: in equilibrium P might ask for *any* bribe above D's maximum, precisely because she knows D will never pay. There is an infinite set of such "babbling equilibria," a game-theoretic manifestation of the fact that, in very low-corruption, high-λ settings, bribery is not a realistic possibility, and both parties know it. In concrete terms, imagine

---

[15] A truly incorruptible police officer would have $b_H^* = \infty$.

getting a traffic ticket in, say, Sweden: there is probably *some* bribe large enough that the trooper would accept it, but it is surely far more than one would be willing to pay to get out of a mere traffic ticket. Both parties know this, and so neither even tries to make a serious offer.

This ideal-type scenario, which I call *peaceful enforcement*, is how law enforcement is supposed to work: police punish infractors without either party seriously trying to strike a bribe agreement. Moreover, under peaceful enforcement, the only effect of a crackdown (i.e., an increase in s) is to increase D's loss to interdiction; the probability of bribery occurring remains at zero (as long as the increase in s is not too big). This is presumably what leaders hope to achieve by cracking down on the drug trade in the first place.

Law enforcement, however, rarely works like this in drug wars, and the peaceful-enforcement condition helps explain why. It says, in short, that to avoid corruption, the state must be able to impose more pain on police for bribe-taking, λ, than police can impose on cartels for trafficking, $h(s)\bar{y}$. Rearranging this a bit, the highest interdiction rate that the state can sustain without inducing police corruption is $h(s) \leq \frac{\lambda}{\bar{y}}$. In many drug-trafficking contexts, especially transshipment markets, criminal profits are immense (implying a large $\bar{y}$), and corruption is rampant (low λ); if leaders give enforcers even moderate capacity to interdict, the peaceful-enforcement condition may not hold, and there will be at least some bribery in equilibrium.

The polar opposite ideal-type scenario can prevail if P expects little sanction for bribe-taking (so that λ is very small): P demands a bribe that D is always willing to pay, and there is no enforcement in equilibrium. This scenario, I argue, formalizes Snyder and Durán-Martínez's (2009b) notion of *state-sponsored protection*; though they do not explicitly define this as a situation in which enforcement *never* occurs, the scenario certainly fits one of their empirical referents: Mexico under the PRI. There, the expected sanction for bribe-taking (λ) was essentially zero because state leaders deliberately built an arrangement where local enforcers could easily strike bribery arrangements with the relevant illicit actors. Under state-sponsored protection, crackdowns simply give more P more bargaining power (at D's expense), raising the size of the equilibrium bribe; the probability of enforcement remains at zero (as long as the increase in s is not too big). This might seem perverse, but if leaders prioritize illicit rent extraction, as the PRI regime seems to have, these might be desirable outcomes.

In between these two extremes, a *hide-and-bribe* scenario prevails, in which D pays the bribe when profits are high enough and hides otherwise. In this scenario, P's "naive" optimum b_H^* is her true optimum, and her equilibrium bribe demand. Crackdowns increase the size of this bribe demand ($\frac{\partial b_H^*}{\partial s} > 0$), since the larger the loss that P can inflict on D through enforcement, the more D is willing to pay to avoid it. This captures a key component of the violent corruption story:

H_1: *Crackdowns—increases in the degree of repression—give enforcers additional bargaining leverage over traffickers.*

Other key outcome variables in this scenario are the equilibrium *ex ante* probability of the bribe demand being paid (Pr_B), and its complement, the probability that P enforces and D hides: $\text{Pr}_H = 1 - \text{Pr}_B$. Crackdowns affect these probabilities, making enforcement less likely and bribes more likely ($\frac{\partial \text{Pr}_H}{\partial s} < 0$), though busts, when they do occur, are larger. This baseline model thus predicts that, in a scenario in which both bribery and enforcement occur with some probability, crackdowns produce larger but less frequent busts, and larger but more frequent bribes.

The probability of bribery occurring is also, naturally, decreasing in anti-corruption efforts or the deployment a less-corrupt force. These increases in λ make enforcement more likely ($\frac{\partial \text{Pr}_H}{\partial \lambda} > 0$), because they make bribe-taking less lucrative for P; if λ is high enough, we get the pure-enforcement scenario, with $\text{Pr}_H = 1$, discussed above.

4.1.2.2 A Basic Fighting Model

To illustrate the core intuitions behind violent corruption, now suppose that if D rejects P's bribe demand, P still enforces, but D now "fights." For now, I ignore the cost to D of acquiring the means of violence (such as arms and soldiers), as well as any increased state repression that fighting incurs due to repression being conditional; I relax both these simplifying assumptions in the full specification below.

Fighting might have two distinct effects: a defensive "loss-reduction" effect, and a coercive, "*plomo*" effect. (This distinction is generally unnecessary in canonical, zero-sum models of war, because one side's territorial gain is by definition the other's loss.) Here, I consider each in turn; the richer specification below parameterizes their relative weight.

First consider the pure-defense case: violence is entirely defensive, reducing D's loss to enforcement compared to hiding, but inflicting no pain on P. Formalize this by replacing the interdiction rate $h(s)$ with $f(s)$; the equilibrium bribe price becomes $b_F^* = \frac{f\bar{y} + \lambda}{2}$. So, if fighting reduces D's loss compared to hiding, so that $f(s) < h(s)$ for all s, then $b_F^* < b_H^*$. That is, the "loss-reduction" effect of violence lowers P's "naive" optimal bribe demand by reducing P's power to hurt D. In this way, *à la* Schelling, what is pure defense at one level affects the coercive negotiation over bribes at another. This in turn increases D's expected payoffs, and the larger the "loss-reduction" effect, the larger these positive incentives to adopt fighting over hiding.[16]

---

[16] Formally, if U_F^D and U_H^D are D's expected payoffs under fighting and hiding, then $U_F^D - U_H^D = \left(h(s) - f(s)\right) \frac{\left(3\bar{y}^2 - 4\underline{y}^2 + \frac{\lambda^2}{f(s)h(s)}\right)}{8(\bar{y} - \underline{y})}$, which is positive and increasing in the size of the "loss-reduction" effect $h(s) - f(s)$.

As before, there are ideal-type scenarios in which bribery never occurs (which I call *violent enforcement*) and where it always occurs (which I call *coerced peace*); these are violent analogues of the peaceful-enforcement and state-sponsored-protection scenarios discussed earlier. I discuss all these scenarios—the conditions likely to produce them, and what they look like in practice—in the subsequent section, in light of the richer specification developed there.

In between these ideal types, we get *fight-and-bribe* equilibria, where P makes a bribe demand that D sometimes accepts and sometimes rejects (leading P to enforce and D to fight in response), so that the probability of fighting, Pr_F, is between zero and one. Assuming that fighting offers a loss-reduction advantage over hiding, but holding all other parameters constant, the probability of bribery occurring is higher under fighting: $\mathrm{Pr}_F < \mathrm{Pr}_H$. Importantly, though, the effect of crackdowns on that probability is still positive: just as with hide-and-bribe equilibria, increases in the degree of repression (s) produce more frequent bribes and less frequent enforcement ($\frac{\partial \mathrm{Pr}_F}{\partial s} < 0$). In short, as long as violence is purely defensive, with no coercive, "*plomo*" effect, the dynamics of bribe negotiation are broadly similar to non-violent bribe negotiation.

Now consider the pure "*plomo*" case: assume, for the moment, that fighting does not reduce D's loss to enforcement (so that $f(s) = h(s)$), but does inflict pain on P to the tune of $-\pi$. I treat π as exogenous and costless for now. Focusing on interior solutions, P's equilibrium bribe demand becomes:

$$b_F^* = \frac{f(s)\bar{y} + \lambda - \pi}{2} \tag{4.1}$$

Because we have assumed (for now) that $f(s) = h(s)$, the initial hiding case can be recovered by setting $\pi = 0$; from there it is obvious that any "*plomo*" effect ($\pi > 0$) reduces b_F^*. Indeed, this reduction in the equilibrium bribe price is the whole point of *plata o plomo* threats: if excessive bribe demands will be "paid" with bullets, P will demand smaller bribes. This translates into a higher equilibrium payoff for D (as long as bribery occurs with some probability); this benefit of fighting over hiding is, not surprisingly, increasing in the amount of pain (π) that D can inflict on P.[17]

As we just saw, purely defensive violence also lowers the equilibrium bribe demand, but the mechanism is different, producing different dynamics. The "loss-reduction" effect physically reduces P's leverage over D, so P gets less out of any potential bribe agreement, leading to less frequent bribes. The coercive, "*plomo*" effect gives P incentives to avoid enforcement, so she "shaves" her demand to ensure bribes occur with greater frequency. Indeed, the probability

---

17 Formally, $U_F^D - U_H^D = \pi \frac{\bar{y}h(s) - \lambda - \frac{\pi}{2}}{4(\bar{y}-\underline{y})h(s)}$, which is positive under the assumption that bribery occurs with positive probability, and is increasing in π.

of enforcement occurring, which now implies "fighting," is clearly decreasing in π:

$$\text{Pr}_F = \frac{\lambda - \pi}{2f(s)(\bar{y} - \underline{y})} + \frac{\frac{\bar{y}}{2} - y}{\bar{y} - \underline{y}} \qquad (4.2)$$

Equation 4.2 reveals that λ and π have opposite pulls on the likelihood of fighting: a higher λ means a greater sanction on P for bribe-taking, which makes enforcement relatively more attractive to her, while a higher π means more "*plomo*" punishment when P enforces, making bribes more attractive. When $\lambda > \pi$, the net effect is fight-inducing, when $\pi > \lambda$, bribe-inducing. Either way, though, this net effect is inversely proportional to the interdiction rate that D faces, $f(s)$, implying that crackdowns weaken it. That is, if $\lambda > \pi$, the net fight-inducing effect grows smaller as s increases, and Pr_F is decreasing in s. Conversely, if $\pi > \lambda$, the net bribe-inducing effect grows smaller as s increases, and Pr_F is increasing in s.[18]

The result is that, whereas the effect of crackdowns on the probability of hiding ($\frac{\partial \text{Pr}_H}{\partial s}$) is always negative, the effect on the probability of fighting ($\frac{\partial \text{Pr}_F}{\partial s}$) is indeterminate. With purely defensive fighting, where $\pi = 0$, crackdowns produce more frequent bribes, as with hiding. But if the "*plomo*" effect is strong enough, so that $\pi > \lambda$, then $\frac{\partial \text{Pr}_F}{\partial s}$ becomes positive, and crackdowns will lead to more frequent fighting. The condition $\pi > \lambda$ means, roughly, that police have more to fear from cartel violence than from internal-affairs investigations or their own guilty consciences. This condition is thus more likely to hold when corruption is common, widely accepted, or otherwise unlikely to go punished. Summarizing:

H_2: *Crackdowns in a context of rampant corruption can exacerbate cartel–state violence.*

This is one of the model's central results, and is robust to the specification below, which accounts for D's costs of fighting.

So far, I have assumed that λ and π are unaffected by crackdowns if we relax this assumption, the result in H_2 is likely to be even stronger. For example, we might think that, just as cartel violence may have a defensive, "loss-reduction" effect for D, increases in s could have a defensive, "body-armor" effect for P, reducing the amount of pain (π) that D inflicts by fighting during enforcement; formally, say that $\frac{\partial \pi}{\partial s} < 0$. Similarly, it might be the case that crackdowns (increases in s) also necessarily involve anti-corruption measures or deployment of less corrupt forces, raising λ (so that $\frac{\partial \lambda}{\partial s} > 0$). In either case, the condition for

---

[18] Formally, differentiating Equation 4.2 gives: $\frac{\partial \text{Pr}_F}{\partial s} = \frac{(\pi - \lambda) \frac{\partial f}{\partial s}}{2f(s)^2 (\bar{y} - \underline{y})}$, which is positive if and only if $\pi > \lambda$.

$\frac{\partial \Pr_F}{\partial s} > 0$ is even more easily met than before.[19] Substantively, if crackdowns not only increase interdiction rates but also make fighting less painful and bribe-taking more risky for P, then they are even *more* likely to produce additional fighting.

4.1.3 To Hide or Fight? A Richer Specification

Thus far, I have considered hiding and fighting separately, as different "outside options" when D rejects P's bribe demand. This illustrated the potential benefits to D of fighting, and the different dynamics that are obtained when corruption is rampant and violence has a powerful "*plomo*" effect, but it ignored D's costs of violence, and never formalized D's choice between hiding and fighting. I now develop a significantly richer but more complicated model to address these concerns. D now chooses an amount of arms to acquire, a, which in equilibrium determines whether he will fight or hide in response to enforcement. I make D pay for his guns, but the more critical cost of fighting is the extra state repression it exposes D to, i.e., the *conditionality of repression*. This richer specification formalizes conditionality, as well as the relative importance of defensive, "loss-reduction" effect of violence, allowing the model to better speak to the trade-off cartels face between violent and non-violent strategies. Derivations and proofs of formal propositions are omitted for brevity, and available by request, but I retain some formal notation when it is clarifying.

4.1.3.1 Setup
The game now starts with D purchasing a quantity of arms a at a price of 1; these costs are sunk, even if no fighting occurs. I assume that P observes a but not realized drug profits, y.[20] The game then proceeds as before: drug profits are realized, with D but not P observing realized y. Since D chooses a before profits, y, are determined, his choice of a cannot act as a signal of the realized value of y. I also redefine the distribution of y in terms of its mean value, μ, and a parameter $\zeta \in (0,1)$ that indicates the degree of P's uncertainty: $y \sim U[\mu(1 - \zeta), \mu(1 + \zeta)]$. This formulation clarifies a necessary condition for the state-sponsored protection ideal-type scenario ($\zeta < \frac{1}{3}$) and, as in Dal Bó and Powell (2009), distinguishes short-term fluctuations (random draws of y) from general market conditions (μ). P then demands a bribe b, and, unlike in the previous iterations of the model, D now has a three-way choice: paying the bribe (B), hiding (H), or fighting (F).

---

[19] The formal condition is $\pi(s) > \lambda + \frac{f(s)}{\frac{\partial f}{\partial s}} \left(\frac{\partial \pi}{\partial s} - \frac{\partial \lambda}{\partial s} \right)$. $f(s)$ and $\frac{\partial f}{\partial s}$ are positive, and the expression in parentheses negative by the assumptions made in the text, so this condition is more easily met than $\pi > \lambda$.

[20] Cartel armament is likely to be more accurately observable than profits, in part because D has incentives to downplay y and to exaggerate a, so it is sufficient to assume that D can costlessly reveal a but cannot create the illusion of having more than a.

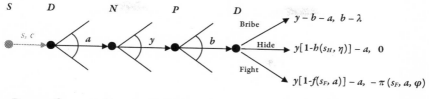

y = Drug profits s = Degree of repression $h(\cdot)$ = Interdiction rate if D hides

b = Bribe price c = Conditionality of repression $f(\cdot)$=Interdiction rate if D fights

a = Cartel arms $s_H = s\,(1-c)$ = Repression if D hides $\pi(\cdot)$ = Pain inflicted on P if D fights

                 $s_F = s$ = Repression if D fights η = Efficacy of hiding (territoriality)

                 λ = P's sanction from bribe-taking φ = Efficacy of cartel coercion

FIGURE 4.1. Violent Corruption Game Tree.

If D pays, he now gets $y - b$ minus his sunk costs for weapons $(-a)$. P receives, as before, $b - \lambda$. If D rejects the bribe demand (playing H or F), P enforces; as before, enforcement causes D to lose some share of realized drug profits, h or f, depending on whether he hides or fights. Both h and f depend on the degree of repression, which I now assume to be weakly greater if D fights—perhaps P can only use deadly force when fired upon, for example. Formally, assume that a state leader (S) now sets both the degree (s) and conditionality (c) of repression exogenously and publicly prior to play. Let s_H and s_F represent the amount of repressive force P brings to bear, respectively, if D hides or fights in the last round; then $s_H = s_F(1 - c) \leq s_F$. Thus $c \in (0,1)$ parameterizes *conditionality*: as repression becomes unconditional $(c \to 0)$, the relative reprieve D gains by eschewing violence evaporates $(s_H \to s_F)$.[21] For expositional simplicity, I further assume $s_F = s$, i.e., violent cartels face the maximum amount of state repression available.

Changes in conditionality, as formalized, change the amount of repression D faces if he hides, leaving unaffected the repression he faces if fighting. This approach reflects a substantive consideration: states usually direct the maximum repression possible at cartels that employ anti-state violence; conditional policies, when implemented, usually take the form of "easing off" on cartels that eschew violence. This formalization also helps distinguish between conditionality "across" and "within" cartels. In both forms, a cartel switching from hiding to fighting incurs additional repression. In conditionality within cartels, there is an added element of "forgiveness": switching from fighting to hiding yields a commensurate reprieve. Under conditionality across cartels, no such reprieve is given, and once a cartel is targeted for additional repression, it has no incentive to go back to hiding. As explicitly formalized here, conditionality is within cartels, and hence can push a violent cartel them to

---

[21] Ruling out $c = 1$ guarantees that non-violent trafficking is always subject to *some* degree of repression.

TABLE 4.1. *Effects of Increased Firepower on Enforcement Outcomes.*

		Effect of increases in		
		State firepower (s):	Cartel firepower (a):	
Enforcement outcomes:	*D*'s loss $f(a,s)$	"Interdiction" $\frac{\partial f}{\partial s} > 0$	"Loss-reduction" $\frac{\partial f}{\partial a} < 0$	☐ Defensive
	P's "pain" $\pi(a,s)$	"Body armor" $\frac{\partial \pi}{\partial s} < 0$	"*Plomo*" $\frac{\partial \pi}{\partial a} > 0$	☐ Coercive

The defensive/coercive distinction occurs because, unlike zero-sum conflicts, P does not "win" D's drug profits via interdiction, nor does D directly gain by hurting P.

eschew violence. We can instead model the effects of increases in conditionality across cartels, where anti-state violence once adopted locks in full-bore state repression, by assuming that c goes to zero for a cartel already employing a fighting strategy.

To endogenize D's choice of a and analyze explicit solutions, I specify contest success functions (CSFs) for h, f and π. It seems natural to assume that s and a have both defensive and coercive effects, with opposite impacts on f and π. The idea, captured in Table 4.1, can be formalized by defining $f \equiv \frac{s}{a+s}$ and $-\pi \equiv -\varphi\frac{a}{a+s}$. $f \in [0,1]$ still represents the interdiction rate, so D's loss to enforcement is $y \cdot f$. In a typical CSF specification, each player wins what the other loses. In drug war, though, neither P (enforcers) nor S (policymakers) "win" the street value of interdicted drugs, ruling out such a zero-sum formulation. Rather, cartel firepower increases, and state firepower decreases, the amount of pain D can inflict on P. The parameter φ scales P's distaste for physical confrontation, capturing the size of fighting's "*plomo*" effect relative to its "loss-reduction" effect, and reflecting Schelling's insight that coercive power "is not unconcerned with the interest of others" but rather "measured in the suffering it can cause" (1966, 2).[22]

Since hiding is a distinct "technology" from simply fighting without arms (which here would yield a total loss), let $h(\cdot) \equiv \frac{s_H}{\eta + s_H}$, where η is a parameter that captures the relative loss-reducing efficacy of hiding. A low η implies that fighting yields significant defensive benefits over hiding; this might be the case if physical territory itself is valuable, so that fleeing leads to large cartel losses. Thus, one substantive interpretation of η is as an inverse measure of the territoriality of the drug trade. In Rio, for example, favela territory contains retail points of sale as well as caches for *matériel*, so that even successfully

22 For technical reasons, assume $\varphi \neq \lambda$.

fleeing from police may leave traffickers substantially worse off, implying low η. In Colombia, by contrast, physically holding territory was probably less useful than securing high-level protection of trafficking routes; this would imply a high η and little purely defensive value to fighting.

In this one-shot setting, subgame perfect Nash equilibrium (SPNE) requires D to choose the highest-payoff action in the last round. Since D gets no intrinsic pleasure from hurting P, he can only credibly threaten to fight if, beyond some level of armament, D retains more profits by fighting than hiding:

$$\exists \, \tilde{a} > 0 : a \geq \tilde{a} \Rightarrow f(a, s_F) \leq h(\eta, s_H) \qquad \text{(Condition } \tilde{a})$$

This condition requires fighting to have at least some defensive, "loss-reduction" effect. To explore the possibility of violent corruption where fighting is purely coercive, we would need to abandon subgame perfection (i.e., permit non-credible threats) or move to a dynamic model where costly punishment in one round is sustained by its effects on future play, possibly through reputation-building. The latter is a promising avenue for future research. Here, I retain SPNE; the CSF specification assumes that cartel firepower produces defensive ("loss-reduction") effects, and thus satisfies Condition $\tilde{a}$: $a > \frac{\eta}{1-c} \equiv \tilde{a} \Rightarrow f < h$. The case where violence has *only* defensive value can be modeled by setting φ to zero; larger values of φ imply a larger coercive effect of cartel violence relative to its defensive effects.

4.1.3.2 Analysis

In the last round, D either pays the bribe demand, fights if he has chosen $a \geq \tilde{a}$, or hides if $a \leq \tilde{a}$. Because arms do not affect the efficacy of hiding, but are costly to acquire, D's best "hiding strategy" is to acquire no arms at all; write this as $a_H^* = 0$. D's best "fighting strategy" will be some $a_F^* \geq \tilde{a}$. P's equilibrium bribe demand depends on whether D has committed himself to hiding (by playing a_H^*) or fighting (by playing a_F^*); write P's potential bribe demands as b_H^* and b_F^*. In the first round, D can thus use backward induction to compare his payoffs to choosing a_H^* (which will induce P to play b_H^*) or a_F^* (inducing b_F^*). Which strategy is preferable depends on parameter conditions, and in particular on the degree (s) and conditionality (c) of repression. First, I show that the main comparative statics results for each strategy type carry over from the baseline model. I then turn to D's choice between strategy types, exploring how shifts in state policy and other factors might push cartels from hiding to fighting strategies or vice versa.

The key outcomes for each strategy remain the equilibrium bribe price (b_H^* or b_F^*) and the probability the outside option is taken ($\Pr_H$ or $\Pr_F$). I focus first on areas of the parameter space in which these probabilities are between zero and one, that is, hide-and-bribe and fight-and-bribe scenarios (which I refer to here as "interior solutions"). I turn to the "ideal-type" scenarios where bribery never or always occurs ("corner solutions") in the following section.

The derivations of b_H^* and b_F^* are essentially the same as in the baseline model. Since $a_H^* = 0$, the hiding case is easy to solve. The effect of crackdowns (increases in s are the same) as before; now, though, we also consider the effect of an increase in the conditionality of repression, c:

Proposition 1. *Assuming an interior solution and $a < \tilde{a}$, the equilibrium bribe price b_H^* is increasing in λ and s, and decreasing in c. The probability of bribery occurring is decreasing in λ, increasing in s, and decreasing in c.*

As before, higher expected sanctions for bribe-taking (λ) deters bribery—this is why police corruption tends to be either rampant or rare—while increases in s (crackdowns) make bribes larger and more frequent because they reduce D's outside option. Thus H_1 still holds: *crackdowns increase the demand for corruption.* Conversely, increases in conditionality (c) diminish s_H, the interdiction rate for under hiding, thus reducing D's incentive to reach a deal. Indeed, there is always some c high enough (but less than one) such that the peaceful enforcement corner solution prevails, and there is no bribery in equilibrium.

The fighting case is more complicated; making a few reasonable but technical assumptions about the relative size of parameters allows us to explicitly solve the model, take comparative statics, explore D's equilibrium choice of hiding versus fighting, and applying these insights to a discussion of the substantive conditions under which different corner and interior solutions might hold in equilibrium.

For interior solutions, the comparative statics results of the basic model are almost identical. The equilibrium bribe price b_F^* is increasing in λ and s, and the probability of bribery occurring ($1 - \text{Pr}_F$) is decreasing in λ, as in the hiding case. However, crackdowns do not always make bribery more likely:

Proposition 2. *Increases in s raise the probability of fighting whenever $\varphi > \lambda$, and decrease it if $\varphi < \lambda$.*

Thus, the key result summarized in H_2 holds here as well: if violence is at least partially coercive (so that $\varphi > 0$ and police expect to suffer a relatively small sanction for bribe-taking (so that $\lambda < \varphi$), then *crackdowns increase traffickers' incentives to fight enforcers.* The finding has particular importance if conditionality is "among cartels," such that once a cartel is targeted as violent (i.e., subject to s as opposed to $s(1-c)$), it cannot gain a reprieve from repression by turning away from violence.

4.1.3.3 To Hide or Fight?
We can now explore the choice between fighting and hiding strategies; formally, D compares U_F^D, his ex-ante expected payoff when $a = a_F^*$ to U_H^D, with $a = a_H^* = 0$. This calculation is sensitive to parameter conditions; mapping the parameter space reveals how changes in state policy (s and c) affect D's choice.

Proposition 2 tells us that once in a fight-and-bribe equilibrium, crackdowns exacerbate fighting; the numerical example developed here shows that crackdowns can also flip D's equilibrium strategy from hiding to fighting. Figure 4.2's vertical and horizontal axes show D's expected utility and choice of a, respectively. U_H^D is maximized at $a = 0$, shown by the dashed horizontal line for comparison. U_F^D is maximized at a_F^* (for interior solutions); D plays a fighting strategy whenever that maximum lies above the dashed horizontal line. Scenario (a) represents a low-enforcement status quo. If D plays $a = a_H^* = 0$, P demands bribe $b_H^* = 4.7$ (which D pays 20 percent of the time). Playing $a = a_F^*$ would reduce P's demand to $b_F^* = 1.9$, but arming and fighting costs outweigh this benefit, so D plays hide-and-bribe ($U_F^D < U_H^D$). In scenario (b), a crackdown has raised s to 1. Now D is better off playing $a = a_F^*$ (since $U_F^D > U_H^D$), and fighting 30 percent of the time.[23] To gain intuition, note that in (a), D expects small total bribe payments ($\text{Pr}_B \times b_H^* = 0.2 \times 4.7 = 0.94$) so can gain little by arming; in (b), expected payments are larger ($0.45 \times 7 = 3.15$), making arming attractive.

Much of the parameter space is susceptible to such violent blowback. Figure 4.3 extends the example above, allowing s and c to vary along the axes,

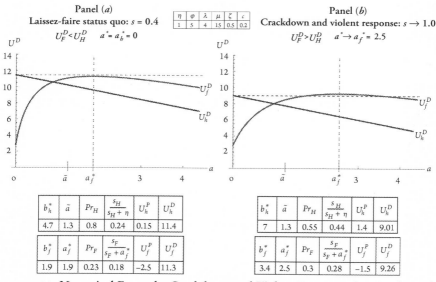

η	φ	λ	μ	ζ	c
1	5	4	15	0.5	0.2

Panel (a) — Laissez-faire status quo: $s = 0.4$; $U_F^D < U_H^D$; $a^* = a_h^* = 0$

b_h^*	$\tilde{a}$	Pr_H	$\dfrac{s_H}{s_H + \eta}$	U_h^P	U_h^D
4.7	1.3	0.8	0.24	0.15	11.4

b_f^*	a_f^*	Pr_F	$\dfrac{s_F}{s_F + a_f^*}$	U_f^P	U_f^D
1.9	1.9	0.23	0.18	−2.5	11.3

Panel (b) — Crackdown and violent response: $s \to 1.0$; $U_F^D > U_H^D$; $a^* \to a_f^* = 2.5$

b_h^*	$\tilde{a}$	Pr_H	$\dfrac{s_H}{s_H + \eta}$	U_h^P	U_h^D
7	1.3	0.55	0.44	1.4	9.01

b_f^*	a_f^*	Pr_F	$\dfrac{s_F}{s_F + a_f^*}$	U_f^P	U_f^D
3.4	2.5	0.3	0.28	−1.5	9.26

FIGURE 4.2. **Numerical Example: Crackdown and Violent Response.** Starting from the peaceful, laissez-faire status quo shown in Panel (a), a crackdown (raising s from 0.4 to 1) shifts D's equilibrium strategy from hiding to fighting, as shown in Panel (b).

---

23 Note the Pareto inefficiency of fight-and-bribe vs. hide-and-bribe: $U_F^D + U_F^P < U_H^D + U_H^P$, in spite of the fact that bribes are more common under fighting: $\text{Pr}_F < \text{Pr}_H$.

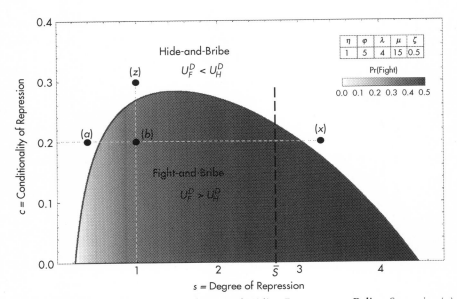

FIGURE 4.3. **Numerical Example: Fighting and Hiding Responses to Policy**. Scenarios (*a*) and (*b*) from Figure 4.2 are shown here as points in the s, c plane. Crackdowns (increases in s) can cause both an abrupt switch to fighting strategies, and a smooth increase in the equilibrium probability of fighting, which is indicated by shading.

and plotting the region for which $U_F^D > U_H^D$. Within this region, the equilibrium probability of fighting ($\Pr_F$) is indicated by shading, and is increasing in the degree of repression (s) as per Proposition 2. Scenarios (*a*) and (*b*) from Figure 4.2 appear as points in this plane. The hump shape reflects both the benefits and two different costs of violence. The value of the additional leverage gained by fighting is proportional to s, but so is the cost of arms needed to achieve that leverage. Thus, even under perfectly unconditional repression ($c = 0$), we get hiding at very low s (where intimidation is cheap but not worth much) and very high s (where intimidation is valuable, but prohibitively costly). As conditionality further increases the relative costs of violence (by offering D a relative reprieve for hiding), the range of s for which fighting is advantageous shrinks.

One interpretation of Figure 4.3 is that cartels fight when the state doesn't crack down hard enough. From point (*b*), the state could expand repression out to point (*x*), inducing D to eschew violence. This is true in general, even when repression is perfectly unconditional ($c = 0$):

Proposition 3. *For any set of parameter values, there is some degree of repression s^* above which D hides; that is, $s > s^* \Rightarrow U_H^D > U_F^D$.*

Substantively, though, high levels of s may be infeasible or undesirable: states face resource and capacity constraints, opportunity and political costs, and at least some democratic limits on repressive tactics. If an upper bound like $\bar{s}$ exists, then moving from (b) to (x) is infeasible, and hiding can only be induced by raising c. In fact, the state could pacify the cartel without raising s at all by increasing conditionality, say to point (z); at this level of conditionality, D hides for *any* s. This too generalizes: increases in conditionality raise D's expected payoff from hiding relative to fighting, thus reducing s^*. Beyond some point, but short of decriminalization (since we have assumed that $c < 1$), s^* reaches zero, and D never fights. Moreover, since increases in c amount to reductions in the amount of force directed at non-violent cartels, there is also a level of c above which the peaceful enforcement corner solution holds, and we get no bribes in equilibrium.

Proposition 4. *For any set of parameter values, if repression is sufficiently conditional, then D plays $a^* = 0$, and no bribes are paid in equilibrium.*

The analysis illuminates the tradeoffs facing the state. Conditionality is an effective violence-reduction policy lever, and can be critical to breaking out of a fighting equilibrium when constitutional and capacity constraints restrict policymaker's choice of s. Moreover, reducing enforcers' discretion to prosecute non-violent traffickers can drastically reduce bribery, even in lieu of traditional anti-corruption efforts (i.e., trying to raise λ).

However, D's utility is strictly decreasing in s and, when hiding, increasing in c. For P, the opposite holds: except at critical points where D flips from fighting to hiding, P would always prefer a higher s and a lower c. This points to the *political* costs to leaders of increasing conditionality: it can generate hostility or insubordination among enforcers,[24] while leaving cartels better off, exposing leaders to the venomous epithet of "accommodating the drug trade."

A prominent alternative (or complementary) explanation for drug violence is changes in profitability, though predictions run both ways: violence in Mexico has been attributed to both increased profits after Caribbean routes were interdicted in the 1990s, and shrinking profits due to tighter border patrols after 2001, paralleling debates over the effects of economic growth on civil war onset (Blattman and Miguel 2010, 10–12). The full model offers some leverage, distinguishing short-term fluctuations (y) from long-term expectations (μ). For fight-and-bribe equilibria, larger realized y means less fighting, echoing Mejía et al.'s (2013) finding that short-term supply restrictions drive drug violence.[25]

---

[24] If enforcers do not realize or believe that cartels will switch to hiding strategies under conditionality, they will always oppose it; convincing enforcers that conditional repression reduces cartel–state conflict could thus alter their political stance. In Rio, police leaders were initially skeptical and divided over the conditional aspects of Pacification, but now explicitly embrace them.

[25] They, however, assume that negative supply shocks *increase* profits, due to supposedly inelastic demand.

Changes in μ are more ambiguous. For fight-and-bribe equilibria, increases in μ first lowers, but eventually raises, the probability of fighting. Similarly, both U_H^D and U_F^D are increasing in μ, and at lower values of μ, it is not clear which increases more. However, a sufficiently large μ always produces fighting:

Proposition 5. *For any parameter values,* $\exists\ \mu^* \in \mathbb{R}^+$ *such that* $\mu > \mu^* \Rightarrow U_F^D > U_H^D$.

This result bodes poorly for settings like Central America where total state resources (with which to buy s) are dwarfed by drug profits. It also suggests that increased profitability alone can induce cartel–state conflict. That said, large increases in μ are needed to push cartels from hiding to fighting; small increases can make hiding *more* preferable. Moreover, since μ represents shared expectations about drug-market size, it probably moves slowly. Thus, changes in μ alone probably cannot explain rapid shifts in cartel–state conflict, though they can clearly complement other explanations. Substantively, the large expansion of Mexico's drug market in the 1990s may have contributed to the slow escalation of conflict there, but it is less plausible that an abrupt increase in profits explains the rapid growth in violence from 2006 onward.

4.1.3.4 Ideal-Type Scenarios (Semi-Corner Solutions) and the Limits of Anti-Corruption Efforts

Thus far, the analysis has focused primarily on regions of the parameter space where the relevant choice for D was between hide-and-bribe and fight-and-bribe equilibrium outcomes; in these, both bribery and enforcement occur with some probability. As in the baseline models presented earlier, though, ideal-type scenarios can occur in which bribe demands are either always paid (so that enforcement never occurs) or bribes are never paid (so that enforcement always occurs). I now explore the conditions under which these ideal-type scenarios occur in equilibrium, and how they map onto real-world cases.

In technical terms, both hide-and-bribe and fight-and-bribe scenarios constitute interior solutions, since (as we saw) small changes in key variables like s, c, and λ affect both of our outcomes of interest: the size of the bribe demand, and the probability of D paying it. Conversely, in ideal-type scenarios, changes in s, c, and λ have no effect on the probability of the bribe being paid (which is either 1 or 0), but do affect the equilibrium bribe price; for this reason, I call them "semi-corner solutions."[26]

First, let us characterize the general conditions under which different scenarios occur. For clarity, Table 4.2 presents these conditions in the general notation used in the baseline models above; the conditions for the richer specification can be recovered by substituting in for h, f, π, and y. For

[26] A true corner solution is one in which marginal changes in variables does not affect any outcomes of interest.

TABLE 4.2. *Conditions for Corner and Interior Solutions under Hiding and Fighting.*

Hiding			Fighting		
Condition	Scenario	Pr_H	Condition	Scenario	Pr_F
$\lambda > h\bar{y}$	Peaceful Enforcement	1	$\lambda - \pi > f\bar{y}$	Violent Enforcement	1
otherwise	Hide-and-Bribe	$\in (0,1)$	*otherwise*	Fight-and-Bribe	$\in (0,1)$
$\lambda < h(2\underline{y} - \bar{y})$	State-Sponsored Protection	0	$\lambda - \pi < f(2\underline{y} - \bar{y})$	Coerced Peace	0

The bottom and top rows correspond to "never-bribe" and "always-bribe" semi-corner solutions; the middle rows correspond to interior solutions. Conditions are given here in general form; to recover the richer specification used above, let $h = \frac{s(1-c)}{s(1-c)+\eta}, f = \frac{s}{s+a}, \pi = \varphi\frac{a}{a+s}$, and redefine the range of y as $[\mu(1-\zeta), \mu(1+\zeta)]$.

both hiding and fighting strategies, there are "never-bribe" and "always-bribe" ideal-type outcomes (where the probability of hiding (Pr_H) or fighting (Pr_F) is 1 or 0, respectively), and interior-solutions where these probabilities are between 0 and 1.

These conditions have natural interpretations. The left-hand sides represent P's reservation value for bribe-taking, i.e., the smallest bribe she would ever accept. Under hiding, this is equal to the expected sanction for bribe-taking, λ. Under fighting, the *"plomo"* effect (here given by π) strictly reduces this reservation value, coercing P into accepting a smaller minimum bribe.[27] For the never-bribe conditions, the right-hand sides represent the largest loss P can impose, i.e., D's reservation value. Unless this exceeds P's reservation value, there is no bargaining range, and we get pure enforcement. If P is hiding, this implies peaceful enforcement, which corresponds to our canonical notion of how policing is supposed to work: police never accept bribes, always enforce, and criminals do not threaten police or fight back when enforcement occurs. If P is fighting, however, a never-bribe outcome implies violent enforcement: police always enforce, but cartels fight back, presumably for purely defensive, loss-reducing reasons, since bribes are never paid and the equilibrium bribe demand has no effect on payoffs.

Always-bribe scenarios occur when P prefers a sure-thing, low-ball bribe to a larger bribe that D rejects with some probability. Under hiding, where P faces no retaliation for enforcement, this can only occur if $2\underline{y} - \bar{y} > 0$, which in turn requires that the minimum value of y is large relative to the range of y: ($\underline{y} > \bar{y} - \underline{y}$). A substantive interpretation of this condition is that P's uncertainty about the range of potential drug profits ($\bar{y} - \underline{y}$) is small relative to

---

[27] This illustrates Acemoglu and Wolitzky's (2011, 560) definition of coercion as lowering someone's outside option so that she accepts an offer she would otherwise reject.

the size of the market. In addition, P must have sufficient interdiction capacity (here represented by h, which is a function of the degree of repression, s) so that the low-ball bribe exceeds her reservation value, λ. This suggests that state-sponsored protection is more likely when drug profits are stable and widely known, and enforcers face little sanction for bribe-taking. As I discuss below, Mexico under the PRI fits this description. Under fighting, an all-bribe outcome is always possible if the "*plomo*" effect is strong enough, producing a coerced peace scenario: D threatens P with violence if P enforces, but these threats are never acted on, because P is effectively bullied into demanding a small, low-ball bribe. This bribe may well be less than λ, leaving P in the red, precisely because the coercive force of π has lowered her outside option.

Which of these six scenarios obtains in equilibrium depends not only on the conditions listed above, but also on whether D plays a hiding or fighting strategy. Figure 4.4 plots equilibrium outcomes for the full model, holding parameter values constant (as shown), and allowing the degree of repression (s) and the expected sanction for bribe-taking (λ) to vary on the x and y axes, respectively. The main plot, Panel A, has the virtue of containing regions where each of the six possible outcome scenarios obtain in equilibrium; Panels B, C, and D show the effects of changes in conditionality (c) and P's degree of uncertainty over the size of drug profits (ζ).

Outcome scenarios clearly depend to a large extent on the value of λ. Successful anti-corruption efforts, or more realistically, deploying a supposedly less-corrupt force (such as the army, in the Mexican case), could both raise λ. Figure 4.4 thus offers insight into how changes in the level of corruption in the relevant force deployed to confront cartels affect predicted outcomes, including shifts from one scenario to another.

One surprising result is that reducing force corruption can, perversely, trigger the onset of anti-state violence, and even *increase* the likelihood of bribery. Panel A offers an example. At point (a), λ is low (likely signifying rampant force corruption), but not so low that an always-bribe, state-sponsored protection scenario obtains. Rather, P makes a bribe demand high enough that D sometimes rejects it, yet not so high that it is worth it to D to fight, and we get a hide-and-bribe outcome. If λ increases, say through deployment of a less corrupt force, and we move to point (b), coerced peace obtains: D now threatens P with violence if P enforces, and in response P demands a bribe low enough that D is sure to accept. Deploying a less corrupt force has, paradoxically, led to an *increased* probability of bribery occurring *and* a shift by D from hiding to fighting strategies. If λ increases further, to point (c), we enter fight-and-bribe territory, in which violence occurs with positive probability.

Obviously, this is not the only possible outcome of reducing corruption; it can, in some circumstances, lead D to switch from fighting to hiding strategies. Moreover, it is only at the critical points where D switches between hiding and fighting strategies that increases in λ can *raise* the likelihood of bribery; everywhere else, they weakly reduce the likelihood. The point remains,

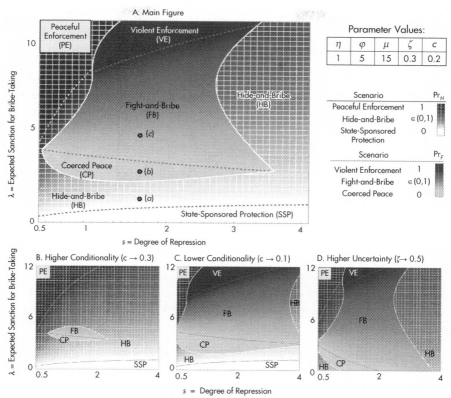

FIGURE 4.4. **Numerical Example: Map of the Parameter Space by Outcome Scenario.** Panel A presents a plot of equilibrium outcome scenarios for different values of s and λ, with other parameters held constant as shown. Shading indicates the equilibrium probability of hiding or fighting; lighter regions indicate a higher probability of bribery occurring. Panels B and C show how the results change when the conditionality of repression increases or decreases respectively. Panel D illustrates that when uncertainty is relatively high (formally, if $\zeta > \frac{1}{3}$), state-sponsored protection cannot be achieved even if $\lambda = 0$.

however, that reducing the general level of force corruption, even if it were easy, can have unpredictable effects on anti-state violence, and in some circumstances even make bribery more common.

A far more reliable means of curtailing anti-state violence is by increasing the conditionality of repression. Panel B of Figure 4.4 illustrates this: all parameter values are held constant relative to Panel A except conditionality (c), which increases from 0.2 to 0.3. This change nearly eliminates the range of values for which D adopts a fighting strategy. Conversely, in Panel C, conditionality falls (relative to Panel A); fighting becomes optimal for D over a much larger range of values. These examples also illustrate how the possibility of cartel violence exacerbates the difficulty of achieving peaceful enforcement—the conventional notion of how law enforcement is supposed to work. Even where cartel violence is mostly deterred by high conditionality (Panel B), Peaceful Enforcement requires that λ be high relative to s; in other words, eliminating bribery requires the state to threaten enforcers with more pain than enforcers can impose on traffickers. As conditionality falls (Panel C), cartels have less incentives to eschew fighting strategies, and the conditions for Peaceful Enforcement become even more restrictive. Thus, in addition to the logistical and institutional challenge of detecting and punishing bribe-taking by police, leaders face the political challenge of holding a large share of repressive capacity in reserve (high c) against traffickers who are often seen as a demonic threat to society.

Finally, Panel D illuminates the importance of reducing uncertainty over cartel profits to sustaining non-violent but high-corruption outcomes like state-sponsored protection. Looking only at Panels A, B, and C, one might get the impression that allowing police to take bribes (i.e., keeping λ very low) guarantees a non-violent outcome. However, in these examples, P has a relatively good idea of the size of D's realized profits, represented by a low ζ; indeed, $\zeta < \frac{1}{3}$ is a necessary condition for state-sponsored protection. In Panel D, P's uncertainty is greater ($\zeta = 0.5$); as a result, not only is state-sponsored protection ruled out, but D may opt for a fighting strategy even if there is no sanction against bribe-taking at all ($\lambda = 0$).

How do these results map onto empirical reality? As noted, peaceful enforcement is rarely achieved in drug wars. State-sponsored protection, however, was approximated by the PRI's regime in Mexico until the 1990s. The state established regular, direct linkages with traffickers, who were allowed to operate in exchange for regularized bribes; while failure to pay was apparently punished enough to ensure regular compliance, it is also clear that repression was highly conditional: incidents of anti-state violence or other unacceptable forms of cartel behavior were severely and swiftly punished. Snyder and Durán-Martínez (2009b) offer compelling reasons why this racket collapsed, but do not fully explain why it collapsed into violent corruption and not into a non-violent, hide-and-bribe or peaceful enforcement scenario. Increases in λ and s, on their own, make enforcement more likely, but they do not necessarily make fighting more advantageous than hiding. Similarly, increased uncertainty over drug profits—a likely by-product of expanding cocaine trafficking in the 1980s and 1990s—might produce occasional bargaining breakdown, as enforcers try to avoid being low-balled, but does not necessarily give traffickers incentives to fight back. Decreases in conditionality (c), on the other hand, strictly raise the relative payoff to fighting. In the case study to follow, I show how Mexico's democratization in the 1990s brought a reduced capacity for conditionality, while Calderón deliberately reduced conditionality further, mostly for political reasons. This, I argue, is the most plausible explanation of cartels' switch to fighting strategies toward the state.

Coerced peace, in which cartel threats of anti-enforcer violence are so credible and effective that they are never acted on in equilibrium, evokes Colombia in the late 1970s and early 1980s when police, prosecutors, and judges were simply too afraid of Pablo Escobar to risk enforcing the law. A threatening note to a judge in a 1985 extradition case, for example, conveys Escobar's coercive power (and strongly suggests he held enforcers to negative reservation values):

> We will DEMAND a favorable decision … We will not accept that you go sick. We will not accept that you go on holiday; and we will not accept that you resign.
>
> (Quoted in Bowden 2001, 70)

In contemporary Mexico, coerced peace seems to occur in smaller municipalities, where overmatched local police forces are not so much bribed as ordered not to interfere with cartel business, on pain of death (Aguayo et al. 2016).[28]

Under coerced peace, marginal increases in the degree of repression, s, have no effect on the probability of fighting, which remains at zero (though they do raise the equilibrium bribe price, making D worse off and P better off); large increases, however, can trigger equilibrium violence. This can be seen in Figure 4.4, where rightward movement from a coerced-peace region eventually leads to a fight-and-bribe scenario with positive probability of fighting. In the late 1980s' Colombia, expansions in police capacity and protective measures for prosecutors and judges, including anonymous (*sin rostro*) status, encouraged intrepid enforcers to go after Escobar;[29] ironically, this may have contributed to the wave of cartel assassinations of officials during the period (CIJL 1990).

Finally, under violent enforcement, both sides prefer a fight to any available bargain; this can only occur in relatively low-corruption settings ($\lambda > \varphi$). At the same time, D must prefer a sure fight to the relevant outcome under a hiding strategy; since "*plomo*" has no traction here (because its effect on the bribe price is moot), fighting must provide a significant defensive benefit over hiding, $f(a_F^*, s) < h(\eta, s(1 - c))$. This is more likely when territoriality is high (low η) and repression is unconditional (low c). Substantively, a cartel facing relatively uncorrupt special forces may fight purely to minimize interdiction losses, especially if territoriality is high and police are licensed to use deadly force irrespective of cartel action. In Rio, the elite BOPE police force initially had all these attributes: a reputation for incorruptibility (high

---

28 Interview, Executive Secretary, National Public Security System (SNSP), Mexico City, September 13.
29 Interview, former *fiscal sin rostro*, Medellín, December 24, 2010; interview, former attorney general, Bogotá, December 13, 2010.

λ),[30] a warrior ethos of physical engagement (low φ), and license to use deadly force irrespective of cartel behavior (low c). Prior to Pacification, traffickers frequently clashed with BOPE forces, despite being overmatched; Pacification's pre-announced occupations effectively increased c, raising the relative payoff to hiding, and traffickers largely eschewed confrontation with the BOPE during these operations.

Overall, these ideal-type outcomes constitute the conceptual bookends of violent corruption. Violent enforcement is violent but not corrupt, and violence plays an exclusively defensive, brute-force function. At the other pole, coerced peace is corrupt but not violent, at least not on the equilibrium path, and violence plays an overwhelmingly coercive role. Everything in between can be fairly characterized as violent corruption.

4.2 A TOY MODEL OF VIOLENT LOBBYING

4.2.1 Overview

Violent lobbying is essentially a war of attrition between cartels and states over de jure policy. In this very simple model, a leader and a cartel have distinct ideal-point policies. If the leader chooses hers, the cartel can either accept this or "fight"—inflicting pain on the leader and generating costs for the cartel—in an attempt to coerce the leader into policy concessions. The two key questions are: (1) can the cartel inflict sufficient pain that the leader prefers to concede? and (2) is the cartel *willing* to do so; i.e., do the expected benefits of concessions outweigh the costs of fighting? With complete information, there are three possibilities: either the cartel is (a) unable or (b) unwilling to fight, in which case the leader simply chooses her preferred policy, or the cartel is willing and able to fight, in which case the leader immediately concedes. In all three cases, no violence occurs in equilibrium. Adding asymmetric information—plausible given the private and volatile nature of conditions (1) and (2)—generates actual fighting in equilibrium. Short-lived, failed violent lobbying campaigns (like that of the Familia Michoacana in Mexico) can be explained by cartel overoptimism about (1); drawn-out but successful campaigns (like Pablo Escobar's) require sustained uncertainty on the part of the leaders about (2).

4.2.2 Model

Violent lobbying is more straightforward than violent corruption, in part because we are already familiar with the logic of coercion in interest group politics (Dal Bó and Di Tella 2003). To violently lobby is, in a sense, to engage in an extremely hard version of hardball politics. Escobar's campaign

---

30 Over time, the BOPE has increasingly suffered from cases of corruption, including the sale of intelligence and weapons to traffickers (*O Globo* 2015).

against extradition leveraged public sentiment and a capacity to severely punish policymakers in order to significantly constrain de jure policy in a way that benefited his externality-producing corporate interests. In doing so, one might ask, how did Escobar differ from other hardball interest groups like, say, the National Rifle Association (NRA)?

Esobar's campaign differs in two key respects: first, the punishment he inflicted was not only electoral but violent, and involved killing innocent civilians. Second, the government responded by trying to destroy him. The key questions that Escobar had to ask himself before launching his campaign were (1) how much pain would the government stand before it caved? and (2) how much damage would the government inflict on him in the meantime? For the licit interest groups waging non-violent pressure campaigns, question (1) is highly relevant (and for the NRA, the answer seems to be "not much"), while question (2) is far less so. In this sense, violent lobbying resembles a war of attrition.

Along these lines, I introduce a very simple formal framework for thinking about violent lobbying. I draw out some basic insights, in particular the role uncertainty may play in generating actual, on-the-equilibrium-path violence. I then discuss these insights in light of the empirical cases.

4.2.2.1 Setup
In this simple framework, a cartel D (he) faces a government leader, G (she). At the outset, G chooses a policy ρ from among three options in increasing order of harshness. Denote these $l, c,$ and m, for laissez-faire, crackdown, and maximum repression, respectively. Assume G has a (weakly) ideal point at c:

$$U_l^G < U_c^G \geq U_m^G$$

while D prefers the least amount of repression:

$$U_l^D > U_c^D > U_m^D$$

Once G announces her policy choice $\rho \in \{l, c, m\}$, D chooses whether to fight (F) or hide (H); in this setting, fighting amounts to a violent lobbying campaign, while hiding amounts to letting G's policy choice go uncontested.[31] If hiding, the game ends and the players get $U_\rho^{i \in \{G,D\}}$ for two periods. By assumption, if D fights in any period, the level of repression goes to m; in addition, D inflicts

---

[31] This approach highlights the conditions under which violent lobbying can succeed and is worth it to cartels, at the cost of downplaying the possibility of non-violent lobbying. This seems justified, since cartels cannot openly lobby the way licit interest groups can, and so generally turn to what I call in Chapter 3 "illicit lobbying." As a leading example shows, illicit lobbying can backfire badly. The Cali cartel's "Champagne Project" involved bribing the president in exchange for a promise of non-extradition, but when the bribes were discovered, the president was forced to crack down on Cali, whose leaders were arrested and ultimately extradited. Because such high-level bribery produces scandal when discovered, it involves an element of risk not present in licit lobbying.

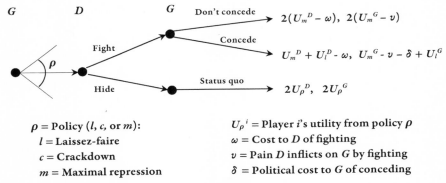

FIGURE 4.5. Violent Lobbying Game Tree.

v in damage on G, at an out-of-pocket cost (apart from any policy effects) of ω. If fighting occurs in the first period, G can then either grant concessions by switching to l, or not, in which case D fights again and repression remains at m for period 2. If concessions are granted, G pays a political cost of δ, over and above her ex-ante policy preferences. I discuss δ at length below; for now, think of it as a placeholder for all potential political effects, both good and bad, of negotiating (successfully) with cartels. If G does not grant concessions, the players get $U_m^{i\in\{G,D\}}$ plus their respective costs of violence for two periods. I assume no discounting.

4.2.2.2 Solving the Game

In this simple model, the key question is whether or not the policy that G chooses in round 1 is *susceptible*: that is, whether D can force G to revoke it through coercion. Working backward, if D has chosen to fight, then at round 3, G will back down and grant concessions if $2U_m^G - 2v < U_m^G + U_l^G - v - \delta$. This yields a *susceptibility* condition:

$$U_m^G - U_l^G - \delta < v \qquad\qquad (R^G)$$

If R^G does not hold, D cannot inflict enough pain on G to induce policy concessions, and therefore has no incentive to fight. In that case, G can do no better than to choose her ideal point, c. This corresponds to the uninteresting case in which c is not susceptible, i.e., the state cannot be cowed, and D knows it.

If R^G holds, then any policy G plays in round 1 is susceptible: D knows that by enduring one period of fighting he can induce G to back down in the second period. D will fight if this leaves him better off than accepting whatever policy ρ is chosen by G at the outset:

$$U_l^D + U_m^D - \omega > 2U_\rho^D$$

TABLE 4.3. *Regions of Parameter Space for Violent Lobbying Game.*

$$R^G$$

	T	F
T R_c^D	G is effectively coerced: $\{l, H\}$	G cannot be coerced: $\{c, H\}$
F	G *could* be coerced but not worth it to D: $\{c, H\}$	

Condition R^G indicates whether the government's choice of policy is susceptible to violent lobbying. Condition R_c^D indicates whether the cartel has sufficient resolve to engage in an effective violent lobbying campaign.

Rearranging this yields a *sufficient resolve* condition for D:

$$U_l^D - U_\rho^D > U_\rho^D - U_m^D + \omega \qquad (R_\rho^D)$$

Condition R_ρ^D has a clear substantive interpretation: the left-hand side represents, for any initial choice of ρ, D's potential policy gains from violent lobbying, while the right-hand side captures the (always positive) costs of violence. Thus R_ρ^D never holds for $\rho = l$ (why fight if the status quo is your ideal point?). Costs can be decomposed into out-of-pocket costs ω, and policy costs, $U_\rho^D - U_m^D$. The latter represents, for any choice of ρ, the additional sanction available to the state should D opt for violence—capturing the idea of *conditionality of repression*. Thus, if the state "maxes out" at the beginning of the game, choosing $\rho = m$, conditionality of repression is effectively zero, and D will always fight (as long as ω is small relative to the potential policy gains).

Whether R_ρ^D holds when $\rho = c$ depends on parameter values, and corresponds to a substantive question about the relative incentives and disincentives to violence that D faces. If R_c^D fails, G simply plays her ideal point c, knowing that D will not fight. If R_c^D does hold, G will play l as long as $2U_l^G > U_m^G + U_l^G - \upsilon - \delta$ which we know is true from R^G. The parameter space can thus be divided into three regions, corresponding to three substantive outcomes, as shown in Table 4.3.

Note that with complete information and no shocks to relative strength and other parameter values between periods, there is no fighting along the equilibrium path. Can G be coerced? Is doing so worth it to D? Intuitively, if the answers to both questions are known to both parties, then either no threat is made because the cartel is too weak (and both sides know it), or the threat is made but never acted on because the government would back down (and both sides know it). Thus far, we have a story of bargaining success, not failure.

One likely culprit in explaining actual episodes of violent lobbying is asymmetric information. Intuitively, R^G depends directly on the government's policy preferences, while R_c^D depends on the cartel's; these are excellent candidates for private information, and both actors have incentives to exaggerate their resolve. Below I explore one simple way to model such a situation.

4.2.2.3 Incomplete Information with Equilibrium Fighting

Fighting along the equilibrium path could be generated in any number of ways. In keeping with the illustrative nature of this very simple model, I focus on a basic private-information mechanism. Assume again that R^G holds, so that c is *susceptible*. Now say that there are two possible types of cartel, strong and weak, for whom R_c^D does and does not hold, respectively. G correctly believes she will face a weak type with probability $\mu \in [0,1]$. D knows his type but has no way to credibly communicate it to G before she chooses ρ. If G plays c, she will provoke a fight (that she will lose) with probability $1 - \mu$, but will otherwise enjoy her ideal-point policy. This is worth the risk if:

$$\mu(2U_c^G) + (1 - \mu)\left(U_m^G + U_l^G - \upsilon - \delta\right) > 2U_l^G$$

This is false if $\mu = 0$ (by R^G) and true if $\mu = 1$, so by continuity there is some cutoff μ^* above which G plays c and a fight ensues with probability $1 - \mu$.

In this world, D only fights when he can win. Further private information would be needed to produce an equilibrium in which D sometimes fights and loses. But the model already illustrates a key point about the relationship of conditionality to susceptibility. From D's perspective, c is a conditional policy, since fighting provokes increased repression (i.e., a move to $\rho = m$). Yet c is susceptible, and D knows it. This means that, at another level of analysis, c is conditional *in the wrong direction*: if D hides, he has to live with c, but if he fights, he will eventually face less repression (l). This captures, in a stripped-down fashion, a logic often attributed to Escobar, namely that the government would only grant concessions once it became convinced that it could not defeat the cartels outright (López Restrepo 2006, 203).

Susceptibility operates at a different level than conditionality. In the model above, c is conditional, m is not; either may be susceptible. Indeed, in this highly simplified setting, c's degree of conditionality (which we might think of as its "distance" from m) has no effect on whether c is susceptible, which is determined by G's tolerance for pain. However, c's degree of conditionality *does* affect whether or not it is worth it to D to fight. Recalling the formula for R_ρ^D, the further c is from m, the higher D's costs to fighting, and the less he stands to gain from coercing a concession. Intuitively, the more conditional a policy the government starts with, the more coercive leverage it has to dissuade a violent lobbying campaign, *regardless of whether that campaign would succeed or fail*.

4.2.3 Discussion

The necessary conditions for violence off the equilibrium path—that is, for the threat of violence, though not ultimately acted on, to influence the actions that leaders take—are captured by R_G and R_D. Before we ask why violence would actually occur in equilibrium, unpacking these highly reduced-form equations helps to focus on the relevant real-world operative conditions for violent lobbying. The government's resolve condition R_G has three components: policy preference ($U_m^G - U_l^G$), disutility of cartel violence (v), and the cost of concessions (δ). The first is relatively straightforward: it represents leaders' ex-ante feelings about engaging in maximal crackdown vis-à-vis laissez-faire. These preferences certainly incorporate a host of political considerations, including assessments about the future consequences of pursuing either policy. However, they are separate from concerns about appearing to have caved in to cartels' demands, which are captured by δ. This captures the idea that, assuming $\delta > 0$, that always having been laissez-faire (U_l^G) is preferable to switching to laissez-faire ($U_l^G - \delta$). Cartel violence is also straightforward: it includes not only the risk of physical damage that leaders face but (more importantly, at least empirically) the political costs of public outrage and panic in the face of cartel attacks, which tend to take the form of terroristic violence.

The parameter δ is, on the other hand, nothing more than a placeholder for a host of potential factors and dynamics that might be at play. Many of these lie outside the model, in the sense that they involve actors or realms not explicitly captured in the game. First among these are audience costs (Fearon 1994), the public's disapproval and political punishment of politicians who back down in the face of a crisis. On the other hand, since actual fighting is occurring, the public may become weary and demand an end to the violence. Related to this is the political saliency of the specific policy issue at hand: if leaders can make a policy concession that remains largely invisible (such as a subtle change to prison policy) then the audience-cost component of δ might be quite low. But a realistic model might also need to partially endogenize δ, since the manner in which leaders announce and enforce their policy choice can affect their "wiggle room" later on. President Calderón, for example, strongly identified his entire presidency with his crackdown on the drug trade, (intentionally) elevating δ so high as to make any overt policy reversal virtually unthinkable.

A more subtle but potentially crucial dynamic also covered by δ has to do with the creation of a pro-crackdown constituency within the state. When leaders initiate large-scale crackdowns, they empower "drug warriors"—bureaucrats; police, military, and intelligence officials—who may then use their acquired position of prominence to push back against any potential concessions or negotiation. A prime example of this was the vocal opposition of General Maza, then director of Colombia's DAS, to the Barco and Gaviria government's attempts to put in place a policy of voluntary submission. Going even further beyond this model, in some cases attempts to back down from hardline positions by leaders can be met with actual obstinacy and insubordination by enforcers, such that de facto policy remains largely unchanged. This seems to have occurred in Rio de Janeiro, for example, when the left-wing Worker's Party (PT) briefly held the governorship (2002–2003), appointed a restraint-minded security czar, but failed to rein in an increasingly militarized and homicidal police force.

As we have seen, an information asymmetry is sufficient to generate violence along the equilibrium path. The relatively few empirical examples of violent lobbying seen in my cases suggest a role for asymmetric information: one-off terror attacks, like the Familia Michoacana's 2009 synchronized attack on police stations and a more complex information structure—in particular one that realistically modeled mutual (though perhaps not symmetric) uncertainty over the true size of δ—would be one interesting avenue of further formal investigation. That said, incomplete information models are widely thought to be better at explaining the outbreak of violence than sustained violence, since fighting over time would presumably reveal the private information that caused the fighting in the first place (Fearon 1994; Powell 2006). In substantive terms, a mechanism like the one shown here seems more compelling as an explanation of the momentary outbreaks of violent lobbying, such as the sporadic terror campaigns launched by the CV in Rio or the handful of examples from the Mexican case than the decade-long war waged by Escobar against the Colombian state.

In the latter case, we might follow the literature in looking to complete information approaches, in which a commitment problem keeps the two sides from reaching agreement. In this strain of models, a group fights today to prevent a shift in power that will leave it unable to fight effectively tomorrow. The counterparty might like to buy off the violent group, but cannot credibly promise not to renege once the group has been weakened in the future. In concrete terms, the problem for the Colombian state was not merely agreeing not to extradite Escobar today, but finding a way to guarantee that it would not turn around and extradite him in the future, once he had disarmed. Strong evidence that such a dynamic was at play is the fact that negotiations over Escobar's voluntary submission dragged on for years, and then abruptly ended on the very day that a Constitutional Assembly approved an article definitively banning extradition. Escobar turned himself in that afternoon. A similar kind of story could be told of Escobar's flight from La Catedral—the prison he built for himself upon surrendering and from which he retained significant control over his operations—rather than allow himself to be transferred to more secure facilities.[32] Further research along these lines would require a more complicated model in which fighting not only imposes costs but also affects future bargaining power.

Finally, important aspects of the empirical cases suggest that a fuller model of violent lobbying might need to take into account third parties. I have already discussed some of the issues around the parameter δ, which depends in large part on the reaction of the public, but may also reflect intra-state friction between enforcers and leaders. Explicitly modeling these actors could help endogenize δ, if only partially. Another consideration along these lines is electoral competition. In the toy model, there is just one G, but the fact that violent lobbying in Brazil has often coincided with election periods suggest a model in which δ has a different value for the incumbent G and some electoral challenger: the incumbent may be too committed to his crackdown to survive concessions, but a challenger could reap the benefits of reducing public violence without paying the political price of backing down.

Is violent lobbying ever successful? A skeptic would argue that Escobar's war ultimately failed: he wound up dead, his cartel dismantled, and extradition was reinstated in the 1990s. Similarly, waves of attacks by Rio's most violent cartel, the Comando Vermelho, in 2010 not only failed to deter state leaders from implementing militarized invasions that led to its expulsion from numerous key *favela* territories. La Familia's attacks in Michoacán had little effect on de jure policy, and probably contributed to the organization's 2010 decapitation and subsequent fragmentation. Moreover, in all three cases, rivals were happy to stand back while the more confrontational cartels took the brunt of state repression. Violent lobbying is problematic for precisely these reasons, and is thus rarer and less central to overall cartel strategy than violent corruption.

That said, characterizing violent lobbying as an ex ante error, or as evidence that cartel violence is irrational, is almost certainly going too far. In Michoacán, the Knights Templar, one of La Familia's splinters, had consolidated its position within the state by 2012 and, if its overt messages to Mexico's new president were any indication, still found violent lobbying a useful strategy.[33] In one of the most spectacular examples of violent lobbying outside Colombia, the São

---

[32] There were certainly information asymmetries involved in what appears to have been a snap decision by Escobar to take state hostages and flee in the middle of the night—the operation was by all accounts a comedy of errors on the part of the government (Salamanca and Garzon 2003) and there was an abject failure to communicate to Escobar any credible information about where he would be transferred to. Nonetheless, even with adequate information, there may have been no mutually agreeable solution: if the transfer would have left Escobar powerless to hurt the government, nothing could stop the government from reneging on any promises it had made.

[33] Since then, the Knights Templar have suffered serious setbacks after paramilitary *autodefensa* groups rose up and—with unofficial state support—quickly routed the cartel from many of its strongholds.

Paulo prison gang Primeiro Comando da Capital, an ally of Rio's Comando Vermelho, launched three successive waves of attacks in 2006 (Adorno and Salla 2007; Bailey and Taylor 2009) that brought the city to a standstill until officials made concessions in carceral policy (Penteado et al. 2006).

As for Escobar, he did manage to negotiate surrender on extremely favorable terms (García Márquez 1997), building his own prison where, by his brother's account, he spent the happiest year of his life (Escobar Gaviria 2000). His rivals in the Cali cartel outlived him, but they were quickly apprehended once their state patrons could no longer protect them; Escobar survived on the lam for far longer. Above all, he avoided extradition; if we take at face value his motto "Better a tomb in Colombia than a jail in the United States," he proved a utility-maximizer after all.

PART II

CASE STUDIES

5

Colombia

Conditionality to Contain a Killer

The war between the Colombian state and Pablo Escobar's Medellín cartel is perhaps the most well-known example of cartel–state conflict on record; this chapter marshals the theory developed in Part I to explain its dynamics. I make the following claims: (1) Colombia's initial crackdown and escalation (1983–1986) were unconditional. This led cartels—united under Medellín's leadership—to adopt increasingly violent strategies toward the state. (2) From 1987 onward, repression increasingly focused on Medellín to the exclusion of Cali because the former engaged in anti-state violence; that is, conditionality across cartels increased. This contributed to Cali's decision to attack Medellín (1988), and permitted it to operate in concert if not cooperation with the state to destroy Escobar (1992–1993). (3) The Sometimiento policy (1990–1991) allowed the state to credibly promise reduced repression on Medellín if it eschewed violence going forward, raising conditionality within cartels. Medellín members responded by eschewing anti-state violence. (4) The rescinding of Sometimiento after Escobar's escape (1992–1993) decreased conditionality within cartels, leading Escobar to re-engage in anti-state violence. I also conjecture that after the fall of Medellín and Cali, an effectively conditional approach has deterred cartel–state conflict. I describe the policy reform process that produced Sometimiento and the failed attempts at reform that preceded it, and discuss the unique role of violent lobbying in Colombia.

5.1 OVERVIEW

In a country wracked by waves of mass violence and civil war, from the nineteenth century to the present day, the *narco-guerra* between Colombia's state and its drug cartels—dating roughly from Pablo Escobar's murder of Justice Minister Rodrigo Lara Bonilla in April 1984 to Escobar's death at the hands of state forces in December 1993—still stands out. Ask most Colombians who were alive at the time, and they will vividly recall the day of Escobar's death. Fernando Botero, Colombia's greatest living artist, mythologized that moment in two iconic paintings. And though non-specialists were often unfamiliar with the details of the period when I first visited Colombia in 2007, everyone became an expert after watching the immensely popular 2012 mini-series *El Patrón del Mal*, based on Salazar's (2001) definitive history.[1] In scholarly studies, photo essays, tell-all memoirs, documentaries, and dramatizations, the story has been told from countless angles by family and associates, bitter rivals, dogged journalists, scholars, filmmakers, and at least one Nobel laureate (García Márquez 1997).

This book offers yet another take on the episode: as *the* leading example of cartel–state conflict, and perhaps criminal war in general. In this comparative theoretical perspective, the Colombian case is critical. First, it speaks to the substantive importance of cartel–state conflict: even amidst active armed insurgencies (some of which continue to the present day), the war between Escobar and the state took precedence. Second, it establishes that cartel–state conflict can break out in the absence of inter-cartel turf war, and subsume turf war when it too breaks out. Third, the Colombian case offers unusually clear examples of both violent lobbying and violent corruption, as well as their non-violent counterparts.

This chapter explores these points in depth, and shows how the theory developed in Part I fits the case-study evidence. Unconditional crackdowns spurred increases in cartel violence against the state—through the logics of both violent lobbying and corruption—while periods of conditional repression saw sharp abatement. Because violent lobbying was uniquely prominent, the case provides some evidence on how its dynamics differ from those of violent corruption. It also provides an important example of successful policy reform: the advent of the *Sometimiento* policy, whose conditional nature, I argue, was the key to its unexpected efficacy. Finally, the collapse of this policy and subsequent resurgence of cartel–state conflict, as well as the eventual "taming" of Colombia's traffickers in the post-Escobar period through a broadly conditional approach, further support my core claims.

The Colombian case is not, however, a quintessential example or ideal type; it differs in fundamental ways from both the Rio de Janeiro and Mexico cases. First and foremost, the number of relevant actors was very small. Indeed, the history of cartel–state violence in Colombia revolves around Pablo Escobar himself and the groups he helped organize and lead: Muerte a Secuestradores (MAS), Los Extraditables, and the Medellín cartel. The rival Cali cartel is the critical foil; initially an ally of Medellín, Cali eventually launched a violent turf war against Escobar, but always avoided anti-state violence. Though other

---

[1] A similar process is underway at the international level with the airing of *Narcos* (2015), which unfortunately fictionalizes many key historical details. The show's Brazilian director, José Padilha, previously chronicled Rio's drug war in the documentary *Bus 174* (2002) and two *Elite Squad* feature films (2007, 2010).

traffickers in the Medellín cartel played important supporting roles, it was more often than not the decisions of Escobar alone—in response to changes in state policy—that determined the onset, abatement, and recrudescence of cartel–state conflict.

As such, conditionality of repression took on highly personalized forms in Colombia. Initially, the state cracked down on all cartels unconditionally. Soon, though, it focused repression on Medellín, rewarding and encouraging Cali's behavior—both its eschewal of anti-state violence and, eventually, its active campaign of violence against Medellín—by turning a blind eye to its trafficking activities. Conditionality had thus increased in a sense, but not for Escobar and his allies. This "conditionality *across* cartels" is preemptive but not reforming; it can deter non-violent groups from adopting violence, but creates no incentives for already-violent cartels to revert to peaceful strategies. Only when the state offered Escobar himself a reprieve from repression conditional on eschewing violence going forward—what I call "conditionality *within* cartels"—did Escobar call off his war.[2]

Colombia also stands out for the prominence and scale of violent lobbying. While violent corruption (captured in the phrase Escobar made famous, "*plata o plomo?*") led to the death of hundreds if not thousands of state enforcers, the highest-impact attacks were driven by violent lobbying over the status of extradition. Cartels waged both a terrorist war and a public relations campaign against extradition, painting it as unpatriotic and "pro-Yankee" (Sanín and Stoller 2001). These political appeals found some resonance with the public, which generally held a negative view of extradition. Moreover, the legal status of extradition was in flux throughout the period. In the terms introduced in Chapters 3 and 4, extradition was highly *susceptible* to violent lobbying. Perhaps most surprising of all, violent lobbying in Colombia *worked*: extradition was banned by Colombia's 1991 constitution, and Escobar was never extradited.

5.1.1 Trajectory and Core Claims

The "peaceful prelude" phase of Colombia's drug war runs up through the early 1980s, when a boom in US demand for cocaine had created a new class of lucrative and well-organized processing and trafficking operations. Escobar established himself as a "boss of bosses" among Colombia's principal drug traffickers by organizing MAS, a collective militarized response to kidnapping and extortion by leftist guerrillas. In fighting insurgents, MAS often collaborated with army forces, which suggested that tacit collusion with the Colombian state might be a viable long-term strategy. When, instead, Colombia launched its first serious crackdown on the cocaine trade in 1984, Escobar

---

[2] See Chapter 1 for a full discussion of this distinction, which arises in the case of Rio's Pacification policy as well.

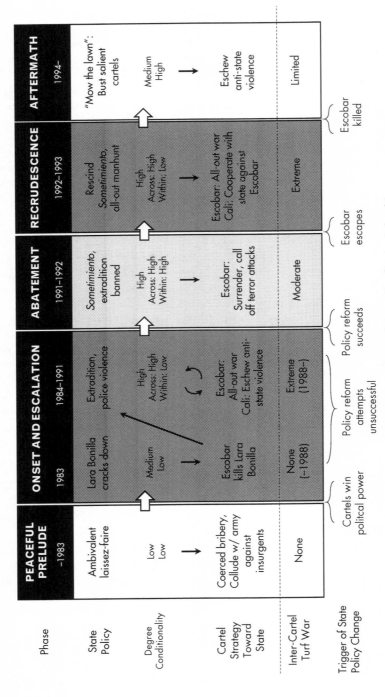

FIGURE 5.1. Trajectory of Cartel–State Conflict in Colombia.

Phase	PEACEFUL PRELUDE	ONSET AND ESCALATION		ABATEMENT	RECRUDESCENCE	AFTERMATH
	~1983	1983	1984–1991	1991–1992	1992–1993	1994–
State Policy	Ambivalent laissez-faire	Lara Bonilla cracks down	Extradition, police violence	Sometimiento, extradition banned	Rescind Sometimiento, all-out manhunt	"Mow the lawn": Bust salient cartels
Degree Conditionality	Low Low →	Medium Low →	High Across: High Within: Low	High Across: High Within: High →	High Across: High Within: Low →	Medium High →
Cartel Strategy Toward State	Coerced bribery, Collude w/ army against insurgents	Escobar kills Lara Bonilla	Escobar: All-out war Cali: Eschew anti-state violence	Escobar: Surrender, call off terror attacks	Escobar: All-out war Cali: Cooperate with state against Escobar	Eschew anti-state violence
Inter-Cartel Turf War	None	None (~1988)	Extreme (1988–)	Moderate	Extreme	Limited
Trigger of State Policy Change		Cartels win political power	Policy reform attempts unsuccessful	Policy reform succeeds	Escobar escapes	Escobar killed

would extend MAS's confrontational approach from insurgents to the state itself.

This initial crackdown was triggered not by inter-cartel violence (of which there was virtually none at the time), US pressure, or domestic anti-drug fervor, but rather by traffickers' penetration into Colombia's political and social elite (Pardo Rueda 1996, 190), epitomized by Pablo Escobar's election to Congress in 1982. Justice Minister Rodrigo Lara Bonilla, dedicated to rooting out corruption, investigated Escobar and got him expelled from Congress in 1983, but also targeted the drug trade more broadly. Escobar responded, to the surprise of even some of his own colleagues, by having Lara Bonilla killed. The state, in turn, ramped up repression and authorized extradition. This "onset and escalation" phase saw seven years of open and increasingly intense cartel–state conflict. Escobar alone assassinated a leading presidential candidate, a standing state governor, an attorney general, chiefs of police, countless judges, and the director of a major national newspaper; he bombed the headquarters of Colombia's intelligence agency, blew up a passenger plane, kidnapped relatives of the political elite, and made a standing offer to the thugs of Medellín of several thousand dollars for every policeman killed.

In the midst of this phase, peace and cooperation among Colombia's traffickers began to erode. The Rodríguez Orejuela brothers, leaders of the Cali cartel, had originally participated in MAS, and were friendly with the Ochoa clan, founding members of the Medellín cartel. As fighting wore on, though, Cali increasingly bridled at Escobar's violent campaign and the taxes he charged other traffickers to carry it out. Open inter-cartel warfare broke out in early 1988 when Cali operatives bombed Escobar's home in Medellín, prompting Escobar to respond with a string of bombings in Cali.

Throughout the onset and escalation phase, numerous high-level commissions tried and failed to negotiate a cartel–state peace agreement. After the four main candidates in the 1990 presidential election were assassinated (not all by Escobar), the eventual winner César Gaviria announced that reducing violence would take precedence over eliminating the drug trade. A new policy called *Sometimiento a la justicia* (voluntary submission to justice) was implemented, increasing the government's room to maneuver. To its formulators' surprise, many top traffickers soon surrendered under *Sometimiento*. After a lengthy negotiation that included a ban on extradition, Escobar himself surrendered and called off his war, ushering in an "abatement" phase.

For roughly a year between 1991 and 1992, Escobar and his crew lived in a posh prison he built on his own land, from which he continued to run his operation. Authorities were aware of this, but were only spurred to action when Escobar murdered, on the prison grounds, two associates suspected of graft.[3] The government attempted to move the kingpin to a more secure location, violating the conditions of his surrender. Escobar easily escaped.

---

[3] Interview, former Attorney General Gustavo de Greiff, December 13, 2010.

President Gaviria, humiliated, rescinded any possibility of a second surrender under *Sometimiento* and launched a massive crackdown on Escobar and his remaining allies, who in turn re-initiated hostilities. In this "recrudescence" phase, cartel–state conflict raged for a year and a half. An intense manhunt, involving both significant US technical assistance and the active if sub rosa cooperation of Escobar's rivals, finally succeeded in wearing down Escobar's defenses; he was killed in a firefight with police on December 2, 1993.

Colombia's varied "aftermath" phase has seen, overall, little anti-state violence by drug cartels. Escobar's death in 1993 left Cali ascendant. For a time, its non-violent approach seemed to pay off, earning a promise of amnesty from incoming president Ernesto Samper in exchange for campaign contributions. However, a public scandal forced Samper to reverse course and actively target Cali (Dugas 2001), leading to the capture of its leaders in 1995. With both the Medellín and Cali cartels left in fragments, the belligerents of Colombia's intensifying civil war became increasingly involved in coca cultivation and trafficking. While this intermingling complicates the analytic picture, Colombia's "pure" trafficking organizations have remained small and non-confrontational; the days of systematic cartel–state conflict ended with Escobar's death.

The following section briefly considers my thesis—that state policy is a central driver of variation in cartel–state conflict—in light of alternative perspectives, particularly ones emphasizing the agency of important, idiosyncratic individuals like Escobar. I then present a detailed chronological account organized by phases, making and defending the following core claims as they arise:

Claim 1: Colombia's initial crackdown and escalation (1983–1986) were unconditional. This led cartels—united under Medellín's leadership—to adopt increasingly violent strategies toward the state.

Claim 2: From 1987 onward, repression increasingly focused on Medellín to the exclusion of Cali because the former engaged in anti-state violence; that is, conditionality *across* cartels increased. This contributed to Cali's decision to attack Medellín (1988), and permitted it to operate in concert if not cooperation with the state to destroy Escobar (1992–1993).

Claim 3: The *Sometimiento* policy (1990–1991) allowed the state to credibly promise reduced repression on Medellín if it eschewed violence going forward, raising conditionality *within* cartels. Medellín members responded by eschewing anti-state violence.

Claim 4: The rescinding of *Sometimiento* after Escobar's escape (1992–1993) decreased conditionality within cartels, leading Escobar to re-engage in anti-state violence.

Conjecture: After the fall of Medellín and Cali (1995–), an effectively conditional approach to the smaller remaining cartels, rather than their fragmented nature, deterred further cartel–state conflict.

These claims correspond roughly to the vertical arrows in Figure 5.1. The horizontal arrows represent shifts in state policy, triggered by a variety of proximate causes. In the sections to come, I focus descriptive attention on the processes by which conditional reform efforts initially failed and finally succeeded with *Sometimiento*, as well as that policy's eventual collapse. Part III analyzes these reform processes in comparative perspective.

5.2 STATE POLICY AS DRIVER OF CARTEL–STATE CONFLICT AND ALTERNATIVE EXPLANATIONS

My core claims—in which shifts in the degree and conditionality of repression drive cartel decisions to use or eschew anti-state violence—are, in a sense, structural. In my theory, cartels respond rationally to the incentives created by their strategic interaction with the state. One important set of alternative explanations, given the prominence of individuals and particularly Escobar in the story of Colombia's drug war, is the agency of key actors. Agency explains important outcomes of interest as the result of the idiosyncratic traits and decisions of powerful individuals. Many people in Escobar's position, an agency-based explanation might posit, would *not* have launched an all-out terrorist attack on the state. In this view, the dynamics of cartel–state conflict in Colombia are better explained by Escobar's personal traits than the strategic situation he found himself in; he is more fruitfully thought of, analytically, as a sociopath, a violent man-child, or a dangerously wounded megalomaniac, than as a rational actor leading a profit-maximizing drug firm. Similarly, Lara Bonilla's initial crackdown on the cartels might better be explained as the suicidal obsession of a martyr-type than any kind of rational response to incentives.

Focusing on agency has its advantages. For one thing, it allows us to avoid describing Escobar's murderous campaigns as "rational." This is not merely a normative concern: the fact that Escobar's assassination of Lara Bonilla made him into a permanent fugitive, and that his campaign of terror ended with his killing by police, both suggest that his decision to go to war with the state was ultimately a rash mistake. On the other hand, the fact that he successfully bullied the state into banning extradition and, for a time, allowing him to run his drug operations from the safety of a prison he built himself suggests that his war was not so irrational after all.

More decisively, an agency approach accommodates the undeniable fact that figures like Escobar and Lara Bonilla really did act differently than similar actors in similar or identical situations. Most of Lara Bonilla's colleagues—including the president who appointed him—thought his crusade ill-advised, and staked out far more accommodating stances toward the *narcos*. Meanwhile, the Cali cartel's consistent avoidance of violent strategies and Medellín's embrace of them are frequently attributed to the different personalities of the cartels' leaders: whereas the Rodríguez Orejuelas were sober businessmen, Escobar and his colleagues José Rodríguez Gacha and Carlos

Lehder were violent, thuggish types (e.g., Chepesiuk 2003). Evidence for this is the fact that Cali did not respond to Lara Bonilla's initial, blanket crackdown with anti-state violence while Medellín did, a fact nicely explained by the alleged temperament and tastes of its leaders. Similarly, the Rodríguez Orejuelas never resorted to anti-state violence, even when repression against them turned unconditional after their payoffs to President Samper became public. Escobar, for his part, was certainly a unique individual, whose resentment toward the economic and political elites that barred his ascension surely contributed to the ferocity of his war.

Of course, agency and structure are not mutually exclusive (Yashar 1997); we can believe that Escobar was temperamentally predisposed to violence while still asking how his use of it was affected by the incentives he faced. The fact that shifts in state policy coincided with important changes in Escobar's use of different types of violence is better explained by my account than by a pure agency view. Similarly, in the sections to follow, I argue that Cali was motivated to remain non-violent by a policy of conditionality across cartels that was focusing repression nearly entirely on Medellín. Evidence of this is the fact that Cali *did* engage in an extremely lethal campaign against Medellín, which the government did not punish, and may have encouraged, suggesting that its avoidance of anti-state violence was not merely the result of temperament.

A distinct alternative hypothesis simply reverses the causal arrow of my core claim: states respond to cartel violence with crackdowns, not the other way around. This argument is a common one among state officials, who have solid political incentives to avoid blame for exacerbating armed conflict. In Colombia it is made explicitly by former Defense Minister Rafael Pardo, who argues that a great deal of Escobar's anti-state violence occurred in the period 1986–1989, precisely when extradition was inoperative. Moreover, Pardo argues, extradition was often imposed in response to cartel violence—in particular, the assassinations of Lara Bonilla in 1984 and presidential candidate Luis Carlos Galán in 1989 (Pardo Rueda 1996, 188–189).

In one sense, Pardo's argument is too clever by half: it is rich to count the assassination of Galán as occurring when extradition was off the table, since Escobar is widely thought to have killed Galán specifically because the latter explicitly campaigned on a platform of re-instituting extradition, and was all but certain to win the election. However, Pardo is correct that there is a kind of paradox here. Surely Escobar must have realized that murdering Lara Bonilla and Galán would set off massive increases in repression. If the goal was to avoid extradition, why give two presidents the perfect excuse to impose it via states of emergency? One view is that Escobar was blinded by fury, vengeance, and wounded pride. Yet the fact that these operations were well planned and involved teams of actors augurs against the idea that Escobar was simply hot-headed. As I argue in the sections to come, Escobar likely anticipated a short-term increase in repression, but believed (correctly) that extradition would prove susceptible to violent lobbying.

A final alternative approach would firmly agree that state policy drove the dynamics of violence, but question my coding of *Sometimiento* as a conditional policy. To be sure, if this were a single-case study, we would simply say that Escobar and the state reached a negotiated settlement, in the juridical form of a plea bargain. Is a policy like *Sometimiento*, which held out the possibility of such a plea bargain, fairly construed as a conditional approach? I argue it is. In a setting where one man had effective control over the single largest cartel in the country, the relevant form of conditionality within cartels was *conditionality for Escobar*. Thus an individual plea-bargain deal under *Sometimiento* constituted a promise to reduce state repression conditional on Escobar's (and hence the cartel's) cessation of hostilities. This is the essence of conditionality.

5.3 PEACEFUL PRELUDE (−1983): OFFICIAL INDIFFERENCE AND INTER-CARTEL COOPERATION

Drug trafficking and particularly contraband have long histories in Colombia, with emeralds and marijuana the largest markets until the late 1970s (Thoumi 1995), and traffickers seen more as colorful, "folkloric" figures than dangerous criminals (Pardo Rueda 1996, 180–184). State anti-narcotics policy was relatively permissive, with Colombia's elites frankly ambivalent, recognizing trafficking as an unseemly activity yet admiring and appreciating the fortunes it created. Indeed, marijuana legalization was hotly debated and actively promoted by key political and civil society actors (Tokatlián 2000), and a "back window" (*ventanilla siniestra*) banking policy allowed illicit profits to be nationalized with virtually no questions asked. US diplomatic pressure to get tough on trafficking was slowly growing, as was the DEA's presence in Colombia, but the need for an ally against communist insurgency both in Colombia and throughout Latin America often trumped the drug issue (Strong 1995, 60). When a confluence of domestic factors and US pressure led to a militarized crackdown in 1978, it was directed entirely at marijuana production in the Caribbean region of the country (Britto 2010).

The upshot was that Colombia's incipient cocaine trade faced only mild repression, and by the early 1980s, expanding cocaine shipments to the United States were generating enormous illicit profits for an assortment of smuggling outfits. Perhaps because the scale of these profits was not yet widely appreciated, traffickers seem to have had little trouble bribing the relevant low-level customs and aviation officials. At least in the case of Pablo Escobar, bribe offers were accompanied by threats of violence, but these threats generally proved effective and hence were rarely acted on (I discuss some important exceptions below). In terms of the model presented in Chapter 4, the situation thus approximated a "coerced peace" scenario, in which neither enforcement of the law nor anti-state violence occurs in equilibrium.

Indeed, the traffickers' main antagonists in this period were Colombia's insurgent groups, and the newly formed cartels initially positioned themselves as allies of the state in the fight against guerrillas. By the late 1970s, some key traffickers, including Escobar and Gacha, had already accumulated landholdings that made them targets for rural insurgencies. Moreover, the nascent M-19 guerrilla movement adopted a strategy of kidnapping traffickers, with the goal of collecting large ransoms to put toward their planned "invasion of Colombia" (Kirk 2003, 104). After an unsuccessful attempt on trafficker Carlos Lehder, the group succeeded in several kidnappings, including the sister of Jorge Luis Ochoa, a major trafficker from Medellín and a prime ally of Escobar. Feeling targeted as a group, Colombia's top drug traffickers—some say as many as 200, including the leaders of the Cali cartel—came together in November 1981 to discuss a united response (Chepesiuk 2003, 64). Lehder and Escobar, both known for their skill in military matters, argued that only by hitting back at the M-19 with violence could the group avoid being victimized in the future. The argument won the day; the traffickers all agreed to pony up money, soldiers, and arms to the collective, which was christened "Muerte a Secuestradores" or MAS ("Death to Kidnappers").

MAS announced its presence by dropping thousands of leaflets over a packed soccer stadium in Cali, but its true debut came when members of the M-19 were found bound and gagged in front of a Medellín newspaper office. MAS operated in covert cooperation with army and police units that were hunting the M-19, often carrying out the kind of brutal and unethical actions that state forces could not. Dozens if not hundreds of other members and associates of the M-19 were captured, tortured, and murdered. Eventually, leaders of the M-19 and MAS met in Panama, the meeting facilitated by Manuel Noriega, then head of Panamanian intelligence.[4] Ochoa's sister was freed and the M-19 abandoned its strategy of kidnapping traffickers.

The MAS incident had diverse and far-reaching impacts. First, the targeting of the leaders of Colombia's burgeoning drug trade ended up unifying what was until then a group of autonomous actors; it imposed on them a sort of class consciousness, both of their vulnerability to extortion and their common interest in cooperation and presenting a united front. Though the immediate goal was to win release of the captives, the formation of MAS—in particular the face-to-face meeting between traffickers who had until then had never met—facilitated collective action and broader cooperation, leading to a peaceful division of both Colombian and US drug turf that held for several years (Strong 1995, 64).

At the same time, the incident made clear to the trafficker class the usefulness of armed force, and consequently elevated Pablo Escobar to a dominant role within the group, as the capo with a comparative advantage in violence and coercion. The rapid success of MAS's operation further consolidated Escobar's position, which resembled that of a Mafia protection racket. Escobar received donations from all MAS members to carry out the military actions needed to

---

4 According to Salazar (2001, 87), Ochoa's contact with the Panamanian government was itself facilitated by none other than Venezuela's Carlos Andrés Pérez.

keep the traffickers "safe." This turn of events, together with his swift victory over M-19, seems to have cemented in his mind the idea that fighting was the best alternative to an endless spiral of extortion at the hands of others. It certainly set a precedent for his leadership: he continued to tax members of the Medellín cartel with the explicit justification that his war against the state created benefits for all traffickers.

A third consequence—concerning the relationship between drug traffickers and insurgencies—is paradoxical and double-sided. On the one hand, the formation of MAS constituted the beginning of armed anti-guerrilla pro-government paramilitarism in Colombia. MAS worked in concert if not active collusion with the army, threatening and murdering lawyers defending M-19 members, for example (CIJ 1992). To those with anti-leftist leanings, the incident taught an important lesson: state forces would gladly ally with traffickers in a battle against an insurgent foe. Indeed, the dominant paramilitary group of the 1990s—the infamous Autodefensas Unidas de Colombia (AUC)—was organized by founding MAS members and early Escobar allies Fidel and Carlos Castaño.

Yet at the same time, the MAS campaign brought Escobar into direct negotiation with the M-19 leadership, yielding a bizarre but important relationship of mutual respect and, according to some, operational cooperation. To Escobar, the M-19 was resourceful, clever, and effective. The personal contact turned a worthy opponent into a fellow traveler, and over the following years the M-19 would come to represent a model of successful violent lobbying, a trailblazer of sorts. Escobar seems to have reasoned that if the M-19 could stand up to the Colombian state, and MAS could stand up to the M-19, then why shouldn't MAS stand up to the state?

The lesson that other traffickers drew was very different. If the M-19 could stand up to the state and MAS could stand up to the M-19, then why not collude with and ultimately subvert the state by doing its dirty work for it? Although it would be years before the highly lucrative and functional pact between the Cali and Medellín cartels would break down into openly declared war, a fundamental divergence in strategy was already apparent. For a time, this divergence was merely an irritant to Escobar and his rivals. By the end of the 1980s, the inexorable logic of paramilitarism would lead the Cali leaders and the Castaño brothers to ally with the state against Escobar, as MAS once had against the M-19.

Before any of that could happen, however, Escobar reached the high water mark in his quest for political power and social legitimacy. Starting in the early 1980s, he had become engaged in social causes in the low-income neighborhoods and squatter settlements of Medellín. These involved not only massive public-goods and infrastructure provision, but also a deep and personal engagement, organizing dozens of neighborhood committees, attending community events, and constructing a populist discourse in his weekly column for *Medellín Cívico*, a local newspaper owned by his union-organizer uncle

Hernando Gaviria (Salazar 2001, 78).[5] Escobar's flagship project, Medellín Sin Tugurios ("Medellín Without Slums"), built an entire neighborhood for a community living in precarious conditions atop a city dump. To this day, the neighborhood is informally known as Barrio Pablo Escobar.

In early 1982, Jairo Ortega, a candidate for Congress, invited Escobar to join his list as a *suplente* (alternate). Ortega had founded the Movimiento de Renovación (Movement for Renovation), which was then allied with the Nuevo Liberalismo (New Liberalism) offshoot of the Liberal Party. Nuevo Liberalismo was headed by the charismatic leaders Luis Carlos Galán and Rodrigo Lara Bonilla, and was founded on the promise of rejuvenating and cleaning up both the Liberal Party and Colombia's electoral system in general. As such, they were adamant about avoiding "hot money" and other improprieties, which soon led them to expel Escobar and Ortega from the movement mid-campaign. Ortega switched to the camp of Alberto Santofimio, an important, traditional Liberal who had almost won the party's presidential nomination that year. Ortega was elected with Escobar as his alternate, while Galán's break with the larger Liberal Party led to the presidential victory of Belisario Betancur, a Conservative. A now infamous puff piece on Escobar in Colombia's top news magazine (*Semana* 1983), "A Homegrown Robin Hood"[6]—published shortly after Escobar won his seat—captures the rather innocent nature of both political campaigns and attitudes toward traffickers at the time.

> Even if at the provincial level [Escobar] is no more than Jaime Ortega's alternate in the House of Representatives, at the national level he is the principal backer of *santofimismo*. Santofimio's charisma, bolstered by Escobar's money, are transforming the political customs of the country. Campaign tours that used to be slow and uncomfortable ... today are done quickly and comfortably in his planes and helicopters. At rallies, speakers stand on daises of wood specially constructed for the occasion ... On important occasions, speeches are transmitted to the country via paid radio time slots.[7]

5.4 ONSET AND ESCALATION (1983–1991): THE FIRST *NARCO-GUERRA*

5.4.1 Initial Crackdown and Response (1983–1986): Taking on the *Narcos*

Claim 1: Colombia's initial crackdown and escalation were unconditional. This led cartels—united under Medellín's leadership—to adopt increasingly violent strategies toward the state.

---

[5] Among the issues that Escobar wrote about in his regular column were housing and sanitation for the poor, environmental education and conservation, keeping Colombia's youth off drugs(!) and, of course, revoking the extradition treaty.

[6] *Un Robin Hood Paisa*, literally "A Robin Hood from Antioquia." Antioquia is the department of which Medellín is the capital.

[7] Author's translation.

Escobar's career as a politician was to be short-lived. President Betancur, obliged to make some appointments from opposition parties, named Rodrigo Lara Bonilla his justice minister. Lara Bonilla announced his intention to investigate and crack down on "hot money," and a confrontation ensued between him and Escobar's patron, Jairo Ortega, on the floor of the House. Ortega presented evidence—arranged for by Escobar—that Lara Bonilla himself had accepted campaign contributions from a trafficker. Lara Bonilla's response was to double down on his anti-corruption crusade, publicly denouncing Escobar as a drug trafficker, and seeking revocation of his congressman's immunity.[8] Escobar mobilized a public campaign of denial of wrongdoing combined with accusations and legal action against Lara Bonilla, who found himself under official investigation. Politically isolated, Lara Bonilla went so far as to offer Betancur his resignation (Strong 1995, 92), which Betancur declined.

Lara Bonilla eventually prevailed, however, when the editor of the *El Espectador* newspaper, Guillermo Cano, located and re-published a 1976 news story in which a young Escobar and five others were arrested for drug trafficking. The case against Escobar was re-opened and an arrest warrant issued. By October 1983, Escobar was out of Congress, his immunity and US visa both revoked; in January 1984 he publicly withdrew from politics. Meanwhile, Lara Bonilla continued his broader campaign against the drug trade as a whole, culminating in the March 1984 raid on Tranquilandia, a cocaine-processing factory town that a consortium of traffickers had built in the heart of the Amazonian jungle. At the time, it was the largest cocaine bust—fourteen metric tons—in world history.

Escobar responded by taking a drastic step: Lara Bonilla was murdered by assassins on April 30, 1984. President Betancur immediately declared a state of emergency, and at Lara Bonilla's funeral announced that he would begin authorizing extraditions. Shortly thereafter, Betancur signed an extradition order for kingpin Carlos Lehder. Many of the top traffickers fled the country.

Escobar, Lehder, and Gacha fled to Panama, where they made a peace offer to President Betancur, an offer they would make again and again over the next six years. In exchange for a definitive revoking of extradition and amnesty (*indulto*), the traffickers would quit trafficking, turn over laboratories, planes, and other infrastructure, and repatriate all of their capital. President Betancur rejected the offer, and, following through on his threat, authorized the first extraditions to the United States in 1985. Nonetheless, exile was risky for the traffickers. Cali leader Gilberto Rodríguez Orejuela and Medellín stalwart Jorge Luis Ochoa had fled to Spain in 1984, but were soon indicted there. Escobar and his allies in Panama rightly mistrusted Noriega, and also faced US indictments for trafficking cocaine through Nicaragua. Thus, in spite of increasing repression at home, the principal traffickers soon returned to Colombia, where they would remain until their capture or death.

[8] Bowden (2001, 35–40) provides a vivid recounting of this episode in English.

Both Lara Bonilla's initial crackdown and the state's doubling down in response to his murder were, I claim, unconditional. Despite Lara Bonilla's very public feud with Escobar, the crackdown was far more than a personal vendetta. Rather, Lara Bonilla saw Escobar's election as the leading edge of a cartel takeover of the state from within, and his removal from office as key to a broader campaign of repression. Indeed, Lara Bonilla had cemented a working partnership with the head of the National Police's anti-narcotics division, Jaime Ramírez Gómez, himself an incorruptible and effective investigator who would be assassinated by Escobar in 1986. Their efforts, typical of states' initial anti-cartel crackdowns, were directed against the drug trade as a whole (Gugliotta and Leen 2011, 116–118), and were in no way conditional on cartels' use of violence. Lara Bonilla directed Ramírez to investigate the top thirty suspected traffickers in the country, resulting in warrants for the arrest and extradition of Carlos Lehder (Salazar 2001, 119) and other traffickers. (President Betancur, however, refused to authorize any extraditions, citing nationalist concerns (López Restrepo 2005, 199) but probably also leery of Lara Bonilla's zeal to unearth questionable campaign contributions (Castillo 1987, 183).) Lara Bonilla also rescinded licenses for some 150 aircraft used by traffickers, and launched public accusations of money-laundering rings involving politicians, soccer teams, and other shadow businesses (*Semana* 1987).[9] Together, Ramírez and Lara Bonilla planned and executed the Tranquilandia bust in March 1984, which affected a large group of traffickers.

It is also significant that the government never signaled any form of conditionality; on the contrary, Lara Bonilla always spoke collectively, of "*narcos*" or the drug trade in general. In the tug of war between Betancur and Lara Bonilla over extradition, neither man advocated using the recourse as a deterrent by punishing excessive violence or other "bad behavior." Indeed, Lara Bonilla was generally critical of Betancur's refusal to extradite even relatively minor traffickers. After signing off on one of Betancur's denial-of-extradition rulings as a show of gratitude for Betancur's support throughout the campaign-contribution scandal, Lara Bonilla made clear that he would henceforth seek maximal repression against anyone trafficking drugs. "The more I investigate, the more I see how much damage the *narcos* cause to this country. I will never again decline to extradite one of these dogs" (Castillo 1987, 184).

The state responded to Lara Bonilla's assassination with an immediate escalation of repressive measures; these too, I claim, were unconditional. In one sense, of course, this doubling down meets the definition of conditionality: anti-state violence was met with increased repression. Yet these new measures were not conditional in the relevant sense of offering relatively less repression to those cartels that eschewed violence. On the contrary, President

---

[9] Gugliotta and Leen (2011) mention a single incident in which fifty-seven aircraft licenses were cancelled; it is not clear if this is the total for the whole period.

Betancur's state of emergency declaration made drug trafficking an offense without bail, to be tried in military tribunals, and, if a conviction were reached, not subject to parole. Betancur also began signing extradition orders, which he had notoriously refused to do during Lara Bonilla's initial crackdown. Again, traffickers were blamed collectively for the violence, and the government made no attempt to distinguish, juridically or verbally, violent trafficking from non-violent trafficking.

Beyond the letter of these decrees and the government rhetoric surrounding them, their observable effects were similar across cartels. In particular, even though Cali had always been a more business-like and less violent cartel than Medellín, and even though its participation in MAS was tenuous, it seems to have been subject to equal repression in the immediate wake of the Lara Bonilla assassination. Consider that in this period, Cali's Gilberto Rodríguez Orejuela fled Colombia for Spain together with Medellín's Jorge Luis Ochoa. By 1990, once the government had begun to focus almost exclusively on Medellín, Rodríguez Orejuela could circulate freely in Cali, while Ochoa turned himself in to avoid extreme state repression. In 1984, however, cartels understood repression to have increased generally and unconditionally.

As for Escobar's murderous response to the initial crackdown, it was not a hot-headed vengeance killing, but rather part of a deliberate strategy; the long list of state officials he assassinated over the course of his career is testament to this. What did this larger strategy consist of? It certainly included Escobar's embrace of violent lobbying, exemplified by the Extraditables' overt declarations of war, to be called off in exchange for policy concessions. But Escobar had been employing anti-state violence well before the Lara Bonilla assassination; this violence flowed, I claim, from the logic of violent corruption. Indeed, Escobar's long association with the phrase "*plata o plomo?*" suggests that he adopted a fight-and-bribe strategy very early on in his career. The earliest documented example is from 1976. Escobar and several lieutenants were arrested for smuggling thirty-nine kilos of cocaine over the border from Ecuador by agents of DAS, the relatively uncorrupt national intelligence agency. Escobar offered a money bribe on the spot, which was refused,[10] and he was imprisoned; the judge assigned to the case received *plata o plomo* threats, but also refused to be bought off.[11] The arresting DAS officers were murdered several months later, and the original judge was the victim of two dynamite attacks (CIJ 1992, 17) and numerous car-burnings. Her statement at the opening of the case, "If I have to die for putting someone, however important, in prison, then I'll die," suggests that Escobar's threats were credible, and that he

[10] Interview, Alonso Salazar, Medellín, June 28, 2012.
[11] This arrest later proved to be Escobar's political undoing, when Escobar's mug shot was republished by *El Espectador* editor Guillermo Cano in 1983, putting the lie to his claims that he had no tie to the drug trade. Escobar later had Cano assassinated and bombed the paper's headquarters.

had already been making them for some time (Salazar 2001, 58–60). Eventually Escobar succeeded in having the case transferred to another judge who accepted his bribe and freed him.

Another early example was given to me by a former judge and public prosecutor from Medellín whom I interviewed. In October 1980, two Medellín judges were murdered and a number of criminal courts burned down (CIJ 1992, 15). Assigned to an investigation of Escobar's brother-in-law for one of these murders, my informant recalled, "They called me saying it was all fixed. 'There's a lot of a money [*plata*] to go around, a lot of bullets [*plomo*] too.' A colleague, a judge, told me not to fight with these types; stay out of trouble."[12] The judge refused the bribe and handed down a conviction; he was followed by hitmen but luckily had been assigned escorts and survived.

With these few exceptions, this early period approximated a "coerced peace" scenario of my model: Escobar threatened local enforcers with violence, but since this was sufficient to induce bribe agreements in the vast majority of cases, little actual violence occurred. The necessary conditions for coerced peace certainly match up with what we know of the period: the degree of repression was low (Escobar was mostly dealing with customs agents who were not targeting the drug trade per se (Castillo 1987, 62)), conditionality was low (judges complained of death threats but this did not lead to increased repression against Escobar), and Escobar's ability to inflict pain on enforcers was high (thanks to his "eyes and ears" throughout the Medellín underworld). For example, the original judge in the 1976 episode made official note of the threats she and the DAS agents had suffered (Salazar 2001, 58–60), but this averted neither Escobar's release, nor the murder of the DAS agents.

Under this interpretation, Lara Bonilla's crackdown had two distinct effects. First, by increasing the degree of repression, it altered the dynamics of violent corruption, increasing the frequency with which Escobar and his more violent Medellín-cartel colleagues carried through on *plata o plomo* threats. As the stakes rose, this logic dictated increasingly harsh reprisal against officials who stood firm, in order to intimidate the rest. In early 1984, for example, Edgardo Gonzáles, a former Justice Ministry official who appealed a government decision not to extradite two traffickers, was murdered; the judges charged with hearing the appeal resigned (Strong 1995, 92). To officials, it became crystal clear that Escobar would respond with violence if they turned down his bribes and enforced the law. For example, in late 1983, when judge Gustavo Zuluaga Serna, at Lara Bonilla's urging, indicted Escobar for the earlier murder of DAS agents, he said "I may have just signed my death warrant" (Salazar 2001, 120); he and his wife suffered death threats until his murder three years later. Lara Bonilla himself, on the eve of his death, had become convinced that he would be killed, and was set to be transferred to a diplomatic post abroad.

---

12 Interview, former judge and anonymous public prosecutor (*fiscal sin rostro*), December 26, 2010.

The second effect of Lara Bonilla's crackdown was to help push Escobar into violent lobbying by forcing his withdrawal from politics, hobbling his ability to influence de jure policy through non-violent means. Many have speculated why Escobar sought office openly when other traffickers like Cali's Rodríguez Orejuela brothers were (and would remain) content to lobby through campaign contributions to friendly politicians. Escobar was surely motivated in part by hubris, but he also harbored a deep mistrust of the political class (Salazar 2001, 120), and may have felt that Cali-style lobbying was a mug's game. What is certain is that losing office vastly reduced Escobar's influence over de jure policy precisely when he needed it most, facing a major crackdown and the authorization of extradition.

Moreover, the two necessary conditions for violent lobbying discussed in Chapter 3 were met. First, in Escobar's judgment (correct as it would turn out), extradition was a sufficiently unpopular policy that it would be *susceptible*—i.e., subject to reversal by leaders if they were made to suffer enough for it. Second, the free-rider problem inherent in all lobbying could be overcome. Although MAS had by this point degenerated into a nascent paramilitary organization, Escobar still retained the power to tax his fellow traffickers to pay for military operations in the common interest. Together with his Medellín cartel allies, he founded the Extraditables, which launched a terror campaign aimed at knocking down extradition. While personality surely played a role (even Escobar's Medellín-cartel allies were wary of a full-blown war against the state), these strategic factors made Escobar's move from non-violent to violent forms of lobbying an entirely logical one.

Like MAS, the Extraditables accompanied violence with public relations. Savvy public communiqués, embossed with an image of the first Colombians to be extradited, heads down and in chains, carried the phrase "We prefer a grave in Colombia to a jail in the United States." In its rhetoric, the Extraditables justified its campaign of violence with passionate and patriotic arguments against extradition and the vile political oligarchy that was imposing it. This amounted to the continuation by violent means of the political campaign Foro Contra la Extradición (Forum Against Extradition) that Escobar had launched while campaigning as a Liberal party candidate in the early 1980s.

Violent lobbying, particularly death threats against judicial officials, soon paid off: the Supreme Court declared the extradition treaty unconstitutional on a technicality in December 1986. President Virgilio Barco immediately signed a new law to replace the treaty, and used it to extradite Carlos Lehder in 1987—widely thought to have been ratted out by Escobar himself. However, by June 1987, the Supreme Court found the new extradition law unconstitutional as well, and extradition was off the table for a time. The legal status of extradition continued to vary over the course of the narco-violence years in Colombia; Figure 5.2 presents a timeline of this variation, coded trichotomously into periods where extradition was in effect, periods in which it was "on the table" as a potential option or of unclear or changing status, and periods in which it had been judicially ruled out (if only temporarily). The timeline also shows key events and presents violent-event data I produced as part of the NRI/OBIVAN project: in this case, daily newspaper reports of bombings and acts of arson from 1986 to 1993.

5.4.2 Turf War Erupts (1987–1988): Conditionality *Across* Cartels

Claim 2: From 1987 on, repression increasingly focused on Medellín to the exclusion of Cali because the former engaged in anti-state violence; that is, conditionality *across* cartels increased. This contributed to Cali's decision to attack Medellín (1988), and permitted it to operate in concert if not cooperation with the state to destroy Escobar (1992–1993).

In Colombia, the onset of cartel–state conflict significantly preceded that of inter-cartel turf war. Indeed, for most of the 1980s, Colombia's drug traffickers were not only at peace but in some sense operated as a true cartel. US retail markets were peacefully divvied up, and traffickers from Cali and Medellín acted more like friendly business associates than rivals. Somewhat surprisingly, inter-cartel peace continued well into the period of mutual escalation between the state and the cartels. This fact alone demonstrates that cartel–state conflict is neither a mere by-product of nor a sufficient condition for inter-cartel turf war.

Nonetheless, inter-cartel peace in Colombia eventually broke down. On January 13, 1988, agents working for the Cali cartel set off a eighty-kilogram car bomb in front of Escobar's home in Medellín, destroying the entire building. Escobar responded with a series of bomb attacks in Cali, often targeting the Rodríguez Orejuelas' drug store chain *La Rebaja*. From that point on, turf war raged between the two cartels. For Escobar, this opening of a second front would ultimately prove disastrous.

The theory developed in this book is intended to explain cartel–state conflict, not inter-cartel turf war, but it nonetheless sheds some light on Cali's decision to attack. The Cali-Medellín war was likely driven by multiple factors, including personal animosity between the well-heeled Rodríguez Orejuelas and the always contemptuous Escobar, as well as shrinking profits due to increased interdiction by US law enforcement (Chepesiuk 2003). That said, the evolution of repressive policy in Colombia also shaped Cali's incentives in key ways.

In 1987, the government stepped up repression against the Medellín cartel, setting in motion two dynamics that, I argue, contributed to the breakdown of Cali–Medellín cooperation and the outbreak of open warfare. The first was financial: as Escobar's war with the state escalated, he increased taxes on his fellow traffickers to cover his expenses. Cali bridled at these payments, and eventually refused to make them. The second dynamic was strategic: as the state focused increasingly on Medellín, it directed ever less repression at Cali.

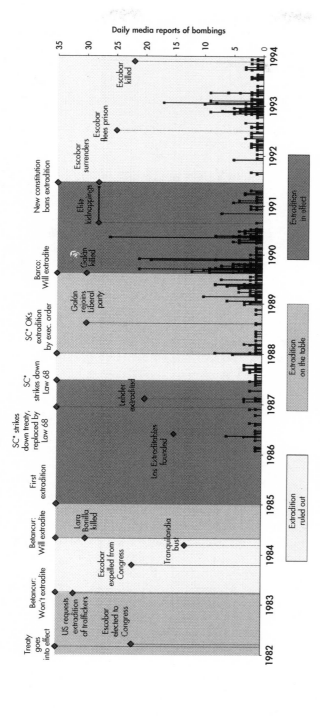

FIGURE 5.2. Colombia's Drug War: Extradition and Narco-Terrorism, 1982–1994. The height of the vertical bars indicates the number of newspaper reports mentioning a terror attack on a given day, not necessarily the number of unique events, and can thus be seen as a rough measure of intensity or public impact.

Source: author's coding of newspaper reports (NRJ/OBIVAN).

139

Because the state's focus on Medellín was due to its use of violence, I consider this a form of conditionality—conditionality across cartels. This preemptive form of conditionality did not deter Escobar, who was already targeted, but gave the Rodríguez Orejuelas incentives to further distance themselves from Escobar, and suggested that if and when they engaged him militarily, the state would largely look the other way.

That the government began focusing increasingly on capturing the kingpins of the Medellín cartel, directing little if any repressive force against the Cali cartel, is an uncontroversial claim. In the words of César Gaviria, who served as cabinet minister in the Barco administration before becoming president in 1990, "We viewed Escobar and the Medellín Cartel as the worst of two evils. That's why the Colombian government directed all its attention and resources against the Medellín Cartel" (Chepesiuk 2003, 130). Escobar complained loudly and repeatedly at the time of the state's unequal persecution of him and his allies, and officials rarely bothered to dispute such accusations. One clear manifestation of the increasingly conditional nature of repression was the advent of the *Bloque de Búsqueda* ("Search Bloc") elite police force. Housed in an armored police academy in central Medellín, the Bloque de Búsqueda was well trained, well equipped (thanks in part to US technical assistance) and enjoyed a wide berth to engage in extremely repressive and extrajudicial tactics (Bowden 2001). It was also formed for the sole purpose of capturing or killing the leaders of the Medellín cartel.[13]

Besides increased repression against Medellín, this shift to conditionality across cartels also involved a deliberate *decrease* in repression against Cali. As then-DEA station chief Joe Toft noted, "We had agents working on both cartels, and the group assigned to the Cali Cartel worked just as hard as the Medellín [cartel] group. *But the Colombian government's focus was on [the] Medellín [cartel], which had declared war on the state.* So we couldn't get the Colombian government to do much on [the] Cali [cartel]" (Chepesiuk 2003, 130; emphasis added). Apparently, the DEA had actionable intelligence which the Colombian government never acted on. This highlights a key operational aspect of conditional repression: since conditionality requires, by definition, holding something in reserve, in practice it often involves *declining to act* even when opportunities for interdiction and arrests arise.

Conditionality across cartels not only persisted after the Cali cartel initiated open hostilities against Medellín, it may have intensified. There is suggestive evidence of collaboration between state officials and Cali operatives in targeting Escobar and his associates (e.g., Chepesiuk 2003, 130). Moreover, as discussed above, the Cali cartel later financed and encouraged the anti-Escobar group Los Pepes, who also acted in concert, if not coordination, with state agents. Officials, unsurprisingly, deny any collaboration, but generally acknowledge that from this period onward repression was focused overwhelmingly on Medellín.

---

13 Interview, Bloque de Búsqueda commander Hugo Martínez, Bogotá, December 2010.

Admittedly, the Cali cartel never willfully adopted a strategy of brazen anti-state violence, even under the initial unconditional crackdown. Thus it is clear that conditionality across cartels alone did not cause them to avoid violence. Rather, Cali leaders Gilberto and Miguel Rodríguez Orejuela seem to have simply been hiding "types." They were educated and entrepreneurial, with neither the interest in overt political power nor, perhaps, the comparative advantage in violence that characterized Escobar and his Medellín partners Carlos Lehder and José Rodríguez Gacha. Indeed, though the Rodríguez Orejuelas apparently contributed to MAS (the group's first public announcement occurred in Cali), its original purpose was to fight insurgents, not the state, and was clearly the initiative of the Medellín traffickers (Gugliotta and Leen 2011, 92–93). By most accounts, the Cali brothers were basically along for the ride, and they were almost certainly opposed to (though probably not consulted about) the murder of Lara Bonilla (Chepesiuk 2003, 124). Another sign that conditionality alone did not determine Cali's strategy is that when the state was finally forced by scandal to direct maximal repression against the cartel from 1994 on, its leaders took hiding approaches, never turning to anti-state violence even in the face of capture and extradition.

That said, state policy surely influenced the Rodríguez Orejuela brothers' strategic choices. At first, it did so indirectly, by setting off Escobar's all-out assault. The Cali traffickers were as frightened of extradition to the United States as anyone—Gilberto Rodríguez Orejuela risked returning from Spain to face arrest and trial in Colombia to avoid it—but with Escobar leading the charge, and organizing the violence, they had little reason to conduct a campaign of their own. Indeed, as discussed in Chapter 3, when violent lobbying works, it works for everyone in the industry; for this reason, Escobar felt justified in demanding contributions to his "war chest." Escobar's increasing tax demands were an important cause of the Cali–Medellín split (Chepesiuk 2003), but conditionality across cartels almost certainly played a role as well. At a minimum, reduced repression on Cali had allowed them to grow stronger, which in turn put them in a better position to reject Escobar's demands in 1986 (Chepesiuk 2003, 127). Two years later, with Escobar feeling the brunt of state repression, these shifts in relative power probably contributed to Cali's decision to launch an all-out war against Escobar, bombing the eight-story building, Edificio Mónaco, where Escobar's family and closest associates lived.

Conditionality may have contributed even more directly to the Rodríguez Orejuela brothers' decision to attack Escobar. They may have anticipated (correctly) that even after attacking him, the state would continue to concentrate repression overwhelmingly on Medellín—that is, they may have (correctly) understood repression to be conditional on anti-state violence, but not inter-cartel violence. They certainly would have been right to anticipate this: in 1989, after more than a year of open warfare between the Cali and Medellín cartels the Rodríguez Orejuelas were subject to so little repression that they felt comfortable circulating freely in Cali. The chief of Cali police justified this by noting that "We have no arrest order" (Long 1989). Moreover, given Cali's many contacts with state officials through (non-violent) corruption, it is entirely plausible that they knew they would not be punished for attacking Escobar; there is even some evidence that key government actors—not necessarily corrupt—deliberately encouraged the outbreak of inter-cartel war for strategic reasons (Chepesiuk 2003, 127).

Whether or not Cali anticipated the state's non-reaction to its attack on Escobar, it certainly felt emboldened after the fact to sustain and intensify its campaign. This included an ultimately failed military strike in 1988 on Escobar involving paid English mercenaries, and the infiltration of a spy into the operations of Medellín capo Rodríguez Gacha that eventually contributed to Gacha's death in a police raid in late 1989 (Chepesiuk 2003, 129–135). Cali further ramped up its efforts after Escobar escaped from La Catedral prison in 1992, including its sponsorship of Los Pepes, a group of former Escobar allies.

5.4.3 Mutual Escalation (1988–1991): Extreme Unconditional Repression

Colombia's 1990 presidential election, initially a hopeful opportunity for political reform, was transformed by the country's ongoing drug and civil wars into a tragic conflagration of violence. The four leading candidates, three representing unprecedented attempts by insurgent groups to engage the political process, were assassinated mid-campaign, and the eventual winner barely escaped with his life from the most lethal terrorist attack in Colombian history. The repercussions of the violence were varied and long-lasting, going well beyond the story to be told here. In particular, Colombia's active insurgencies—their political wings exterminated—turned definitively away from electoral politics, contributing to the escalation of civil war in the 1990s and 2000s. In terms of cartel–state conflict, Escobar's murder of frontrunner Luis Carlos Galán and airplane bombing intended to kill Galán's successor César Gaviria probably represent the height of anti-state violence by cartels. If there was a silver lining, it lay in setting the political stage for Gaviria's turn toward violence reduction as the primary objective of repressive policy.

Escobar's enmity toward Galán went back to the 1982 elections, when Galán and Lara Bonilla expelled him from their New Liberalism movement. That year, Galán broke with the mainstream Liberal Party and ran as a third-party candidate, contributing to the victory of Conservatives under Betancur. Galán then sat out the 1986 election, permitting the Liberals, under Barco, to retake the presidency. Throughout the 1980s, he remained a very popular figure, though he stood little chance of winning as an independent. Thus, for the 1990 election, he proposed to re-join the Liberals on condition that the party select its nominee via primary, rather than by party elders. In late 1988, the Liberal leadership agreed, and Galán was restored.

For Escobar, beyond any lingering hurt feelings, Galán posed a very real threat. Like his murdered fellow traveler Lara Bonilla, Galán was a vocal proponent of extradition and a fierce anti-corruption crusader. He was also a skilled campaigner and a magnetic personality. Over the course of 1989, it became clear that he would not only win his party's nomination, but was the clear frontrunner for president. On August 19, 1989, while delivering a campaign speech, Galán was assassinated. The event was, even more than the murder of Lara Bonilla, a watershed. Galán's assassination, like John F. Kennedy's, shocked and silenced a nation, cutting down a transformative political figure in his prime.[14]

Unlike the Kennedy case, however, there was little mystery as to who had killed Galán, or why. President Barco immediately "declared war" on the Medellín cartel, cutting off back-door negotiations being carried out by various high-level commissions and announcing that he would conduct extraditions via executive order. Although the legal basis for extradition was still unclear, the Supreme Court had previously signaled that it would not interfere, and indeed some twenty extraditions occurred within four months of Galán's murder (Bowden 2001, 65). Barco also ramped up street-level repression, forming elite anti-narcotics police corps including the Bloque de Búsqueda team that, years later, would eliminate Escobar.

In terms of the trajectory in Figure 5.1, cartel–state conflict had entered another round of mutual escalation. Escobar responded with an intensification of his terror campaign, carrying out some eighty-eight bombings between Galán's assassination in August and the end of 1989 (Pardo Rueda 1996, 201). In one spectacular attack, a truck carrying one ton of dynamite completely destroyed the headquarters of DAS. In another, Escobar downed a commercial jetliner on which Galán's successor, César Gaviria, was meant to be traveling. Gaviria survived and went on to win the presidency, but 110 other passengers were killed. It was also during this period that Escobar hit on the tactic of kidnapping members of Colombia's political elite, an approach that turned out to be more effective than bombing in driving the state to the bargaining table.

Not all of Escobar's anti-state violence was driven by the logic of violent lobbying, however. As the state ramped up the degree of repression, Escobar ramped up his *plata o plomo* threats. Justice ministry officials warned Barco of the threat to judges and public prosecutors, but little protection was offered, and many were killed in the immediate wake of his declaration of "war."[15]

[14] Incredibly, the electoral violence of the 1990 election was only just getting started. Two candidates of the Unión Patriótica (the political wing of the FARC insurgency) and one from the M-19 movement (which by then had demobilized and transformed itself into a political party) were murdered in early 1990, most likely by right-wing paramilitary leaders.
[15] Interview, former anonymous public prosecutor (*fiscal sin rostro*), December 26, 2010. Of Barco's declaration of war, the interviewee added: "Imbecile! It's not a war between two countries. You have to generate fear in them [i.e., the cartels], do something, but [declaring war] didn't change anything. It just exposed us."

Gaviria implemented the constitutionally dubious practice of anonymous ("faceless") judges and investigators (*jueces y fiscales sin rostro*), a technique borrowed from Italian anti-Mafia investigations, as a means of protection. Judges' case assignments were coded by number, with the codebook hidden under lock and key. Such measures were intended to protect judiciary agents, but did not always prove effective, as a former *fiscal sin rostro* explained to me:

> Judge #13 was a *juez sin rostro*. I [was] a *fiscal sin rostro*. We were smoking a cigarette in the hall. "I heard that Pablo Escobar is offering 50 million [pesos][16] to know which judge was assigned the case of the seizure of the cocaine laboratory in..." She went pale. "Why do you ask me that?" "Because I was having a coffee and I heard this conversation." "Unfortunately, I have [that case]. Now what?" "You go to the president of the tribunal and ask that they increase your security detail." They gave her more security, changed her car, gave her a special car just for her. Within a month the [*sicarios*] had killed her while she walked out of her house. They came by on a moto.[17]

5.5 ABATEMENT (1991–1992): CONDITIONALITY *WITHIN* CARTELS, BY PRESIDENTIAL DECREE

Claim 3: The *Sometimiento* policy allowed the state to credibly promise reduced repression on Medellín if it eschewed violence going forward, raising conditionality *within* cartels. Medellín members responded by eschewing anti-state violence.

Gaviria's presidency began in August 1990 with a vocal shift in state anti-narcotics strategy toward violence reduction. Extreme electoral violence itself was surely one factor; another may have been a unilateral truce declared by the Extraditables on July 27, 1990, just prior to Gaviria's inauguration. If this move allowed Escobar to "claim political protagonism and impose dialogue on Barco's successor" (Pécaut 2006, 405), it also gave Gaviria room to maneuver politically (Pardo Rueda 1996, 266). In any case, Gaviria's inaugural address not only discussed alternatives to extradition but also made a critical distinction between ending narco-terrorism—his government's immediate goal—and the larger problem of drug trafficking per se, on which "no progress will be possible as long as consumer countries do not substantially reduce their demand" (Gaviria 1990). This reframing of the problem, I argue in Chapter 9, helped the Gaviria administration tack toward a conditional policy that (inevitably) involved going easier on Escobar and his Medellín allies conditional on their eschewal of violence.

[16] About $180,000 in 2015 dollars.
[17] Interview, former anonymous public prosecutor (*fiscal sin rostro*), December 26, 2010.

In any case, Gaviria's speech breathed new life into policy reform efforts that had been brewing for some time. In one sense, these stretched back to the first efforts to negotiate a truce or surrender with the Medellín cartel in 1984. More immediately, during a negotiation effort in early 1990, officials within President Barco's security team had begun to sketch out a new policy initiative. The idea was similar to plea bargaining, except that the traffickers were not in state custody, and in most cases, had no outstanding indictments or even open cases against them. In Pardo's words, "If an extraditable turned himself in, surrendered, and there were no legal case against him in Colombia, he would go free. This was my concern." Pardo "prepared a brief and schematic memorandum ... the rendition to which the Extraditables referred would be defined as voluntarily turning themselves in (*entrega voluntaria*) to an authority, and in order for this to be usable by the justice system, whoever turned themselves in would have to make a confession that would permit the judge to indict them. In exchange for the confession and turning themselves in, there would be a reduction in sentence" (Pardo Rueda 1996, 264).

When the 1990 negotiations collapsed, Pardo put the memo in his briefcase, where it remained all summer. However, when Pardo heard Gaviria's inaugural address, he returned to his policy idea. Gaviria had drawn a clear conceptual distinction between the crisis of narco-terrorism and the larger problem of drug trafficking in general. He argued that the former had to be solved immediately, by Colombia itself, while the latter was a far more intractable problem that, at minimum, would require demand reduction in the wealthy consumer countries. For Pardo, this opened the door to a *judicial* solution.

Pardo, together with Gaviria and Minister of Justice Jaime Giraldo, hammered out a first draft a policy known as *Sometimiento a la justicia* ("[voluntary] submission to justice"), which won unanimous support from Gaviria's cabinet. Gaviria himself announced the policy, lending it the heft of a presidential decree. The juridical details, however, proved complex. Issues arose over whether the state should make a one-time or a standing offer, how to deal with suspected traffickers for whom insufficient judicially valid evidence existed to get a conviction, and what promises to make around the possibility of future extradition for other crimes. Over the course of the next five months, the government would refine the *Sometimiento* policy through a series of three more decrees, ultimately negotiating the policy's final form with Escobar himself.

Around the time of the original decree, in late August 1990, Escobar (acting in the name of the Extraditables) took hostage a group of journalists including Diana Turbay, daughter of former president Júlio Turbay. Shortly thereafter, he kidnapped additional high-profile targets including the editor of *El Tiempo*, the country's leading daily, and two cousins of the president. Although the timing of the Turbay kidnapping suggests that Escobar was not specifically responding to the *Sometimiento* policy when he began his campaign (Pardo Rueda 1996, 272), the hostages proved to be very powerful bargaining chips in Escobar's negotiations with the government. By focusing on targets who were both well-known journalists and members of Bogotá's tight-knit elite, Escobar induced a media frenzy that captured the attention of the nation (García Márquez 1997). Indeed, another commission of prominent political figures, including former presidents Turbay and Alfonso López Michelson, soon opened a line of back-door negotiations with Escobar for the hostages' release; talks collapsed when Gaviria ruled out a political amnesty.

Nonetheless, as *Sometimiento* began to take shape—and particularly after Escobar's Medellín ally Fabio Ochoa turned himself in under the new policy in December 1990—Escobar increasingly saw the policy as a vehicle for a successful peace negotiation. Government officials insisted, and still insist, that this was not a negotiation at all, simply an offer of leniency in exchange for submission; by any reasonable standard, this stance was mere posturing (Leal Buitrago 2006). In reality, the nearly nine months between the Turbay kidnappings and the captives' release in late May 1991—overlapping with the Notables' failed efforts—saw an intense back-and-forth between the state and Escobar (through his intermediaries) over details related to the terms of his surrender and confinement (García Márquez 1997).

The terms Escobar insisted on are often portrayed as whimsical, most infamously the right to build his own luxurious prison, La Catedral, on his property overlooking Medellín, but they (mostly) reflected key strategic considerations. Under active attack by the Cali cartel, and anticipating police reprisal after his murder of hundreds of officers, he rightly feared for his life in a state prison. He also insisted that any agreement extend to crimes committed between the emission of the *Sometimiento* decrees and the moment of surrender. The government had initially refused to offer such extensions, fearing it would give cartels carte blanche to commit score-settling murders and then surrender. Escobar nonetheless insisted on the provision, acutely aware that until the moment of surrender he would be guilty of, at a minimum, armed hostage-taking. The government gave in, incorporating the provision in its fourth *Sometimiento* decree in January 1991.

Meanwhile, for reasons going beyond the drug war, a constitutional assembly had been convened. By early 1991, there were indications that the new constitution might address the issue of extradition. While some assembly members faced *plata o plomo* threats from the Extraditables, and non-violent bribe offers from Cali (Chepesiuk 2003, 135), many also genuinely opposed extradition, especially those hailing from the M-19 (which had demobilized and become a political party). This gave Escobar incentives to hold out, even though most of the technical details of his surrender had been worked out with the emission of the final *Sometimiento* decree. On June 19, the day the assembly approved a new constitution banning extradition, Escobar handed himself over to the authorities and took up residence at La Catedral. The hostages were freed, and the bombings abruptly stopped.

This abatement phase would prove ephemeral, a strange interlude in what might appear in hindsight as a continuous conflict from Lara Bonilla's death in 1984 to Pablo Escobar's in 1993. Escobar's year of captivity in a prison of his own design is now commonly dismissed as a farce (e.g., Bowden 2001), in part because of the sumptuous and permissive conditions in which he was discovered to be serving his sentence, in part because, as soon as the government did something about it, he handily escaped. The 498-day manhunt that ensued brought a return to the narco-terrorism that had raged from 1989 to 1991; to many it seemed that the episode left the state back at square one, or perhaps even worse off than before. The *Sometimiento* policy, in short, can be read as a total failure.

However, from the perspective of 1991, *Sometimiento* looked more like a surprising and resounding success. Originally conceived as a way to "pick off" lower-level traffickers from cartel organizations, *Sometimiento* had led first to the Ochoas' peaceful imprisonment, and now, it seemed, the resolution of an incredibly violent and disruptive conflict. Escobar's surrender, and the release of the elite hostages he was holding, came as a huge relief to the nation. Some 75 percent of the population supported some sort of "peace deal," the Gaviria administration claimed it as a major achievement, and even the US government cautiously approved (Pardo Rueda 1996, 269). Some, of course, took issue. "Can we honestly speak of traffickers submitting to the State? Would it not be more precise to speak of the State submitting to the will of the traffickers?" wrote the staunchly pro-extradition *El Espectador* (Cardona 2009). Public opinion, though, probably echoed the relief and approval expressed by Gabriel García Márquez: "The secret police of the whole world has been searching for this guy for ten years, and Gaviria captured him with a decree" (*El Tiempo* 1991).

García Márquez's pithy assessment is ingeniously ingenuous; after all, it was *because* of the international manhunt that Gaviria's decree worked. Conditionality requires both high levels of repression for violent trafficking and a credible reprieve for cartels that switch to nonviolence. Nonetheless, García Márquez nicely captures the striking and surprising turnaround in cartel behavior that policy shifts can occasion. Did the *Sometimiento* policy have a causal impact on the situation? Or was it simply the policy at hand when Escobar, for other reasons, decided to surrender?

The main evidence that *Sometimiento* itself played a profound, and not merely proximate, causal role in bringing about abatement is that so many previous attempts to reach such similar terms failed. Between 1984 and 1991, at least four distinct "negotiations" between members of the Medellín cartel and key political actors occurred (which the government denied were actual negotiations), and each of them collapsed. In all these episodes, the traffickers' demands were broadly similar: no extradition and some form of amnesty (*indulto*) for their outstanding crimes, precisely the terms of Escobar's surrender under *Sometimiento*. The reasons why the earlier negotiations failed are complex, but in each case the parties representing the state either could not or did not make credible offers to Escobar and his allies of reduced repression once they surrendered. The difficulty of making a promise that will remain binding after one party suffers a loss of relative power—what game theorists call the commitment problem—is an endemic problem in reaching negotiated settlements (Powell 2004; Walter 2009). *Sometimiento*, I argue, solved this commitment problem, allowing the state to effectively increase the conditionality of repression within cartels.

In May 1984, just a few days after Lara Bonilla's assassination, Escobar and several other Medellín cartel stalwarts met in Panama with López Michelson, apparently with the approval of President Betancur. This led to a subsequent meeting with several top officials of the Betancur administration, in which a six-page "peace" deal was drafted. In exchange for a promise of non-extradition and amnesty, the traffickers offered to return to Colombia, quit trafficking, turn over laboratories, planes, airstrips, and other infrastructure, and repatriate all of their capital.[18] Though Betancur's officials seem to have been enthusiastic about the offer they brought back, it was leaked to the press, causing a scandal among a public still shocked by Lara Bonilla's assassination. Betancur dismissed the offer out of hand and denied having known about or authorized any negotiation (Castillo 1987).

For much of 1988, another drawn-out attempt to negotiate occurred, this time through an intermediary on behalf of President Barco's secretary general Germán Montoya. These negotiations eventually stalled, and then collapsed when Galán was assassinated; worse, evidence including draft resolutions and recorded "narcodialogues" came to light, causing another public scandal. Former minister of defense Rafael Pardo's explanation of the scandal illuminates the difficulty of negotiating peace settlements, particularly in drug wars. "People could not understand that the same government that had led a fight which the country saw as crucial to its survival as a Nation, could at the same time pursue dialogues with the cartel leaders' spokespeople" (Pardo Rueda 1996, 201).

In early 1990, after Escobar took his first elite hostages, a group of prominent politicians known as *Los Notables* (The Notables),[19] again involving López Michelson and two other former presidents, opened a line of negotiation. The Notables suggested that the Extraditables take the opportunity not only to free the hostages but to negotiate a peaceful surrender. (It was at this point that Rafael Pardo began sketching out the idea behind *Sometimiento*.) Surprisingly, the Extraditables responded with an astonishing offer of self-rendition,

18 An urban legend has it that they also offered to pay off Colombia's external debt.
19 A similarly named Commission of Notables had previously formed to negotiate with insurgent groups.

acknowledging the "triumph of the State." Escobar even released a number of hostages and handed over several laboratories, all as a sign of goodwill in the run-up to a regional summit in Cartagena featuring US president George H. W. Bush. While press reports emphasized the non-official and hence tenuous nature of the proposed deal (e.g., *Semana* 1990), FBI documents assert that "Escobar and President Virgilio Barco had reached an agreement to call-off the 'war'"; again, Escobar's terms involved non-extradition and trial in Colombia, as well as retention of his family's wealth (FBI 1990, 2). Yet Barco, facing pressure *not* to negotiate with Escobar, in part because of his own declarations of war in the wake of the Galán assassination, neither publicly condoned the Notables efforts nor acknowledged any deal. He ramped up repression after the meeting with Bush, and by April 1990, the Extraditables were back at war.

The fourth and final attempt at negotiation occurred in late 1990 and early 1991, after Escobar had expanded his campaign of elite kidnappings. A reconstituted group of Notables formed and began a kind of shuttle diplomacy, urging Gaviria to offer Escobar the same amnesty that Barco had conceded to the M-19 guerrillas. Gaviria refused, and the Notables' back-door efforts at mediation went nowhere.

How was *Sometimiento* different? For its intellectual author Rafael Pardo, the key to *Sometimiento* was that it was a *presidential* policy. Gaviria took political ownership of *Sometimiento*, personally issuing the decrees that defined it, giving it a legitimacy that previous back-door negotiations lacked. Of course, back-door negotiating occurred with *Sometimiento* as well, but the policy's legalistic nature gave government officials a useful rhetorical device: Gaviria, Pardo, and others could insist that the policy offered no amnesty (something only available to guerrillas), but was simply a promise to treat with clemency any criminals who accepted "submission" (*El Tiempo* 1991). More importantly, the lengthy back-and-forth concerned important but secondary details, such as the logistics of Escobar's confinement, the status of extradition, and the question of crimes committed between the implementation of *Sometimiento* and any potential surrender. The core offer, forgiveness and leniency for past crimes in exchange for surrender and confession, was guaranteed by public, presidential decrees.

The *Sometimiento* policy thus largely solved the government's commitment problem. Escobar knew that by surrendering, he would become significantly weaker; the government could then renege on any cheap-talk promise not to prosecute or extradite him. *Sometimiento* bound the hands of the government on the first point, as the constitutional assembly's banning of extradition did for the second. And what did these devices allow the government to commit to? In a word, conditionality—a reprieve from state repression conditional on eschewing violence. Critically, this conditionality was *within* cartels, implicitly offering forgiveness for past violence conditional on nonviolence going forward. Once the state could credibly commit to this type of conditional repression, Escobar surrendered.

5.6 RECRUDESCENCE (1992–1993): CONDITIONALITY COLLAPSES

Claim 4: The rescinding of *Sometimiento* after Escobar's escape decreased conditionality within cartels, leading Escobar to re-engage in anti-state violence

Escobar's time in La Catedral is painted in idyllic terms by his brother and fellow inmate Roberto, who called it one of the happiest times in their lives (Escobar Gaviria 2000). The prison was lavish, and regularly hosted family, friends, business associates, prostitutes, and even the Colombian national football team, against which the imprisoned traffickers played scrimmages. Escobar is also thought to have regularly left La Catedral to attend events and meetings in Medellín. Initially, the government was content to turn a blind eye to Escobar's cheeky prison lifestyle, largely because this was also a peaceful time for the nation, which saw an abrupt drop in cartel-related violence of all types. Medellín's homicide rate had grown at an average rate of 30 percent from already high levels in 1987 to an unheard of 400 per 100,000 people in 1991 (nearly twice that of Mexico's Ciudad Juárez at its 2010 high-water mark); finally in 1992 it dropped by 15 percent, beginning a long-term downward trend.

The government's implicit tolerance of Escobar's lax conditions of confinement changed in 1992, when he brought two of his own lieutenants, Fernando Galeano and Gerardo Moncada, to La Catedral for questioning. Suspecting them of embezzling money from him, Escobar ended up murdering them on site. Their families made a public stir, accusing the state of bearing responsibility (Bowden 2001, 118). At the same time, the office of the Fiscal General (Attorney General)—a newly created post that had enormous autonomy of action—opened an investigation into the murders and the conditions at La Catedral in general. Under pressure, Gaviria and Pardo decided to address the situation.

Gaviria ordered Escobar to be transferred to a more secure facility. In a tragicomic episode, the army general and vice-minister who headed the government delegation sent to do the job were immediately taken hostage by Escobar's men within La Catedral, who it turned out were quite well armed. After a tense and failed telephone negotiation with leaders in Bogotá that dragged into the night, Escobar and several henchmen walked out of the prison and disappeared into the urban labyrinth of Medellín.

Immediately upon his escape from La Catedral, Escobar began making a series of increasingly less demanding offers for a second negotiated surrender under *Sometimiento*. At first, he seemed to take it for granted that such a new deal would be welcome. Indeed, Attorney General Gustavo de Greiff was sympathetic, opening channels of communication and even offering protection for his family members.[20] President Gaviria, however, completely ruled out any further negotiations. He was apparently deeply humiliated and angered, not only by the severely bungled attempt to relocate Escobar but by subsequent exposés that revealed Escobar's lush living conditions and near total freedom of action at La Catedral. Moreover, Gaviria faced strong pressure to abandon the *Sometimiento* approach from two key sectors that had been strongly opposed to the policy in the first place: the US embassy, and the Colombian police chiefs that Gaviria, and Barco before him, had empowered to combat Escobar. For both US and Colombian law enforcement, Escobar's surrender had prematurely squandered their shot at capturing or killing the capo; they had unsurprisingly characterized the *Sometimiento* policy that facilitated it as a cowardly and ill-advised capitulation to his abominable terror tactics. Escobar's escape now gave them the moral high ground. Gaviria, with unprecedented assistance from the United States (Bowden 2001), committed himself to an all-out unconditional crackdown.

For Escobar and his lieutenants, the degree of repression increased but conditionality evaporated. When some of them, including Escobar's brother, turned themselves in at his urging (he was afraid for their lives), they received harsh sentences (Bowden 2001, 306). Escobar himself went on the lam, apparently aborting several attempts to surrender for fear that he would be killed by police or extradited if he turned himself in without guarantees of his safety (Strong 1995, 282). His fears were not unfounded. The unstated but widely acknowledged objective of the Bloque de Búsqueda and the other state forces hunting him was to kill, not capture, Escobar (Bowden 2001). They may even have deliberately thwarted his surrender. According to Strong (1995, 281), "Whenever it was suspected that Escobar might hand himself in to the Envigado council, the town was invaded by the Search [Block]. The same was true around Igaüí's maximum security jail [where the Ochoas and Escobar's brother were being held], whose nearby streets were occupied upon the slightest rumour of his surrender there." For former Attorney General De Greiff—who was conducting shuttle diplomacy between Escobar and Gaviria to negotiate a second surrender—the fixation on killing Escobar came from the very top: "[Gavira] put up every obstacle [to surrender] possible. Gaviria wanted Escobar dead."[21]

Escobar responded to the situation, almost immediately, by reinstating his campaign of bombings and assassinations of police. These would continue, accompanied by threats and demands for negotiations, virtually until his death in December 1993. In one interesting gambit, Escobar announced the extinction of the Extraditables and the formation of a new guerrilla group, Antioquia Rebelde. The logic of this move is patent in the letter he sent to Attorney

[20] Interview, Bogotá, December 13, 2010.
[21] Interview, Bogotá, December 13, 2010.

General De Greiff announcing it. "As on previous occasions, I will always be open to dialogue and the search for peace, but from this day forward, the conditions of this dialogue will be the same as those employed with all rebel groups known as subversives or guerrillas." Unsurprisingly, this final attempt to win "political status" also failed. A later offer to surrender if his family was given asylum in the United States was rebuffed by the US embassy.

Escobar's killing of Galeano and Moncada had a second important consequence. Surely intended as a signal to other Medellín affiliates that betrayal or failure to pay taxes would be severely punished, it ended up inducing defection. In early 1993, a group of estranged Medellín cartel members, some connected to the Galeano and Moncada families, banded together to launch a counter-attack on Escobar, using his own nefarious tactics against him. This included not only car bombs and assassinations, but *narcomanta*-like messages left on corpses and public communiqués signed with the collective *nom de guerre Los Pepes*, an acronym for "Persons Persecuted by Pablo Escobar." Los Pepes met with and received financial support from the Cali cartel, who provided its own intelligence on Escobar as well as contacts with the government (Mollison and Nelson 2007, 223–224).

Los Pepes and their Cali backers were free to target Escobar, since conditionality *across* cartels remained high during this period; indeed, it may have increased. During the year-and-a-half-long manhunt that followed Escobar's escape, the government directed very little repressive action against Cali; Strong (1995, 283) reports some evidence of an explicit deal between Cali and the Colombian attorney general's office. There also appears to have been, at a minimum, active information sharing between police and Los Pepes. Officials denied Escobar's claims of active collaboration, but incidents like the October 1993 close-range grenade attack on his family, while under police protection in a supposedly undisclosed location, suggest Escobar was right (Strong 1995, 285). Months later, fear of another such attack led Escobar to park his family in Bogotá under state supervision; a traced phone call to them would lead to his downfall.

Evidence strongly suggests that Los Pepes came to collaborate directly with the Bloque de Búsqueda, though the precise nature of this collaboration remains controversial. Castaño and Don Berna, another Los Pepes founder who would go on to a long career as a paramilitary leader, were regularly seen in the Bloque de Búsqueda's headquarters (Mollison and Nelson 2007, 227). Los Pepes' attacks often seemed to have required both classified information and police complicity (e.g., *El Tiempo* 1993), while Escobar lieutenants under DEA and CIA surveillance were systematically left alone (Bowden 2001, 194). Escobar repeatedly made accusations of active collaboration; Hugo Martinez, the commander of the Bloque de Búsqueda, denies there was ever any direct collaboration, and some top officials dismissed the allegations as a ploy by Escobar. However, Attorney General De Greiff, based on reports from his field officers stationed within the Bloque de Búsqueda, became convinced Los Pepes were not only cooperating with the police but actually "calling the shots," and told US officials he had enough evidence to issue arrest warrants against Martinez and his lieutenants. Ultimately, President Gaviria intervened to ensure that Martinez was neither arrested or transferred.[22]

Whatever its degree of collaboration with the state, Los Pepes' brutal attacks were essential in wearing down Escobar's defenses over the course of 1993, and may well have been decisive on the final outcome. True, this period saw important increases in the Colombian state's repressive capacity, particularly through US financial and logistical support for the Bloque de Búsqueda. Yet by some accounts, state forces had become desperate before the entrance of Los Pepes (e.g., Bowden 2001, 220), and it is not unreasonable to wonder how long Gaviria would have held out before considering a second surrender negotiation, particularly with an election looming in 1994.

Perhaps most critical were Los Pepes' attempts to assassinate Escobar's family; more than twenty such attacks occurred in 1993 (García 1993). In November 1993, after Los Pepes blew up a Medellín apartment building where his wife and children were hiding, Escobar took a major risk by trying to move them to Germany. Detained at the border, they ended up back in Bogotá, under the protection of state agents from De Greiff's office. In late November 1993, De Greiff threatened to rescind state protection of Escobar's family, increasing the pressure on Escobar to surrender. During this period, Escobar made brief phone calls to his family, surely aware they were being traced, but during one conversation in early December he forgot himself and stayed on the line too long. The Bloque de Búsqueda was finally able to pinpoint his location, and Escobar was killed in a gunfight.

5.7 AFTERMATH (1994–): "MOWING THE LAWN" AS CONDITIONALITY

Conjecture: After the fall of Medellín and Cali, an effectively conditional approach to the smaller remaining cartels, rather than their fragmented nature, deterred further cartel–state conflict.

Cali reaped the benefits of Escobar's downfall, and the policies that led to it. Because repression was still conditional across cartels, the Rodríguez Orejuela brothers' "we don't kill judges, we buy them" (Lee 1994, 205) approach to corruption shielded them from virtually any meaningful repression. With

---

[22] Bowden (2001, 198–220) provides a detailed and fascinating account of conflicting US interests in this matter. US Ambassador Morris Busby pressured Gaviria to remove Martinez to avoid possible accusations of US support for terrorists, while the DEA lobbied against any action that would impede the Bloque de Búsqueda's efforts. Apparently, the DEA's arguments won the day.

Escobar out of the way, Cali monopolized cocaine exports, and soon launched what Miguel Rodríguez Orejuela called the "Champagne Project," offering huge donations to both major candidates of the 1994 presidential elections in exchange for a *Sometimiento*-type amnesty. This attempt to shift de jure policy without violence, an example of non-violent (if illicit) lobbying by a cartel (Chapter 3), was initially successful. Samper accepted the offer, and Rodríguez Orejuela declared "We've got ourselves a president" (Chepesiuk 2003, 190). However, when the donations came to light shortly after Samper won the election, they became politically toxic (Dugas 2001), leading Samper to launch a targeted crackdown that resulted in the capture of the Rodríguez Orejuelas in 1995 (Serrano Cadena 1999).[23] We can only guess whether a counter-factual *pax caleña*—a Colombian drug trade monopolized by the relatively pacific Cali cartel through systematic, non-violent corruption—would have proved sustainable.

In the void left behind by the fall of Cali (and Medellín before it), numerous smaller cartels arose. At the same time, the belligerents of Colombia's intensifying civil war became increasingly involved in drug production and trafficking. The remnants of Los Pepes went on to form the United Self-Defense Forces of Colombia (Autodefensas Unidas de Colombia, AUC), a paramilitary umbrella organization that, under the banner of counterinsurgency, terrorized and displaced huge numbers of civilians and deeply penetrated the state throughout the 1990s and early 2000s (Morales and La Rotta 2009), while never ceasing to traffic cocaine (Saab and Taylor 2009). The FARC, for its part, turned to protecting and taxing coca cultivation—then migrating en masse from Peru—as a source of funding in a post-Cold War world (Labrousse 2005). While these groups regularly clashed with state forces, the remaining "pure" drug cartels generally eschewed anti-state violence.

Many observers—including advisors to Mexico's President Calderón—attributed this reduced violence to the fragmentation of Colombia's cartels. However, fragmentation of Mexico's cartels under Calderón failed to curb anti-state violence, suggesting that this interpretation was incorrect. Conditionality of repression may provide a better explanation. With the Colombian state focused on fighting a three-way civil war, its anti-narcotics forces adopted a strategy described by the director of the DEA's Bogotá office as "mowing the lawn," i.e., targeting only the most prominent and troublesome traffickers for repression and extradition.[24] While this approach was likely motivated more by resource constraints than a strategic attempt to curtail violence, it nonetheless gives traffickers incentives to keep a low profile and avoid confrontation. In this view, it was conditionality, and not fragmentation of cartels per se,

[23] Ironically, the Rodríguez Orejuelas were eventually extradited to the United States in the mid-2000s, after the constitutional ban Escobar had fought for was removed.
[24] Interview, February 22, 2013.

that "tamed" Colombia's drug trade, at least with respect to cartel–state conflict.

5.8 CONCLUSION: POLITICS BY OTHER MEANS

History loves an outlaw and Escobar's exploits are, true to type, both terrifying and engaging. The prolonged frontal battle with the Colombian state he waged over the course of three presidencies is by far the longest and most brazen episode of violent lobbying by a criminal organization on record. With its limited number of protagonists, it also makes for a coherent and compelling narrative that has spawned a cottage industry of popular but well-researched accounts (e.g., Bowden 2001; Cañón 1994; García Márquez 1997; Morales and La Rotta 2009; Salamanca and Garzon 2003; Salazar 2001).[25] As a result, this aspect of the narco-violence period has received the most attention, and in many ways come to stand for the drug war as a whole. The idea that a drug trafficker could go, as DEA Bogotá station chief Jay Bergman puts it, "toe-to-toe with the state"[26] is indeed chilling, so it is perhaps understandable that much of the analytic focus has been on explaining why Escobar fought such an overt war, and whether it was an ex-ante mistake. I return to these questions below.

This standard reading, however, risks missing part of the story: cartel–state conflict in Colombia was not driven exclusively, and perhaps not even primarily, by the logic of violent lobbying. Violent corruption—the *plata o plomo* strategy that Escobar made infamous—pre-dates violent lobbying and narco-terrorism by at least eight years, if we take Escobar's 1976 arrest by and subsequent murder of DAS agents as the earliest observation. If I am correct that a "coerced peace" scenario held prior to that failed bribe negotiation, violent corruption started even earlier, even if anti-state violence remained off the equilibrium path.

Moreover, Escobar's assassination of Lara Bonilla, in some sense the opening shot of his war on the Colombian state, is better thought of as a case of violent corruption—the following through on a *plata o plomo* threat—than of violent lobbying, since Escobar had yet to make any demands for de jure policy change. Indeed, Escobar was a member of Congress, and extradition was not in effect. He was largely in agreement with the de jure policies of the day. Lara Bonilla's campaign amounted to an increase (from nearly zero) in the enforcement of a policy against "hot money," and it was this enforcement which Escobar sought to influence, first through bribery, and when Lara Bonilla refused to be bought, through violence.

---

[25] The compelling nature of the narrative comes clear in the subtitle of Bowden (2001), *Killing Pablo: The Hunt for the Richest, Most Powerful Criminal in History*, as well as a blurb from the back cover: "10 times better than any fictional crime story."
[26] Interview, February 22, 2013.

Disentangling the logics of violent lobbying and violent corruption can help make sense of the microdynamics of drug conflict. Though not mutually exclusive (Escobar clearly engaged in both), these logics of violence come into play under different conditions and predict different empirical patterns of violence. From 1984 onward, Escobar was a fugitive from justice, whose overriding concern was to avoid being killed or extradited. At times, he found it worthwhile to put pressure directly on leaders to affect the formulation of de jure policy—in particular, to knock down extradition and to push for some form of amnesty or pardon. Escobar experimented with different forms of violence to achieve maximum pressure, eventually shifting from assassinations and car bombs to elite kidnappings. The intensity of these terror tactics also varied over time, following the intricate rhythms of sub rosa negotiation over the status of extradition and, eventually, his surrender under *Sometimiento*. Sometimes Escobar would up the ante, in order to force the state back to the bargaining table; sometimes, when the state seemed to be cooperating or once he was ensconced in La Catedral, Escobar stood to gain little or nothing from additional leader-directed violence, and terror tactics would abate.

Lulls in violent lobbying did not mean that Escobar had no use for violence in general: the logic of violent corruption was still operative. Escobar continued to devote significant resources to maintaining an enormous network of corrupt officials and informants, as well as a private army of *sicarios* (assassins) culled from the slums of Medellín. Moreover, and crucially, the violence followed the pattern predicted by the theory of violent corruption modeled in Chapter 4: state crackdowns led to an increase in violence against enforcers. In particular, the increase in repressive capacity in the judicial sector, through the appointment of new *fiscales* and the advent of *jueces sin rostro*, may have disrupted a coerced peace among judges hitherto too frightened to take on Escobar, thus contributing to the dozens of assassinations of judicial officials in the escalation phase.

The model of violent lobbying, in turn, helps explain why Escobar engaged in spectacular assassinations and bombings even though he surely knew that these brazen attacks would result in further crackdowns. That is, he must have known that repression would be at least in some sense conditional; why did this not deter him? One reason is that this form of conditionality offered no reprieve for past crimes; another is that the government may have already been close to maxing out repression. A third possibility, however, is that Escobar anticipated that these crackdowns, conditional or not, were, in the language I developed in Part I, *susceptible* to violent lobbying. Indeed, a more sophisticated, longer-term view—based on the Colombian government's actual dealings with insurgent guerilla groups—may have *encouraged* Escobar to fight on.

Colombian scholar Andrés López Restrepo points out that cartel–state conflict began in a period in which President Betancur was making very generous offers of amnesty to violent guerrilla groups in hopes of a settlement. The government justified these offers by claiming that the guerrillas' violence had been political, ultimately in the service of the nation, and hence pardonable. Yet only a few years earlier the state had been actively trying to destroy these groups at all costs. To Escobar and his colleagues, the lesson was simple: "If the government had defeated the guerillas, it would not have had to recognize them as a political cause. The traffickers saw the possibility to take advantage of the situation: if the state could not defeat them, then it would recognize them as a political cause and negotiate their incorporation into legality" (López Restrepo 2006, 203).

Susceptibility, or the perception of susceptibility, creates incentives for violent lobbying, since however hard the state cracks down in the short run, additional fighting by the cartel will eventually pressure the state into *reducing* repression. Interestingly, Escobar seemed to hold to this belief even as the state escalated repression throughout the 1980s in response to his campaign. Thus even when President Barco cracked down hard in the immediate aftermath of Galán's assassination in 1988, Escobar continued to escalate, betting that he could win the war of attrition with the state. The terms of his voluntary submission in 1991—while he never received full amnesty, the state certainly gave in on many of his other demands—suggest he was right.

6

Rio de Janeiro

Conditionality, One Favela at a Time

In Rio de Janeiro, the 1980s' cocaine boom coincided with the advent of a new form of organized crime—the prison-based Comando Vermelho (CV) drug syndicate and its rivals—to produce unusually concentrated and territorialized retail markets based in the city's numerous favelas (slums). Police institutions built during authoritarian rule delivered both brutal repression and rampant corruption. The result was an increasingly violent but resilient system of illicit rent extraction and escalating repression, punctuated by a handful of locally successful policy experiments. Starting in 2008, a new strategy, Pacification, significantly altered this dynamic, vastly reducing cartel–state conflict. I make three key claims: (1) Between democratization (1983) and Pacification (2008), the degree of repression varied but trended upward, while conditionality remained low. Syndicates responded to unconditional crackdowns with violent, "fight-and-bribe" strategies. (2) The GPAE policing program (2000–2001) raised conditionality locally, leading affected traffickers to eschew anti-state violence until the program eroded and collapsed. (3) The initial implementation of the Pacification strategy (2008–2012) significantly increased the conditionality of repression at a city-wide scale, leading cartels to eschew anti-state violence. I conjecture that Pacification's initial success and rapid expansion led to an erosion of effective conditionality, contributing to a resurgence of violence since 2013. I discuss the reform processes by which GPAE and Pacification were implemented and the difficulties of sustaining them. I also conjecture that Rio's numbers racket (1940s–1980s) was kept relatively peaceful through a moderately conditional approach.

6.1 OVERVIEW

Rio de Janeiro is known as "the marvelous city" for many reasons, including its natural beauty and imperial history, but Rio would not be Rio—socially,

158

culturally, or politically—without its *favelas*.[1] Over the last hundred years, these squatter communities have spread across rainforested hillsides and muddy mangroves, sprouted amid the high-rises of wealthy beach-front neighborhoods, and filled in vast interior tracts far from the city center. The favelas are the cradle of *carioca*[2] culture—samba, carnaval, and now *baile funk*—and home to hundreds of thousands of workers who came to Rio from rural Brazil to build much of the formal city we see today. The favelas are also, tragically, the site of an unusually violent, territorialized, and resilient urban armed conflict.

For more than a generation, most of Rio's favelas have been under the militarized dominion of prison-based drug syndicates.[3] Nowhere else in Brazil, or in much of the world for that matter, is the retail drug trade so concentrated and territorialized, and nowhere else have retail drug syndicates—above all the Comando Vermelho (CV)—systematically engaged the state in armed confrontation for so long.[4] The capacity to organize the retail drug trade of an entire metropolis makes the CV more akin in firepower and manpower to cartels involved in international smuggling than typical urban drug gangs. From its beginnings, the CV has responded to state repression with an armed, confrontational stance; as policing grew more brutal and corrupt, a quarter-century of escalating cartel–state conflict set in. So entrenched was the violence that envoys from Colombia's Cali cartel, sent to Rio in the 1990s

[1] Like New York, Rio de Janeiro is a city, a metropolitan area, and a state (though with a far smaller "upstate" or *interior*). For simplicity, and to avoid confusion between two senses of the word "state," I generally refer to all three as "Rio." For the most part I am referring to the city, which is the epicenter of cartel–state conflict. However, since policing and prisons are organized at the state level, and controlled by governors, much of the political and policy analysis actually refers to state-level data or decisions. Meanwhile, it should be borne in mind that a significant and growing share of cartel–state clashes occur in the surrounding municipalities of Greater Rio, as well as the much smaller cities of Rio state's *interior*.

[2] *Carioca* is the adjective for someone or something from Rio de Janeiro.

[3] There is no good English term for Rio's drug-trafficking organizations. In Portuguese, they are called *facções criminosas* (criminal factions), reflecting their origin as rival gangs in prison. Their names often include "Command" as in Comando Vermelho (Red Command), but they are not referred to collectively as *comandos*. In any case, neither "factions" nor "commands" are accurate or useful terms in English. Analytically, "cartel" is no less accurate a description of Rio's DTOs than Mexico's or Colombia's, but Rio's DTOs are neither named nor referred to as cartels, so the word sounds awkward when used in isolation. Thus, I use "prison-based syndicates" or simply "syndicates" when discussing Rio's DTOs in isolation, as in this chapter, and "cartel" when considering them together with Mexican and Colombian DTOs.

[4] São Paulo's criminal underworld underwent a major change from 2000 onwards as the Primeiro Comando da Capital (PCC) prison gang—itself inspired by and allied with Rio's Comando Vermelho—achieved hegemony inside the prison system and eventually throughout the urban periphery (Denyer Willis 2015). Nonetheless, the PCC has not established territorial dominion or local monopolies over retail drug trafficking, focusing instead on wholesale and consignment to a broad network of affiliates.

to explore ways to normalize and streamline retail distribution for the city's booming cocaine market, quickly abandoned their efforts (Soares 2011).

Besides its uniquely urban, retail-based nature, Rio's militarized drug war stands out in comparative perspective as providing the clearest observations of the dynamics of violent corruption. While Pablo Escobar is credited with the phrase *"plata o plomo"* ("the bribe or the bullet"), it is often difficult to distinguish empirically between his intimidation of police and judicial enforcers from his larger terrorist campaign of violent lobbying, which included political assassinations and open contracts on all police officers. In Rio, violent lobbying is not only rarer, but almost always takes place *outside* the favela, on the *asfalto* ("asphalt," the formal part of the city), where violence is more likely to create political costs to leaders. In contrast, the violent dynamics of the *arrego* (arrangement)—the weekly or monthly bribe paid by incumbent syndicates to local police battalions in exchange for non-enforcement—take place inside, on the traffickers' turf, an open secret of favela life.

On good days, the police are nowhere to be seen and law-abiding residents can go about their business as teenage traffickers patrol with automatic rifles and openly sell packets of cocaine and pot from street corners and narrow alleys. On bad days, police enter en masse to capture or kill traffickers who, unlike retail traffickers throughout the world, usually fight back. Shootouts go on for hours or even days—residents lock themselves inside to avoid stray bullets, knowing that anyone killed by police will be automatically registered as an "armed opposer"—and end only when the police withdraw, often carrying bodies. The police have superior firepower and training, but the favelas' defensive advantages—high ground, byzantine streets and alleys, and cooperative if cowed residents—mean traffickers rarely have to fully retreat. Hundreds of such clashes per year generate civil-war levels of casualties (including significant police losses), as well as enormous seizures of drugs and weapons, but have neither permanently dislodged traffickers nor deterred them from trafficking. This repeated mutual punishment may seem pointless, but my model of violent corruption shows how it is part of an equilibrium, a costly but unavoidable counterpart to the successful bribe negotiations that allow for the "good" days.

Rio's nexus of drug trafficking and regularized police corruption can be understood as a stable "system of illicit rent extraction," occupying a theoretical middle ground between the top-down state-sponsored protection racket organized by the PRI in Mexico (roughly 1950–1990) and the fragmented, idiosyncratic corruption seen in Colombia and post-democratization Mexico. Rio's system lacks the centralized political control exerted by the PRI, and perhaps as a result fails to deter trafficker violence. Yet it has proven remarkably stable, a chilling demonstration of how violent corruption and militarized drug war more broadly can become permanent fixtures of the sociopolitical landscape. I consider some of the implications for state formation and other bodies of theory in Chapter 11.

Finally, Rio stands out for its clear variation in both dimensions—degree and conditionality—of state repressive policy. For some twenty-five years, conditionality remained low while the degree of repression trended upward but oscillated in time to a political pendulum. In line with my model of violent corruption, cartels adopted fight-and-bribe strategies, with periods of greater repression producing more clashes. Then, in 2008, the Pacification strategy—the most obviously conditional policy considered in this study—fundamentally reoriented repressive tactics. As a result, cartels abruptly switched to non-violent hiding strategies, and clashes plummeted. Pacification replicated on a city-wide scale the results of a previous conditional pilot program that virtually eliminated cartel–state violence in a single favela complex, before succumbing to political pressure and collapsing. Tragically, Pacification—whose formulators explicitly sought to avoid the mistakes of previous reform efforts—also began to suffer setbacks in 2013, for similar reasons, with cartel–state violence rising for the first time since 2007. While disheartening, conditionality's ups and downs in Rio provide key evidence of its effect on cartel violence, and a rich opportunity to explore why conditional approaches are difficult to implement and sustain.

6.1.1 Trajectory and Core Claims

Rio's "peaceful prelude" is peaceful only in comparison with what followed. Brazil's military dictatorship (1964–1985), engaged in a dirty war against subversives and militants, built enduring police institutions that still bear the stamp of authoritarian design. The investigative Civil Police relied principally on torture and confession rather than evidence collection, while the "ostensive" (i.e., patrolling) Military Police contained and repressed popular protest. When the leftist threat abated from the mid-1970s on, state repression shifted toward "protecting" the middle class by containing and often brutalizing the growing favela population, who were often forcibly relocated to distant government housing projects. Meanwhile, organized crime, dominated by the *jogo do bicho* (a numbers racket), was managed through a system of regularized bribery and illicit rent extraction that largely deterred anti-state violence and may have helped reduce turf war over time.

This peaceful status quo was upset by the same early 1980s' cocaine boom that birthed Colombia's cartels, interacting in Rio with a powerful new form of prison-based criminal organization. Drug retailing, especially cocaine, soon overtook the numbers racket as the city's primary illicit economy. Sporadic turf wars among neighborhood-level trafficking outfits made headlines (Zaluar 1985), but they rarely engaged state forces. Meanwhile, the Comando Vermelho, a prison gang spawned in the dungeons of the military dictatorship—where it gleaned techniques of cooperation and organization from jailed leftist militants—began expanding beyond the prison walls to establish a criminal network on the streets. The CV initially focused on property

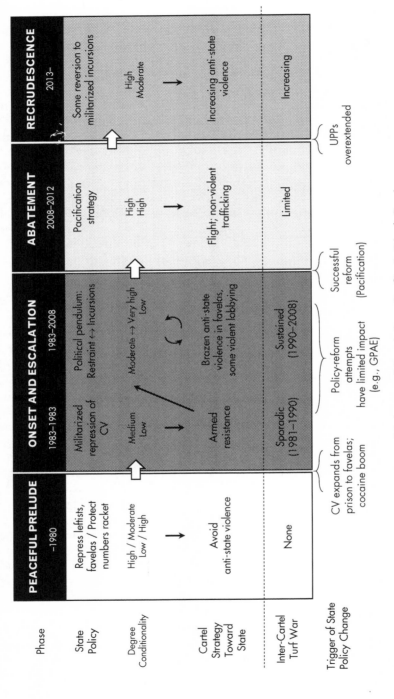

FIGURE 6.1. Trajectory of Cartel–State Conflict in Rio de Janeiro.

162

crime, but soon came to dominate the lucrative retail drug markets of Rio's favelas. Hegemony was short-lived, however; by 1990 several rival syndicates, some born out of schisms within the CV, had arisen, and inter-cartel turf war for favela territory set in.

From its inception, the CV responded to Rio's authoritarian, militarized police repression with armed resistance, even before the outbreak of sustained inter-cartel turf war. The state's response followed a post-democratization (1983) political pendulum: progressive governors attempted to restrain authoritarian policing practices and protect favela residents' rights, while hardliners promised to restore order and exterminate the CV and its rivals through militarized incursions into the favelas. Overall, the degree of repression rose, with elite police corps of highly trained "killing machines" in armored vehicles coming online in the early 2000s. Yet over three decades of escalation, the syndicates neither disappeared nor adopted non-violent strategies toward the state. Rather, they continued to fight back (and fight each other), building military arsenals and standing armies of child "soldiers" (Dowdney 2003),[5] and adopting a combination of homespun guerilla and medieval siege tactics.

To observers of Rio's drug war in the mid-2000s, including the author at the outset of this study, two seemingly contradictory characteristics stood out: the extremity of the violence, and the stability of the system that produced it. From 1993 to 2007, police killed more than 10,000 civilians in thousands of armed confrontations, and federal forces intervened at least seven times. Yet as 2007 drew to a close, the majority of the city's favelas were still dominated by the CV and its rivals.[6] Corruption was a constant presence: the paradoxical flip-side of brutally violent policing in the favela is the regularized bribing of local police battalions through the *arrego*. Equally entrenched was syndicates' social control within the communities they dominated, which saw their political aspirations and organizations co-opted by traffickers. It is not only the CV and its rivals but an entire sociopolitical dynamic (including, many believe, the flow

---

[5] Dowdney's work not only shed invaluable light on the use of children in Rio's drug trade, but also helpfully distinguished the phenomenon he called Children in Organized Armed Violence (COAV), often overshadowed by international concern for child soldiers in "official" civil wars and armed conflicts. The similarities and important differences in the drivers and consequences of COAV vs. child soldiers (Dowdney 2005) constitute one manifestation of the larger distinction between civil and criminal war highlighted in Chapter 2.

[6] The only significant inroads into syndicate territory were being made not by the state but rather the violent, police-linked paramilitary groups known as *milícias*. The *milícias* have expanded rapidly since 2004, and now may collectively control as much or more territory than the CV. Their expansion suffered a setback in 2008, after a *milícia* group tortured a group of journalists triggering a congressional investigation (Freixo 2008) and several high-profile arrests, but they lost almost no territory. Today, the *milícias* remain a grave threat, principally because of their far greater power to penetrate the political system, an issue I have explored in co-authored work (Hidalgo and Lessing 2014) and discuss briefly in Chapter 11. Ignacio Cano's work provides an excellent empirical overview (Cano and Iooty, 2008) and an analysis of the effects of anti-*milícia* crackdowns on *milícia* behavior (Cano and Duarte, 2012).

of drug money into higher echelons of government) that proved surprisingly resilient, a violent yet stable system for producing, extracting, and distributing illicit rents while subcontracting governance in the urban periphery to criminal groups.

Another regular feature of this long escalatory phase were attempts to reform policing policy. These too followed Rio's political pendulum, producing a series of well-meaning pilot experiments in community policing that rarely outlived a single governor's term. The most successful was GPAE,[7] which drastically curbed violence in a complex of smaller favelas from 2000 to 2002 and was extended to several larger favelas thereafter. However, a lack of support within the police and heavy criticism from elected officials as a "pact with the traffickers" undermined the program: leading to a reversion to traditional police practice, the resurgence of cartel–state conflict, and ultimately the project's demise. In 2007, police killed 1,330 civilians in armed confrontations, a record; escalation seemed to know no end.

Then a felicitous surprise occurred. Starting in 2008, the state government began experimenting with a new policy—Pacification—using overwhelming force to first militarily occupy a favela, then implant a permanent proximity-policing unit (Unidade de Policia Pacificadora, UPP) there to maintain state control and provide social order.[8] Critically, Pacification also shifted the stated goal of policing from eradicating the drug trade to eliminating the armed presence of traffickers and associated violence. Pacification succeeded beyond anyone's expectations. Over the next five years, the state reclaimed enormous amounts of favela territory while police killings of "armed opposers" fell by nearly two-thirds. Compared to the intense escalation of the previous decade, and the larger conflict stretching back a generation, this "abatement" phase was an astonishing and radical reversal.

Beginning in 2013, Pacification stalled and cartel–state conflict entered a disheartening "recrudescence" phase. Recruitment and training of new UPP units could not keep pace with the program's expansion, so traditional police were sometimes used. Several UPP commanders were sacked for corruption, police brutality, or both, eroding favela residents' hard-earned trust. Traffickers began to re-engage militarily, attacking UPPs in larger favelas; deaths from cartel–state confrontations—in sharp decline from 2008 to 2012—rose by 40 percent in 2014. Such incidents of violence and corruption fed public disenchantment and demands for a return to traditionally aggressive policing. As of this writing, Pacification is in limbo; expansion has stopped, and a return to *status quo ante* policing in the sprawling Maré complex could prove a tragic bellwether of the policy's impending collapse.

---

[7] GPAE stands for Grupamento de Policiamento em Áreas Especiais, or Policing in Special Areas Unit.

[8] Usually, police battalions are located outside the favela.

"Tragic" because, as this chapter argues, Pacification succeeded not only in raising conditionality at scale but also, and as a result, in significantly curtailing cartel–state violence in Rio after decades of escalatory stalemate. The following section considers this claim and my larger argument—that changes in conditionality of repression are the key driver of variation in cartel–state conflict—against alternative perspectives, particularly ones emphasizing state efforts to win the "hearts and minds" of favela residents. I then present the chronology of the case, organized by phases, making the following core claims as they arise:

Conjecture: A de facto conditional approach toward Rio's numbers racket (1940s–1980s) successfully deterred anti-state violence by its leaders, and may have contributed to a reduction in fighting among them.

Claim 1: Between democratization (1983) and Pacification (2008), the degree of repression varied but trended upward, while conditionality remained low. Syndicates responded to unconditional crackdowns with violent, fight-and-bribe strategies.

Claim 2: The GPAE policing program (2000–2001) raised conditionality locally, leading affected traffickers to eschew anti-state violence until the program eroded and collapsed.

Claim 3: The initial implementation of the Pacification strategy (2008–2012) significantly increased the conditionality of repression at a city-wide scale, leading cartels to eschew anti-state violence.

Conjecture: Since 2013, the effective conditionality of repression under Pacification has eroded, leading cartels to reengage in anti-state violence.

These claims correspond roughly to the vertical arrows in Figure 6.1. The horizontal arrows represent shifts in state policy, triggered by a variety of proximate causes; I zoom in on the processes by which conditional reforms were implemented, first locally in the case of GPAE, then at a city- and state-wide scale with Pacification. I consider these processes of reform in comparative perspective in Part III.

6.2 STATE POLICY AS DRIVER OF CARTEL–STATE CONFLICT AND ALTERNATIVE EXPLANATIONS

Common explanations of cartel–state conflict during Rio's long escalation phase invoke structural factors like Rio's mountainous geography, endemic police corruption, economic decadence, and the unique prison-based structure of its syndicates. While these factors certainly constitute permissive conditions, none of them changed quickly enough to explain the rapid abatement in cartel–state conflict seen after 2008. The contemporaneous rollout of the Pacification strategy, however, was abrupt and significant; the timing alone is prima facie evidence that abatement was driven primarily by a shift in state policy. Case details further strengthen this claim: for example, two major militarized invasions of the CV's main favela stronghold—one just prior to the advent of the Pacification approach and another two years into its implementation—saw traffickers respond with opposite strategies.

While few observers would object to the claim that these sharp changes in cartel–state dynamics were due to Pacification, there is disagreement over the mechanism. For many, including US officials, Pacification "closely resembles U.S. counterinsurgency doctrine in Afghanistan and Iraq"; they locate the program's success in its "clear and hold approach" (Bailly 2011), pushing criminal elements out of favelas, then providing public goods and social programs for residents to win hearts and minds (Gloudemans 2010; Stahlberg 2011). This, in my view, attributes too much agency to favela residents, and too little to the syndicates.

Pacification worked, I argue, because of the incentives it created for syndicates to avoid violence; it was less Baghdad's counterinsurgency than Boston's Ceasefire; less Helmand than Hamsterdam.[9] I present qualitative evidence for this specific claim in the discussion to come, but the debate over mechanism speaks to a larger theoretical concern over the sociological context of drug war worth addressing here. Downplaying the role of Rio's more than one million favela residents may strike some readers as a grave oversight, particularly in light of recent work within conflict studies on civilian agency in shaping rebel governance (e.g., Arjona 2016; Mampilly 2011). As I make clear in the remainder of this section, my approach is not meant to discount civilians' struggles and suffering, or deny the importance of the syndicates' provision of governance to them, but rather focus attention on less static factors more likely to explain observed variation in cartel–state conflict.

Whereas several bodies of scholarship view Rio's drug war through the lens of insurgency, with significant analytic emphasis on the role of the civilian population, I draw on a tradition that sees Rio's drug markets as a system for illicit rent extraction (Misse 1997, 2003) to argue that cartel–state conflict is largely driven by the logic of violent corruption. As in my model, I focus on three principal actors: syndicates, police, and political leaders. Favela residents play important roles in the overall dynamic, as consumers, coerced collaborators, and recruits; there is no doubt that the CV provides a form of governance, and surely gets much in return. This is a fascinating relationship, but, empirically, a largely stable one, and hence unlikely to explain sharp variation in cartel–state conflict. In Rio, residents have rarely been in a position to challenge syndicate rule, instead seeing their civil organizations

9 Operation Ceasefire was a conditional policy that dramatically reduced gang violence in Boston and influenced policymakers in both Rio and Mexico; I include it in the comparative analysis of policymaking in Part III. Hamsterdam, in *The Wire*'s fictionalized portrait of Baltimore's drug trade, was a policy experiment instituted by a rogue police captain, offering non-repression in exchange for non-violent trafficking and consumption. This fictional policy is clearly conditional, and as with many real-world conditional policies, was both effective in reducing violence and so politically toxic that it quickly collapsed.

systematically coopted by traffickers (e.g., Arias 2006; Leeds 1996; McCann 2013) and used for their own gain (Arias 2013). This perhaps explains why, in residents' own accounts, the CV's early "defender-of-the-people" ethos quickly gave way to violent and often arbitrary rule (Dowdney 2003). For at least a generation, CV capos have not seemed much concerned with winning hearts and minds. Favela residents, like other disadvantaged groups caught between traffickers and state forces, not only bear the brunt of drug-war violence but are severely lacking in avenues of meaningful resistance and contestation.

My approach contrasts with a "traffickers-as-insurgents" theme that is common to several relevant literatures. A strong line of Brazilianist scholarship sees the violence as the fruit of the dictatorship's original sins, and the democratic state's war against favela-ensconced syndicates a disturbing and perhaps deliberate translation of the authoritarian right's struggle against an "enemy within" from the realm of politics (leftist insurgents) to economics (urban poor), allowing it to live on in the face of democratization (e.g., Batista 2003; Coimbra 2001; Zaluar 1985) and even thrive under the post-Cold War, pro-market "consensus" (Wacquant 2003). Interestingly, Brazil's reactionary right makes no bones about advocating highly repressive and authoritarian measures against drug syndicates and the areas they dominate; it simply blames the leftist insurgents of yesterday for creating the syndicates and the human-rights advocates of today as traitorous defenders of criminals (de Carvalho 1994). Meanwhile, security scholars have focused on the syndicates' use of guerrilla tactics; their establishment of territorial dominion over the favelas; their provision of social order and other public goods to marginalized residents at the price of silence and complicity; their recruitment from the local population; their use of the favelas as a physical base from which to occasionally launch invasions of rival territory, strikes against state forces, or terrorist attacks against the civilian population; and their sustained defiance in the face of militarized and brutal state repression. These scholars see Rio's drug war as a prime example of "criminal insurgency" (Burgoyne 2012; Killebrew 2011; Sullivan 2000), "criminal urban guerrillas" (Pinheiro 2009), and other novel subtypes.

These perspectives have important merits. They draw attention to the plight of residents, and address fundamental questions of consolidating the democratic rule of law in post-authoritarian Brazil (Pinheiro 1997), and third-wave democracies more generally (O'Donnell 1993). They also speak to the undeniable fact that the CV's armed resistance to state power has proven more resilient than probably any other group in Brazil's history. This fact was not lost on the CV's founders, who often invoked ideological language in the syndicate's early days:

> We conquered something the guerrillas never did: the support of the poor. I go to the favelas and I see kids involved, smoking and selling pot. In the future,

they will be 3 million adolescents, who will kill [the police] on the corners. Have you thought what it will mean to have 3 million adolescents and 10 million unemployed with guns?[10]

(Quoted in Amorim 1993, 255)

The revolution, however, never came; the CV's ideological shine quickly wore off while its confrontational stance toward the state abided. The traffickers-as-insurgents lens generally fails to provide a compelling explanation for this fact. This is the result, I would argue, of two analytic oversights: first, a tendency to reify the state as a unitary actor, treating rampant police corruption as (at best) an afterthought; second, a failure to take seriously the economics of the drug trade and the resulting incentives facing the syndicates.[11]

An alternative approach, pioneered by sociologist Michel Misse (1997; 2003), views Rio's traffickers less as crypto-Maoist insurgents swimming in a sea of favela residents than as illicit economic actors within a system of state-provided protection. Taking a very different historical point of departure, Misse notes that for decades prior to the rise of Rio's drug trade, a territorialized system of bribery peacefully governed the city's numbers racket (1997, 16). This system was largely replicated for the drug trade when it overtook the numbers racket as the city's primary illicit activity; the puzzle is why the former became violent when the latter did not. In Misse's framework, increased police repression of markets for illicit goods generates concomitant growth in shadow markets for "political goods" (*mercadorias políticas*) (Misse 1997, 11–16)—roughly speaking, bribes. Though Misse does not have explicit theoretical predictions of when corruption is likely to turn violent, he was a pioneer in arguing that the two were related.

My formal model of bribe negotiation, and the resulting claim that violent corruption is a key driver of cartel–state conflict, flow directly from this analytic approach. To be sure, the combination of a marginalized favela population with an incredibly violent and unaccountable police apparatus still plays an important role. However, where others focus on normative aspects and consequences for the democratic rule of law (e.g., Ahnen 2007; Caldeira 2002; Pinheiro 2000), my analysis is instrumental and strategic, highlighting the immense extortionary power that a well-equipped, unaccountable, and thoroughly corrupt police force wields over traffickers. This yields an intuitive explanation for drug syndicates' startling consistency in opting for confrontation in the face of overwhelming losses inflicted by police over the decades. Favela-bound, without legal or social protection against militarized police forces bent on extorting away their profits, traffickers adopt a fight-and-bribe strategy to

10   Author's translation.
11   The "criminal insurgency" literature does emphasize economic aspects; however, as I have argued in Chapter 2, by stretching the concept of insurgency to include cases where armed groups have no revolutionary or secessionist intent, it fails to fully appreciate the very different logics driving cartels' decisions to confront the state.

Rio de Janeiro 169

reduce the burden of bribe payments. Syndicates' willingness to bear the costs of the resulting confrontations makes more sense when understood as a means of escaping coerced wage-slavery.

These two analytic perspectives are not mutually exclusive. Rio's police really are an institutional legacy of the dictatorship; they are instilled with a repressive "warrior ethos," and all too prone to see favela residents as criminals and criminals as "enemies" to be destroyed through frontal combat. Sustained abuse of marginalized population by state forces helps armed groups win their allegiance; this is just as true for Rio's syndicates as it is for insurgent groups. In the poignant commentary of a favela resident in the 1997 documentary *News From a Private War*: "The good thing about the armed presence of the traffickers is that the police are now afraid to come in here and mistreat us." Even once the CV's "defender of the community" rhetoric began to ring hollow as local *crias* (syndicate members native to the favela where they work) were replaced by more violent outsiders in the 1990s (Dowdney 2003), it continued to provide basic social order in the favelas, which generally enjoyed low rates of property crime.

None of this, however, is incompatible with the logic of violent corruption. The compliance of favela residents, however much coerced, is surely valuable to the syndicates, contributing to the "territoriality" of Rio's drug trade and thus making fighting attractive (in part) on purely defensive grounds. Low police accountability and the strong warrior ethos, meanwhile, raise the extortionary power of the police by increasing the pain they can credibly threaten to inflict on cartels if a bribe agreement is not reached. Moreover, my model predicts that corrupt cops' bargaining position also improves the greater their taste for physical confrontation.[12] Going beyond the model, even if "warrior" cops are themselves not corrupt, more corrupt elements within the police probably benefit from their existence, if they can be counted on to fight ferociously if and when no bribe deal is struck.

On the other hand, over time and in general equilibrium, the warrior ethos has also helped syndicates by creating a supply of potential recruits who feel, in their words, "*revolta*" (Dowdney 2003; Zaluar 1985)—a roiling animus—toward the police. My model assumes that cartels' threats of violence are credible; in the real world, syndicate bosses must ensure that their foot soldiers will actually fire on police. Since this often constitutes suicide, it helps if doing so feels like a justified act of revenge.

In sum, my approach glosses over the rich sociology of favela life in order to focus on the strategic interaction between syndicates and police, and the effect of repressive policy on it. To be sure, building a police force that treats favela residents as citizens is of utmost normative importance; providing real public security, formal property rights, and basic infrastructure would

---

[12] In the model, the parameter φ captures police "distaste" for violence, so a warrior ethos would correspond to a lower φ and a higher equilibrium bribe price.

quite simply transform the lives of favela communities. Such a transformation could empower residents and increase their trust in police and the state more generally, potentially making it harder for syndicates to re-establish armed control. But Pacification did not accomplish this; after decades of police brutality, trust in police remained elusive (Cano 2012). The sharp variation in cartel–state conflict brought about by the widespread adoption of the Pacification strategy and its more recent erosion is most plausibly explained by its direct impact on cartels' incentives.

6.3 PEACEFUL PRELUDE (–1980): AUTHORITARIAN ROOTS OF RIO'S DRUG WAR

Though Brazil's period of military dictatorship (1964–1985) was free from cartel–state conflict (and cartels for that matter), it was a tumultuous time in the history of Rio and Brazil in general. It was also a formative period for many of the eventual protagonists and dynamics of Rio's drug war: a police apparatus designed by the junta for maximal repression and minimal accountability; a nascent criminal syndicate inadvertently exposed to the organizational know-how of leftist insurgents in the bowels of the dictatorship's dungeons; a large, populous, urban periphery accustomed to neglect and abuse by the military government; and a post-authoritarian political pendulum that swung between progressive, human-rights concerns and a reactionary embrace of hardline repression. In Rio, it also produced another key legacy, a territorialized state-sponsored protection racket that evolved around the city's numbers racket that would eventually be replicated, in violent form, around the drug trade.

6.3.1 Managing the Numbers Racket (1940s–1980s)

Conjecture: A de facto conditional approach toward Rio's numbers racket successfully deterred anti-state violence by its leaders, and may have contributed to a reduction in fighting among them.

For most of the twentieth century, including the authoritarian period, Rio's *jogo do bicho* numbers racket far outshone drug trafficking as the largest and most powerful illicit market (Misse 2003). Until the 1980s' cocaine boom and the simultaneous rise of the CV, Rio's drug trade was simply too small to sustain anything like cartels, and hence cartel–state conflict. The numbers racket, by contrast, has been a regular part of Rio's urban life and culture since the late nineteenth century (Chazkel 2011), despite being criminalized in 1941. It is relevant here because the system of territorialized control and regularized bribery that evolved around the racket was a critical precursor to the dynamics of violent corruption that came to dominate Rio's drug trade after democratization.

Like the retail drug trade, the numbers racket involves a large number of retail points of sale, with overall market concentration depending on the ability of the bosses—known as *bicheiros*—who paid out winning bets and claimed the residual profits, to control large numbers of points. The numbers racket was initially fragmented after its prohibition, but went through an important process of internal organization in the 1950s (Misse 2007). *Bicheiros* came to control fixed territories, usually entire neighborhoods or, in Rio state's interior, whole municipalities. Under the *bicheiros* were managers who oversaw the operations of multiple bookmen (each working a point of sale) as well as salaried gunmen and lookouts to protect territory from rival groups. With the restructuring of police institutions that came under the military dictatorship in the late 1960s, responsibility for patrolling passed to the uniformed Military Police (PM). With state repression now overwhelmingly focused on countering the perceived communist threat (Misse 1999, 186), the PM largely allowed the numbers racket to operate without interference, in exchange for regularized bribes.

In some ways, this system resembles the state-sponsored protection racket that operated in Mexico under the PRI for much of the twentieth century: police wielded significant repressive power that was mostly held in reserve, in exchange for a portion of illicit profits. State policy was not, as far as scant historical sources indicate, explicitly conditional—as it would later come to be under Pacification. However, it seems likely that *bicheiros* understood that any anti-state violence would incur a serious increase in repression, precisely because the military government was focused overwhelmingly on fighting armed urban insurgents rather than crime per se, especially the popular numbers racket. In any case, busts were rare enough to make headlines (Misse 1999), and when they occurred, criminals rarely offered resistance (Misse 2007, 143). In terms of my model, this suggests a "hide-and-bribe" equilibrium in which criminals did not threaten state agents with violence should bribe negotiations fail. Indeed, the *bicheiros* never adopted confrontational strategies toward the state or police, but rather sought and often obtained social legitimacy, in large part through their patronage of Rio's samba schools and the annual Carnaval parades (Chinelli and Machado da Silva 1993).

That said, Rio's system falls short of Mexico's full-blown state-sponsored protection racket insofar as it does not appear to have been centrally organized by the political leadership. We do not know how far up the echelons of political power the *bicheiros*' bribes went, but networks of corruption appear to have developed from the bottom up (e.g., Misse 1999, 242–243). This decentralized system prevented anti-state violence, but lacked the political coordination to ensure the type of fluid bribe negotiations enjoyed by Mexico under the PRI, resulting in more frequent enforcement. Rio's system also did not prevent occasional turf wars among *bicheiros* in the 1950s and 1960s, though by the late 1970s they formed an effective and peaceful union that facilitated their transformation into semi-legitimate businessmen. This transformation

172   *Case Studies*

was surely also aided by the rise of the drug trade, which made *bicheiros* and the numbers racket in general seem relatively anodyne by comparison. In this context, it is plausible that the state's willingness to let *bicheiros* operate freely as long as they avoided violence contributed to the end of inter-*bicheiro* conflict.

In sum, since police corruption was rampant, but not necessarily encouraged or "sponsored" by leaders, Rio is perhaps best thought of as a "police-provided protection racket" or what I call a "system of illicit rent extraction." In terms of state policy, I code repression toward the numbers racket during this period as low in degree but high in conditionality, a form of active management that, as my model predicts, largely deterred anti-state violence.

6.3.2 Authoritarian Policing: Containing the Favelas (1970s–1980s)

Beyond the numbers racket, policing during the authoritarian period could be brutal. Indeed, the modern juridical and institutional structure, as well as the quotidian praxis, of law enforcement in Brazil were laid down during the military dictatorship, and remain largely unchanged to this day. Concerned first and foremost with leftist insurgency, the regime built a highly repressive police apparatus that democratic governors and reform-minded officers have struggled with ever since (Cerqueira 1996).

Policing in Brazil is concentrated at the level of state governments. Most cities lack armed municipal police, though many have municipal guards (*guarda municipal*) who have limited, order-keeping functions. A specialized federal police corps has jurisdiction over highways, while the main Federal Police (*Polícia Federal*, PF) has an investigatory function like that of the FBI, which can overlap with, and frequently targets corruption within, state police corps. At the state level, the most important structural feature is the division of the "ostensive" policing functions (*policiamento ostensivo*)—patrolling, maintaining order, responding to situations, and so on—from investigative and juridical functions. The former is the responsibility of the confusingly named Military Police, so christened because it was originally a subaltern branch of the military, taking its commands directly from the ruling generals in Brasília (Buarque de Hollanda 2005, 80). The PM was designed primarily to crack down on public protests, maintain order, and physically confront whatever armed resistance to the regime should occur—one reason it has proven hard to transform into an effective preventive, community policing force. Investigative duties and evidence collection fell to the Civil Police (*Polícia Civil*, PC), which carried out the detentions and interrogations of Brazil's limited but nonetheless brutal dirty war. The PC's modus operandi for obtaining evidence and convictions was, essentially, torture and confession, a practice supported by a legal code also designed during the dictatorship (Costa 2011).

A related legacy of authoritarian police institutions is the legal denomination for cases of civilians killed by police during operations, *autos de resistência* (literally "acts of resistance," ARs). Introduced into the criminal code in 1969 by the military regime (Souza 2010, 157), the denomination's subtitle reads "resistance followed by death of the opposer," implying a resort to lethal force by police in self-defense. Thus, simply registering the death of a civilian from police action invoked a (generally uncontestable) official assertion that the victim had reacted violently. Only in the rarest cases would such an assertion be investigated, giving police a very effective mechanism for legally masking summary executions (Verani 1996, 33–37). Forty years later, ARs remained a cornerstone of police activity in Rio de Janeiro.[13] In the 1990s the government began tracking them and from 1998 has included them in its official statistics. Though problematic, I use them throughout (together with data on police killed while on duty) as my preferred measure of cartel–state conflict (e.g., in Figure 6.2).[14]

The PM, in addition to violently shutting down pro-democracy demonstrations, often directed concentrated and unaccountable repressive force at Rio's favelas. This was increasingly the case as the communist threat dissipated, and favelas expanded rapidly with the arrival of new migrants, in the late 1970s and early 1980s. Numerous studies of this period describe a societal shift in which property crime came to replace subversion as the primary threat to Rio society, and extremely violent policing and even extrajudicial killing of "marginals" became more frequent and normalized (e.g., Machado da Silva et al. 2005; Misse 1999; Zaluar 1985). Rio de Janeiro state's public security secretary from 1975 to 1977, for example, sought to build a cordon of battalions between favelas and the formal city "to avoid an invasion of Rio de Janeiro"; he openly endorsed police abuse of suspected property criminals (quoted in McCann 2013, 101). Police Colonel Nazareth Cerqueira, who would later head major

---

13 In 2012, a resolution from the federal Human Rights Secretariat (under the president) recommended extinguishing *"auto de resistência"* as a legal category, replacing it with "homicide resulting from police intervention." Although a bill implementing these changes at the federal level faced resistance from law-enforcement lobbying groups, the norm was put into place through state-level executive orders in São Paulo and Rio in 2013. This complements longer-term efforts by high-level security officials in both states to reduce police lethality (of which the Pacification strategy in Rio was a part). It probably also reflects a deeper shift in public awareness and, increasingly, rejection of abusive policing that is at least partially due in part to the proliferation of cases caught on video. As in the United States, these videos generate outcry if not always punishment of officers involved or concrete changes in policing practice.

14 Not all armed resistors were necessarily drug traffickers, and a fair number of ARs likely represent police killings of citizens who were not offering armed resistance at all (Alston 2007). Moreover, ARs only account for the share of cases where police filed reports admitting responsibility for the killing; some police killings may end up reported as stray bullets, "unknown causes" (Cerqueira 2011), missing persons, or never get reported at all, particularly if they are carried out by off-duty officers (Alston 2007, 4). Still, each AR represents a civilian killed by an active-duty police officer and reported by that officer as an act of self-defense in an armed confrontation. With more than 10,000 over the last decade, the AR data offer a shocking and yet conservative estimate of the scale of cartel–state violence. Moreover, the regularity and length of the AR time series provides the best available measure of the dynamics of cartel–state conflict over the past two decades.

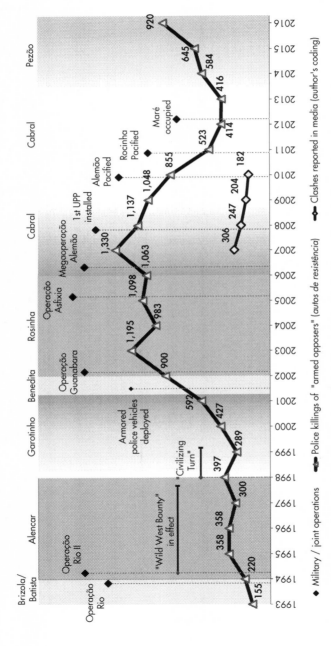

FIGURE 6.2. **Rio's Drug War: Police Killings and Major Militarized Operations by Governorship, 1993–2016.**

Sources: ISP-RJ (2016); SSP-RJ (2003); Author's coding of media reports (NRI/OBIVAN). Shading represents, roughly, how hardline a governor's tenure was.

reform efforts under Rio's first democratic governorship in 1983, was part of police high command (*estado maior*) during the military period; he describes favela policing thus:

> Of the celebrated and traditional *blitzes* in the favelas (police know them well), recall that they consisted of a large police apparatus that would shut off the entrances and exits of those areas, so that the so-called "penetration groups" could enter the area, breaking down shanty doors, entering them, searching residents, and "arresting suspects" without any judicial authorization whatsoever.
>
> (Cerqueira 2001, 166)

Police posts inside favelas, anthropologist Alba Zaluar noted in 1981, "don't even bother to hide their use of torture. Everyone knows, everyone sees" (Zaluar 1994, 10).

In these early days, the drug trade was both small and unorganized; within a few years, it would largely replicate the territorial structure, local hierarchies, and regularized police bribery that characterized the numbers racket (Misse 2003). The decentralized system of illicit rent extraction that developed around the *jogo do bicho* carried over into the drug trade, producing a similar pattern of sporadic but not uncommon busts against a backdrop of bribery. What differed dramatically was the extent of violence, and in particular anti-state violence, associated with this new system.

In the sections to come, I argue that the dynamics of this system can be understood in terms of my model of violent corruption, with variation in the degree and conditionality of state repression the key explanatory variables driving the onset, escalation, abatement, and recrudescence of cartel–state conflict. However, a key antecedent condition, and hence one more tragic legacy of the authoritarian period, was the advent of a criminal organization capable of organizing Rio's retail drug trade, accumulating enough firepower to confront the state, and surviving three decades of militarized repression.

6.3.3 The Rise of the Comando Vermelho (1970–1981)

The story of Rio de Janeiro's anomalous drug war revolves around the Comando Vermelho, and the story of this prison-gang-cum-drug-syndicate is a tale of unintended consequences as ironic as they were tragic. Born as a by-product of the military dictatorship's efforts to crush an armed resistance movement, the CV grew to become a far graver and more resilient threat to state power than the leftists ever posed.

In the early 1970s, Brazil's military dictatorship, invoking the newly passed National Security Law (*Lei de Segurança Nacional*, LSN), began convicting and incarcerating leftist militants together with common criminals, in an attempt to obscure the militants' political status and, it was hoped, delegitimize their cause. All the new convicts were housed in a makeshift, open-plan "LSN wing" within Cândido Mendes prison, a dilapidated and anarchic tropical Alcatraz located some forty kilometers from the Brazilian mainland. The insurgents responded with a disciplined campaign to physically separate and politically distinguish themselves from the common criminals in the wing. By the mid-1970s, they were granted amnesty, though by that time armed resistance to the regime was on the wane.[15]

The true beneficiaries of the junta's ill-conceived policy were the common criminals of the LSN wing, who learned and adopted many of the leftists' organizational and collectivist tactics, forged a strong group identity, and eventually decimated all rival gangs at Cândido Mendes.[16] The "LSN gang," as it was then known, recognized that the leftist militants' strategy of isolation coupled with outside political pressure for amnesty could never work for common criminals. Rather, in the words of CV co-founder William da Silva Lima, "Our path could only be the opposite: integration with the prison masses and the fight for liberty using our own resources" (Lima 1991, 43). The LSN gang imposed a rough-hewn social order throughout the prison: it banned rape and theft, provided rudimentary welfare and health services, and won important concessions from authorities that ultimately made it immensely popular among inmates. Through misguided government attempts to break up the gang by transferring its leaders, it established outposts, and eventually control, throughout Rio de Janeiro's prison system.

Soon dubbed "Falange Vermelho" (the "Red Gang," for its association with the leftist militants and its often politicized rhetoric), the group began to plan its outward expansion, organizing mass prison breaks and individual escapes. Freed members were obliged to contribute money and resources to the prison collective and to participate in rescue attempts. Mutual aid and cooperation among freed members facilitated joint criminal ventures, but since most were property criminals, and the militants they had learned from relied heavily on bank robberies for operating funds, the group initially engaged mostly in risky and frequently disastrous bank heists.

---

15 The British later used the same technique with the Irish Republican Army (IRA), to (arguably) even worse effect. The IRA was, by some accounts, galvanized and rejuvenated by the so-called prison wars, and the immense media attention generated by IRA hunger strikes won many new sympathizers (English 2005, 187–226).

16 It remains controversial how complicit leftist militants were in passing on such volatile human capital to the other LSN inmates. When the CV first attracted public attention, the media and the military government assumed that its members had been deliberately indoctrinated and trained by the leftists as part of a long-term strategy to re-ignite armed resistance to the regime (Amorim 2003)—this association is thought to be the origin of the name "Red Command," which founding members say was imposed by authorities (the group began life as the "Falange LSN" or "LSN gang"). Leftists generally deny any such deliberate training or assistance, emphasizing that their political strategy involved minimizing contact with the common criminals, and that they successfully mobilized to have their wing physically divided, points on which CV members concur (Lima 1991, 45).

6.4 ONSET AND ESCALATION (1981–2007): A QUARTER-CENTURY OF DRUG WAR

6.4.1 Onset (1981–1983): The Red Command Takes Over

Both inter-cartel turf war and cartel–state conflict began around 1980, in the twilight of the dictatorship, but initially constituted distinct historical threads. Turf wars emerged among local favela-based trafficking groups who generally eschewed anti-state violence, while anti-state violence was initiated by a criminal group—the CV—that had yet to enter the drug trade.

Inter-cartel turf war seems to have been driven by a rapid expansion of profits due to the cocaine boom. Increased supply from the Andean region went hand in hand with increased demand as the drug became financially accessible, and soon thereafter fashionable, to the working and middle classes (Misse 1997, 4). As marijuana lost ground to cocaine, drug dealing went from being mildly to extremely lucrative, and drug "lords" arose with the financial power to hire not only managers and dealers but small standing "armies." A few extended turf wars—including the one dramatized in the book and film *City of God* and recounted in the anthropological research that undergirded them (Lins 1997; Zaluar 1985)—drew the attention of the media and authorities. There is no evidence, however, that these traffickers systematically confronted state forces, even as systematized police extraction of illicit rents shifted from the numbers racket to the drug trade.

Meanwhile, the CV was taking its "struggle" against state officials from the prisons to the streets, where things quickly grew violent. Officials inferred that the CV was some sort of leftist militant group: it had emerged from the LSN wing where leftists had been grouped with common criminals; it appeared to operate in well-organized cells reporting to a central leadership; and its modus operandi—armed heists—was a common fundraising technique of Brazil's militants (Amorim 2003, 145). This mis-reading led authorities not only to name the group "Red Falange" and later "Red Command" but to adopt an anti-guerrilla, unconditional-crackdown policy that quickly resulted in armed confrontation. In April 1981, when police learned of a CV cell in Conjunto dos Bancários, a middle-class apartment complex, and sent seven heavily armed officers to make the arrests, CV members fought back with automatic weapons. Police reinforcements invaded the building, leading to a spectacular twelve-hour gunfight in which five people were killed and another twenty-four wounded, ending only with the death of the lone CV leader remaining (Amorim 2003, 145–154). The incident—christened "Four Hundred Against One" in the title of one CV founder's autobiography (Lima 1991)—marked a turning point: a purely criminal group had confronted the state with significant military force.

Over the next few years, these two historical strands came together, as the CV turned to drug trafficking and rapidly took over the city's retail markets, while maintaining its violent stance toward the state. As the ranks of the CV's founders thinned, newer members with a background in drug trafficking gained sway over the organization. This coincided with the cocaine boom that made trafficking into Rio's primary illicit economy and was already leading local outfits to amass arsenals and occasionally clash for turf. The CV set its sights on expansion, developing a kind of "incubator" micro-credit program:

> The Command supplied anyone who wished to open a *boca* [drug retail point] with everything they needed to set up the movement in a new area, including guns, contacts for the purchase of the drugs and cash. In return, the new "owner" would pay a regular and sizable chunk of his earnings into the Command's common "fund" and agree to respect the rules of mutual support, alliance against enemies, respect, support and "protection" for the locals and, especially, for the "friends". Any attempt to defraud the network on any level was punishable by death.
>
> (Misse 2007, 150)

This new system had a transformational effect, humorously hinted at in the very last scene of the film *City of God* (2002). Non-Brazilian viewers may have missed the joke: an impossibly young member of the newly ascendant local gang asks his leader if he's heard the rumors of "some Falange Vermelha coming this way?" "No," says the leader, "but if he tries, we'll whack that guy too." Of course, the Falange (i.e., the CV), was not a "guy" and the locals would not "whack" him. They and other groups like them would be overwhelmed: by the mid-1980s, CV bosses controlled 70 percent of Rio's favelas (Amorim 1993, 203). But the joke reflects how unforeseeable the CV's collective structure and modus operandi would have been to traditional, autonomous, single-favela incumbents. The CV's hegemony was only challenged in the late 1980s with the advent of schism-born rival syndicates, most prominently the Terceiro Comando and Amigos dos Amigos. By the early 1990s, inter-cartel turf war would reach new levels of intensity as Rio's favelas and prison units were divvied up among the CV and its smaller rivals, an arrangement that largely persists as of this writing.

Outside the prison system, the CV became, and remains, a loose affiliation of autonomous drug firms whose bosses engage in mutual aid and occasional coordinated actions. There is no central treasury or clear hierarchy among bosses, and the politically tinged rhetoric of the early days has long given way to an overriding concern for profits (Coelho 1988); this is even truer of its schism-born rival syndicates. This book focuses largely on the syndicates' "favela side": the retail drug trade and the massive armed presence they have amassed to defend it.

However, the CV's "prison side" continues to play an important, if less visible, role in perpetuating the CV and its rivals. First, arrestees are assigned to jail and prison cells based on the syndicate-affiliation of the community they are from, so someone from a CV-dominated favela will be sent to a

CV-dominated prison, regardless of whether they are actual CV members. This aids recruitment and socialization of new members. Indeed, even those who enter prison as autonomous criminal actors may well leave as respected leaders of the organization, with the right to a lucrative position within the drug trade.[17] Second, imprisoned leaders continue to wield important influence over outside members. The clearest cases are imprisoned CV drug bosses, who usually continue to run their drug operations directly from prison, delegating only the necessary amount of authority to their right-hand men. Orders are almost always followed, since those on the outside know that sooner or later, either the boss will be released or they will go to prison.

A more subtle form of influence is also at work. The prison system provides a forum for CV leaders to coordinate their strategies, share information, agree on mutual aid policies, plan invasions, and come to agreements. The greatly respected older CV leaders, especially those with links to the founding members, are particularly important (Barbosa 1998). Their praise or disdain can alter the fortunes of an up-and-coming CV member, or decide the fate of a proposed course of action. They are frequently called upon to settle disputes, appoint successors, broker deals between bosses, and evaluate alternative strategies.[18] As I have argued elsewhere (Lessing 2013), imprisoned leaders exert influence on outside members not just through coercion (the promise of reward or punishment once incarcerated) but as "focal points" on whose signals it is mutually beneficial for outside actors to coordinate (Myerson 2005; Schelling 1960).

These mechanisms help explain why Rio's retail drug trade has its anomalous character. In the urban periphery of three other Brazilian cities, I found that local drug markets are usually characterized by shifting degrees of market concentration: from time to time, one group expands and becomes dominant, only to draw the attention of authorities and rivals, while the lack of resilient succession mechanisms leads to the re-fragmentation of the market after the upstart's demise or imprisonment (Lessing 2008). Similar dynamics are reported in other contexts (e.g., Dorn et al. 1992; Hagedorn 1994), leading to the observation that drug retailing organizations in general tend to be small, informal, and short-lived. By contrast, Rio de Janeiro's (at the time) *sui generis* syndicates used the coordinating power derived from their control over the prison system to neutralize many of these centrifugal forces, organizing a united front against police and rivals, pooling resources, and resolving succession and other intra-syndicate disputes. This prison-based power—rather than hilly geography, police corruption, and market size—is the most plausible explanation of the consistently concentrated nature of Rio's drug market and

---

[17] Interview with non-trafficking ex-CV member and prison capo, August 14, 2009.
[18] Interview with ex-CV drug boss and inmate, August 14, 2009.

the unusual persistence of large, articulated, well-armed "cartels" in a retail setting (Lessing 2008).[19]

6.4.2 Escalation (1983–2007): A Political Pendulum

Claim 1: Between democratization (1983) and Pacification (2008), the degree of repression varied but trended upward, while conditionality remained low. Syndicates responded to unconditional crackdowns with violent, fight-and-bribe strategies.

The CV's takeover of Rio's drug market roughly coincided with the end of military rule in Brazil, beginning in 1983 with the democratic elections of state governors. This had important implications for state repressive policy, since most policing and anti-narcotics policy is made at the state level. Besides Rio's repressive police institutions and the CV, the authoritarian period also engendered a political pendulum that, after democratization, drove both public opinion and the resulting state governments. On the one hand, two decades' resistance to and ultimate victory over Brazil's military dictatorship drove a left-leaning concern for protecting human rights and restricting the repressive reach of the police and the state more broadly. On the other, a growing sense of fear and anomie drove conservative, even reactionary, calls for repressive state action against "marginals" (*marginais*) to reduce crime and violence and protect "honest citizens" (*cidadãos do bem*). Cartel–state conflict, turf war, and crime in general contributed to this political dynamic. If it was a perception of progressive tolerance or even sympathy for favela-based criminal behavior that fueled hardline reactions, then it was public outrage at the inevitable excesses of repressive police action that eventually swung the pendulum back (partway) toward restraint.

My core argument is that cartel–state conflict was also shaped by this oscillation in repressive policy. In particular, with a few important exceptions, what varied was the overall *degree* of repression, not its *conditionality*. Hardline governments generally gave police ever-increasing leeway, capacity, and even incentives to use deadly force; progressive governments in turn attempted to restrict violent police practice in general, not make it conditional on the use of violence. Traffickers faced more or less brutal police raids, but never a clear signal from the state that they would only face the full brunt of repression if they insisted on using violence.

The first elected governor of Rio de Janeiro was Lionel Brizola (1983–1987), a returned political exile and founder of the socialist PDT.[20] His progressive agenda included an explicit focus on the rights of favela residents, declaring

[19] Similar coordination by large, articulated prison gangs of retail drug sales on city- and region-wide scales has been reported in California and Texas (US Department of Justice 2010).
[20] Partido Democrático Trabalhista, Democratic Labor Party.

an end to forced removals and improving favela infrastructure and schools. Informed by his own activism against the dictatorship and eventual exile, Brizola and his visionary security chief Nazareth Cerqueira implemented an ambitious "democratizing" police-reform agenda, including imposition of civilian control and important restrictions on police action in favelas, effectively reducing the degree of repression (Soares and Sento-Sé 2000, 7–9). Overall, Brizola vastly improved the lives of favela residents, who began replacing wooden shanties with brick houses; his approach to policing, however, inadvertently contributed to the entrenchment of CV power over favela life, and possibly the increase in property crime seen throughout the city. A sense of lawlessness and fear on the part of the middle class, along with vocal opposition from police leaders, led to Brizola's defeat in 1987.

Governor Moreira Franco (1987–1991) of the more conservative PMDB,[21] ran on a promise to end the violence within six months of taking office. Franco's victory marked a return to repressive police tactics and the explicit belief that public safety and respect for human rights (at least those of criminals and suspects) were incompatible (Machado da Silva et al. 2005, 9). In addition, it raised the professional profile of old-guard police leaders whose careers had begun during the dictatorship, and granted them a wide berth for discretionary action (Soares and Sento-Sé 2000, 16). Increased repression, however, did not reduce either crime in general nor the increasingly brazen violence of the syndicates, which fought a protracted turf war for a large favela in the heart of the city's wealthier region (Barcellos 2003). The failure of the Franco government to stem the growing turf war among syndicates and restrain crime rates in general made his government unpopular, allowing Brizola to return to office (1991–1995).

Brizola's second term, though less ambitious than his first and hobbled by his exit from office to run (unsuccessfully) for president in 1994, saw renewed efforts to restrict police brutality, reform the corps from within, and develop the first community policing programs (Cerqueira 1996). These efforts met with a great deal of internal resistance from hardline police officers (Soares and Sento-Sé 2000); such discontent likely contributed to the growth of death squads (*esquadrões de morte*) and proto-paramilitary groups known as *polícia mineira* during this time, culminating in several brutal massacres.

The growing sense of disorder led to Operação Rio, the first large-scale use of the armed forces to address Rio's drug war. Originally envisioned as a temporary measure to guarantee public safety during the 1994 elections, akin to the army's role providing security for hundreds of foreign heads of state during the Rio-92 environmental summit, Brizola and acting governor Nilo Batista first opposed, then grudgingly accepted the operation in a clumsy and unsuccessful bid to cover their flank on security issues (Machado da Silva

---

[21] Partido do Movimento Democrático Brasileiro, Party of the Brazilian Democratic Movement.

et al. 2005, 12). They lost to right-wing Marcello Alencar of the PSDB,[22] who stayed true to his campaign promise of severe repressive action. Alencar arranged for the redeployment of the army to favelas in Operação Rio II, put an army general in charge of policing, authorized unconstitutional "collective search warrants"[23] and instituted an infamous "wild west bounty" (*premiação faroeste*), paying police bonuses for each (alleged) trafficker killed. Eventually, outrage from civil society, quick to compare these tactics to those of the dictatorship, helped push the pendulum back toward some degree of restraint.

In 1998, Anthony Garotinho, then a political heir of Brizola and rising PDT star, won the governorship in part on the promise of a "civilizing turn" (*inflexão civilizatória*) in policing, laid out in a detailed manifesto co-written with a team of progressive social scientists led by Luiz Eduardo Soares (Garotinho and Soares 1998). Soares and his team took leadership positions, implementing a number of reform projects including the Mutirão pela Paz (Mobilization for Peace) project, an early precursor of Pacification, which combined police occupation of a target favela with community outreach and a raft of new social programs (Soares 2000, 280–284). However, opposition and increasing insubordination from within the police corps made continued reform a costly political proposition for the governor. Garotinho publicly sacked Soares, who fled Brazil in the wake of police death threats, and replaced his team with hardliners, part of Garotinho's larger tack into right-wing populism. A major escalation in police firepower and tactics followed, including the expansion of the elite BOPE Special Operations Battalion.[24] According to Soares (2011), it was around this time that the BOPE adopted an essentially murderous "no surrender" policy, which gave traffickers every reason to fight to the death. Garotinho left office in 2002 to run for president, leaving vice-governor Benedita da Silva to finish out his term.

Benedita[25] was a hero of the left-wing PT[26] and had lent credibility to Garotinho's originally progressive platform, but by the time she took office Garotinho had left the PDT and was running against the PT's Luiz Inácio Lula da Silva for the presidency. Hostility from him and his remaining appointees combined with Benedita's inexperience to make her brief tenure frustrating and ineffective. On the security front, her call for a return to the "civilizing turn"

---

22 Partido da Social Democracia Brasileira, Brazilian Social Democratic Party.
23 Of dubious legal standing, these supposedly authorized police to carry out invasive house-by-house searches in entire favelas.
24 BOPE stands for Batalhão de Operações Policiais Especiais. It is the subject of the film *Tropa de Elite* (Elite Squad) (2007).
25 Like President Dilma Rousseff and Rio Governor Rosinha Mateus, Benedita is known publicly by her first name. While not unheard of with respect to male politicians (such as Getúlio Vargas or Juscelino Kubitschek), the practice seems near universal with female politicians. Given the many chauvinist attacks against Dilma during her 2016 impeachment ordeal, one wonders if this practice might be part of the problem.
26 Partido dos Trabalhadores, Workers Party.

and re-appointment of Soares yielded a few positive experiences (Machado da Silva et al. 2005, 18), but fed opposition within the rank-and-file (Câmara 2009, 8) just as important increases in police tactical power were coming online (including further expansion of the BOPE and the first operational deployment of the armored vehicles known as *caveirões*[27]). Garotinho's wife Rosinha Mateus easily won the 2002 election, reinstating what had by then become Garotinho's signature hardline approach (*Pressão Máxima*, or "Maximum Pressure"), and soon appointing him public security secretary. With the BOPE and its *caveirões* becoming the go-to state response, police killing of civilians (ARs) reached a record high of 1,195 in 2003 and held steady for the rest of Rosinha's term.

Surprisingly, Rosinha's successor Sérgio Cabral was able to win on a law-and-order campaign, largely because of serious corruption scandals involving the Garotinhos and corrupt police chiefs, as well as the general ineffectiveness of their security policy in reining in violence. While Cabral presented himself as a pro-human rights reform type during the campaign, terror attacks by the CV at the outset of his governorship provoked a turn toward repression. For most of 2007, Cabral's rhetoric, as well as that of his public security secretary, former Federal Police investigator José Mariano Beltrame, recalled that of earlier crackdowns (Ribeiro et al. 2008), while the coalition between Cabral's PMDB and Lula's PT facilitated an extensive deployment of federal troops to favela hotspots.

The centerpiece of this initial crackdown was a June 2007 joint operation of police and federal troops in the Complexo do Alemão favela, the CV's stronghold. For a month, over 1,300 troops laid siege to Alemão, while "traffickers circulated carrying assault rifles and pistols ... and impudently pointed them at federal soldiers, challenging them to a confrontation in the favela" (Costa et al. 2007). Finally, troops invaded the area, leaving nineteen civilians (all allegedly drug traffickers) dead and yielding some arms seizures but no arrests. Incredibly, while this operation—the largest ever in Brazil's history according to officials—drew severe criticism from human rights organizations and even the United Nations (Alston 2007), it left the favela under the dominion of the CV (Costa et al. 2007). The year marked the high-point of cartel–state conflict, with a record 1,330 civilians killed in armed confrontations with police.

Thus, despite occasional reform efforts, the secular trend over this twenty-five-year period was a steadily increasing degree of repression, and consistently low conditionality. Police action in favelas was, on the whole, extremely violent and to a large extent indiscriminate, with little effort made to distinguish actual traffickers from non-participants, much less hinge decisions about the use of lethal force on the behavior of traffickers. As a popular saying has it, "The only good criminal is a dead criminal." The following anecdote

---

[27] Literally "big skulls," they were named this because they often carried the emblem of the BOPE, a skull with a bowie knife thrust through it.

attracted attention because of the age of the victims, but it also conveys the reality facing both active traffickers and innocent residents caught in the middle.

> The young boys Welington Santiago Oliveira Lima, 11, and Luciano Rocha Tavares, 12, were killed by Rio Military Police during an operation in the Estado favela in Niterói (15km from Rio). Another two minors and a youth also died. The police claim the victims were drug dealers, including the two children. Residents, however, deny the accusation. ... Welington's mother ... says that he had gone to buy a soda when the shootout started: "a policeman started shouting that he was a drug dealer, dragged him by the leg like a pig and killed him with a shot in the head."
>
> "History shows that children do participate in the drug trade. In May, we captured a 12-year-old boy who confessed to killing a PM sergeant. I am certain they were part [of the drug trade]," said the commanding officer.
>
> (Figueiredo 2005)[28]

Even granting the commanding officer's claim that these pre-adolescents were traffickers, his statement is quite telling: if simply being involved in the drug trade is enough to warrant summary execution at the hands of the police, then traffickers have every incentive to fight back when police enter the favela. Indeed, no effort was made to determine whether the children had actually shot at the police before being killed:

> The bodies of the five dead—among them four minors—were released from the Legal Medical Institute [Instituto Médico-Legal, IML], without having been examined for gunpowder traces on their hands, which would have shown if in fact they participated in a shootout, as the police allege.
>
> (*O Globo* 2005)[29]

This suggests that police officers face little pressure to condition their use of lethal force on the behavior of traffickers. Consequently, traffickers—or even favela youth who might be mistaken for traffickers—have no reason to eschew violence, since doing so will not earn them a reprieve from potentially lethal police action.

Systematic assessments confirm this. Cano (1997, 2010) studied the universe of incidents involving police that ended with firearm deaths or wounds over a thirty-month period. Among many intriguing findings, he calculates *lethality indices*: the ratio, among all incidents in which police shot "opposers" (not innocent bystanders), of deaths to woundings. Presumably, if police were trying to apprehend or incapacitate criminals, rather than kill them, this index would be less than one, and Cano reports that for most US cities, it is (1997, 31). In Rio, however, it is significantly higher. Even for whites in non-favela areas, there were about two lethal shootings for every non-lethal shooting; for non-whites

---

28 Author's translation.
29 Author's translation.

in favelas, there were more than eight (2010, 40). Cano also reports that forensic examinations were carried out in only 26 percent of cases with civilian victims, and that even among those, tests for gunpowder on hands were rare (1997, 57).

The title of a 2005 Amnesty International report vividly captured favela residents' experience of police actions in their communities: "They Come in Shooting" (Amnesty International 2005). Residents also consistently reported being treated by police with disrespect and suspicion as "accomplices of the criminals." As the report points out, such police behavior was often encouraged and protected by the dubious legal practice of obtaining collective search and seizure warrants for entire favela communities. Comments like "[The police] beat and beat and beat you, then say 'Sorry, you're not the one we're looking for'" (Amnesty International 2005, 25) make clear that for residents, even those not involved in the drug trade, violence at the hands of the police was hard to avoid. This was undoubtedly true for youth actually involved in the drug trade: of more than 200 traffickers interviewed in a 2004 study, 74 percent reported suffering violence at the hands of police, while only 53 percent reported having ever been arrested (Silva 2006, 35–37).

If the unconditional nature of repression in Rio created no disincentives to violence, what created the positive incentives for cartels to fight back? I claim that the CV's (and to a lesser extent, its smaller rivals') embrace of anti-state violence constitutes a fight-and-bribe strategy as per the logic of violent corruption. That is, syndicates used armed force against state enforcers as part of a larger strategy to maximize profits, and in particular as a means of keeping police bribe demands reasonable. The most important piece of evidence is simply the aggressive and confrontational behavior of CV outfits throughout this period. Over and over again, traffickers showed themselves willing to engage not only Rio's Military and Civil Police rank-and-file but also its well-armed elite corps.

Novel violent-event data reveals that cartel-police clashes inside favelas in response to police incursions are the modal form of drug violence in Rio (Figure 6.3). Clashes, as opposed to unilateral cartel attacks,[30] accounted for 46 percent of all reports of drug violence in Rio (compared with 10 percent in Mexico). As the left-hand panel of Figure 6.3 indicates, the vast majority of clashes were between police and cartels, not among traffickers; as the right-hand panel shows, roughly half of all clashes were directly preceded by a police action, almost always a police incursion into a favela in order to capture traffickers and drugs (note that police incursions in response to ongoing violence are counted as cartel-initiated). At least 80 percent of clashes occurred within favelas.

---

[30] Violent actions are coded by type; a single category, "clash," covers *any* situation in which two or more actors exchange lethal force. See Appendix A for details.

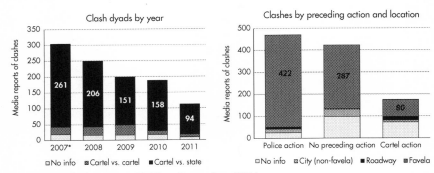

FIGURE 6.3. **Clashes, June 2007 to December 2011.**
Sources: Author's coding of newspaper reports; see Appendix A for details.
*Includes only June to December 2007.

This strongly suggests that the driving force behind cartel–state conflict in Rio is the *plata o plomo* logic of violent corruption. Clashes in favelas impose costs on enforcers, but not so much on political leaders, who have even benefited politically from "taking the fight to the bandits." This augurs against the logic of violent lobbying, whose footprint—terror tactics and calls for changes to de jure policy—have occurred in Rio, but make up a relatively small share of cartel violence. What about a purely defensive logic of loss-minimization? Might syndicates fight back solely in order to physically prevent police from arresting members and seizing merchandise, rather than in an effort to intimidate police and strike cheaper bribe agreements in the future? Since we rarely if ever observe bribe negotiations when they do occur, it is difficult to answer this question directly.

The model of violent corruption from Chapter 4, however, provides some analytic purchase, suggesting that while loss-minimization may play a role, it is almost certainly not the primary factor. To see why, first recall that the model characterizes an ideal-type scenario in which violence is purely defensive: in such "violent enforcement" equilibria, police are functionally incorruptible, and cartels have no motive to intimidate police into lowering their bribe demand, because bribe agreements will never be struck. Nonetheless, cartels fight back simply because fighting is (significantly) more effective than hiding at reducing their losses under enforcement. "Violent enforcement" predicts constant clashes between police and traffickers, and essentially no occurrences of successful bribe negotiation. This may characterize syndicate interactions with the BOPE in its early, low-corruption days; indeed, its "no surrender" policy gave traffickers little choice but to fight. However, the violent enforcement scenario simply does not match the overall empirical pattern of violence seen in Rio. Clashes between traffickers and police, while common enough, are very far from constant. On any given day, hundreds of favelas patrolled by openly armed traffickers are *not* the scene of shootouts, even though nearby police patrols certainly knew where to find the traffickers. Popular and ethnographic accounts almost universally attribute such non-enforcement to the *arrego* bribes paid by incumbent traffickers to local police battalions. Even the BOPE has become thoroughly corrupt, if arrests of its officers for selling information and weapons to traffickers (*O Globo* 2015) are any indication.

This pattern of intermittent enforcement met with trafficker violence is better explained by the model's fight-and-bribe equilibria, in which cartels' use of anti-state violence is part of a larger strategy aimed at keeping police extortion in check. When corruption is rampant, and bribes likely to be struck, the equilibrium bribe price is very important to both sides. For cartels, both defensive and intimidatory functions of cartel violence play a role in reducing the equilibrium price of bribes: the former reduces the pain police can inflict on cartels, while the latter makes police less willing to inflict that pain. Taken together, these effects lead police to demand a lower bribe that is more likely to be paid. To reiterate one of the model's central findings, rampant corruption and the possibility of successful bribery in exchange for non-enforcement can make violence *more* useful to cartels than it is in a world where corruption is off the table.

Additional evidence of the centrality of the logic of violent corruption comes from traffickers' own accounts of their business. In a longitudinal study of 230 drug traffickers, 54 percent reported having suffered extortion by police, while only 53 percent reported having been arrested and 28.5 percent had actually been imprisoned (Silva 2006). This regularized corruption transpires in a context of mutual violence: a full 73.5 percent of the sample reported having suffered extralegal police violence, while 68 percent had been involved in at least one armed confrontation with police (compared to only 53 percent in confrontation with rival groups). In an earlier survey, traffickers were asked to name their main fear in their line of work. Among those under the age of eighteen, fear of death ranked first (35 percent) followed by fear of police extortion (30 percent); among those over eighteen fear of extortion ranked first; in both cases, fear of arrest was third.

Interviews and statements of higher-ups in the drug trade corroborate this view of anti-state violence as a safeguard against police extortion. The boss of Rocinha said in his statement upon arrest in 2011 that he regularly paid half of his revenue in bribes, and often had zero net profits (Werneck 2011). One of my informants, a high-level manager in a large non-Pacified favela, also reported extortionate demands and explicitly tied it to a motivation for the use of anti-state violence:

> There's no way to pay [the police] everything they demand; if we did we'd end up just working for them. ... So when there's not enough money to pay them with, well then, there will be bullets.[31]

---

[31]   Interview, mid-level CV manager, Rio de Janeiro, March 29, 2010.

Luis Eduardo Soares transcribes an interview with a syndicate member describing a dynamic that goes beyond the simplifying assumptions of my model—rotation of police leading to the breaking of a bribe agreement and the kidnapping of traffickers for ransom—but the fundamental logic of using violence to avoid extortionate bribe demands is still operative:

> Say [a cop] is behind on his car payments, and he's no longer at the police post [in the favela], so he's not part of the *arrego*. So he comes to … arrest a dealer who has already paid the *arrego*. … When they break the *arrego*, they always arrest one of us. Then they want R$15,000, R$20,000 [US$7,500–8,000], above and beyond the *arrego*. So, some of these guys get shot, and what happens when you shoot them, they call for reinforcements. And then the shit that has to go down goes down.
>
> (Soares et al. 2005, 259–260)

These testimonies nicely capture both the presence of the *plata o plomo* logic in Rio de Janeiro, and also its very different cast from the Colombian case. Whereas Pablo Escobar sought out judicial officials and police chiefs, proactively making his offer, Rio's traffickers are physically circumscribed within their favela bases, sitting ducks for well-armed police officers with the power to, if not permanently expel them, seriously disrupt their drug business. Bargaining theory tells us that in general, the player who makes the offer has more bargaining power; in Rio it certainly seems as though police held the advantage in the negotiation of the *arrego*.

On the other hand, the manager of one large operation told me that his *arrego* cost one million *reais* per week,[32] on revenue that could go as high as seven million, a relatively low percentage. Intriguingly, he claimed that the size of the *arrego* was rarely if ever renegotiated, even when profits rose. When I asked why the police did not ask for a larger share, he said "If they tried to raise the bribe price, we would fight them. So it's better for him to want a little than to get greedy and end up fighting."[33]

6.4.3 GPAE (2000–2001): Conditionality in One Favela

Claim 2: The GPAE policing program raised conditionality locally, leading affected traffickers to eschew anti-state violence until the program eroded and collapsed.

Alongside the fitful militarization of repression that characterized Rio's escalation phase, a second and less visible trend was developing: repeated attempts at police reform, often taking the form of experimental pilot projects undertaken in partnership with civil society organizations and residents'

---

32 About US$300,000.
33 Interview, August 4, 2014.

organizations, and informed by international trends in community and proximity policing. Early experiments mostly took place outside the favela, in middle-class neighborhoods in the formal part of the city. Policing of favelas, meanwhile, remained repressive, and increasingly relied on (temporary) militarized occupations when violence became particularly extreme. These two strands came together in the GPAE program in 2000, in the wake of an episode of civil disorder in a group of three neighboring favelas after police killed five youths. Working together with the Brazilian NGO Viva Rio and local community organizations, reform-minded police major Antônio Carballo Blanco designed an experimental police intervention that combined permanent, physical occupation with community-policing practice within a favela.

GPAE had to tackle the question of how to do deal on a daily basis with an armed, violent, organized criminal group. The answer its creators came up with—prioritize repression of trafficker *violence* and *ostentation of arms* over trafficking itself—made it the first truly conditional policing project to be implemented in Rio. Though it drew on previous community policing experiments in Rio, GPAE's conditional component was most directly and deeply influenced by Boston's Operation Ceasefire. After observing Ceasefire first-hand, Viva Rio director Rubem César Fernandes organized a return visit to Boston with a Brazilian delegation including Carballo Blanco. Both Fernandes and Carballo Blanco clearly understood that the key to Ceasefire's success in reducing gang violence was its differential repression of such violence over and above other criminal activities, including drugs (Fernandes 2003, 95). Chapter 9 further explores Operation Ceasefire and its influence on GPAE.

GPAE's guiding idea was to reduce violence by shifting the stated goals of policing, from eradicating the drug trade to eliminating its armed presence. GPAE's mission statement called for a differentiated strategy of "qualified repression" and described its approach as "essentially preventive and, when necessary, repressive" (quoted in Albernaz et al. 2007, 40). This translated into a change in tactics. Rather than invade favelas in large coordinated actions aimed at capturing or killing traffickers, the GPAE battalion was installed within the favela, maintaining a regular, preventive police presence that did not actively target drug dealers, as long as they followed a few simple rules: "Don't walk around openly armed, don't sell drugs near school, and don't employ children."[34] These clearly conditional directives were complemented by a commitment to restraint over police themselves: "zero tolerance of police inside the community committing violent or arbitrary actions, abuse of power, or complicity with criminal practice " (Albernaz et al. 2007, 42).

The program was initially very successful: the homicide rate in the community fell to zero during the first year, and residents overwhelmingly approved of the program. Moreover, conditional repression worked as predicted: it did not eliminate the presence of traffickers, but proved effective at altering their

---

[34] Interview, Major Antônio Carballo Blanco, June 2003. See also Carballo Blanco (2003).

behavior. Traffickers carried out few if any armed patrols and rarely threatened residents; their relationship with GPAE police was summed up by one resident as "I pretend not to see you and you pretend not to see me" (quoted in Novaes 2003, 114).

GPAE was widely seen as a policy success within Brazil (Albernaz et al. 2007, 40). However, it also came under attack as a pact with the drug trade from Rio's mayor and other political rivals of the governor at the time (Fernandes 2003, 98). This put the program's advocates on the defensive; while the "pact" charge was not literally true, reducing the relative amount of repression directed against non-violent traffickers—a principal point of criticism—was central to GPAE's strategy.[35] When Carballo Blanco was transferred to a post in Brasília, he was replaced with a hardliner, who reverted to traditional, repressive police practice (Fernandes 2003, 98), and cartel–state violence soon erupted again (Ungar and Arias 2009, 418).

Nonetheless, GPAE's success led to its hasty replication and deployment in four other communities between 2002 and 2005, each time in response to local crises. Overall, these new GPAE units were not effective in reducing violence; Ungar and Arias (2009) attribute poor performance to a lack of support from state leaders, police, NGO activists, and local leaders, while Fernandes (2003) argues that the later GPAEs were deployed in communities that were far too large and violent to be manageable. Critically, though, these new GPAEs, like the original unit after 2003, generally lacked commanders committed, or even sympathetic, to a conditional approach (Albernaz et al. 2007). Carballo Blanco had personally administered the GPAE program, firing dozens of police who he considered truculent, corrupt, or otherwise incompatible with the program's aims. The only other successful GPAE unit, which virtually eliminated shootouts in a small favela in neighboring Niterói, was led by a young commander who clearly adopted "the end of shootouts" rather than "the end of drug trafficking" as his metric of success, and used repressive force to impose rules on incumbent traffickers (Albernaz et al. 2007, 44). Ultimately, though, rising violence in other GPAE communities led to the degradation of the program's image (Fernandes 2003, 95) and eventually its extinction.

The GPAE episode is an object lesson in the political difficulties of implementing and sustaining a policy of conditional repression; I examine these more fully in Part III. The key point here is that a move to a conditional approach—however localized and temporary—produced sharp abatement in cartel-related violence in general and cartel–police clashes in particular; furthermore, when repressive policy reverted to a more unconditional form, violence returned. The GPAE episode thus supports the overarching argument of this book. More importantly, it demonstrated to real-world decision-makers in Rio that shifts in the way repressive force was applied could radically alter the behavior of criminal groups; years later, this would inspire Governor Cabral

[35] Interview, Major Antônio Carballo Blanco, June 2003.

and Secretary Beltrame to implement a conditional approach on a much larger scale.

6.5 ABATEMENT (2008–2012): GETTING TO CONDITIONALITY THE CARIOCA WAY

Claim 3: The initial implementation of the Pacification strategy significantly increased the conditionality of repression at a city-wide scale, leading cartels to eschew anti-state violence.

The security policy of the Cabral government, or at least its outward manifestation, was quite erratic at the outset of his first administration. During his campaign, Cabral positioned himself as a reformer and protector of the rights of favela residents (Ribeiro et al. 2008, 8). While meeting with community activists on election day in 2006, for example, he promised to retire the armored *caveirões*. Yet Security Secretary Beltrame soon contradicted his boss, citing the vehicles' usefulness in rescuing wounded officers, and Cabral later announced that the *caveirões* would stay.

On December 28, 2006, just days before Cabral's inauguration, imprisoned CV leaders ordered a wave of terror attacks on police stations and posts, as well as bus-burnings, that left eighteen dead, including two police officers.[36] The administration thus took office in a climate of insecurity, and responded with a familiar hardline approach. Beltrame and Cabral adopted a rhetoric of war, secured the support of President Lula in the form of federal troops, and launched a series of violent operations in key favelas that would culminate in the controversial June 2007 "mega-operation" in Alemão. Even after the failed invasion, Beltrame maintained his public posture, warning Rio's citizens in October of that year that "to eliminate the criminals' firepower, lives will have to be decimated. This is a war, and in war there are wounded and killed" (Soares 2007).

Unknown to the public at the time, 2007 also marked the beginnings of the Pacification program. Cabral, unlike many previous governors who treated public security as a signature policy issue, had given Beltrame a high degree of autonomy. Beltrame, a former Federal Police officer, used it to appoint a team of close colleagues, many also from the Federal Police. Stationed in Rio since 2003, Beltrame and his team were familiar with Rio's problems—including police corruption, which they had investigated—yet remained outsiders, insulated

---

[36] Such coordinated attacks ordered from prison are the modal form of violent lobbying in Brazil, and are common around elections. That said, the December 2006 attacks were not accompanied with a clear demand for de jure policy change, and officials publicly disagreed about the traffickers' motives. The leading hypotheses were (a) an attempt to pressure the new government, and (b) retaliation for state complicity with the rise of *milícias*, police-linked paramilitary groups that had expanded quickly between 2004 and 2006, expelling traffickers from numerous favelas (Gomide and Torres 2006).

from Rio's internal politics and the sullied reputation of its police. This team had already begun to fundamentally rethink repressive policy. According to Intelligence Sub-Secretary Roberto Sá:

> We had to engage frontally to bring an end to the [traffickers'] attacks. If we hadn't adopted that hardline rhetoric, their audacity would never have ended. But the results showed us that it was just more of the same. We had to do it, but that alone was not going to deliver the results we wanted.[37]

Beltrame and a group of his top officials, including communications manager Dirceu Vianna, began holding brainstorming sessions over lunch. "The UPP project was born as an internal discussion," said Vianna. In operational terms, the basic outlines of the Pacification strategy took shape in late 2007, when Beltrame's team began to draw up security plans for a major federal infrastructure program known as PACs.[38] These were to be installed in some of the largest and most troubled favelas, including Rocinha, Manguinhos, and Complexo do Alemão. Beltrame's team believed that some form of occupation would probably be necessary, knew that the standard operating procedure of temporary occupation was falling out of favor politically, and saw this as an opportunity to put into practice some of the ideas that had been percolating through the lunch sessions.

In the plans that emerged, many of the eventual elements of the Pacification/UPP strategy were already present. A document from November 2007, for example, calls for a three-phase approach: occupation by special forces (*grupos táticos*), sweeps of the community to seize guns and arrest traffickers, and finally the implantation of a form of community policing. Similar PAC-related plans from early 2008 already use the word "*pacificação*." However, the PAC project ended up being somewhat less extensive than originally conceived, and the ambitious proposals to occupy Rio's largest favelas were shelved.[39]

As when Colombia's Rafael Pardo put his *Sometimiento* policy proposal back in his briefcase after the 1990 negotiations with Escobar collapsed, Beltrame and his team now had concrete plans awaiting an opportunity for implementation. That opportunity was Dona Marta, one of the oldest favelas in the city, and site of vicious urban warfare between two drug factions in the 1990s. By the 2000s it was a largely peaceful favela, but its physical location, next door to the mayoral mansion and across the street from a major police battalion, gave it an iconic presence. In late 2008, Governor Cabral's wife became involved in a publicly funded day care center that had been prevented from opening by local drug traffickers. This offered a pretext for the state to occupy the favela. According to Sub-Secretary Sá: "Dona Marta presented itself as a good place to begin. It's small, there are no cars, few routes of access, it offered less adversity. We decided to do an experiment."

[37] Interview, August 1, 2014.
[38] Programa de Aceleração do Crescimento, Growth Acceleration Program.
[39] Interview, Sub-Secretary Roberto Sá, Rio de Janeiro, August 1, 2014.

The elements of what would become the Pacification policy were not yet all present. In fact, all Beltrame's team really knew was that they intended to keep state forces in Dona Marta indefinitely. The policy did not even have a name; press reports at the time referred to it simply as an "occupation." Shortly thereafter, two more favelas—City of God and Jardim Batam—were unexpectedly occupied by police commanders acting on their own authority, in response to violent episodes in each.[40] Beltrame seized the moment and announced that new "proximity policing" units, eventually christened UPPs, would be installed in all three communities on a permanent basis.

It was in the run-up to the fourth Pacification, of Chapeu Mangueira/Babilônia, that Beltrame first pre-announced the impending occupation. He was widely criticized (Beltrame 2014, 120) and the move drew resistance from within the police. Old-guard officers argued that pre-announcement allowed dangerous criminals to escape, and that UPPs' prolonged contact with drug traffickers would inevitably lead to collusion (*conivência*) with traffickers and, more generally, "laxity" (*frouxidão*). These concerns had to be taken with a grain of salt, since corrupt police stood to lose from a policy that reduced their discretion over traffickers. Still, the rank-and-file's position was probably not entirely cynical given the warrior ethos that had become entrenched in the PM, in part because of significant police causalities over the years. For Beltrame, however, pre-announcing favela occupations was critical to the goal of minimizing violence; indeed, it was a pillar of the program's overall conditionality. He overruled police commanders and insisted on pre-announcing invasions.

With Chapeu Mangueira/Babilônia, Pacification had become an identifiable government policy. While it would continue to evolve, its basic elements had been defined, and with observable security improvements in the Pacified favelas, a proof-of-concept had been established. The strategy, in its "ideal" form, consisted of the following steps:

1. Announce the impending Pacification of a given favela or group of favelas. While exact dates were never given, announcements came far enough in advance to give traffickers a chance to flee.
2. Occupy with overwhelming force. This was usually carried out by the elite BOPE, with the armed forces offering support, especially in the form of tanks.
3. Hold, clear, and install a UPP unit. BOPE forces generally remained for a month or so after the initial occupation, searching for arms and drugs and deterring traffickers from attempting to retake the community. During the transition, a UPP unit is installed, usually in a new building built to purpose.

---

[40] Jardim Batam had been dominated by one of the police-linked *milícia* groups discussed in note 6; the *milícia's* torture of a group of journalists led the local BOPE commander to occupy it.

4. BOPE withdraws, UPP stays. In an effort to break the culture of corruption and brutality of the Military Police, the UPPs were composed entirely of fresh recruits who had gone through a separate, specialized training program in human rights and community relations. A large share of UPP officers were women, and all of them received bonuses, intended to raise the profile of work that traditional, hardline officers tended to view as "soft."[41] In some communities, the project was reinforced with a "Social UPP" component, a raft of social programs.
5. Move on to the next community.

This ideal characterizes the program's early, highly successful rollout (2008–10), in which about forty UPP battalions were installed, covering about 200 Pacified communities. The Pacification of the larger favelas, and those that came later in the process, tended to have more involvement of the armed forces, and the "occupation" period was often extended while waiting for new UPP recruits to be recruited and trained.

Two aspects of the Pacification strategy made it clearly conditional. First, the government announced Pacification-related occupations ahead of time; it also generally maintained only loose perimeter patrolling between announcement and occupation, and declared the operational goal of the occupation itself the retaking of territory rather than the capture or killing of traffickers. In this way, the state essentially gave syndicates a "hiding option," i.e., a chance to flee or, for those unlikely to be identified by police, disarm and melt into favela society. Second, once established, the UPP battalions, while not exactly tolerating the drug trade explicitly, made interdiction and arrest of traffickers a minor priority.

Both these aspects of the policy represent strong breaks with previous practice, and, as with GPAE before it, the Pacification program initially came under criticism for turning a blind eye to traffickers. But whereas GPAE's backers often found themselves on the defensive, Secretary Beltrame forthrightly defended both aspects of the Pacification strategy. In an absolutely crucial piece of rhetorical innovation, he repeatedly stressed that the primary goal of public security policy should be to establish state control and presence within the favelas, and that the goals of arresting kingpins and eradicating the drug trade per se should be considered secondary.

> We cannot guarantee that we will put an end to drug trafficking nor do we have the pretension of doing so. [The idea is] to break the paradigm of territories that are controlled by traffickers with weapons of war.
>
> (Quoted in Phillips 2010)

Criticized for allowing kingpins to escape by pre-announcing occupations, he said:

[41] Interview with UPP police academy instructor, December 20, 2011.

What difference does the arrest of a drug lord make to the life of people who live in a given community? ... Will it reduce crime rates? Arresting drug lords is important, but it isn't the most important thing. Without territory, they are much less "lords" than they were before.

(Quoted in Bastos 2011)[42]

When confronted by journalists with footage of drugs being openly sold in a Pacified favela, Beltrame did not apologize for what is perhaps the most difficult-to-swallow aspect of conditional repression, the need to use less than the full brunt of the state's repressive apparatus against non-violent traffickers:

The basic mission was to disarm the drug dealers and bring peace to the residents. The footage doesn't appear to show anyone armed. ... I can't guarantee there is no drug dealing going on, in some dark corner, in a place as large as [the] City of God [favela] ... That positive outcome is worth infinitely more than the sale of a half dozen packets [of cocaine].

(Quoted in Araújo 2010)[43]

Pacification's trial by fire came in late 2010. The CV launched a wave of bus-burnings, similar to those at the outset of Cabral's term in 2006, this time aimed at discrediting Pacification and pushing Cabral to abandon the policy. Instead, the government announced the imminent Pacification of the CV's principal favela strongholds, including the sprawling Complexo de Alemão, well ahead of schedule. This was the same complex of favelas where Cabral had launched his lethal but unsuccessful 2007 "mega-operation." By the time of the 2010 invasion of Alemão, Pacification was well-established, and cartel–state conflict had been in abatement for over a year. Nonetheless, the consensus view was that traffickers had simply been falling back to Alemão and neighboring Vila Cruzeiro. After Cruzeiro was occupied and state forces amassed on the periphery of Alemão, concern grew from virtually all quarters that the impending invasion would result in a "bloodbath" in which CV soldiers, now gathered in one place, would make their final stand. A coalition of eight prominent human rights and community groups released a public note on November 27 entitled "We will not accept another massacre," making explicit reference to the 2007 failed invasion.[44]

Beltrame, for his part, had told US officials that he expected his planned invasion of Alemão to be lethal and "traumatic" (Fraga 2010), indicating both that prior to the 2010 Alemão invasion, syndicates were understood to be entrenched in a fighting strategy, and that even the formulator of the Pacification strategy did not anticipate the extent to which the CV would switch to hiding strategies. On November 28, the commanding officer in charge of

---

[42] Author's translation.
[43] Author's translation.
[44] "Nota Pública—Não aceitamos mais uma chacina," available online at http://global.org.br/ programas/nota-publica-nao-aceitamos-mais-uma-chacina.

state forces made a public ultimatum, giving the traffickers until sundown to turn themselves in. A prominent cultural figure and experienced mediator, who entered Alemão at the behest of the traffickers and with the permission of state authorities, said he was motivated to take such a risky action by a desire to avoid a massacre.

The attempt at mediation failed, and the next morning a combined force of 2,700 police and soldiers entered Alemão. However, to the surprise of the media, analysts, and even force commanders, there was next to no resistance: the entire operation lasted only a few hours, and produced three fatal casualties. Prior to the invasion, estimates of the number of armed traffickers in Alemão ran from 500 to more than 1,000. The invasion produced no more than two dozen arrests. Most of the traffickers, including the local CV boss, successfully fled. Although the official line is that the state sought to corral the traffickers and bring them to justice, and that the escapes occurred via genuinely successful subterfuge or the corruption of individual officers, this seems implausible given the sheer number of traffickers. A more likely hypothesis is that, as had become standard practice during previous Pacifications, state forces essentially allowed the traffickers to either flee or to disarm and melt into the local population.

If this relative lack of armed confrontation during the 2010 invasion was a happy surprise, its aftermath was even more so. The operation left the CV's principal stronghold firmly in the hands of the state for the first time in more than a generation, ending what Beltrame called Alemão's "illusion of invincibility" (Carneiro 2010). Moreover, in the wake of the successful Pacification of Alemão, the state managed to retake enormous amounts of important favela territory without firing a shot. The next scheduled pacification, in the São Carlos favela, in February 2011, took place almost nonchalantly. Residents said that the traffickers had either fled or disarmed a week in advance of the operation (Costa et al. 2011). The most spectacular example of cartels' shift toward non-violent strategies, however, was the Pacification of the Rocinha–Vidigal–Chácara do Céu group of favelas in November 2011. Rocinha, one of the largest favelas in Latin America, sits in the heart of the city's wealthy southern zone and is widely thought to be the single most lucrative drug market in the city. After arresting the head of the favela's drug operation under somewhat bizarre circumstances (he was riding in the trunk of a car the occupants of which claimed to be Congolese diplomatic officials), the state announced the imminent Pacification of the community. Several days later, an enormous task force of police and army units took all three favelas in a matter of hours without firing a shot.

My core claim is not just that Pacification brought about this radical reduction in cartel–state conflict, but that it did so by increasing the conditionality of repression, creating incentives for traffickers to adopt non-confrontational strategies. One prominent alternative explanation credits the program's outcomes to the UPP units themselves, composed of new, uncorrupted recruits trained in human rights and proximity-policing techniques. In this line of argument, Pacification is a form of counterinsurgency, not only because of its territorial "clear and hold" methods but because the UPPs won the hearts and minds of favela residents, undercutting the social base of the traffickers (Bailly 2011). To be sure, the UPPs' goal of more humane policing and mutual respect with favela residents is crucial to the consolidation of democracy and the full expansion of citizenship in Rio de Janeiro, and the project certainly made some forward progress.

However, it is simply not plausible that this aspect of the Pacification strategy was the primary cause of syndicates' abrupt change of strategies away from anti-state violence, any more than government neglect of the favelas was the sole factor that pushed criminals there to take up arms against the state in the first place. Timing alone makes this clear: the syndicates shifted very quickly to hiding strategies once the nature of Pacification became clear, at a time in which many Pacified favelas were still occupied by BOPE and army forces. Moreover, it is not clear that residents' hearts and minds were ever won, even where UPPs were successfully installed. Little of the promised public investments were effectively delivered, the drug trade abided (by design), and many residents remained skeptical that the UPPs would remain after the 2016 Olympics. More broadly, the syndicates' rule had long been relatively brutal and unpopular among residents; while they certainly relied on residents' compliance and silence, they were long content to obtain it through coercion rather than persuasion. In sum, however normatively important the UPPs' "hearts and minds" mission, it is empirically unlikely that state public-goods provision under Pacification was so effective at winning over residents, or that residents' sentiments were so critical to syndicate strategy, that syndicates were forced to turn away from confrontational strategies. Rather, it was Pacification's explicit focus on eliminating the armed presence of the syndicates and downplaying of efforts to eliminate the drug trade per se that created—for the first time in a sustained and credible fashion—incentives for traffickers to eschew violence.

6.6 RECRUDESCENCE (2013–): PACIFICATION OVERSTRETCHED

Conjecture: Since 2013, the effective conditionality of repression under Pacification has eroded, leading cartels to re-engage in anti-state violence.

In 2013, Pacification began to show signs of trouble. Recruitment and training of new UPP cadets and commanders could not keep pace with the program's expansion. Several UPP commanders were sacked for corruption, police brutality, or both; in one particularly painful episode, an innocent worker in Rocinha was killed by UPP police, leading to widespread protest and a collapse in slowly accumulated public trust. Above all, cartel–state violence has risen steadily since 2013. While not limited to Pacified favelas, this violence seems to be driven in large part by increasingly common trafficker attacks on UPP units. These had never fully ceased in Alemão, but have grown more serious and spread to other Pacified areas, including Rocinha (which was dominated by the Amigos dos Amigos syndicate prior to Pacification, not the CV), City of God, and Cantagalo and even Dona Marta, the first favela to be Pacified.

Partly in response to these setbacks, Secretary Beltrame halted the expansion of the Pacification program in 2015. The Maré complex of favelas, occupied in preparation for implantation of a UPP unit, was instead simply left unguarded when army troops left in 2015; traffickers quickly reclaimed the territory. There has been no official talk of dismantling the UPPs that are already installed, but these units are increasingly facing armed attacks from traffickers, and in some cases are forced to physically retreat.

Despite these setbacks, Pacification still stands as perhaps the most successful conditional program on record. The UPPs have stopped expanding, but thus far are not in active retreat. Pacification successfully survived a change of governor (albeit of the same party), which in Brazil is itself an accomplishment. Nonetheless, the long-run fate of Pacification is now, sadly, in question. And while the UPPs already in place have not yet been dismantled—outliving the end of the 2016 Olympic Games that many assumed would mark their demise—the longer they remain targets for what are essentially guerrilla attacks by traffickers, the harder it will be to maintain them. Whatever happens, though, it is clear that Pacification fundamentally altered the dynamic of cartel–state violence in Rio, after decades of escalatory stalemate. It should be accounted for by any broader analysis of criminal war.

My theory offers some leverage on understanding the resurgence of cartel–state conflict in Rio. In particular, I conjecture that while Pacification still represents an increase in conditionality over the *status quo ante*, the effective conditionality of day-to-day policing may have fallen over time. The rapid expansion of Pacification, from a few well-planned occupations of smaller favelas to encompass the sprawling and mountainous regions of Alemão, Vila Cruzeiro, and Rocinha simply outstripped the state's capacity to provide properly trained UPP units and commanders, and in some cases police rank-and-file were used instead. Cases of police abuse and corruption undermined residents' support for Pacification in some favelas, and may have also signaled to traffickers that repression was decreasing conditional there. Furthermore, limited ethnographic evidence suggests that, after an initial period in which the drug trade became highly mobile and non-territorial, new *arrego* arrangements were struck in which traffickers occupied fixed points of sale and made regular bribe payments to local UPP officers (Grillo 2013).[45] This

[45] Author's conversations with residents of Babilônia and Chapeu-Mangueira residents in 2012.

may have set (back) in motion the dynamics of violent corruption that characterized the *arrego* in the pre-Pacification status quo. Local UPP commanders may be tempted to increase repressive pressure on local traffickers—even if they are unarmed or peaceful—to extract larger bribes. As the differential between the daily repression of the drug trade practiced by the UPP and the threat of a BOPE incursion in response to anti-state violence grows smaller, effective conditionality of repression falls, increasing cartels' incentives to fight back.

Another potential factor is the decreasing public support for Pacification as a whole. The original Pacification of Vila Cruzeiro and Alemão was undertaken in response to a wave of violent lobbying attacks by the CV in the autumn of 2010. These attacks presumably sought to undermine support for Pacification, but badly backfired. In terms of my model of violent lobbying, the Pacification policy was simply not susceptible to violent lobbying, because it enjoyed widespread support from the public, the media, and the political coalition that ran from the mayor through the governor to the federal government in Brasília. The climate in the recrudescence phase has been quite different: scandals undermined public and resident support, and the federal government was embroiled in a major political crisis and far less supportive of Cabral's successor, Luis Fernando Pezão. Indeed, in the 2014 gubernatorial election, several of Pezão's competitors for the office—particularly former governor and hardliner Anthony Garotinho—voiced deep skepticism about Pacification's future. Security officials suggested that traffickers may have believed that Garotinho's election would lead to the weakening or rollback of Pacification. Garotinho lost and Pezão continued to defend Pacification, but with the 2016 resignation of Beltrame, Pacification's founder, the program's future is unclear. CV leaders' assessment of Pacification's susceptibility to violent lobbying has thus probably risen, creating incentives to use violence to further undermine the policy. Such lobbying has a realistic chance of success, since it undermines the fundamental appeal of Pacification: that it had made such violence a thing of the past. This reveals an inherent political weakness of conditional repression: a violence-reduction policy can be "spoiled" by anyone capable of committing extensive violence.

6.7 CONCLUSION: TO PACIFY A DRUG WAR

Rio de Janeiro's drug war has a fractal structure, with different patterns emerging and echoing across different spatial and temporal scales. Reading the newspaper (or systematically coding it), one observes a nearly constant stream of shootouts and confrontations, both among syndicates and—more frequently—between traffickers and police. Looking beyond the headlines, though, most syndicate-controlled favelas on most days were *not* the site of shootouts, seizures, and arrests; attempts to aggressively enforce drug laws, however violent their outcome, are an exception to the rule of the *arrego*.

This pattern of regularized bribery punctuated by intermittent armed clashes, I have argued, constitutes a stable equilibrium: even though anti-state violence is costly for traffickers, it ultimately serves to keep the demands of corrupt police from growing too extortionate.

Taking a slightly longer view, the seemingly endless stream of police–trafficker clashes is peppered with less frequent but more severe sorts of violence: full-scale invasions by one syndicate with the intent of permanently taking another's territory; shocking police massacres of civilians; and syndicate violence *outside* the favela, often attacks on police stations or government buildings but also bus-burnings, grenade attacks, and syndicate-ordered closures of schools and businesses. The first two phenomena lie outside the explanatory scope of this study, but the CV's occasional resort to "terror tactics" fits the theory of violent lobbying laid out in Chapters 3 and 4. When de jure state policies become susceptible to cartel pressure for change, whether because they are not salient or simply not popular, cartels may find public violence an effective way to impose costs on political leaders.

At the time-scale of governorships, one perceives an oscillation in de jure policy between liberalizing restraint and reactionary crackdown; a longer view, however, reveals two secular trends behind this political pendulum. First, there was a steady escalation in the drug war's armament and tactics; second, a remarkable stability of its "battle lines." In the two decades since the advent of Rio's drug war in the mid-1980s, Brazil democratized, state governors came and went, the presidency switched hands from the privatizing reformer Fernando Henrique Cardoso to the leftist hero Lula, and both the police and the syndicates went from pistols to assault rifles to armored vehicles, barricades, grenades, and anti-aircraft weapons; besides driving ever-higher death tolls, none of this seemed to fundamentally alter the dynamics of the syndicate–police–favela nexus. At the outset of 2008, the CV and its rivals controlled the same swathes of critical urban territory—including the massive favelas Complexo do Alemão and Rocinha—that they had for some twenty years, and the state seemed no closer than ever to dislodging them. The situation was so grim that when police-linked *milícias* began to "liberate" outlying favelas only to establish their own violent and exploitive rule, Rio's mayor publicly declared them to be the lesser of two evils (Bottari and Ramalho 2006).

To the pleasant surprise of residents, policymakers, and researchers (present company included), this decades-long escalatory trend abruptly reversed course between 2008 and 2012, during the heyday of the Pacification strategy. Pacification began as a local policy experiment, but its initial success led to rapid development and replication, producing a sharp change in the state's overall objectives and strategies vis-à-vis Rio's drug syndicates: a discontinuous increase in the conditionality of repression, to use the theoretical terms developed here. This increase in conditionality, I have argued, was the primary cause of the fundamental shift in the dynamics of Rio's drug war. The scale and starkness of that shift was, by any measure, quite extraordinary. As a former

Brazil specialist for Amnesty International put it to me in 2012, "This city is becoming normal."[46]

The erosion of Pacification since 2013, and the resurgence of cartel–state conflict that has accompanied it, suggest that what seemed like a definitive break might in fact be part of yet another pattern of oscillation. Pacification is not the first case of reform efforts initially succeeding in reorienting policing policy toward the goals of violence reduction, establishing state presence, and protecting the rights and lives of vulnerable citizens—with demonstrable reductions in armed violence—but ultimately succumbing to forces that push policy back toward invasive policing and the attendant violence of open cartel–state conflict. One hopes that this pattern is not so much an endless cycle as a rising helix. GPAE built on earlier failed efforts, and the architects of Pacification later learned from GPAE's mistakes; even if Pacification is entirely abandoned in the years to come, it could make important contributions to future reform efforts. One contribution is as a proof-of-concept; as an NGO director in Maré said of the favela's temporary occupation and the reversion to trafficker dominion that followed, "Well, at least it showed what can be done. The question now is whether Rio will ever put up the money to really do it."[47] Not all the costs are monetary, though: as I explore in Part III, the politics of drug war play a critical role in undermining conditional reforms once implemented.

In comparative perspective, Rio highlights three sobering realities of cartel–state conflict. First, unconditional crackdowns aimed at crushing drug cartels can not only fail but can result in *decades* of entrenched militarized drug war, including cartel–state conflict with crippling effects on large populations. Second, conditional crackdowns can rapidly curtail cartel–state conflict and produce profound changes in the dynamics of the drug trade, but require institutional and political support for a reorientation of policy goals. Finally, even well-planned and successful conditional crackdowns face difficult long-term challenges: rapid expansion and shifting political optics can quickly undermine support and lead to resurgence of cartel–state conflict. By no means do these challenges invalidate conditional repression as an approach: Pacification has improved the lives of hundreds of thousands of favela residents, and pointed the way toward a future in which Rio is no longer home to a full-blown urban armed conflict. One hopes that deeper understanding and further investigation of these self-undermining dynamics can contribute to that future.

---

[46] Interview, Rio de Janeiro, January 5, 2012.
[47] Interview, Rio de Janeiro, August 17, 2016.

7

Mexico

Conditionality Abandoned

Mexico has become known for drug violence, which escalated dramatically from 2006 to 2012, including a ten-fold intensification of cartel-state conflict. However, large DTOs operated peacefully in Mexico for more than a century. Since its advent in the 1930s, the hegemonic Partido Revolucionario Institucional (PRI) actively managed cartels through a highly conditional state-sponsored protection racket. This system began to erode in the late 1980s and eventually collapsed with Mexico's democratization in the 1990s. Though cartels grew stronger from the 1990s onward due to market forces, the triggering factor for cartel–state conflict—and possibly inter-cartel turf war—was shifts in state policy. This chapter makes four key claims: (1) Under single-party PRI rule (1930s–1989), conditionality was high, leading cartels to eschew anti-state violence. (2) Democratization (1990–2000) weakened conditionality, pushing cartels toward violent strategies, though actual anti-state violence remained rare. (3) Fox's limited, unconditional crackdown (2003–2005) pushed cartels to fight back, triggering the onset of cartel–state conflict. (4) Calderón's massive crackdown (2006–2012) severely reduced conditionality, leading to full-blown cartel–state conflict. I also conjecture that attempts to reform policy in a more conditional direction in 2010 and 2011 mostly failed, but modestly increased conditionality in some repressive agencies. This may have induced some cartels to adopt less confrontational strategies. Under Enrique Peña Nieto, state policy seems to have remained largely unconditional, and cartel–state conflict abides.

7.1 OVERVIEW

Between December 2006, when President Felipe Calderón led Mexico's armed forces into a "war without quarter" against drug cartels, and the end of his term six years later, some 75,000 lives were lost to cartel-related violence. Mexico's drug war began before Calderón's time in office, and has certainly outlived it. Yet Calderón's crackdown and the explosion of violence that followed it both represent radical breaks with the past. What had been a growing but minor concern at the outset of Calderón's presidency became an enduring crisis of national proportions, altering Mexico's perception in the eyes of the world and its own people. Moreover, Calderón's unconditional, militarized approach was quietly adopted by his successor, Enrique Peña Nieto, despite initial vows to reverse course. As of this writing (late 2016), cartel violence—including anti-state violence—is down from its 2011 peak and no longer widely reported on, but continues at levels unheard of prior to 2006. The ten-year anniversary of Calderón's war momentarily sparked renewed public debate, ironically highlighting the conflict's transition from a polemical to a permanent feature of Mexican life. Calderón's crackdowns seems to have pushed Mexico into a new, harrowing equilibrium in which militarized drug war is the new normal; if Rio de Janeiro's thirty-year conflict is any indication, it is an equilibrium that could prove all too stable.

It is easy enough to blame the bloodletting on geographical misfortune, a tragic new twist on the long-standing lament, "Poor Mexico, so far from God, so close to the United States." Caught between the coca fields of the Andes and the unquenchable cocaine markets of the United States, Mexico became the obvious path northward after US interdiction efforts shut down Caribbean routes in the early 1990s. Those same efforts helped dismantle Colombia's hegemonic Medellín and Cali cartels, leaving Mexican DTOs dominant and further fueling their growth. Adding injury to insult, lax US gun laws give Mexican cartels easy access to firearms, even more so after the 2004 expiration of an already porous Federal Assault Weapons Ban (Dube et al. 2013). Cartels even benefited, perversely, from US anti-narcotics know-how and fervor: members of Mexico's elite GAFES (Grupo Aeromóvil de Fuerzas Especiales, Special-Forces Airmobile Group) force took their School of the Americas training with them when they defected to form the Zetas, the private militia of the Gulf cartel. By the early 2000s, Mexico's cartels had grown into some of the richest, most powerful, and best-armed criminal organizations in the world—a fitting if depressing capstone to a fifty-year history of US-backed repression inadvertently pushing the cocaine trade from Chile ever northward (Gootenberg 2012).

Yet Mexico's drug war must ultimately be understood as a product of domestic politics and policies, above all the end of single-party rule under the Partido Revolucionario Institucional (PRI) and the dynamics that democratization set in motion. For most of the twentieth century, the PRI actively managed and pacified Mexico's always sizeable drug trade, proving that the mere existence of well-organized cartels need not produce militarized drug war. On the other hand, the PRI accomplished this—as it did so much else—through a praxis of systematic corruption, with authorities at all levels of government regularly extracting bribes from traffickers. As the PRI's hegemony eroded in the 1990s, so too did this state-sponsored protection racket and the highly conditional repression that supported it. Political competition destabilized corrupt protection arrangements, inter-cartel pacts collapsed, and an incipient turf war began. As violence worsened and the first opposition presidents Vicente Fox and Felipe Calderón came to power under the Partido Acción Nacional (PAN), their repressive responses were strongly shaped by effects of democratization both pragmatic and political: fragmented control across municipal, state, and federal governments; newfound electoral concerns; and the ever-present shadow of the PRI's corrupt past. These factors, more than US pressure, led to the deliberate abandonment of conditionality in favor of a "no quarter" approach that, I will argue, triggered the onset of cartel–state conflict.

In comparative perspective, Mexico stands out in three ways. First, inter-cartel turf war is preeminent in Mexico; unlike in Colombia and Rio, fighting among cartels triggered the initial state crackdown and continues to account for the bulk of the violence. This has understandably led scholars to focus explanatory work almost exclusively on inter-cartel violence, or even overall homicides, downplaying, in my view, both the substantive importance and the unique puzzle posed by cartel–state conflict. Second, whereas in both Colombia and Rio reform efforts ultimately succeeded in implementing conditional policies, ushering abrupt abatement phases, similar attempts at reform in Mexico were mostly thwarted. Finally, Mexico's PRI period represents the clearest example of a stable "state-sponsored protection" scenario, in which highly conditional repression kept the drug trade peaceful while enforcement of the law rarely occurred in equilibrium. Top-down control of bribery was institutionalized, and likely strengthened rather than undermined the state. The collapse of this system in the 1990s was a key driver of inter-cartel and eventually cartel–state violence, offering important insights into the murky linkages between corruption, violence, and state capacity.

On balance, democratization and the end of the PRI's repressive and increasingly corrupt regime are surely positive developments; Calderón's claims of an ethical imperative to crack down on cartels and definitively end state-sponsored protection are, in light of the ensuing violence, harder to evaluate. This book argues that leaders face hard trade-offs, since they cannot minimize drug flows, corruption, and violence at the same time. The PRI's approach combined a deliberate and resource-intensive focus on reducing cartel violence and active encouragement of corruption with a blithe indifference to drug flows; however morally dubious those objectives, the PRI's policies largely achieved them. The PAN's unconditional crackdowns, by contrast, were sometimes sold as a means to achieve all three goals; sometimes as a devil's bargain that would reduce drug flows and corruption at the cost of short-term violence; and sometimes as a struggle for Mexico's soul in which ending the corrupting, *political* influence of cartels was paramount, whatever the cost in blood and treasure and however ineffective at stanching the flow of drugs. Shifting goalposts notwithstanding, the tragedy of Mexico's drug war is how little progress has been made on *any* of these dimensions.

Perhaps the greatest tragedy is that Mexico is not a particularly violent society. While it has known armed conflict, autocratic government, and persistent crime, it never suffered either the full-fledged civil wars or the debilitating violent crime rates that have scarred many of its Latin American neighbors over the last sixty years.[1] Its national homicide rate has historically been low by regional standards, and fell steadily from twenty per 100,000 habitants in 1992 to under ten in 2007 (Escalante 2009). The explosion of drug-war violence since then contributed to a sharp turnaround, but even in 2012, Mexico's national rate (twenty-two) was dwarfed by those of Honduras (ninety) and Venezuela (fifty-four), and remains well below Colombia (thirty) and even Brazil (twenty-five) (UNODC 2014).[2] Yet in places where cartels fought one another for turf, or fought state forces for power, whole cities became war zones, populations were decimated and displaced, and, in the language Calderón came to adopt, the "social fabric" was rent. Even the political and economic elites ensconced in Mexico City, which somehow escaped the drug war's ravages, were not wholly immune: extreme violence ravaged Acapulco (the nearest coastal city) and even reached the popular resort town of Cuernavaca only an hour away. In scale, duration, and impact, the drug war is surely the country's most severe conflict since the Mexican revolution.

7.1.1 Trajectory and Core Claims

Unlike Colombia and Rio's initially laissez-faire approach to drug repression, Mexico's "peaceful prelude" phase was marked by an elaborate state-sponsored protection racket (similar to Rio's management of its numbers racket). For much of the twentieth century, and increasingly from the 1950s forward, an historically extensive drug trade of significant size (though small by current standards) was incorporated into a larger system of economic and political corruption sustained by, and sustaining, the PRI's hegemonic party apparatus.

Expansion of the Mexican drug trade (especially the diversion of cocaine flows from the Caribbean to the overland Mexican route) and the breakdown of state-sponsored protection (largely driven by the collapse of PRI hegemony) set the stage for a burgeoning inter-cartel turf war in the late 1990s and early 2000s. Whereas turf war emerged only after cartel–state conflict in the Colombian and Brazilian cases, it was a triggering factor in Mexico. It provoked an increasingly militarized state response starting in 2003, sparking the first incidents of systematic anti-state violence by cartels. Military deployments were reduced in early 2006, but turf war continued to escalate,

---

[1] As for state killings, Mexico's reputation for having avoided the "dirty wars" of other Latin American authoritarian regimes collapsed when government archives were opened in 2001, revealing systematic torture and thousands of extrajudicial killings and forced disappearances.
[2] Figures rounded to nearest whole number.

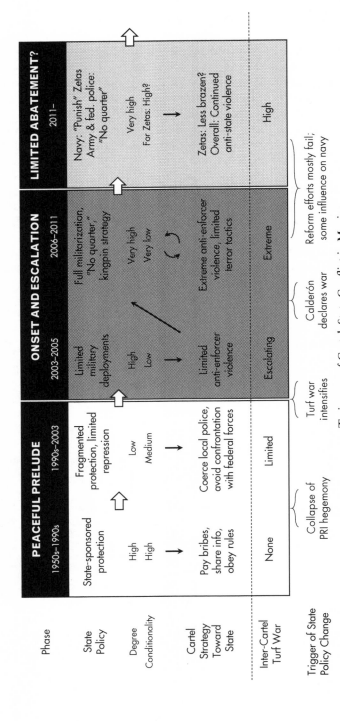

FIGURE 7.1. Trajectory of Cartel–State Conflict in Mexico.

provoking the full-blown militarization of the drug war that President Calderón launched at the outset of his presidency.

Calderón's crackdown was explicitly and deliberately unconditional, promising "no quarter" to any cartel (whatever its behavior), in part to avoid suspicions of favoritism or collusion. The "kingpin" strategy he adopted, based on Colombia's experience, successfully fragmented many cartels by arresting or killing their leaders, yet both cartel–state and inter-cartel violence surged dramatically between 2007 and 2011. This prompted reform efforts by Calderón's own staff to reorient repressive policy toward violence reduction by adopting a more conditional approach. Broadly speaking, these efforts failed, though they seem to have allowed the navy and the national intelligence agency, CISEN,[3] to "punish" the Zetas cartel for its extreme violence. Publicly, however, Calderón doubled down on his stance against selective enforcement, while both the army and Federal Police remained committed to a "frontal combat" approach.

Whether these efforts pushed Mexico into a phase of "limited abatement" is unclear, in part because the government has not released data on cartel-related violence since late 2011. Some argue that the Zetas adopted less violent strategies in the wake of the navy's targeted repression, and even attribute the overall decline in homicide rates since 2011 to generalized if unacknowledged conditionality of repression. Yet while Calderón's successor Enrique Peña Nieto initially feinted in the direction of a more conditional approach, he largely hewed to the militarized, kingpin strategy of his predecessor (Hope 2015). This has produced high-profile arrests and the further fragmenting of Mexico's cartels, but inter-cartel and anti-state violence, as far as we can tell, continue at historically high levels. Moreover, newly formed splinter cartels still engage in brazen armed violence against state forces. In sum, Mexico has neither adopted a clearly conditional approach nor witnessed the sharp "abatement" phase seen in the other cases.

The following section broadly considers my central thesis—state policy is a key driver of variation in cartel–state conflict—against alternative perspectives. I then present the details of the case, organized by phases, making the following core claims along the way:

Claim 1: Under single-party PRI rule (1930s–1989), conditionality was high, leading cartels to eschew anti-state violence.

Claim 2: Democratization (1990–2000) weakened conditionality, pushing cartels toward violent strategies, though actual anti-state violence remained rare.

Claim 3: Fox's limited, unconditional crackdown (2003–2005) pushed cartels to fight back, triggering the onset of cartel–state conflict.

Claim 4: Calderón's massive crackdown (2006–2012) severely reduced conditionality, leading to full-blown cartel–state conflict.

---

[3] Centro de Investigación y Seguridad Nacional (Center of Investigation and National Security).

Conjecture: Reform efforts in 2010–2011 mostly failed to shift policy, but modestly increased conditionality in some repressive agencies, possibly inducing some cartels to adopt less confrontational strategies.

These claims correspond roughly to the vertical arrows in Figure 7.1. The horizontal arrows represent shifts in state policy, triggered by a variety of proximate causes; I provide details on the processes of policy reform that, in Mexico, mostly failed to shift state policy, and consider these in comparative perspective in Part III.

7.2   STATE POLICY AS DRIVER OF CARTEL–STATE CONFLICT AND ALTERNATIVE EXPLANATIONS

To many observers, the violence in Mexico is unsurprising given the underlying conditions: enormous profit margins, organized cartels angling for primacy, a ready supply of weapons from the United States, widespread police corruption, weak institutions (especially in border areas), and few legitimate economic opportunities that might keep youths from entering the drug trade. While these ingredients do seem like a natural recipe for violence, they have all been characteristics of Mexico for years, if not decades. The increase in violence from 2006 onward, on the other hand, was precipitous, and the eruption of cartel–state conflict in particular marked an abrupt break with the past.

Many factors conventionally blamed for drug violence are simply too static or slow moving to explain the rapid escalation of violence that began in 2007, though they certainly may constitute permissive conditions or intensifying factors. As with the sharp decline in cartel–state conflict in Rio de Janeiro since 2008, the sharp increase in cartel–state conflict in Mexico points to explanatory variables that underwent important and large shifts just prior. Calderón's crackdown is the obvious candidate, and I am hardly the first to suggest so. That said, it is certainly not the only relevant factor, and even if it did increase violence, there is an important debate about *how*, as well as *what kind of violence*, inter-cartel or cartel–state. This section examines these alternative hypotheses with respect to my core claims.

One key factor that does vary considerably is the drug market itself; its dynamics surely play some role in drug violence. At the macro level, cocaine flows through Mexico, starting in the 1980s and increasingly significantly in the 1990s, led to qualitative increases in the size and organizational capacity of Mexican cartels (Valdés 2013). Such scale effects could plausibly drive violence in a number of ways. First, they permit cartels to amass firepower; the levels of violence seen in Mexico from 2004 onward simply could not have occurred had cartels not acquired standing armies of salaried soldiers, often with military training. Second, larger drug flows could give cartels more incentives to fight; both with each other, for market share, and with corrupt enforcers, over the size of bribes.

However, higher profits do not necessarily imply more violence. The Colombian cocaine bonanza in the early 1980s demonstrates that cartels can become wealthy and sophisticated, and even amass significant firepower, without either turf-war or systematic cartel–state conflict breaking out. Violence is always a costly way to divide *any* pie, whatever the size (Fearon 1995b); sometimes, a larger pie just means there is enough to go around. For this reason, large and powerful DTOs—and the lucrative drug markets that sustain them—are best thought of as necessary but not sufficient conditions for militarized drug war.

Micro-scale variation in market conditions may also exacerbate violence, but appears not to be a sufficient condition. There is a very high correlation, for example, of US street prices for cocaine and cartel-related killings in Mexico from 2007 to 2009, indicating a possible causal relation; however, this correlation all but disappeared in 2010–2011 (Figure 11.2). Moreover, killings in Mexico might be the cause of changes in prices, not the other way around. In a brilliant study, Castillo et al. (2014) get around this endogeneity problem by regressing drug seizures in *Colombia* on homicides in drug-trafficking municipalities in Mexico. They thus convincingly demonstrate that these negative supply shocks caused increases in violence. Critically, though, their results are significant *after* 2006, but not before. In other words, supply shocks apparently exacerbate violence only under certain conditions, conditions which held only once Calderón's crackdown was underway.

The claim that changes in state policy caused an escalation of drug violence in Mexico is far from novel. Almost from the outset of Calderón's crackdown, critics argued that it was exacerbating the violence, and key Calderón advisors essentially admitted as much. Publicly, however, Calderón insisted his crackdown was constraining violence, restoring order, and protecting Mexicans, and his spokesman Alejandro Poiré published statistics purporting to show that capturing kingpins did not lead to increased violence (Poiré and Martínez 2011). However, numerous analyses employing broader temporal and geographical windows contradicted these claims (e.g., Guerrero 2011a; Merino 2011). Since then, scholars have produced more sophisticated research designs demonstrating a causal impact of increased state repression on cartel violence. Most prominently, Dell's (2015) regression-discontinuity approach showed that increased repression due to the presence of PAN mayors led to increased turf-war violence, while Calderón et al.'s (2015) synthetic cohort approach similarly found that "beheadings" (arrest or killing of kingpins) increased cartel violence and possibly anti-civilian spillover violence. Importantly for present purposes, neither study examines the effects of state repression on cartel–state violence. Since the vast majority of killings in Mexico are among cartels, this is justifiable both in terms of substantive importance and the technical need for statistical power. However, it leaves unexplained a distinct and critical form of cartel violence.

Available measures—such as cartel–state homicides from the SNSP database and a grab bag of Freedom of Information Act reports from the army on cartel attacks on army soldiers—reveal that cartel–state conflict also escalated by an order of magnitude over the course of Calderón's *sexenio*.[4] Yet the bulk of the increase in cartel-related killings consists in inter-cartel killings related to battles for turf; it is simply undeniable that Mexico's drug war remained, in numerical terms, overwhelmingly a war among cartels. One important alternative hypothesis to my core argument is that cartel–state conflict was essentially a by-product of inter-cartel turf war. Even if government policy contributed to the escalation of turf war, it may have had no independent effect on cartels' decisions to attack the state. This argument is made explicitly by Calderón's former head of intelligence in his influential history of narco-violence in Mexico: "78% of deaths from cartel–state clashes occurred in the context of the conflict between the Gulf Cartel and the Zetas ... teams of assassins from both organizations would continually move along highways, to attack or defend [positions] ... It was along these stretches where they would run into federal forces, which provoked the clashes" (Valdés 2013, 405–406).

In contrast, the overarching argument of this book is that cartel–state conflict is driven directly by unconditional crackdowns, following logics that are distinct from inter-cartel war turf war. This was patent in the case of Colombia, where cartel–state conflict broke out prior to the onset of turf war. It is less clear in the Mexican case. After all, it was an escalating turf war that led first Fox and then Calderón to deploy the armed forces in the first place. Could Valdés be correct that state forces in Mexico are simply caught in the crossfire?

A straightforward correlational analysis of official data casts doubt on this position, revealing that the intensity of turf war is a surprisingly poor predictor of cartel–state conflict. Figure 7.2 presents a panel regression of monthly state totals from 2007 to 2011 of cartel–state homicides (the sum of *enfrentamientos* and *agressiones*) vs. cartel–cartel homicides (*ejecuciones*). The relationship is quite weak, and if we focus on times and places with the highest concentration of cartel–state violence, actually becomes negative.[5] Similarly, crossing the same homicide data with a panel of data on cocaine seizures gives us some sense of whether simply carrying out repressive activity somewhere necessarily leads cartels to fight back. While neither relationship is terribly strong, interdiction efforts seem better correlated with turf war than cartel–state conflict. The lack of a straightforward correlation between enforcement and anti-state violence suggests that more complicated mechanisms are at work.

This jibes with intuition. Attacking public officials, police, or army troops is not an obviously winning strategy, even for heavily armed drug cartels at war with one another. Cartels need good reasons to confront the state,

---

[4] Mexico's single presidential terms of six years are called *sexenios*.
[5] A slightly stronger but hardly robust relationship holds among the middle half of observations ($R^2 = 0.28$). Of course, from a normative perspective, it is precisely the outliers at the top of the distribution we care most about.

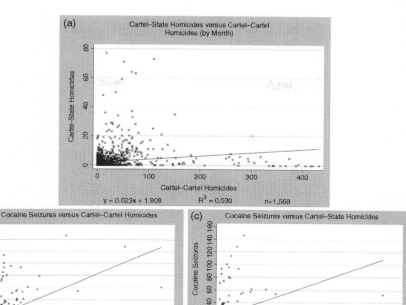

FIGURE 7.2. **Relationships among Cartel–State Homicides, Cartel–Cartel Homicides, and Cocaine Seizures, 2007–2011.**
Source: government dataset of organized-crime-related killings (SNSP 2011). "Cartel–State Homicides" is the sum of *enfrentamientos* and *agresiones*; "Cartel–Cartel Homicides" is *ejecuciones*. Panel (a) shows a scatterplot for these two types of violence; each data point is a state-month. The correlation is very low, and decreases further if we truncate the sample to those state-months with more cartel–state homicides. Panels (b) and (c) show similar scatterplots of cocaine seizures versus each type of violence, by state-year. Neither correlation is strong, but seizures are more strongly correlated with cartel–cartel homicides.

particularly when the state has decided to crack down. The logic of violent corruption modeled in Chapter 4 provides precisely such a reason: crackdowns under conditions of thoroughgoing corruption give cartels an incentive to fight back, as a way of intimidating corrupt enforcers into accepting smaller bribes. Only by making repression conditional can leaders counter these incentives and induce cartels to adopt non-violent strategies. As the following sections detail, Calderón's crackdown was unconditional by design, and reform efforts to increase conditionality largely failed. My theory thus offers a more plausible account of cartels' decisions to confront the state than a simple "caught in the crossfire" account.

7.3 PEACEFUL PRELUDE (1930S–2003): AUTHORITARIAN CONDITIONALITY AND ITS DEMOCRATIC DEMISE

7.3.1 The *Pax Priista* (1930s–1989): Conditionality Through Corruption

Claim 1: Under single-party PRI rule, conditionality was high, leading cartels to avoid anti-state violence.

Mexico's drug trade, and the state's fraught relationship to it, stretch back further than even Colombia's. Marijuana and opium production in Sinaloa state began in the nineteenth century (Osorno 2009), and both products were regularly exported to the United States well before they were prohibited in the early part of the twentieth century. During the Mexican revolution and the period of instability that followed it (1913–20), repression against the drug trade was not a priority. Yet with US prohibition came illicit profits for Mexican drug traffickers, and those profits attracted the attention of police and local caciques. As Astorga (1999) documents, the practice of state governors providing protection to traffickers, or even *being* traffickers, began as early as 1916, and was widespread by the 1930s. Early Mexican anti-narcotics agencies also appear to have been corrupt at their founding, with agents "paid with the drugs they seized" (Astorga 1999, 13).

Political violence and unrest were finally quelled with the founding of the Partido Revolucionario Nacional (PRN), eventually renamed PRI, in 1929. Corruption was, and would remain, central to the PRI's governance and state-building approach: "the clashing gears of interest were lubricated by the heavy oil of graft" (Needler 1961, 311). Particularly important for pacifying post-revolutionary Mexico was the distribution of governorships to military commanders, who exchanged obedience to the president for the liberty to pursue opportunities for personal enrichment. Taxing the drug trade came to be seen as an informal right of governors and other powerful politicians, who kept traffickers in a subordinate position and banned them from participating in politics (Astorga 1999, 14).

From 1947 onward, this decentralized system became federalized with the founding of the Federal Security Directorate (Dirección Federal de Seguridad, DFS), a political police force that also had jurisdiction over drug issues; the Attorney General's Office (Procuraduría General de la Republica, PGR) and the army also became involved. While some arrests were made, and the army did carry out eradications from time to time (Astorga 1999; *CNNMéxico* 2011), these repressive agencies largely served to mediate the corrupt relationship between traffickers and the political system. The DFS took the lead (Aguayo 2001); its mission "was to be twofold: on the one hand, it ensured that part of the [traffickers'] profits was levied in exchange for protection; on the other, it served as a mechanism for containing the violence and any political temptations on the part of the traffickers" (Astorga 2001, 428). Former CISEN director Guillermo Valdés describes the arrangement this way:

> The model of relations between the State and organized crime from the 50s to the 70s consisted in an accord of mutual benefits: handing over franchises or *plazas* to drug trafficking organizations with permission to operate and police protection, both federal and state, in exchange for sharing with authorities the profits from the business and the most "civilized" criminal conduct possible to minimize the impact on society.
>
> (Valdés 2013, 215)

Critical to the ability of the DFS, and the PRI behind it, to dictate these rules of the game was a credible threat that breaking the rules—including the injunction against anti-state and anti-civilian violence—would bring swift and certain punishment (Lupsha 1991; Poppa 2010).

Federal law enforcement agents' bribe-taking was, in turn, regulated from above; they were free to keep a share of the profits, "but not so big as to become autonomous themselves, and certainly not without sharing profits with their superiors in the political structure" (Astorga 1999). This informal yet top-down regulation of bribery and graft was a central mechanism of PRI rule, and an example of how corruption can be state-strengthening by reinforcing bureaucratic hierarchies (Darden 2008). As I discuss in Chapter 11, it may have significantly increased state revenue—bribes meant that enforcers' official salaries could remain low—an unorthodox form of extraction usually overlooked in the state-formation literature.

For decades, the PRI's corrupt but clearly conditional approach produced a steady stream of bribes, very little actual enforcement (Andreas 1998), and essentially no anti-state violence, approaching the "state-sponsored protection" ideal-type scenario identified by my model of violent corruption. Like the "coerced peace" ideal type, approximated by 1970s Medellín under Pablo Escobar's reign, bribe agreements are always reached under state-sponsored protection, and enforcement never occurs. Under coerced peace, however, enforcers *would* face punishing violence if no bribe were paid and they actually enforced the law; under state-sponsored protection, cartels would respond to enforcement with non-violent, evasive strategies. This distinction becomes manifest as we move from ideal-type scenarios, where enforcement never occurs and thus threats are never acted on, to the real world where, inevitably, bribe negotiation sometimes fails. As we saw in Chapter 5, the few intrepid enforcers who refused Escobar's bribes were either murdered or barely escaped with their lives.

Parallel evidence that Mexico's cartels were not making Escobar-style *plata o plomo* threats comes from the 1989 surprise arrest of Miguel Ángel Félix Gallardo, undisputed godfather of the then-hegemonic Guadalajara cartel. Though the traffickers' account of the arrest (a fait accompli during a bribe-negotiation meeting with his official protector) differs from the official version (a thirty-man police operation at Gallardo's home), in both versions the capo responded with neither resistance nor posterior reprisals (Osorno 2009, 184, 216; Valdés 2013, 206–208). As Ioan Grillo says of this episode, "That the Mexican government could take down the biggest gangster in the country without firing a shot was telling … officers could take out narcos when they needed to" (Grillo 2011, 77–78). Critically, though, it is also evidence that cartels were playing "hide-and-bribe" strategies, and thus that in the far more common cases where bribery "worked" and no enforcement occurred (such as Gallardo's frequent and friendly meetings with police prior to his arrest), no credible threat of anti-state violence lay off the equilibrium path. One need only compare Gallardo's peaceful arrest to the contemporaneous string of assassinated and threatened judges who dared to investigate and indict Pablo Escobar to see the difference.

The formal analysis of Chapter 4 reveals several necessary conditions for sustained state-sponsored protection. First, enforcers must face little or no sanction for bribe-taking—surely the case here since the protection racket was official state policy. Second, enforcers' uncertainty over the true size of profits must not be too large;[6] intriguingly, specific mechanisms to reduce such information asymmetries appear to have been in place. Lupsha (1991, 50), quoting US grand-jury testimony, offers a vivid example from the heyday of the lucrative Rancho Búfalo marijuana plantation in the early 1980s: "once the processed marijuana arrived at the warehouse it was weighed in the presence of the various police agencies to be paid off. … After weighing, the payoffs were made in U.S. dollars; $12.00 a pound to the [Mexican Federal Judicial Police], and $17.00 a pound to the Rural State Police." Federal agents were permanently stationed in Chihuahua to monitor the group. This coordinated information sharing was likely key to avoiding the kind of bargaining breakdown that drives the frequent breaking of *arrego* deals in Rio, producing (violent) episodes of enforcement there.

The model shows that while these two factors facilitate bribe negotiations, they do not on their own dissuade cartels from resorting to violence. After all, cartels had to share a significant portion of their profits with multiple state agencies; why not use *plata o plomo* threats to drive down the bribe price? To maintain a peaceful state-sponsored protection racket, as opposed to coerced peace or fight-and-bribe equilibria, requires both a high degree and high conditionality of repression: the state must wield enough force to extract large bribes, while maintaining enough in reserve to dissuade traffickers from resorting to bribe-reducing violence.

---

[6] Formally, these two conditions are captured by the inequality $\lambda < h(2y - \bar{y})$; that is, the sanction to bribe taking (λ) must be smaller than the interdiction rate (h) times $2\underline{y} - \bar{y}$, which is positive only when enforcers' uncertainty is small relative to average profits.

Such accumulation and control over repressive force was made possible by the PRI's political hegemony (Diaz-Cayeros et al. 2003; Valdés 2013). Mexico's security institutions are deeply fragmented, with more than 1,000 police corps spread across municipal, state, and federal levels of government. One-party rule, however, rendered this fragmentation largely moot. Overlapping federal and local jurisdictions, which were critical in reducing police corruption in US cities (Reuter 1995), did not complicate this scheme because the highest-level officials were in on it. At the same time, fluctuations in the market structure of the drug trade were not terribly disruptive because, as individual traffickers' turf grew, the locus of state control could move fluidly from local to state to the national level:

> Should a trafficker have a major business success with resulting notoriety, he would then likely be visited by the "Judicales" (State level agents law enforcement) and later by the "Federales" (agents of national police agencies) and operating "franchises" would have to be also purchased directly from these agencies.
>
> (Lupsha 1991, 44)

Thus, at least until the 1990s, all the necessary conditions for a state-sponsored protection racket were met. The state established regular, direct linkages with traffickers, who were allowed to operate in exchange for regularized bribes. While failure to pay was apparently punished enough to ensure regular compliance, it is also clear that repression was highly conditional: incidents of anti-state violence or other unacceptable forms of cartel behavior were severely and swiftly punished. The most spectacular example of this occurred in 1985, after Félix Gallardo and his Guadalajara cartel co-founder Rafael Caro Quintero had DEA agent Enrique "Kiki" Camarena kidnapped and murdered. With help and pressure from the United States, Mexican authorities cracked down hard on Guadalajara, capturing several top capos, imprisoning Caro Quintero after his arrest while on the lam in Costa Rica, and ultimately arresting Gallardo himself.

The Camarena episode set in motion two important dynamics that would ultimately undermine Mexico's mostly peaceful modus vivendi. First, it brought about the arrest of Félix Gallardo, which led him to repartition the Guadalajara cartel's turf among his lieutenants. While Gallardo originally intended this to prevent succession battles, the end result was the fragmentation of Guadalajara's near monopoly into an oligopolistic market of powerful cartel-clans. Though many of these new cartels would unite in a federation for much of the early 1990s, and a large grouping of capos under the banner of the Sinaloa cartel[7] remains a cohesive group until the present day, the breakup

---

[7] The Guadalajara cartel itself was born from a previous incarnation of the Sinaloa cartel; Gallardo and most of his lieutenants were from Sinaloa, and had only relocated to Guadalajara after fleeing the Operation Condor eradication campaign in the 1970s.

of the hegemonic Guadalajara cartel laid the foundation for the turf wars that would sprout in the 1990s and explode in the 2000s.

The second change was the dismantling of the DFS in the wake of the international scandal that Camarena's death sparked (Grayson 2010, 138). The DFS's extinction in 1985 pre-dated the fall of the PRI, which was able to reorganize its state-sponsored protection racket under the auspices of the PGR for a time. However, this system quickly eroded as the PGR became decentralized (Snyder and Durán-Martínez 2009b) and the once hegemonic PRI began to lose local and state elections in the 1990s, then control of Congress, and finally in 2000, the presidency for the first time in seventy years (Magaloni 2005).

7.3.2 Democratization (1990–2003): Conditionality Eroded

Claim 2: Democratization weakened conditionality, pushing cartels toward violent strategies, though actual anti-state violence remained rare.

The period from the breakup of the Guadalajara cartel (1989) through the election of Mexico's first non-PRI president, Vicente Fox (2000–2006) of the PAN, saw the outbreak and steady intensification of inter-cartel turf war, along with a stark buildup of cartel firepower and organizational capacity (Trejo and Ley 2016). Cartel–state conflict, however, only began to emerge in the wake of the first large deployments of federal troops and police, sent to quell a pitched cartel battle in Nuevo Laredo that erupted in 2003. A key factor in explaining this latter development, I argue, is the reduction in the conditionality of repression brought on, inadvertently, by democratization. Reduced conditionality probably also played a role in the rise of turf war as well, though this was clearly also driven by changes in market conditions. Either way, it was turf war that eventually triggered an increase in state repression, which, under conditions of low conditionality, produced the first instances of cartel–state conflict.

In terms of market conditions, the period brought Mexican cartels a massive windfall, in one of the greatest examples on record of the "balloon effect." In the early 1990s, US law enforcement managed to largely shut down the Caribbean trafficking routes used by Colombian cartels. This led the Colombians to rely increasingly on Mexican trafficking organizations that could transport shipments overland at US border crossings such as Juárez, Laredo, and Tijuana (Meiner 2009). These routes, as well as the contacts between Colombian and Mexican cartels, had been established for some time. Indeed, Félix Gallardo, the "boss of bosses" of the Guadalajara cartel, was described by his lawyer as not just a business associate but a close personal friend of Pablo Escobar (Osorno 2009, 244). However, as an increased share of the cocaine trade shifted to Mexico in the 1990s, the value of these border crossings increased, as did the size and organizational capacity of the Mexican cartels that controlled them.

Another trend that began in this period was an increasing—though limited by today's standards—militarization of anti-narcotics efforts. During the final

PRI presidency of Ernesto Zedillo (1994–2000), military officers took over important positions within the Procaduría General de República (PGR), the principal anti-narcotics investigative agency, and the share of drug seizures carried out by the army rose, though was still small compared to the PGR (Borjón Nieto 2010, 4). Whether this actually produced increased repression is unclear: several high-profile corruption cases involving military officers erupted, including drug czar General Gutiérrez Rebello, whose links to traffickers were portrayed in the popular film *Traffic* (2000). Meanwhile, desertion rates were astronomical—tens of thousands per year according to Turbiville (2010)—allowing cartels a highly trained recruitment pool from which to build private armies. This practice seems to have been the brainchild of Osiel Cárdenas, head of the Gulf cartel, who managed to "flip" members of the Grupo Aeromóvil de Fuerzas Especiales (GAFES), an elite US-trained anti-narcotics unit. The group came to be known as the Zetas and would eventually break with the Gulf cartel in 2010 to become an autonomous, extremely violent cartel of its own and overshadow its former boss.

For some, the increased profitability of the cocaine trade is a sufficient explanation for the outbreak of inter-cartel turf war. Purely economic arguments stress fixed costs of contesting turf, such that a sudden increase in profitability can suddenly make it worthwhile to hire private the armies and amass the arsenals necessary to forcefully seize rivals' territory (e.g., Castillo et al. 2014). Yet increased profits do not necessarily provoke turf war, as the early 1980s cocaine bonanza in Colombia shows. Indeed, from a purely theoretical point of view, it is not clear whether a growing pie favors more fighting, since there is more to fight over, or less, since there is more surplus with which to buy off rivals.

Equally important, surely, were the collapse of PRI hegemony at the state and local levels and the decentralization of the PGR, spreading enforcement authority over a broader array of political and bureaucratic actors. In their insightful analysis, Richard Snyder and Angelica Durán-Martínez (2009b) show how democratization and the PGR's adoption of force rotation and a new geographical division of its field offices multiplied the number of relevant protectors cartels needed to buy off; this, they argue, destabilized Mexico's state-sponsored protection racket, leading to increased violence. Building on this argument, Trejo and Ley (2016) show that the election of non-PRI governors, and the consequent replacement of key state-level enforcement officials, is strongly associated with increases in state-level inter-cartel violence. Both these findings are consistent with my model of corruption: increases in sanctions for bribe-taking (including anti-corruption measures and the overlapping-jurisdictions problem), as well as increased uncertainty over drug profits—also driven by overlapping jurisdictions as well as expanding cocaine flows—can render a "state-sponsored protection" scenario unviable.

Critically, though, bargaining breakdown alone does not guarantee violence. The PRI system did not merely provide protection to cartels from state enforcement; it also kept cartels peaceful by conditioning repression on cartels' use of violence. Repression was certainly conditional on anti-state violence; to the extent that the "rules of the game" included restrictions on inter-cartel competition, they likely also deterred inter-cartel violence. Conditionality, as I have argued, requires the logistical capacity to identify cartel misbehavior and respond to it with significant repressive force. The PRI's political hegemony was critical in producing this logistical capacity, providing smooth, centralized control over enforcers across Mexico's highly fragmented and corrupt police institutions. Democratization did not eliminate corruption, but meant that bribe-taking was no longer part of an institutionalized, hierarchy-reinforcing system (Darden 2008). In this way, by weakening the "mechanisms for the reduction of violence" (Astorga 2001) inherent in the old DFS system, democratization made state threats of swift and certain punishment for cartel misbehavior less credible, reducing conditionality.

Whether or not this reduction in conditionality was a driver of turf war, it certainly affected cartels' stance toward the state. For example, whereas Félix Gallardo offered no resistance to his 1989 arrest "despite having in his power several high-caliber firearms" (Osorno 2009, 216), Osiel Cárdenas, backed up by his Zetas, fought a pitched battle—with automatic weapons and grenades (Grillo 2011, 99)—against the army detachment that finally arrested him in March 2003 (García et al. 2003). Such direct confrontation of state forces came as a shock when it began occurring in 2003, suggesting that it was quite rare before this. In reality, cartels had probably already shifted to violent strategies toward state forces at the local level. However, because municipal and even state police were increasingly outgunned, and because even a small cut of cartels' increasing profits was good reason to keep quiet, a coerced peace scenario likely obtained in which local enforcers were basically cowed into accepting moderate bribes on pain of death. As the model of violent corruption reveals, an increase in the degree of repression—such as the deployment of the army to arrest Cárdenas—without a corresponding increase in conditionality can produce a shift from coerced peace, where no violence occurs on the equilibrium path, into actual cartel–state violence. This is a plausible explanation of the eruption of anti-state violence during Cárdenas' arrest.

7.4 ONSET AND ESCALATION (2003–2011): DECLARING A DRUG WAR

In the popular imagination, Mexico's drug war is often dated to Calderón's crackdown in December 2006; this is misleading in several ways. First, as noted, the dynamics of drug trafficking, state repression, and rampant corruption stretch back to the founding of the PRI. Second, inter-cartel violence began in the 1990s, and rose dramatically during the presidency of Calderón's predecessor Vicente Fox. Third, and most importantly, Fox launched what I consider Mexico's first unconditional crackdown, deploying federal troops to arrest Cárdenas in 2003 and more extensively to Nuevo Laredo in 2004 to quell a turf war between the Sinaloa and Gulf cartels. This crackdown, I argue, produced the first sustained episodes of cartel–state conflict, and prefigured many of the dynamics of the larger conflict. Indeed, the failure of Fox's crackdown to curtail rising cartel violence during his presidency contributed directly to Calderón's decision to radically ramp up state repression at the outset of his own, setting off a vertiginous escalation.

7.4.1 Onset (2003–2005): Reluctant Crackdown, Violent Cartel Response

Claim 3: Fox's limited, unconditional crackdown pushed cartels to fight back, triggering the onset of cartel–state conflict.

Though the simmering cartel violence of the late 1990s appears mild from today's perspective, it was becoming something of a concern as Mexico's first non-PRI president in seventy-one years took office. Fox's instincts, however, were in the direction of reform, not repression (indeed, he would eventually become a vocal proponent of drug legalization). Fox saw the problem as arising from the increasing militarization of anti-narcotics work over the previous decade, which he associated with the authoritarian tendencies of the PRI, and was troubled by potential corruption of military officers. He proposed a number of measures intended to reverse this trend, and specifically called for the withdrawal of the army from the fight against the drug trade; however, strong opposition from US drug czar Barry McCaffrey led Fox to abandon this course (Astorga 2004, 98).

Instead, as the turf war among Mexico's cartels escalated, Fox found himself reluctantly deploying federal police and eventually army units to hot spots. The buildup of cartel firepower—including private militias and military-grade weapons—that had begun in the 1990s under Zedillo began to boil over into major armed clashes for territory (Trejo and Ley 2016). The most extreme was the "war" between the Gulf cartel, backed up by the Zetas, and the once-hegemonic Sinaloa cartel, which had by then acquired an armed wing of its own, known as Los Negros (Thompson 2005). Starting in 2003, and building throughout the following two years, these groups clashed for control of Nuevo Laredo, a border town and key trafficking route into the United States.

In my account, the battle for Nuevo Laredo, rather than Calderón's crackdown, marks the true onset of cartel–state conflict in Mexico, and in a sense, the drug war writ large. The episode constitutes a microcosm of the larger conflict to come, incorporating the intertwined dynamics of both turf war and cartel–state conflict. Besides the fighting between the Sinaloa and Gulf cartels, there were numerous clashes between traffickers and police, as well as conflict between municipal police (thought to be in the employ of cartels) and the federal forces that Fox deployed (Grillo 2011, 103–104).

An early but clear turning point was the July 2003 shootout in which a group of Los Negros gunmen, accidentally coming upon a federal police patrol, attacked them with military-grade firepower (Turbiville 2010). As with Osiel Cárdenas' violent response to the army troops sent to arrest him, this incident fits the model of violent corruption. The feds had come to Nuevo Laredo to replace the municipal police, some 200 members of which had been suspended for corruption. Given the firepower of Los Negros, the *status quo ante* was likely a coerced peace in which local police dared not enforce the law for fear of cartel violence. The federal takeover then increased the degree of repression and, perhaps, lowered corruptibility, both of which predict a shift toward fight-and-bribe or violent enforcement scenarios.

Ominously, Fox's federal crackdown throughout 2004 and 2005 did not quell the violence, and may have exacerbated it. In yet another harbinger of things to come, Fox launched Operation México Seguro in June 2005, the first so-called joint operation, sending some 700 army troops and federal police officers to Nuevo Laredo and later expanding the operation throughout the country (Grillo 2011, 102). Despite, or because of, these unprecedented militarized deployments, annual drug-related homicides nearly doubled over the course of Fox's term. Rising violence throughout 2006, in turn, contributed to the decision of Fox's successor in the PAN, Felipe Calderón, to double down on a policy of militarized repression. Equally important, as we shall see, was Calderón's need to shore up his presidency in the wake of a divisively contested election.

7.4.2 Escalation (2006–12): Calderón's "War Without Quarter"

Claim 4: Calderón's massive crackdown severely reduced conditionality, leading to full-blown cartel–state conflict.

Calderón and the PAN won the July 2006 presidential election by the slimmest of margins (0.58 percent, just 240,000 votes) over leftist Party of the Democratic Revolution (PRD) candidate and mayor of Mexico City Andres Manuel López Obrador. López Obrador, invoking the infamous election-night fraud in 1988 that had prevented leftist hero and eventual founder of the PRD Cuauhtémoc Cárdenas from winning the presidency, declared the result invalid, called for a full recount, and mobilized a mass of supporters in a semi-permanent street protest that stretched on for months. The legal impasse was only resolved in August, when Calderón secured a judicial victory, but his refusal to endorse a full recount kept López Obrador's movement alive straight through the December inauguration (Albarrán 2012, 31). A few days before Calderón took office, López Obrador was proclaimed "Legitimate President" in a mass rally in Mexico City's *zócalo*; in his "acceptance" speech, he laid out a shadow agenda and called for a parallel cabinet to serve in protest. Calderón's inauguration ceremony was marred by an actual brawl on the floor of Congress, and the new leader's hasty exit from the building.

The details are colorful, but Calderón's position was truly precarious. His need to establish legitimacy and support quickly and decisively would lead to the most important single decision of his presidency, publicly declaring war[8] on the drug trade, and ordering the Mexican army to crack down on cartels in urban areas and along major land routes. In some ways, this was a second-best solution, since the public saw economic problems as far more pressing than crime and security, and would continue to until the violence peaked in 2011 (Tiro and Parrales 2013). However, as a conservative, Calderón's attempts to outflank López Obrador's economic populism had proven futile (Albarrán 2012, 32). Meanwhile, cartel-related violence *was* becoming more intense and, importantly, more visible. A grisly, multiple decapitation in Uruapán, Michoacán in September 2006 was particularly shocking, leading the governor to personally request help from fellow *michoacano* Calderón. While this offered Calderón an opportunity to shift public debate away from the contested election and economic issues, the question remains why Calderón thought that a militarized drug war would constitute more favorable political terrain. The answer, in a word, is Colombia.

Colombia's experiences with armed conflict had two related and ultimately tragic effects on Calderón's thinking. First, at the time, Colombian president Álvaro Uribe had an approval rating of over 80 percent, roughly as high as that of Brazil's once-in-a-lifetime leftist hero Luiz Inácio Lula da Silva, and probably about as popular as any right-wing president has ever been in Latin America. The key to Uribe's unprecedented level of support was straightforward: his "Democratic Security" policy—centered around a massive crackdown on the country's guerrillas—had made Colombians feel safer, after decades of seemingly unending civil war. In so doing, he proved by example that public security could be one, and perhaps the only, path to mass popularity for the right.

Calderón visited Bogotá in October 2006 while still president-elect (though he was nonetheless "treated as head of state due to his personal friendship with Uribe" (Jiménez 2015)). After a two-hour private talk with Uribe, the two headed a joint staff meeting "dedicated exclusively to reviewing the Colombian model of combatting the drug trade," particularly the role of the army (Albarrán 2012, 44). Calderón emerged declaring that, inspired by Colombia, he would prioritize a frontal fight against Mexico's cartels, which could not be allowed to "challenge the authority of the state" (Jiménez 2015).

[8] Calderón would come to deny that he framed his policy as a war, insisting that he had always used the terms *lucha contra la delincuencia organizada* and *lucha por la seguridad pública* (fight against organized crime, fight for public security). This is both factually incorrect—as a simple search of his speeches demonstrates (Bravo 2011)—and disingenuous, given Calderón's repeated use of martial language and even attire.

In December, within weeks of taking office, Calderón sent a delegation of top security officials, including Attorney General Medina Mora and Public Security Secretary Genaro García Luna to Colombia, to meet with Uribe and his cabinet "to learn from the Colombian experience" in Medina Mora's words (Bailly 2011; Pérez-Plá 2007).

Thus Calderón, only a month into his presidency, publicly declared war on the drug trade and launched a major militarized crackdown. He thoroughly and personally identified himself with the policy, making it in many ways the centerpiece of his presidency. This served both a political and a strategic end. By tying his political fate to the persecution of his war, such that any reversal of course would signify political suicide, Calderón effectively tied his own hands through audience costs (Fearon 1994). This may be one reason that there has been little violent lobbying—and the terror tactics associated with it—in Mexico: there was never much chance that Calderón would call off his crackdown. On the other hand, as we will see, it made course correction in the face of setbacks and unintended consequences significantly more costly.

Colombia's experience influenced Calderón in a tactical sense as well. Uribe had indeed improved security by striking hard and unrelentingly at the leftist guerrillas of the Fuerzas Armadas Revolucionarias de Colombia (FARC)—whom Uribe characterized as "narco-terrorists" and "criminals" in order to rule out negotiations—while simultaneously demobilizing the most violent paramilitary groups. In short, he had shown that a centralized crackdown can be successful both militarily and politically. Equally important, though, was a conventional wisdom that had solidified around the narco-violence period analyzed in this study (1984–1993). In this line of thought, the end of "pure" narco-violence (committed by drug cartels as opposed to guerrillas or paramilitaries involved in the drug trade) was the result of having shattered the giant cartels of the 1980s, Medellín and Cali. What were left behind were smaller organizations that lacked the firepower to "go toe-to-toe with the nation-state."[9] To prominent drug warriors like former DEA chief Robert Bonner, Colombia's narco-violence period constituted a success story, a "victory" that Mexico would be able to learn from and ultimately repeat (Bonner 2010). Calderón took the Colombian experience to heart, ultimately adopting a "kingpin" or "decapitation" strategy that sought to capture and kill cartel leaders with the aim of breaking up the organizations into fragments too small to fight the state (Guerrero 2011b).

Calderón's first deployment—to Michoacán, in December 2006—was relatively successful, but was quickly followed by multiple joint operations across Mexico's trafficking zones in 2007 that seemed to exacerbate, not contain, trafficker violence. Indeed, cartels were if anything emboldened in their confrontation of state forces. In January 2008, for example, traffickers in Ciudad Juárez hung, on a police monument in a public square, a list of executed

---

[9] Interview, DEA Bogotá station chief, October 3, 2011.

police officers under the caption "for those who did not believe," and another seventeen targeted for future execution under the words "for those who still don't believe" (Figure 7.3a). The chief of police, whose name was on the second list, was assassinated a few months later (Cano 2008). Such *narcomantas* (narco-banners) became ubiquitous, frequently addressed to politicians and state agents in threatening and brazen tones. Alternatively, in an act of extreme chutzpah, banners were hung in Nuevo Laredo in 2008 enticing active and former military officers to defect and join the Zetas, offering better food and salary than the state, and including a phone number (Figure 7.3b).

Much of this early anti-state violence was dismissed by Calderón and his supporters as to be expected. One of Caledrón's key advisors and intellectual architect of his strategy was Joaquín Villalobos, a former FMLN guerrilla commander from El Salvador and self-styled "international conflict-resolution consultant," advisor to and staunch defender of Uribe (Navarro 2010), as well as a key backer of El Salvador's ultimately disastrous Mano Dura crackdown (Holland 2013, 57). In a widely read article from June 2008, Villalobos argued that "frontal combat" with the cartels was necessary to re-establish the rule of law and the integrity of the state, and that "the violence that Mexico is living now is the end of a regime of coexistence with organized crime, an end that is obviously bloody and painful" (Villalobos 2008). He confidently predicted such violence would end with the fragmentation of the cartels:

> The defeat of the cartels is foreseeable … In three years, the coercive power of the state will have grown considerably, its territorial deployment will be consolidated; the criminals will have lost financial power; the cartels will be fragmented; and violence will go down substantially.

> (Villalobos 2008)

Villalobos was right about some things: three years on, the state's coercive power had grown (thanks in part to the US-funded Mérida Initiative), more troops than ever were deployed, many of the country's top kingpins had been killed or arrested, and the cartels had been fragmented into at least sixteen smaller organizations (Guerrero 2011a). Yet he was dead wrong about abatement: in 2011, there were an astonishing 16,800 drug-related homicides, roughly ten times as many as 2005, and over 1,000 cartel attacks on army troops and installations (Muro 2014). The intervening years had brought a stream of headlines and shocking scenes, each more grisly than the next, and an accelerating escalation in the intensity, lethality, and brazenness of cartel attacks. In Mexico, at least, fragmentation turned out to exacerbate violence; Calderón et al. (2015) find that the neutralization of a cartel leader in this period caused significant increases in both cartel-related killings and general homicides. More broadly, upstart and splinter organizations, far from switching non-violent strategies, often invested heavily in armament and soldier training, and frequently announced their presence with spectacular, attention-grabbing attacks.

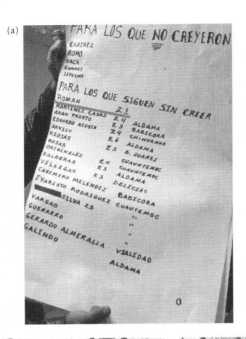

FIGURE 7.3. **Examples of Brazen, Anti-State "Narco-Banners."** Panel (a): banner found on a police monument in Ciudad Juárez in January 2008, with the names of five assassinated police officers under the caption "For those who did not believe"; below this are the names of seventeen officers still alive at the time, under the caption "For those who still don't believe." The officer at the top of the list, then chief of Juárez police, was assassinated four months later (Cano 2008); photo credit: © NOTIMEX, Agencia de Noticias del Estado Mexicano. Panel (b): banner hung from a highway overpass in Nuevo Laredo in 2008. It reads: "Operational Group 'Los Zetas' wants you, soldier or ex-soldier. We offer a good salary, food, and benefits for your family. You'll no longer suffer mistreatment or hunger. We won't feed you instant noodle soups. Make sure to call 8671687423" (Hawley 2008); photo credit: *El Mañana de Nuevo Laredo*.

Why did fragmentation fail to curb violence, particularly anti-state violence, in Mexico, when it seemingly succeeded in Colombia? In Chapter 5, I conjectured that the decisive factor in Colombia was an increase in conditionality, a "mowing the lawn" approach that only targeted the most salient cartels, creating incentives to eschew violence. Likewise, I claim that Calderón's crackdown was highly unconditional: fragmented cartels were offered no reprieve from state repression if they eschewed anti-state violence, while the repression itself created positive incentives via the logics of anti-state violence developed in Chapters 3 and 4.

Conditionality of repression had already decreased considerably in the wake of democratization in the 1990s. Without PRI hegemony, the vertically fragmented nature of Mexico's security institutions—with more than 1,000 police corps across local, state, and federal levels—became very salient. Any crackdown that a PAN president could have launched in 2006 would have been fairly unconditional, simply because he or she could not count on the support of opposition governors and mayors. Moreover, the PRI system left behind a legacy of thoroughgoing police corruption at the municipal and state levels that made operational coordination—critical for effective conditional repression—extremely difficult. Horizontal fragmentation among federal security institutions was also acute: low capacity within the federal Public Security Secretariat (which houses the Federal Police) and the PGR (which had its own police force) led Calderón to deploy the army and the navy as well.

Yet Calderón's approach was unconditional by design, in two key senses. First, Calderón deliberately and repeatedly framed his crackdown as unconditional and impartial—in his words, a "war without quarter,"[10] "without distinctions or nuances among cartels or organizations."[11] Second, in implementing his kingpin strategy, Calderón prioritized generating demonstrable victories quickly and fostered competition rather than coordination among repressive agencies. This gave force commanders incentives to apply repression immediately and maximally, rather than in proportion and response to cartel violence. I take these two points in turn.

Calderón had strong personal and political reasons to adopt a "no distinctions" policy when designing his crackdown. Even in a corruption-free context, a blow against one cartel is almost by necessity a boon to its rivals. This fact takes on toxic tones in light of Mexico's long history of cartel collusion with state officials at the highest levels. Even today, virtually any crackdown or bust raises suspicion among Mexicans, including cartel leaders, of a corrupt deal to aid one cartel at the expense of another. Of particular importance to Calderón were long-standing rumors that his predecessor Fox had facilitated the escape of Sinaloa cartel boss Joaquín "El Chapo" Guzmán from prison in

---

[10] Speech, June 26, 2008. Available at calderon.presidencia.gob.mx.
[11] Interview with Adela Micha, December 1, 2008. Available at calderon.presidencia.gob.mx.

2001. Fox's deployment of troops to Nuevo Laredo was interpreted by many, including the Gulf cartel, as a corrupt attempt to hand the territory to El Chapo (Grillo 2011, 93). Calderón was temperamentally sensitive to any accusations of corruption, and set out from the beginning to dispel the suggestion that he, as PAN successor to Fox, favored the Sinaloa cartel. His martial rhetoric came in part from the view, shared by many of his top security advisors, that a reputation for impartiality would be critical to the legitimacy, and ultimately the efficacy, of his war.

Ironically, such a reputation was never established. Calderón continued to be dogged by accusations of collusion, not only in the form of narco-banners hung by cartels, but also journalistic investigations, including a prominent one by National Public Radio (Burnett et al. 2010). In a response that typified the government's obsession with the issue, it vehemently denied the reports' conclusion, and insisted that cartels were being "attacked in a manner proportional to their size" (Burnett et al. 2010). At least in terms of Calderón's public stance, conditionality was the baby thrown out with the bathwater of corruption.

Operationally, Calderón's kingpin strategy was shaped not only by the general notion that fragmenting the cartels would reduce violence, but by the specific advice of Colombian anti-narcotics officials to "net some big fish" quickly in order to demonstrate capacity and win public support.[12] However, he inherited a deeply fragmented security apparatus, and no single agency had enough capacity to fight a nation-wide drug war. Moreover, the army, navy, Federal Police and PGR each had their own hierarchies, protocols, budgets, and intelligence sources, jealously guarded by leaders chary of cross-agency cooperation and inclined to put the interests of their respective institutions above all. Calderón apparently lacked the political clout or personal charisma to overcome these parochial interests; on the contrary, he faced the political problem of motivating his own security agencies to cooperate with his signature campaign.

The solution Calderón eventually hit upon—distributing a list of most-wanted capos among the different agencies, each of which would pursue its targets independently—bought him motivation at the price of coordination and, ultimately, conditionality. The presidency fostered inter-agency competition for high-profile busts through media-friendly "perp walks," in which the responsible agency proudly showed off fallen kingpins and seized drugs and weapons, spurring the other agencies on. For example, one high-level security official explained to me that the navy's 2009 lethal attack on kingpin Arturo Beltrán Leyva left the army contemptuous and anxious to have a trophy *golpe*[13] of its own; this motivated the army attack that killed Sinaloa cartel kingpin Ignacio "Nacho" Coronel Villarreal seven months later. When, a few months after that, the Federal Police arrested Edgar "La Barbie"

12 Interview, DEA Bogotá station chief, February 23, 2013.
13 Literally "blow" or "coup"; a successful operation against a cartel.

Valdez Villarreal, their reaction was characterized as "We got one too, and we didn't kill ours."[14]

By many accounts, this team of rivals lacked an effective captain, making conditionality a logistical impossibility. Agencies' operational decisions were often taken autonomously from the presidency,[15] which increasingly lacked a means of coordinating the overall anti-cartel effort. Information-sharing across agencies was almost nonexistent, and intelligence was often acted on immediately not only in pursuit of fast glory but for fear of leaks or even inter-agency poaching (Felbab-Brown 2009). Conditionality relies precisely on holding this sort of actionable intelligence in reserve, as a coercive threat to compel cartels to behave; any conditional approach would have required subjecting agencies' operational decisions to a centralized command that doled out repressive actions in response to cartel violence. Instead, this system encouraged agencies to strike against their targets as soon as possible, and certainly without regard to those targets' behavior.[16] Cartel leaders thus had little reason to believe that using less violence would materially increase their chances of survival.

In line with my theory, cartels' use of violence toward the state increased tremendously during Calderón's unconditional crackdown. In 2007, the first year of the SNSP dataset, there were 231 deaths from confrontations between cartels and state forces (*enfrentamientos*) and unilateral cartel attacks on state forces (*agresiones*); in 2010 there were 2,099. Figures from the army confirm a similarly abrupt rise in the number of attacks on army troops (Figure 7.4), on the order of two or three per day in 2011. Between the beginning of Calderón's presidency and July 2011, cartels killed 2,886 state agents, of which 45 percent were municipal police, 33 percent were state police, and 22 percent from federal agencies including the armed forces (*Proceso* 2011). During that same period, the army alone killed some 1,700 "presumed aggressors" (Barragán 2013a); if no more than half of federal agents killed were army troops, this suggests a ratio of more than five traffickers killed for every soldier.

This violence was probably driven by a mix of logics. The preponderance of violence against local and state police—generally thought to be more corrupt than federal forces—suggests that the logic of violent corruption is a major factor. Because the army is thought to be less corrupt, and because cartel attacks, though brazen, generally cause few army casualties, some see a signaling motive, as one army commander suggests: "[B]y attacking the army, they are trying to show the population that they have power." This same lieutenant colonel, though, attributes a second, purely defensive function to the violence:

14 Interview with member of the Technical Secretariat of the National Security Council (Secretaria Tecnica del Consejo de Seguridad Nacional), October 22, 2010.
15 Interview, Director, National Security Council Technical Secretariat, October 22, 2010.
16 Interview, National Security and Intelligence Center (CISEN) officer, September 28, 2010.

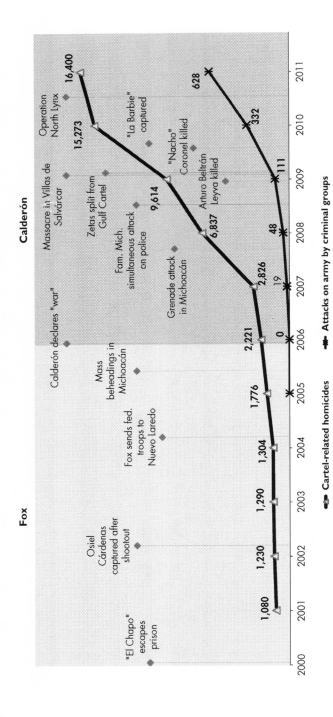

FIGURE 7.4. **Mexico's Drug War: Homicides and Attacks on Army, by** *Sexenio*, **2001–2011.**
Sources: Homicides: Shirk and Ríos (2011). Attacks on Army Troops: SEDENA data cited in Aranda (2011); Attacks on Army, alternate
series: SEDENA data reported in Muro (2014).

> We will go on patrol and face an ambush by these young kids who don't even
> know how to shoot. When you have disciplined soldiers they are going to win
> in these shoot-outs. But then maybe the troops are being held up, while the bad
> guys are moving drugs or carrying out a murder somewhere else.
>
> (Quoted in International Crisis Group 2013, 14)

This is an important point: even a unilateral attack by cartels on army troops
can be driven by the logic of loss reduction if it impedes interdiction elsewhere.

That said, both signaling and defensive violence are consistent with the logic
of violent corruption. If attacking the army shows the population that cartels
have power, it might also show the *army* that cartels have power, and thus
make *plata o plomo* threats credible. It may also weaken the army over time,
by contributing to what is an astoundingly high rate of defection: some 179,000
in twelve years, including almost 2,000 officers (Barragán 2013b). As the model
of Chapter 4 showed, even purely defensive violence—that is, violence which
does not "hurt" commanding officers—still reduces those commanders' implicit
bargaining leverage; if in addition commanders dislike violent engagement, so
that the threat of it makes them more likely to accept bribes, then all the more
reason to engage in it. In short, the logic of violent corruption creates additional
incentives beyond pure defense for anti-state violence.

Of course, we do not observe bribe negotiations; we cannot rule out the
possibility that, at least with respect to the army, a "violent enforcement"
scenario prevails in which no bribery ever occurs and the only function
of violence is pure defense. The jailing of high-ranking army generals for
cartel-related corruption in 2012 suggests this is not the case (Archibold 2012),
but those officers were eventually freed for lack of evidence, and in either
case could represent either the exception or the rule. All we can say is that
if *any* corruption occurs within a security agency, then attacks on that agency's
enforcers, beyond any defensive value, is likely to lower the price of bribes for
cartels. Either way, the unconditional nature of repression gives cartels little
reason *not* to engage in this kind of violence.

Other forms of cartel violence are more clearly driven by the logic of
violent corruption. A glaring example was the assassination of Federal Police
Commissioner Edgar Millán in a Mexico City safehouse in 2008. Because only
his close associates knew his location, it was immediately clear that high-level
police officers had collaborated with Millán's killers. The official explanation of
Millán's murder was that he had refused to take a bribe from the Sinaloa cartel,
a classic case of *plata o plomo*. Countering the popular vision of Millán as
fallen "narco-hero," the journalist Anabel Hernández (2010, 502–508) presents
evidence that he and his successor Gerardo Garay Cadena (who was later
arrested for taking cartel bribes) had been on the Sinaloa cartel's payroll for at
least a year, and that Millán was killed not for his honesty, but for his failure to
live up to his bribe agreement. As with most allegations of high-level corruption,
the truth is difficult to adjudicate, particularly at short historical remove. But
note that whichever was the true motive for Millán's assassination, the logic of

violent corruption still applies: it was Calderón's crackdown that turned bribe arrangements into matters of life or death.

At the other end of the spectrum, corruption within municipal police forces continued to be rampant; indeed, on numerous occasions, federal forces deployed to hotspots would simply decommission or even arrest entire municipal corps for being in the service of traffickers. While an institutional history of corruption was the legacy of the PRI period, in situations such as these, trafficker coercion and intimidation probably played a key role as well. Mexico's often poorly armed local forces almost surely faced threats of violence from cartels, who likely enjoyed significant military superiority. One potential indication of the vulnerability of municipal police is the fact that they make up the plurality of state agents killed in Mexico through 2011. Strictly applying my model, this violence suggests that despite heavy cartel coercion, police refused to be bribed sometimes. A more realistic assessment might go beyond my model—which assumes only a single cartel—and argue that the presence of competing cartels means that police are sometimes unable to avoid anti-enforcer violence even by taking one cartels' bribes.

Some rarely well-documented evidence of violent corruption comes from Aguayo et al.'s (2016) study of the Zetas' massacres of civilians. Drawing on official inquiries and testimony, they demonstrate the Zetas' thoroughgoing use of *plata o plomo* threats. According to one police officer, "we all receive money from the Zetas, some by obligation and others by choice." Evidence of this coercion is the type of work police did for the Zetas and the astoundingly small bribes they received in exchange. Police were obliged not only to ignore citizens' complaints but to act as lookouts, allow Zetas to enter the local jail and remove or beat prisoners, collect protection payments from the businesses the Zetas extorted, and help the Zetas kidnap individuals. For this, they received monthly payments ranging from $1,000 for the chief of police to a mere $100 for low-level officers; those who refused to actively work for the Zetas received only $25. Even taking into consideration their abysmal official monthly salaries, about $320, these figures strongly suggest that the Zetas used threats of violence to induce police to accept smaller bribes. It is simply hard to believe that a sworn police officer, however few qualms about bribe-taking he or she had, would freely choose to commit serious crimes to aid a criminal organization for just a few dollars a day.

7.5 LIMITED ABATEMENT (2011–2012): RESPONDING TO THE ZETAS

Conjecture: Reform efforts mostly failed to shift policy, but modestly increased conditionality in some repressive agencies, possibly inducing some cartels to adopt less confrontational strategies.

For the first two years of the Calderón administration, rising violence was not seen as a major problem. In fact, it was widely interpreted by top officials as an indicator that the war on the cartels was working. Joaquín Villalobos, for example, readily admitted that the crackdown he had helped design was provoking anti-state violence.

> The blows [against the cartels] have been constant and significant, provoking a violent reaction from the criminals, which may come to include terrorism. But the violence is not only a sign of the desperation of the delinquents, but permanently cements the rupture between organized crime and the State.
>
> (Villalobos 2008)

Like former US Vice President Dick Cheney's characterization of 2005's spike in anti-US violence in Iraq as "the last throes of the insurgency," Villalobos' interpretation conveniently implied that rising violence was a positive signal that the government's approach was working. Adopting this rhetorical tactic, top army and Federal Police and even US officials took to defending the "frontal combat" approach by warning that violence would increase, and framing such increases as a positive metric. As then US Ambassador Garza put it in January 2009:

> Calderón must, and will, keep the pressure on the cartels, but look, let's not be naïve – there will be more violence, more blood, and, yes, things will get worse before they get better. That's the nature of the battle, the more pressure the cartels feel, the more they'll lash out like cornered animals.
>
> (Quoted in Corchado 2009)

Garza's prediction was borne out: cartel-related killings more than doubled from 2008 to 2010, and anti-state attacks became increasingly bold. Supporters of Calderón's crackdown publicly interpreted such attacks as indicators of progress. For example, when the Familia Michoacana cartel ambushed and nearly killed Michoacán state's chief of police, attacking her convoy with fragmentation grenades and more than 2,700 rounds of automatic gunfire, the federal government declared:

> This cowardly act shows the desperation of organized crime, whose room to maneuver and conduct illicit activity has been increasingly closed off by state authorities.
>
> (Quoted in Notícias EFE, 2010)

Yet these "last-throes" predictions of imminent cartel collapse proved no more prescient than Cheney's assessment of Iraq. Anti-state violence continued to accelerate through 2010, including a record fifteen mayors assassinated. Meanwhile, as media coverage of cartel violence grew increasingly intense and graphic, and civil society groups began denouncing what they saw as government indifference to violence and human rights violations by state forces, the "frontal combat" approach came under increasing criticism. Calderón's public security secretary Genaro García Luna urged him to stay the course, arguing that the "'last throes" could still be years away:

> International experience ... in Italy, in Colombia, in New York, in Chicago, the curve [of violence] was upwards for the first five or ten years [after the initial crackdown].
>
> (Quoted in Rama 2010)

Villalobos, also a strong supporter of staying the course, advocated for improved government communication and PR, arguing that Mexican society simply did not understand the complexity of what the government was doing (Villalobos 2010).

For a growing group of security officials, however, escalating violence was a problem in its own right, normatively, strategically, and politically. Starting in 2009 and gaining steam throughout 2010, reformers within the state security apparatus began advocating for a shift in repressive policy (Valdés and Hope 2013). While this reform effort failed in the broadest sense, it appears to have led to some limited operational changes that increased effective conditionality, if only marginally.

At the core of the reform effort was a working group of analysts and officials convoked by the director of the national intelligence agency CISEN, Guillermo Valdés. Valdés was particularly concerned about the causal impact of violence itself, and the potential for a downward spiral in which an increasing sense of chaos and loss of state control fueled further increases in criminal activity. In 2009, he formed a working group of CISEN analysts and outside consultants, tasked with generating proposals for re-orienting security policy in a way that might reduce violence. It included some of Mexico's top security analysts, including Alejandro Hope, Eduardo Guerrero, Maria Bertolucci, and Jaime Trewartha, "a group so good," in the words of US-based scholar and policy expert Mark Kleiman, "that you would never see anything like it in Washington."[17] The CISEN group became the center of gravity for a large if loose network of reform-minded actors throughout the government.

The CISEN working group was not tasked with drawing up a specific policy proposal, but rather focused on "diagnostics, evaluation, and description."[18] Members freely discussed different analyses, their own and others; Valdés drew on these ideas to make arguments within the Security Cabinet in favor of a greater focus on dissuasion and selective targeting. Perhaps the closest this process came to major policy reform occurred in 2010, when members familiar with Kleiman's work on Boston's Operation Ceasefire and other conditional approaches (Kleiman 2009), invited him to meet with the group during a visit to Mexico. Kleiman eventually met with Valdés and other senior figures and, at Valdés's request, drew up a proposal for a violence-reduction strategy focused

---

17 Interview, Cambridge, July 24, 2015.
18 Interview, Eduardo Guerrero, Mexico City, August 7, 2014.

specifically on "increasing the cost of violence for cartels."[19] Though the plan "went nowhere" with the higher levels of government, the core ideas, eventually published in *Foreign Affairs* (Kleiman 2011), clearly influenced Valdés and his team.

Another important outcome of the CISEN group was Eduardo Guerrero's work. Guerrero's proprietary dataset of violent events based on media reports was one of the best data sources available until the federal government released its own toward the end of 2010. Drawing on this data, Guerrero argued that the government's kingpin strategy and policy of "indiscriminate arrests" were driving the escalating violence by creating power vacuums and exacerbating competitive pressures. In August 2010, Guerrero made this argument at a public audience with Calderón; the president interrupted and strongly rebuked him. Meanwhile, with Valdés's reform efforts having little immediate impact on actual policy, Guerrero took to the pages of *Nexos*, an influential weekly magazine, with a series of articles laying out his case and urging changes to the government's approach (e.g., Guerrero 2010, 2011a). This led the government to take a hostile and defensive position, arguing that it was absurd to blame the state for the violent actions of criminal groups. Guerrero left the working group, which found itself supporting a position that had become associated with a public critic of the government.

Despite these setbacks, and though no policy proposal as specific as either *Sometimiento* or Pacification arose in the working group, Valdés had distilled a clear argument that reframed the problem as violence reduction and linked this to a set of clearly conditional policy principals. As he described it to me:

> In 2010 there was in important turn, in which we said, "We have to have a deliberate policy of violence reduction, punishing the most violent organization ... to increase the cost of violence for cartels." That is, sending the signal that this organization, in virtue of being the most violent, will receive a harsher punishment from the state.[20]

Both Valdés in his contacts with Security Cabinet members, and mid-level reform advocates associated with the CISEN working group, began building support for pro-conditionality policy reforms, which they variously referred to as "selective enforcement," "targeting," or "focalization."

Although the navy and the PGR were generally receptive to these ideas, neither the army nor the Federal Police under García Luna showed much enthusiasm—"too much work," in the words of one working-group member. Indeed, strategists within the Federal Police were openly dismissive of Valdés's efforts.[21] Moreover, at the level of official discourse, the reform effort clearly failed. Calderón himself seems to have been the critical figure here;

several sources recall him declaring that pursuing all cartels equally was the non-negotiable centerpiece of his security policy. Kleiman recalls being told by a high-ranking advisor that his 2010 proposal was rejected because "there was no way they could stomach politically anything that looked like a backing away from the kingpin strategy."[22]

Nevertheless, after two gruesome 2011 massacres of civilians by the Zetas, which apparently personally infuriated the president, "[Calderón] came around to the idea, at least, that you needed to do something with the Zetas."[23] Repression on the Zetas intensified, and a dedicated army operation ("Lince Norte," or "Northern Lynx"), led to several high-level arrests and busts (Gómora 2011). Multiple reports attributed these actions to an inherently conditional government strategy to target the Zetas for being the most brazen and violent cartel (Corchado 2011; Guerrero 2011b, 89–90). Meanwhile, reformers had succeeded in having the first "fusion center," a kind of intelligence clearinghouse and command center for anti-cartel actions, dedicated to operations against the Zetas. In another effort to increase pressure on the Zetas, Calderón apparently rescinded the rule that targets could only be arrested or killed by the agencies to which they had been assigned, clearing the way for the navy to act. Possibly drawing on actionable intelligence from the fusion centers, the navy captured and killed several top Zetas in late 2011 and 2012.

The presidency, however, continued to deny and publicly reject any departure from an "impartial," and hence unconditional, approach. After critics like Guerrero claimed the government had finally decided to do what he and other reformers had been telling it to, the president's office launched a major PR effort to debunk "Ten Myths of the Fight For Security," brought to life in a series of professionally animated webinars featuring newly appointed national security spokesman Alejandro Poiré. The fourth and fifth episodes implicitly equated "targeted" and "selective enforcement"—i.e., conditional approaches—with corrupt pacting with cartels, and collusion with the Sinaloa cartel in particular (Figure 7.5). Poiré, writing on the President's Blog, explained:

> The federal government does not favor any criminal organization; it weakens them all systematically without distinction. To benefit any criminal group …is to validate the outdated argument that crime can be "managed."
>
> (Poiré Romero 2011)[24]

The upshot of this inchoate and incomplete policy reform might thus be called "conditionality in deed but not in name." There is some evidence that it contributed to an important shift in Zeta strategy in 2012: where Zeta narco-banners previously sought to intimidate, they now downplayed

22 Interview, Cambridge, July 24, 2015.
23 Interview, Alejandro Hope, January 29, 2014.
24 Author's translation.

FIGURE 7.5. **Stills From "10 Myths of the Fight for Security" Government PR Campaign.**
Panel (a): "To believe that by pacting [with criminals] we will restore peace is equivalent
to giving permission to the criminals to continue harming society." From *Myth #4:*
The Solution to the Violence is a Pact With Criminals. Panel (b): "It is FALSE that
the Federal Government favors the Pacífico criminal group [i.e., Sinaloa Cartel]. This
Government does not apply the law selectively. To tolerate or favor any criminal
group is a crime and has never been an option. Authentic citizen security necessarily
requires the weakening of all criminal organizations. We continue to advance along
this path." From *Myth #5: The Government Favors Joaquín "El Chapo" Guzmán.*
The ten myths were: 1. The government has no strategy, just the use of force; 2. The
Armed Forces usurp the job of the police and systematically violate human rights; 3.
The presence of state authority sets off violence; 4. The solution to the violence is
a pact with criminals; 5. The government favors Joaquín "El Chapo" Guzmán; 6.
The battle is Calderón's alone; 7. This is a fight that nobody agrees with; 8. The
government does not listen to criticism; 9. We can only achieve security by legalizing
drugs; and 10. Mexico is one of the most violent countries in the world. Available at
http://calderon.presidencia.gob.mx/tag/10-mitos-de-la-lucha-por-la-seguridad/.

Zeta antagonism toward the state, *denied* responsibility for major acts of violence, and expressed sympathy for victims (Corcoran 2011). One captured Zeta leader, at his May 2012 deposition, described ordering his operatives in Veracruz to lay low during a federal intervention to avoid confrontations (*Reforma* 2013), a hallmark of a hiding approach. Hope argued that the Zetas were effectively "deterred," becoming more cautious and less violent as a result of the government's increased focus (which, since it was due to Zeta violence, amounts to an increase in conditionality) (Hope 2011). Valdés was more skeptical, in part because the government never sent a clear signal that the additional repression was being applied in response to Zeta violence.[25] Indeed, for Valdés, who saw messaging as essential to the effectiveness of a conditional approach, the contradiction between operational and communication policy was "a little exasperating"; he left his post in September 2011.

7.6 CONCLUSION: WHITHER MEXICO'S DRUG WAR?

Historically, Mexico has been a place where the drug trade functions through extremely thoroughgoing corruption (Andreas 1998). Indeed, corruption was so central to the way the PRI governed, and not only in the realm of drugs, that there was little room for lobbying—i.e., attempts to influence de jure policy formulation—except through the party. In general, part of how the *pax priista* worked was to dole out corrupt rents and patronage of all sorts in return for submission to the political hegemony of the PRI,[26] and the drug trade was no exception. Traffickers were permitted to operate mostly free of interference, so long as they played by the rules laid down by the political elite: pay your "taxes" (i.e., bribes) and stay out of politics (Astorga 2001, 428). Like the rent-extraction system of Rio de Janeiro, drug traffickers occupied a subordinate position with respect to state enforcers, with little bargaining leverage. However, for most of the twentieth century, this only rarely led to anti-state violence.

---

[25] Interview, September 12, 2013.

[26] In many contexts, corruption can be fruitfully conceived of as a principal–agent problem: enforcers' preferences diverge from those of leaders, and so the former fail to carry out the policies specified by latter. In such a world, leaders must tolerate, work around, or spend scarce political capital and resources to directly combat corruption. This is reasonably seen as reducing state capacity, particularly the dimension Mann (1986) calls "infrastructural capacity." However, as many authors have noted, the PRI's system of governance did not work *in spite* of corruption but *thanks* to it. Where rents from corruption form the principal glue that binds lower echelons of a pyramidal state party to the central leaders, minor principal–agent problems may still exist without constituting the central feature of corruption (which was ultimately in both leaders' and enforcers' interest). In such a setting, it is misleading to view corruption as a measure of state weakness. Indeed, the collapse of the PRI, and with it its state-sponsored protection racket, almost certainly *reduced* state capacity, at least in the short run.

During Calderón's tenure, corruption continued to play a central role in the drug trade in Mexico. Whole municipal police forces were fired; high-level assassinations occurred that clearly involved inside participation; and six top military officers—including four generals—were arrested in 2012 for facilitating drug trafficking and providing cartels with classified information (Fausset and Sanchez 2013). The shadow of past corruption also had causal power: the idea that Calderón or his lieutenants were secretly protecting El Chapo and the Sinaloa cartel, even if false, was plausible enough to directly affect the administration's actions and rhetoric. It may not have been false: in 2008, the federal police commissioner (the third-highest post in the corps) was arrested and jailed for allegedly receiving $70,000 a month in bribes from the Sinaloa cartel. This arrest now appears to have been a farce: it came immediately after the commissioner wrote to Calderón accusing his boss, Federal Police Chief Genaro García Luna, of himself being on the payroll of Sinaloa since 2005. After three years in prison, the commissioner was found innocent and released, as the state's case rested almost entirely on the testimony of a Gulf cartel member arrested for kidnapping but given witness protection in exchange for his testimony (García 2014). The case strongly suggests that at least one of these two high-ranking Federal Police officials, with significant control over a central arm of the state's repressive apparatus in the midst of the largest crackdown Mexico has ever known, was deeply corrupt. With stakes so high, and with leaders explicitly promising *not* to condition repression on cartel behavior, is it any wonder that bribe negotiations became violent?

At first, the end of Calderón's presidency and the 2013 return to PRI rule under incoming president Enrique Peña Nieto seemed to promise a convenient test of my theory. Peña Nieto vowed to make violence reduction the primary goal of his security policy, which suggests a move to a more explicitly conditional approach. Moreover, the history of the PRI suggested that it would re-establish "rules of the game," fostering the implicit pacts among traffickers that existed through much of the twentieth century. A clear shift toward conditionality would have provided a "hoop test"[27] of my theory: if violence worsened, it would strongly undermine my theory. If violence diminished, on the other hand, it would not definitively confirm my theory; however, it would add to the evidence already presented in this study, in particular the Rio de Janeiro case, that conditional approaches can rapidly curtail cartel–state conflict.

Once in power, however, Peña Nieto did not clearly formulate or implement a policy shift. Rather, he has remained mostly silent on the issue, focusing instead on major economic and political reforms. Public security quietly fell off the public agenda, in part through appeals to the media to stop sensationalizing

---

[27] In a hoop test, "The hypothesis must 'jump through the hoop' to remain under consideration, but passing the test does not by itself affirm the hypothesis. ... Hoop tests do not confirm a hypothesis, but they can eliminate it" (Collier 2011, 826).

violence. As a result, both the independent and dependent variables—state policy and cartel-related violence—have become harder to measure. To be sure, the capture of El Chapo and other kingpins have made headlines. But more systemically, it simply is not clear *what* the government is doing, much less how conditional is repression. Meanwhile, official time-series of cartel-related homicides has not been updated since late 2011, and media-based tallies have become increasingly erratic, probably because of shifts in editorial practice (Shirk et al. 2014). Where newspapers were once overflowing with press releases about death tallies, arrests, and troop deployments, information has become scant. Valiant attempts to cobble together estimates suggest that violence has fallen from its 2011 peak, but the extent of that reduction remains unclear. As the tenth anniversary of Calderón's crackdown passed in December 2016, Mexico's drug war had receded from the headlines, but seemed to be going nowhere.

What is clear is that as Peña Nieto's *sexenio* winds down, cartel–state conflict is still raging. The Nueva Generación Jalisco cartel announced its rise to prominence by launching a synchronized series of attacks on state forces and civilians. This is prima facie evidence that from cartels' perspective, anti-state violence is a good strategy. Meanwhile, despite the sweeping political changes that the PRI's return to presidential power portended, and despite rapidly shifting conditions on the ground, state repressive policy under Peña Nieto has proven disappointingly "rigid" in Alejandro Hope's words (2015). Until *that* changes, there is no end in sight for Mexico's drug war.

PART III

CONDITIONAL REPRESSION AS OUTCOME

8

The Challenge of Implementing Conditionality

Where conditionality of repression increased, it did so through reform efforts by actors within the state security apparatus. These efforts succeeded in Colombia and Rio de Janeiro but not Mexico. This chapter lays out a framework for explaining why. Agency—the strategic choices of decision-makers—is clearly important: President Felipe Calderón's commitment to a policy, or at least a public stance, of combatting all cartels "equally" proved firm, ultimately hobbling reform efforts. President César Gaviria and Governor Sérgio Cabral's willingness to pursue new approaches was equally critical. Yet the institutional and political contexts in which these leaders made their decisions also varied in important ways. In particular, I argue that leaders face similar obstacles to implementing conditional policies—what I call logistical *and* acceptability *constraints. Overcoming these is the key to successful implementation of conditional reforms.*

Thus far, I have argued that conditionality of repression is a key determinant of whether cartels respond to state crackdowns with increased or decreased violence. Part I lays out several logics of anti-state violence, showing how unconditional crackdowns give cartels increased incentives for anti-state violence, and arguing that conditionality of repression could counter these incentives and induce cartels to eschew violence. Part II presents case-study evidence supporting my theory: unconditional crackdowns tended to trigger or exacerbate cartel–state conflict, while turns toward conditionality seem to have had strong, violence-reducing effects. The case studies also provided descriptive narratives of the efforts of reformers that, to differing degrees in each case, succeeded in in raising the conditionality of repression.

The natural next step is to turn our attention back to the state and ask why and when leaders adopt unconditional versus conditional policies in the first place. Indeed, given the success of conditional approaches where they have been tried, one might wonder why they have not been adopted more universally.

Of course, leaders may not understand the potential for unconditional repression to spark cartel–state conflict, or they may simply not prioritize minimizing violence. Both factors probably played some role in the unconditional nature of initial state crackdowns on cartels and subsequent "doubling down." Across cases, initial crackdowns were essentially reactive: cartels had grown stronger due to changing market conditions, upsetting peaceful status quos; decision-makers felt they had to take drastic action, and so unleashed what repressive force they had at hand—usually the armed forces or militarized police—with little strategic planning or intelligence gathering. Leaders framed such crackdowns as efforts to cripple or destroy out-of-control cartels, and their surprise when cartels responded with sustained anti-state violence was probably genuine. On the other hand, leaders quickly began spinning such violence as a positive metric of cartels' desperation and doubled down on unconditional repression; as is often the case, the political optics of "staying the course" could be quite advantageous. All in all, while these policy decisions may seem unwise in light of subsequent events, they are not terribly puzzling.

As the conflicts dragged on and violence escalated, however, the aggravating effect of unconditional repression became clearer, and public exasperation gave leaders good reasons to want to minimize violence. Moreover, in all three cases, actors within state security apparatuses began making concerted efforts to reform repressive policy in a more conditional direction, with the declared goal of reducing violence. At a minimum, then, some state actors both wanted to curb cartel–state conflict and thought that conditional repression could accomplish this.

Thus, it is puzzling that the success of these very similar reform efforts varied starkly: in Mexico, the push for increased conditionality basically failed, while in Colombia and Rio, after initial failures, reformers eventually succeeded in implanting conditional repression. Why did reform efforts succeed in some cases and not others? And what factors contributed to the erosion or collapse of conditional approaches in the "recrudescence" phases in Colombia and Rio? To address the first question, this chapter lays out a theoretical framework for explaining the success and failure of policy reform, while Chapter 9 draws on the empirical details of successful and failed reform processes to build a conjectural account of which factors were most decisive in achieving implementation. Chapter 10 then explores the dynamics that have made it difficult to sustain conditional policies once in place.

8.1 THEORETICAL FRAMEWORK: CONSTRAINTS AND MITIGATING FACTORS

This section introduces a framework for explaining the observed variation in the success of pro-conditional reform efforts. The main reform efforts to be examined are shown in Table 8.1; in addition, I discuss some of the failed efforts that preceded reform success in Colombia and Rio de Janeiro.

TABLE 8.1. *Conditional-Repression Reform Efforts: Implementation and Long-Term Outcomes.*

	Reform Policy	Implemented?	Long-Term Outcomes
Colombia	*Sometimiento*	Yes	Collapse
Rio	Pacification	Yes	Replication → Erosion
Mexico	Selective Repression	No	n/a
Boston	Ceasefire	Yes	Consolidation → Replication
Rio	GPAE	Yes	Replication → Erosion → Collapse

In addition to the conditional policies discussed in the case studies, I consider Boston's Operation Ceasefire, which influenced both Rio and Mexico's conditional approaches. Rio's GPAE, a small-scale precursor to Pacification, is included as a subordinate case; though its implementation was limited, its erosion and collapse are particularly illustrative.

Rio's GPAE[1] program, an important precursor to Pacification, was successful at a very local level, bringing an immediate and drastic reduction in violence in the favelas where the original pilot was implemented in 2000. However, it soon eroded and eventually collapsed. As such, it occupies a middle ground between what I code as reform success (Pacification in Rio, *Sometimiento* in Colombia) and the truly failed reform attempts that preceded success. I include it as a subordinate case.

I also include Boston's Operation Ceasefire—a successful, influential, and highly conditional policy in which Boston gangs were credibly threatened with extra, indeed extreme, enforcement if murders occurred on their turf—as a kind of check on the logic. This is not a true out-of-sample case, since the project directly influenced reformers in Rio and Mexico, as I discuss. Moreover, Ceasefire was aimed at a different problem (relatively low-level violence among street gangs) in a different setting (relatively high state capacity), so it is not always fully comparable along every relevant dimension. Yet Ceasefire's very importance as a "proof of concept" for the actors pushing for reform in Mexico and Rio warrants including it here, even if in a qualified way; the fact that similar dynamics were at play in its formulation, implementation, success, and eventual consolidation as a valid policy approach is heartening.

I distinguish initial implementation from longer-term outcomes because the dynamics at play are potentially quite distinct. The initial implementation of conditional policies generally has more to do with the internal political dynamics of governments and their security agencies, while their long-term

---

[1] Grupamento de Policiamento em Áreas Especiais (Policing in Special Areas Unit).

success depends in large part on the outcomes they produce—the topic of the first two parts of the book—as well as on many idiosyncratic factors. GPAE, for example, ultimately collapsed in part because of the same political obstacles that make conditional reforms difficult in the first place. *Sometimiento*, on the other hand, collapsed because Escobar fled from prison—a fact that tells us little about the challenges of the initial reform stage. I analyze the conditions for successful policy reform and implementation here; Chapter 10 considers some of the common dynamics that have made conditionality difficult to sustain in practice.

Why did pro-conditionality reform efforts succeed in Rio and Colombia, but fail in Mexico? The most parsimonious answer is agency: in this view, President Felipe Calderón of Mexico was just not open to taking a conditional approach, while President César Gaviria of Colombia and Governor Sérgio Cabral of Rio de Janeiro were. The preferences of individual leaders probably play an outsized role here: in all three cases, the power to formulate repressive policy lay largely in the hands of these executives. Had Gaviria and Cabral virulently objected to the very idea of conditionality, it is doubtful that the conditional reforms pushed by either Rafael Pardo or José Beltrame (their respective security officers) would have gained traction. Had Calderón been more amenable to the idea, perhaps reform advocate and intelligence chief Guillermo Valdés's efforts would have flourished.

Agency—the strategic choices of powerful individuals—is a compelling explanation as far as it goes, but, on its own, it does not go very far. We deepen our analysis when we take an integrative approach that considers how institutional endowments and political contexts form "the constraints within which and against which actors maneuver" (Yashar 1997, 3). How did the strong variation in the institutional structure of police and military agencies across cases shape leaders' options? What political factors may have made it less costly for Cabral to change course than for Calderón? How did reformers' ability to point to successful conditional policies elsewhere or in the past change those political calculations? Grappling with these questions does not diminish the causal importance of agency, but rather fleshes it out.

Methodologically, treating state policy not as an explanation of cartel behavior but rather as an outcome to be explained in its own right—in other words, as a dependent rather than independent variable—requires a looser analytic approach than the instrumental logics of violence employed in Parts I and II. Indeed, the formal analysis of violent corruption in Chapter 4 treated leaders' policy decisions as exogenous precisely because the plethora of factors that might shape those decisions could not be usefully included in a parsimonious formal model. The literature on policy formulation has long placed importance on factors that are not purely strategic, such as the "acceptability" of policy options (e.g., March and Olsen 1984, 2004) and the institutional mechanisms of reform itself (Hacker 2004; Schickler 2001). Kingdon's classic account of policy formulation (1984) is also relevant here.

Policy change, in his view, occurs when several factors come together: not only a political opening but a new (or newly understood) problem to be solved, and good ideas for solving it. We miss something if we simply read decision-makers' preferences from policy outcomes, without first exploring how the problem at hand has been framed and the way relevant policy alternatives have been articulated and specified.

Building on these ideas, I argue that conditional approaches are, by their nature, subject to two sets of obstacles or constraints that unconditional crackdowns are not, and that reform attempts were successful when these constraints were mitigated by certain factors. First, *logistical constraints* limit leaders' ability to implement conditionality, which requires more intelligence gathering and centralized operational decision making than unconditional blanket crackdowns. Conditionality is hard work: authorities must credibly threaten to correctly identify and attribute cartel violence, and respond to it swiftly and proportionally. This may simply be unfeasible under conditions of weak state capacity in general and fragmentation in the institutional structure of security sector in particular. Second, and quite apart from logistical concerns, adopting conditional approaches exposes leaders to a broad, shifting set of political and diplomatic costs. These *acceptability constraints* can be quite acute, reflecting the unique politics and optics of drug wars. Negotiating peace settlements with insurgents is never easy, but negotiation with criminal groups is widely seen as fundamentally immoral, while proposing anything short of total eradication of the drug trade as the goal of drug policy can be politically toxic.

In describing how conditional approaches were designed and (sometimes) implemented, reformers often attributed success (or failure) to the presence (or absence) of certain contextual or idiosyncratic factors. Applying my theoretical framework, these factors can be seen as potentially mitigating one or both types of constraints, thus facilitating the implementation of conditional repression. For example, successful reform generally followed a reframing of the problem to be solved, from ending the drug trade completely to reducing the violence associated with it. This factor, I would argue, eases the acceptability constraints associated with conditional repression. To assess which of these factors were most likely to have been decisive in practice, Chapter 9 explores in detail how each played out across cases.

8.2 LOGISTICAL CONSTRAINTS

Conditional repression requires a credible threat of extra state repression in response to cartel violence. Leaders must effectively condition the actions of enforcers on accurate assessments of cartels' violent actions. This in turn requires accumulating solid and actionable intelligence, holding that intelligence safely in reserve until a repressive action is ordered, and ensuring (in a way cartels will believe) that such orders depend on cartel action and will be effectively obeyed. "Operationally," as one reform advocate in Mexico put it, "it's a [expletive] nightmare."[2]

Fragmented police and security institutions are a prime source of logistical constraints. Where there are multiple security agencies involved in anti-cartel efforts, it may be impossible to effectively condition repression on cartel behavior without strong centralized coordination, often across different levels of government. This is clearest in Calderón's Mexico, where effective coordination between municipal, state, and federal police proved virtually impossible. To the contrary, several highly corrupt municipal police corps were arrested en masse by federal forces, and incidents of actual armed confrontations between different police forces were not uncommon. This led Calderón to rely almost entirely on federal forces. Even there, though, no single agency had sufficient capacity, so targets were distributed among police, military, and judicial agencies. This produced, perhaps intentionally, inter-agency competition for the limelight and strong incentives to capture their respective targets.[3] Such competition, however, also made repression less conditional: strikes were not carried out in response to cartel actions but rather according to the vagaries of actionable intelligence within each agency, and often in response to successful strikes by rival agencies.[4]

In comparative terms, Mexico has by far the most fragmented security institutions, not only vertically, with literally thousands of police corps spread across three levels of government, but horizontally: at the federal level, at least four main agencies—the Federal Police, the army, the navy, and the attorney general's office (Procuraduría General de la Republica, PGR)—are involved in major anti-cartel operations. Brazil's institutional structure is only moderately fragmented: the split between the Civil (investigative) and Military (uniformed) Police is severe and at times crippling (Bicudo 2000), but both are under the direct control of state governors. There are no municipal police forces, and the Federal Police are more focused on international crimes and high-level political corruption. The Brazilian armed forces have played a critical supporting role in many crackdowns; however, they rarely act autonomously from state governors. Colombia, meanwhile, enjoys a single police force under control of the national government. Although there are police designated as municipal forces, mayors do not exercise operational control over them.[5]

Still, even in Colombia logistical constraints existed. The lack of capacity and experience with respect to high-security prison facilities became a stumbling

---

2   Interview, CISEN working group member, July 2, 2014.
3   Interview, director of the Federal Ministerial Police (Policía Federal Ministerial, PFM), previously known as the Federal Investigations Agency (Agencia Federal de Investigación, AFI), October 20, 2010.
4   Interview with member of the Technical Secretariat of the National Security Council (Secretaría Técnica del Consejo de Seguridad Nacional), October 22, 2010.
5   Interview with former mayor of Bogotá, Enrique Peñalosa, October 4, 2008.

block during the *Sometimiento* negotiations with Escobar. Notwithstanding Escobar's chutzpah in providing his own lush prison resort on land he purchased for the purpose, he was correct that the Colombian state could not keep him safe from his enemies in the Cali cartel. Another threat to the negotiations was vocal dissatisfaction from prominent state enforcers at having to halt their efforts (Salazar 2001, 273), raising the specter of insubordination and the inability to credibly promise less repression in exchange for submission.[6] Insubordination in the form of excess police violence also haunted efforts in Rio to implement community policing in the early 2000s, and more recently has seriously compromised the UPP[7] units' public image and acceptance among favela residents.

8.3 ACCEPTABILITY CONSTRAINTS

In 2011, a high-ranking Calderón official, serving as a discussant on a symposium panel where I presented my core findings on conditionality and violence, said "Your proposed policy is unrealistic." He was not referring to logistical constraints at all. "Of course we could end the violence, but it would be impossible politically."

Why are the politics of conditional repression so vexed? The main problem, I would argue, is not one of competing interests per se, but rather public morality. For many people, conditional approaches are not just logistically daunting, strategically risky, or resource-intensive, but in some sense morally unacceptable. Conditional approaches are much more likely to be criticized on ethical than on pragmatic, cost–benefit grounds. Such normative concerns can have real constraining power over policymakers, whether they find conditionality morally unacceptable themselves, or merely seek to placate other key actors that do (such as voters, US officials, or UN agencies).

Conditionality generates three normative problems simply by virtue of its basic mechanics—applying less repressive force against cartels that eschew violence than those that engage in it. The logical necessity of "going easy" on non-violent drug traffickers raises the first normative concern: the state is turning a blind eye, or becoming complicit in, systematic violation of its laws. The second normative problem is impartiality: by hurting the most violent cartels, or more subtly, by dissuading violent challengers, the state inevitably "helps" less violent, incumbent cartels. This raises non-normative issues as

---

[6] It is easy to understand why a true, uncorrupt drug warrior would not want leaders cutting deals; it is worth noting that the model of violent corruption presented in this study predicts that a corrupt police officer intent on extorting traffickers for bribes would also oppose a move to conditionality, as it would undercut the officer's bargaining leverage. Perhaps it should thus be less surprising that General Maza Márquez, one of the most vocal critics of *Sometimiento* and perhaps the prime public antagonist of Escobar, was later accused of having worked for Escobar.

[7] Unidades de Polícia Pacificadora (Pacifying Police Units).

well: strategic concern over strengthening incumbents, as well as the specter
of corrupt deals between incumbents and leaders. But on a moral level, helping
one cartel by hurting another seems to violate fundamental notions of equality
before the law. Finally, for many people, conditionality amounts to appeasing,
negotiating, or "pacting" with the drug trade. This violates a powerful norm—a
taboo, I would argue—against negotiation with criminal groups as opposed to
insurgencies and other "political" groups.

In public discourse, these three concerns often meld together into generalized
dismissal of *any* move towards conditionality as "appeasement," institutionalized impunity and corruption, or even outright surrender. For example, Rio's
mayor successfully attacked the GPAE program by characterizing it as a "pact"
and—because it physically occupied favelas without seeking to eradicate the
drug trade—functioning as "the traffickers' bouncer" (Fernandes 2003, 98).
Similar discursive tactics can be seen in the Calderón government's explanation
of its insistence on "weaken[ing] all [cartels] systematically without distinction.
To benefit any criminal group, directly or indirectly, would mean allowing its
illegal activities to go unpunished. The Federal Government has made clear
that it offers neither pacts nor impunity to criminals; rather, it brings them to
justice."[8]

Political scientists are often skeptical that rhetorical and normative concerns
have real causal power. A historical quirk of the Colombian case offers some
evidence that they do. In the late 1980s, President Virgilio Barco's government
engaged in two negotiation processes simultaneously, one with Pablo Escobar's
terrorist group the Extraditables, another with the M-19 guerrilla movement.
The government's subterfuge, mixed signals, and lack of credibility stymied
Escobar's efforts to strike an amnesty deal, while its public negotiation with
the M-19 led to the group's successful demobilization; as the former generated
a public scandal, the latter became a feather in the administration's cap. The
contrast is striking considering that only a few years earlier, the M-19 had
launched perhaps the most spectacular terrorist attack in Colombia's history,
seizing the Ministry of Justice, which led to its destruction and the death of
most members of the Supreme Court. Moreover, doubts lingered (and linger to
this day) over whether the M-19's attack was carried out on behalf of Escobar,
who stood to gain with the destruction of the Ministry of Justice archives.
Nonetheless, the government granted "political status" to the M-19, meaning
that it could negotiate with them, while consistently denying such status to
Escobar (who, desperate, even sought unsuccessfully to enlist as a member
of the M-19). As former Defense Minister Rafael Pardo, who personally
negotiated the M-19 deal, put it: "For the government, it was absolutely

---

[8] From the government's "10 Myths of the Drug War" series, available at: http://cald
eron.presidencia.gob.mx/tag/10-mitos-de-la-lucha-por-la-seguridad/. See Figure 7.5 for other
examples.

critical to separate negotiation with the insurgency from non-negotiation with narco-terrorists."[9]

By 1990, the results of this "separation" were glaring: Carlos Pizarro, former commander of the M-19, was a leading contender in that year's presidential election, while Escobar had just bombed the headquarters of Colombia's national intelligence agency[10] in Bogotá. Even when *Sometimiento* facilitated Escobar's surrender, the details had to be worked out secretly and in contradiction of the government's stated policy of non-negotiation (Leal Buitrago 2006, 112). This caused delay and, eventually, inter-agency confusion about Escobar's freedom of action within La Catedral,[11] which in turn contributed to Escobar's escape, the collapse of *Sometimiento* as a solution, and return to extreme terrorist violence until Escobar's death in December 1993. By that time, the M-19, a fearsome insurgent group only a few years earlier, had become a docile and surprisingly ineffective political party.

Why was it legitimate for the Colombian state to openly negotiate with one violent armed group and not another? In qualitative interviews, top officials from the Gaviria administration all drew a sharp moral distinction between fighting for social change and using violence in pursuit of illicit profits. In the words of Gaviria's vice attorney general, "The guerrillas had, originally, an altruistic purpose. ...The drug trade is just a business."[12] This view was unanimous among Gaviria administration officials I spoke to, despite sharp divergences in opinion over other aspects of state strategy. The distinction was not lost on Escobar, who had long portrayed his war as fundamentally political and even obtained an official affiliation with the M-19 in an attempt to qualify for demobilization.[13] Whatever the merits of this position from a normative point of view, it is clear that differing acceptability constraints left the Colombian state with vastly more room to maneuver in its dealings with the M-19 than with the drug cartels, leading to very different outcomes.

---

[9] Interview, Rafael Pardo, Bogotá, December 16, 2010.
[10] Known as DAS (Departamento Administrativo de Seguridad, Administrative Department of Security).
[11] Interview, former Attorney General Gustavo de Greiff, December 13, 2010.
[12] Interview, former Vice Attorney General Francisco José Sintura, Bogotá, December 17, 2010.
[13] Interview, Rafael Pardo, Bogotá, December 16, 2010.

9

Explaining Reform Efforts' Success

Key Factors and Alternative Hypotheses

> *Why were reformers able to overcome logistical and acceptability constraints and implement conditional repression in Colombia and Rio de Janeiro, but not Mexico? Reformers themselves suggested a number of candidate factors they saw as important; yet the presence of these varied considerably across cases. A comparative analysis suggests that three factors are particularly decisive: (1) the successful reframing of the problem as violence minimization, as opposed to ending the drug trade per se; (2) institutional cohesion, or where institutional structure is fragmented, political cohesion; and (3) the ability to hone and build support for conditional policies through a process of trial and error. Other factors may have played a more limited and idiosyncratic role in individual cases.*

Why were some reformers able to overcome logistical and acceptability constraints and successfully implement conditional repression, while other reform attempts failed? During the qualitative interviews that inform the descriptive accounts of reform efforts in Part II, reformers and other state actors suggested a number of potentially decisive factors. In this section, I evaluate the relative importance of the most commonly proposed factors. Three of these factors, I will argue, were the most decisive in facilitating the formulation and adoption of conditional approaches:

1. *Reframing the Problem*: The officials leading anti-cartel efforts redefined the problem that repressive policy was supposed to solve, from drug trafficking writ large to drug-related violence.
2. *Political/Institutional Cohesion*: Police and other repressive agencies were unified by their institutional structure, by political cohesion across levels of government, or both.
3. *Layering/Trial and Error*: Reformers could experiment at a local or small scale, honing and building support for conditional policies before expanding them.

Three other factors may have played idiosyncratic roles in some of the cases, but were not decisive: a large pool of policy ideas to draw on, the largest cartel also being the most violent, and a leader not tied politically to status quo policies. Finally, three factors that reformers frequently emphasized appear to have played little role in practice: a forum for brainstorming without fear of superiors, delegation of responsibility by decision-makers to provide political cover, and what I call "Sino-Nixonian Effects"—the idea that, just as it took a known anti-communist like Nixon to open diplomatic relations with China, it takes a known hardliner on drug policy to implement conditional repression.

I draw on two types of evidence support these findings. First, the most decisive factors were present in all three cases of highly successful reform (Rio's Pacification, Colombia's *Sometimiento*, and Boston's Ceasefire) and absent in the case of unsuccessful reform ("Selective Repression" in Mexico); other factors were either absent in some of the positive cases or present in the negative case. Second, drawing on details of my case-study observations, a process-tracing approach elucidates the pathways by which these three factors eased political constraints, logistical constraints, or both; other candidate factors failed to consistently or significantly ease these constraints. The results of this comparative analysis are summarized in Table 9.1.

Obviously, the small number of cases and the large number of plausible factors create a severe degrees-of-freedom problem, which process tracing and counterfactual analysis can only partially alleviate. The analysis here is conjectural, a first cut at the problem. Future scholarship on additional cases could help test these structured conjectures.

9.1 MOST DECISIVE FACTORS

9.1.1 Reframing the Problem

In Colombia and Rio, leaders made deliberate efforts to reframe the problem that repressive policy was supposed to address. They adopted public stances that differentiated drug trafficking writ large from the more specific and urgent problem of cartel violence, and in particular cartel–state conflict. These efforts to reframe the problem as principally one of reducing violence as opposed to ending the drug trade, seem to have been largely successful. This in turn vastly reduced acceptability constraints. In Mexico, by contrast, problem reframing was far less successful. While reformers were originally motivated by a grave concern at the rapid escalation of violence from 2009 on, and sought to make violence reduction a central if not top priority of repressive policy, they faced strong resistance to a fundamental reframing of the problem from many quarters, including their own ranks. The result was a limited, incomplete, and consequently fractious reframing, recognizing the need to respond to the most heinous and "high impact" of crimes, without abjuring the drug trade (i.e., the existence of cartels) itself as the core problem.

In Colombia, a key moment in the development of *Sometimiento* was Gaviria's agenda-setting inaugural speech of August 7, 1990:

TABLE 9.1. *Factors Affecting Chances of Pro-Conditional Policy Reform.*

Factors	Cases (Reform Successful?)				Effects on Constraints:		Overall Importance
	Rio (Yes)	Colombia (Yes)	Mexico (No)	Ceasefire (Yes)	Logistical	Acceptability	
Problem Reframed	Yes	Yes	No	Yes		+++	High
Political / Institutional Cohesion	High	High	Low	High	++	+	High
Layering / Trial and Error	High	High	Low	High	++	++	High
Pool of Ideas	High	Low	Medium	High	++	+	Medium
Largest Cartel Also Most Violent	Yes	Yes	No	Yes	+	++	Medium
Leader Not Tied to Status Quo	Low	High	Low	High		+	Medium
Brainstorming / Non-Hierarchy	High	High	High	High		+	Low
Delegation	High	Low	Low	Low		+	Low
"Sino-Nixonian" Effects	High	High	High	High		+	Low

Factors suggested by reformers as important appear on the left. Drawing on case-study evidence and counterfactual analysis, factors were scored for their presence/relevance in each case, and for mitigating effect on logistical and acceptability constraints (from zero to +++). Based on these scores, each factor was rated for overall importance.

> Narcoterrorism is today the principal threat to our democracy. We will confront
> it without concessions. ... But if narco-terrorism is our problem, drug trafficking
> is an international phenomenon which will only be solved through joint action
> by all affected countries, and no progress will be possible as long as consumer
> countries do not substantially reduce their demand. Extradition cannot be the
> only, or even the principal tool in the fight against drug trafficking.

According to Rafael Pardo, one of the key architects of *Sometimiento*, this
conceptual separation of the immediate problem of debilitating violence from
the longer-term and likely insoluble problem of drug trafficking was essential
to building support for the policy. Besides easing the acceptability of offering
reduced sentences to known traffickers, it did so in a way that was seen
to strengthen Colombia's autonomy vis-à-vis the United States (Pardo Rueda
1996).

In Rio, José Beltrame, and to a lesser extent Sergio Cabral himself,
aggressively sought to reframe the problem. Soon after the first, failed invasion
of Alemão in 2007, Cabral echoed Gaviria by declaring that "The aim of the
operation was not to end the drug trade. That's something nobody has ever
done. Trafficking hasn't ended in Paris, New York, or Stockholm, places with
many more resources than us. Our goal is to reach civilized levels of criminality"
(Fernandes 2007).

This phrasing clearly reflects Beltrame's own thinking, repeatedly reinforcing
the notion that ending the drug trade was not the goal of policing; he also
gave a more specific definition of the positive objective: territory and reducing
violence. As he explained it to reporters, at an early press conference on
Pacification, "We can't guarantee that we'll put an end to the drug trade, nor
do we have the intention of doing so. Our objective is breaking the paradigm
of territory controlled by traffickers with military-grade weapons" (quoted in
Phillips 2010).

The savvy with which Beltrame and his team introduced the ideas behind
Pacification to the media and Rio society was certainly due in no small measure
to the close involvement of Dirceu Vianna, Beltrame's communications head
and a former campaign advisor to Cabral. Beltrame's effort to reframe the
problem benefited from both his own natural facility for plain speaking and
his above-average media coaching. But as Vianna explained to me, there was
a natural fit between the secretary's new discursive strategy and the logic of
Pacification itself.

> [The reframing of the problem] was born together with the very conception of
> the Pacification project. "Are we going to get rid of the drug trade? No. So let's
> try to get rid of the assault rifles." We had maps of the favelas marked with the
> radius of an assault rifle's range, two kilometers. Our enemy is the assault rifle's
> shot. That's where we got the idea that we had to retake the territory.[1]

---

[1]   Interview, Rio de Janeiro, March 17, 2014.

In Mexico, the effort to reframe the problem was a major component of the overall reform effort, as Alejandro Hope explained:

> What we tried to do, a bunch of people ... within pretty much every agency, was to make the argument that violence reduction was an end by and of itself.[2]

This view was consonant with increasing popular revulsion over the brutality and escalation of drug-related violence. Public anger at the government's apparent lack of concern for the victims of violence led Calderón to seek a reorientation of his administration's discourse, particularly after the disastrous Villas de Salvarcar incident—in which Calderón's hasty dismissal of the January 2010 massacre of sixteen innocent youth as nothing more than "gang rivalry" led to outcry and an official apology. The extant framing of violence as a positive signal of cartels' desperation—violence as "the last throes of the insurgency" as I put it in Chapter 7—began to fade from public sight.

In its place, Calderón and newly appointed security spokesman Alejandro Poiré sought to craft a more nuanced and empathic discourse, emphasizing the need to respond to "high-impact crimes" and "rebuild the social fabric."[3] This new discourse certainly went some distance in acknowledging violence as a problem. Yet Calderón was adamant that debilitating the cartels remain a central goal of his security policy, and neither he nor his top operational chiefs were willing to explicitly adopt violence minimization as the primary problem frame. Indeed, within the army and the Federal Police, the "violence as last throes" view was still widely and openly held. As one high-ranking advisor to Security Secretary Genaro García Luna told me, "[Intelligence Chief Guillermo] Valdés was anguished by the number of deaths. We were not. We knew violence was going to go up. This vision [of Valdés's], this effort to change the policy, failed. But we at the Federal Police never paid any attention to it."[4] For these actors, the problem was (still) not cartel violence, but the need to stay the course in the face of growing weakness of popular will. As key Calderón security advisor Joaquín Villalobos (2010) put it in his widely read article "Twelve Myths of the War Against the Narcos":

> The process of self-destruction fragments the cartels ... this in turn increases their violence and accelerates their self-destruction. The problem is that, in the meantime, political pressure demands a reduction in violence ... In Mexico, it will still take time before violence falls. But the self-destruction process is accelerating and that is a positive signal.

These contradictory gestures toward reframing the problem led to an increasingly confused relationship between government discourse and action, the genesis of "conditionality-in-deed-but-not-word." In 2011, even those

committed to a larger vision of a *guerra frontal* ("frontal battle") could see
the appeal of forcefully responding to Los Zetas' increasingly barbaric acts.
Moreover, officials from the navy, whose territorial preeminence in Veracruz
and other Zeta areas made it the logical front-line responder, were among the
most sympathetic to the logic of selective enforcement. Yet, as one member of
Valdés's CISEN working group put it, "Bureaucratically there was little to win
by gaining a more nuanced vision of the problem." To implement an explicitly
conditional approach, he said, would be "an uphill battle against the official
narrative, politically fraught."[5] Instead, the navy went ahead with its Operation
Norte Lince and other anti-Zetas strikes without any official statement linking
the increased repression to the Zetas' own violent behavior. When Eduardo
Guerrero and others argued that this in fact constituted a turn toward selective
enforcement (e.g., Guerrero 2011b), the government repeatedly denied it.

Problem reframing in the post-Calderón period has been vexed. President
Enrique Peña Nieto, at the outset of his term, pledged openly (if vaguely) to
make violence minimization a priority, provoking strong rebukes and accusations of corrupt intent from hardline US drug warriors. Security issues quickly
disappeared from Peña Nieto's public agenda, replaced by ambitious economic
and political reform initiatives. His security officials, to the extent they laid
out any kind of strategy at all, mostly talked of improving coordination and
capacity, and increasing human-rights safeguards. Even opposition figure and
Calderón nemesis Andrés Manuel López Obrador never advocated a radical
break from a frontal-combat approach. In Alejandro Hope's view, this reflects
the fact that "in some ways, Calderón won the culture war: people are wary of
moving away from his discourse."[6]

Finally, the architects of Boston's Operation Ceasefire explicitly recognized
the importance that problem (re)framing had in the success of their project:

> Youth homicide in Boston could have been accurately and variously described
> as a problem of: gun violence; violence in poor minority communities;
> minority-male-on-minority-male violence; gang violence; drug-related violence;
> violence by young people with little respect for authority; or violence by young
> people with poor values. All these descriptions were put on the table and seriously
> addressed in the Working Group process. But *until the Working Group settled
> on yet another accurate description of the problem*—1,300 more or less chronic
> offenders well known to the authorities, in 61 gangs, who largely hurt one
> another, principally through gang feuds—*it was unable to make real progress in
> designing a solution.* (Kennedy et al. 2001, 47; emphasis added)

That said, problem reframing in the Boston case was surely a far easier
needle to thread than in cases of outright cartel–state conflict. Gang members,
however negatively seen by society, have not been demonized to nearly the
extent that cartels have. Thus, Kennedy et al. (2001) could write "the key

---

[5] Interview, February 7, 2014.
[6] Interview, January 29, 2014.

insight in the Boston [Ceasefire] Project remains ... that gang members need, and indeed deserve, both help and control," simultaneously capturing the core logic of conditional repression—using repressive force to give criminal groups incentives to avoid violence—and successfully reframing the problem in paternalistic terms. Vastly greater acceptability constraints are at work in militarized drug war; to see this, one need only imagine any of the relevant reformers in my cases writing, "*drug lords* need, and indeed deserve, both help and control." Instead, those reformers who succeeded had to find ways to reframe the problem as violence minimization without challenging an ingrained view of cartels as demonic and sometimes existential threats.

9.1.2 Institutional-Political Cohesion

Powerful political coalitions or centralized political control can help overcome logistical constraints by mitigating the effects of institutional fragmentation. The prime example of this is Mexico under single-party rule. The PRI's political hegemony in Mexico was so thoroughgoing that the formal institutional fragmentation of the coercive apparatus was largely irrelevant. The state did not "feel" fragmented because police at every level of the system were under the control of a central, hierarchical system.

In the wake of the collapse of the PRI, cooperation and coordination among agencies occured more sporadically. For example, Mexico City's former Attorney General Miguel Ángel Mancera told me that relations between his agency (the Procuraduría General de Justicia, PGJ) and the state Secretariat of Public Security (SSP) had long been uncooperative, but that this had recently improved. When I asked why, he said "I have a good relationship with the director of the SSP. We went to school together." Mancera is, as of this writing, mayor of Mexico City,[7] leaving one to speculate that PGJ–SSP cooperation has probably reverted to the mean.

The larger point is that when cooperation among pieces of the state's coercive apparatus depends largely on personal relationships among officials, the state cannot credibly commit to a policy that requires sustained coordination. The PAN's weakness among mayoralties and governorships, as well as Calderón's own weakness within the PAN, meant that the endemic horizontal and vertical fragmentation of Mexico's security institutions came to the fore with a vengeance. Lack of cooperation from governors and lack of coordination among security agencies were mentioned by virtually every federal security official I spoke with.

In Rio, on the other hand, a felicitous alignment of political forces—Cabral's party was in a formal coalition with those of Mayor Eduardo Paes and Presidents Luiz Inácio Lula da Silva and Dilma Rousseff—unified what were already relatively cohesive security institutions. Such a coalition is not strictly

---

7 The official title is Jefe del Gobierno del Distrito Federal.

necessary in administrative terms: in Brazil, control over policing and public (as opposed to national) security is overwhelmingly held by state governors. However, the alliance with the federal government facilitated both increased funding for the new UPP police battalions and, more critically, the participation of the armed forces during occupations, a crucial factor in the taking of Alemão and Vila Cruzeiro. Mayoral support was also important: besides avoiding the kind of public controversy that tarnished the image of the GPAE project, the city government has contributed financially to the UPP program, paying officers a bonus that has been an important incentive for recruitment.

Moreover, the political coalition, by signaling a higher likelihood of success, helped attract support from other key sectors, including the media and business elites. Eike Batista, a Rio entrepreneur and billionaire who donated some $12 million per year to the project, explicitly pointed to the political coalition as a factor in his support: "When I felt the force of [Governor] Cabral together with the mayor ... and his connection to the federal government, [I said] 'ah ... now this is a team.' Without that, nothing ever works. If it hadn't been all three engaged, I wouldn't have contributed."[8] Donations from Batista and other outside contributions were especially important to the early success of Pacification because, officials at the Public Security Secretariat explained, they were mostly in kind: by donating buildings, computers, and other critical equipment, UPPs could be installed quickly, without going through lengthy requisition and bidding processes.

The centralized nature of Colombia's security institutions meant that political cohesion per se was not a major factor. Nonetheless, cohesion under Gaviria was fairly strong: after the assassination of four presidential candidates in the 1990 election, he governed as a uniter, including members of the M-19 and other opposition parties in his cabinet.

9.1.3 Layering/Trial and Error

As aficionados of *The Wire* can tell you, institutional practice, especially that of police departments, is difficult to change. As a result, successful reform efforts to implement conditional repression have often taken the form of "layering" (Schickler 2001), in which new practices or institutions are added on top of, rather than replacing, old ones. The advantage of layering is that it enables policy reformers to simply sidestep, if temporarily, institutional deficiencies and vested interests (Hacker 2004). On the other hand, as the case of Pacification clearly shows, layering leaves those deficiencies and interests unresolved, which can fundamentally threaten the long-term success of a conditional policy once it is consolidated and scaled up.

---

[8] *Roda Viva* (television program), TV Cultura, August 30, 2010. Available online at: www.youtube.com/watch?v=Qix2DMDqcKw&feature=relmfu. The quote above appears from 17′50″ to 18′30″.

In the case of Rio's GPAE, by focusing on a single favela, reformers could put an innovative, differentiated policing regime into practice quickly, without first having to reform a deeply corrupt and violent institution. With Pacification, as the UPP project expanded, layering took the form of essentially building a parallel police force within the existing institutional structure. Beyond expediency, this led to a nearly ideal quasi-experimental setup: not only was the "treatment" (namely, the Pacification process) applied within well-circumscribed areas, but the UPP units themselves were built of new recruits and bureaucratically isolated from the rest of the police force, minimizing the risk of contamination. As we will see in the following chapter, however, this approach left unreformed a still-powerful "old guard" of police who grew increasingly hostile as the UPP contingent grew to constitute a significant share of the police force.

In Colombia, *Sometimiento* can be seen as a form of layering since it did not depend on reining in enforcement agencies—which were pursuing Escobar in a violent and out-of-control way at that point—but rather offered a carrot to their stick. In Mexico, whatever move to conditionality ended up occurring, mostly on the part of the navy, was certainly layered over the unmoved practices of the army and the Federal Police. What is not clear is the extent to which selective enforcement, as advocated for, would have been layered. Kleiman's published proposal, in any case, suggests a wholesale reformulation of national security policy.

Layering's direct effect is to alleviate logistical constraints, but it can also ease acceptability concerns—in particular the charge that conditionality constitutes "turning a blind eye"—by reassuring both traditional police forces and the public at large that regular policing of criminal activity will continue. The architects of Operation Ceasefire were careful to make precisely such assurances:

> The energies that went into implementing the new strategy would represent a fraction of the total criminal justice activity in Boston; normal enforcement by police, probation officers, prosecutors, and others would continue as before. The new reality—it was hoped—was that violence would now bring a special response in addition to "baseline" enforcement activities.
>
> (Kennedy et al. 2001, 37)

More importantly, layering allows reforms to conduct small-scale policy experiments within the limited or controlled realm in which the new policy is first introduced. This trial-and-error approach can in turn ease acceptability constraints, through several related mechanisms. First, it provides some political room to fail: early setbacks need not threaten the entire effort, but can serve as "teaching moments" that help improve the policy before wider implementation. Second, local experimentation allows for a clear attribution of credit in the case of success. Experimentation and adjustment seem to have been critical to both Pacification and *Sometimiento*. Pacification, as Dirceu Vianna put it to me, "wasn't born ready. First came [the favelas] Dona Marta, then City of God. They were experiments. After, we stopped and took stock of what worked and what did not. But the first four [Pacifications] were complicated and messy experiments."[9]

By 2010, Pacification's architects could point to four favelas that had received a clearly differentiated treatment, and plausibly attribute the visible improvements in those favelas to that treatment. This in turn was critical in winning over the support of both the media and the entrepreneurial class.

Similarly, the *Sometimiento* policy evolved over the course of 1990 and 1991 via a series of decrees that altered key details; while some of these adjustments were the result of occult negotiations with Escobar's lawyers, others arose from the government's own trial and error while negotiating the surrender of the three Ochoa brothers in December 1990 and January 1991. These "experiments" also provided critical information for Escobar, in particular that the juridical foundation of the decrees was solid.

Such trial and error was not possible in the Mexican case. One key reason is that the intelligence agency CISEN, the epicenter of the reform effort, lacked any operational forces of its own. It was, and remains, beholden to other agencies to act on the intelligence it gathers and analyzes. If CISEN had had its own troops, and in particular if it had been assigned responsibility for a given cartel or region, it is possible to imagine some form of selective enforcement being put into practice. This in turn could have produced a "proof of concept" that might have encouraged further expansion of the policy, and so on. Instead, because CISEN could not know with whom it would eventually work, its policy prescriptions remain relatively abstract. This made Valdés's proposals easier targets for those in the administration resistant to change: how could abstract notions of "targeting" and "punishing cartels" could be translated into operational rules of engagement? Or, as one dismissive Federal Police official put it, "What would the menu of punishments look like? How much for a beheading? A car bomb?" Some members of the working group admit, a bit sheepishly, that their ideas may have been impractical, but having never had the opportunity, indeed the necessity, to put those ideas into practice, it is hard to know.

9.2 LESS DECISIVE FACTORS

9.2.1 Pool of Ideas

Ideas play a major role in Kingdon's classic analysis of policymaking, constituting one of his three "streams" that must come together for policy change to occur. "The content of the ideas themselves, far from being mere smokescreens or rationalizations, are integral parts of decision-making" (Kingdon 1984,

---

[9] Interview, March 13, 2014.

125). How important was it for reformers to be able to draw on a pool of previous conditional policy successes?

More than in any of the other reform efforts analyzed here, Pacification's architects could draw on such a pool of policy ideas. "We didn't need to reinvent the wheel. Just redo, better, what had been done before but failed."[10] This included not only Rio's history of community policing initiatives, but also some of the projects implemented in Bogotá and Medellín under the progressive mayoralties of Antanas Mockus and Sergio Fajardo. Beltrame also invited numerous social scientists, policy specialists, and civil-society actors to working-group meetings, fostering a dialogue that was an important source of ideas.

Pride of place in this pool of ideas clearly goes to the GPAE program, which provided a kind of proof of concept that favela occupation combined with conditional repression could produce stable, low-violence outcomes. Indeed, the core mechanism for creating conditionality in a context of retail drug trading can be traced back, in a clear line of idea-transmission, to Operation Ceasefire:

> the great inspiration of Boston [was] a strategic principle, the difference between drugs and arms ... I heard a Boston police chief [tell] the gangs: "If you are going to deal drugs, do it right, because if I catch you, I'll arrest you. Now, if you kill someone here, you are totally screwed, you won't sell anything, you won't buy anything, you won't have a moment's peace, I'll come after you with everything I've got." ... This differential strategy is a part of GPAE.
>
> (Fernandes 2003, 95)

Interestingly, though the Ceasefire working group itself was mostly working in *terra incognita*, without a rich pool of policy ideas to draw on, in the end its defining tactic—threatening gang members with extra repression if violence occurred on their turf—had already proven itself in practice with the so-called Wendover strategy, developed and implemented years before by some of the officers in the working group.

Operation Ceasefire also influenced the CISEN working group, albeit indirectly, via Hope's interest in Kleiman's work on "dynamic concentration." Moreover, Ceasefire, a policy centered around policing a single city's gang-ridden neighborhoods, was not directly applicable to a national context like Mexico's, and so served more as a theoretical model than an operational one. Rio's Pacification program itself was known in Mexico, but would have been similarly difficult to directly adapt. Overall, while the CISEN working group had some ideas to draw on, the pool was far thinner and less developed than in the Rio case.

This suggests that a rich pool of policy ideas *can* play an important role; in Colombia, however, it did not. *Sometimiento* appears to have been invented

---

10 Interview, Roberto Sá, August 2014.

by Gaviria's team with little reference to similar statutes elsewhere. While this may have to do with the judicial nature of the policy reform, overall it suggests that a pool of ideas is not a necessary factor.

9.2.2 Largest Cartel Also the Most Violent

One key normative concern contributing to acceptability constraints is that conditional repression ultimately favors some cartels over others. This is particularly problematic for conditionality "across" cartels, in which once a cartel is designated as violent, it receives the full brunt of repression until it is decimated. If there is a single cartel that is both a market leader and clearly the most violent, this concern should be mitigated: such cartels make obvious candidates for additional repression. Where the most violent cartel is *not* the largest, however, conditional repression among cartels will inadvertently but necessarily help the position of the incumbent market leader, by harming a smaller but more violent rival. In sum, conditionality among cartels should be easier to implement when the largest cartel is also the most violent.

The comparative evidence supports this conjecture—conditionality among cartels was accepted more readily in Colombia and Rio (where the largest cartels were the most violent) than in Mexico (where it was not). However, the critical policy reforms in Colombia and Rio involved conditionality *within* cartels—in which violent cartels can earn a relative reprieve from repression by eschewing violence. Conditionality within cartels raises other normative issues—especially the concern that it lets once-violent cartels "get away with murder"—that this factor is unlikely to mitigate. As such, this factor probably played only a middling role in the overall success of reform efforts.

In Colombia, Escobar's Medellín cartel was widely understood to be both the largest cartel and the primary public menace. When the state began to focus on it to the exclusion of the Cali cartel, there was little if any public opprobrium, despite Escobar's tireless efforts to draw attention to what he portrayed as unequal enforcement of the law and collusion with Cali. Similarly, in Rio, the Comando Vermelho (CV) was the dominant cartel—its rivals were born of schisms and never achieved territorial parity—and was also well known to be the most aggressive, particularly with respect to state forces. The decision of Pacification's architects to focus first and almost exclusively on CV-held favelas did occasion some criticism, and even accusations of collusion with its rivals or the police-linked paramilitary *milícias* that now control a significant share of the city's favelas. However, Beltrame's typically forthright admission and explanation of his prioritizing the CV—"we are trying to minimize confrontations, and the CV is the most confrontational"—mostly neutralized such criticisms. In both cases, the fact that the largest cartel was also the most violent plausibly contributed to public acceptance of conditionality within cartels.

However, in both Colombia and Rio, most of the key violence-reducing traction came from conditionality *within*, not among, cartels, reducing the effective importance of this factor. That is, focusing on Medellín to the exclusion of Cali did little on its own to make Medellín less violent (though obviously it gave Cali reason to remain pacific toward the state). It was only when *Sometimiento* gave Escobar a relatively attractive "hiding option" that he turned away from violent strategies. Similarly, the decision to focus Pacification on CV-controlled areas may have given its rivals incentives to remain relatively peaceful, but it also *reinforced* the CV's incentives to fight back, likely contributing to the CV's failed attempt to use violent lobbying in 2010 to scuttle Pacification. It was the conditional-within-cartels components of Pacification—pre-announcement of invasions and conditional repression of trafficking within Pacified favelas—that created incentives for even CV traffickers to eschew violence. In both cases, conditionality within cartels had to overcome strong normative criticism for letting previous trafficker violence go unpunished; however, the fact that the largest cartels were the most violent did not mitigate, and may have exacerbated, this concern.

In Mexico, by contrast, the upstart group Los Zetas was widely seen as the most violent cartel, while the more traditional Sinaloa cartel was understood to be the largest, most powerful, and best connected. Moreover, the policy ideas on the table were essentially, and in the case of Kleiman's plan explicitly, conditional among cartels. Indeed, the underlying desire of many of the reformers was to refocus repressive force on and possibly destroy Los Zetas, which would have inevitably "helped" the Sinaloa cartel, as well as many of its rivals. This rather unfortunate circumstance magnified the effect of long-standing rumors that Calderón, and his PAN predecessor Vicente Fox, were in cahoots with Sinaloa. Calderón was extremely sensitive to these accusations, and minimizing them seemed to constrain his policy choices. As one of Calderón's speechwriters put it, "If it hadn't been for the accusations [of collusion with Sinaloa], it would have been easier to change policy at both the operational and discursive level."[11] In a counterfactual world in which Sinaloa were clearly the most violent cartel, a move to conditionality among cartels would have mitigated this normative concern considerably.

With Boston's Operation Ceasefire, this factor almost certainly carried less importance, since the object of repression was not militarized drug cartels but street gangs, about whose relative size and strength the public probably knew and cared little. Nonetheless, it is interesting to note that when the Ceasefire working group put the project into action, its first target was the Intervale Posse, "widely regarded as perhaps the worst crack-era gang in Boston" (Kennedy et al. 2001, 32) and, it proved, the hardest to teach a lesson.

---

[11]   Interview, Mexico City, February 11, 2014.

9.2.3 Leader Not Tied to Status Quo

Moving from unconditional to conditional repression can involve, at some level, a recognition that years of crackdowns and escalation were ineffective or even counterproductive. Pro-conditionality reform efforts might thus be more likely to succeed when the relevant leader is not strongly associated with a *status quo ante* characterized by unconditional repression. President Gaviria, for example, announced the *Sometimiento* policy within a few weeks of his inauguration; nobody could accuse him of backtracking or betraying his principles.

Conversely, a leader who was personally identified with an unconditional status quo policy might be more hesitant to adopt a conditional reform. One key feature of what I've called "Calderón's war" is that it was Calderón's: he identified himself personally and politically with it from the very outset, making it the defining feature of his government. It seems plausible that this raised the potential political costs to accepting any kind of reform or course adjustment, and hence played a role in his recalcitrance.

Yet there are reasons to doubt that this factor is generally decisive. For one thing, Calderón's association with an unconditional status quo was in some sense endogenous or self-inflicted: by repeatedly insisting on the "impartial" character of his crackdown, Calderón explicitly tied himself to an aspect of his approach that the broader public might not otherwise have focused much attention on. It is easy enough to imagine a counter factual in which he slowly distanced himself from the unconditional aspects of his crackdown, or simply let the entire issue of the drug war drop off the public agenda as his successor Enrique Peña Nieto has done.

Alternatively, Calderón could have simply changed course; the case of Rio suggests that doing so might not have been so costly in political terms after all. Despite campaign promises of more humane policing, Governor Cabral began his term with an unconditional crackdown that quickly came to define him and Security Secretary Beltrame. In the wake of their failed 2007 mega-operation in Complexo do Alemão, a prominent Rio human rights organization characterized Cabral and Beltrame's security policy as "eugenicist" and "based on actions of extermination." The former epithet came in response to infelicitous comments Cabral made after reading *Freakonomics*, but the latter was based on autopsies of the nineteen civilians killed during the Alemão operation, showing that many had been summarily executed by police. Indeed, the scale of Cabral and Beltrame's war was unprecedented: 2007 marked a record 1,330 civilians killed in armed confrontations with police.

In light of this, it is perhaps not surprising that Pacification was initially criticized by human rights activists as an excessively militarized and even genocidal policy. Yet Cabral and Beltrame quickly overcame these criticisms when the nature of Pacification became apparent, and paid little political cost for changing course. On the contrary, Cabral won great praise and Beltrame came to be seen as a visionary. In the counterfactual world, Calderón's often vicious public attacks on those who criticized his approach, his unwillingness to admit errors, and the "doth protest too much" quality of the PR campaign he launched late in his presidency (see Figure 7.5) all suggest that the unwillingness to change course was more a question of personal temperament than a cold political calculation.

9.2.4 Brainstorming/Flattened Hierarchy

In Rio and Mexico, as well as with Boston's Ceasefire, reform efforts began within small working groups that had a nonhierarchical structure and fostered brainstorming; the Colombian case is not quite parallel, but similar in many respects. In all four cases, reformers themselves emphasized the importance of the creative environment and free flow of ideas that these working groups provided.

In Colombia, the original "working group" was made up of just three people: Rafael Pardo (then Security Councilor), Justice Minister Jaime Giraldo, and President Gaviria himself. Pardo had sketched out the core idea of *Sometimiento*—basically, a plea bargain in the absence of an indictment—in a memo in early 1990, which Giraldo, working without staff, adapted into a suitable legal decree overnight (Pardo Rueda 1996, 266). The three then further revised the proposal, adding demobilization and disarmament mechanisms, and coining the term *sometimiento a la justicia* ("submission to justice"). The draft decree was then presented to Gaviria's closest advisors, and later discussed with his entire cabinet. This larger group grappled with a series of difficult logistical questions, not for the last time (there would be three additional decrees, adjusting the policy), but approved the decree unanimously.

The outlines of Rio's Pacification strategy first took shape in an informal working group made up of Beltrame and his closest sub-secretaries and advisors, including Dirceu Vianna. Unhappy with the nearby lunch offerings in the neighborhood of the Security Secretariat's office buildings, Beltrame and his team agreed to split the cost of a private cook.

> Those lunches naturally became a space for the most open and creative discussion. "How to explain the logic of the drug trade?"; "Why is Rio different than the rest of Brazil?"; "See, Rudolph Giuliani nailed it in New York but failed in Mexico"; "Rio is Rio, Colombia is Colombia". We could speak totally openly, never any hierarchy at the table, and everyone opined and disagreed openly.

> (Beltrame 2014, 103)

Vianna echoed this sentiment, emphasizing the importance of being able to voice criticism openly:

I remember I told the Secretary, "We need a new instrument." We were using straight repression, "let's really smash them." Nothing is getting better in the long run. I complained a lot. In our lunches, we had no hierarchy.[12]

With the success, both operational and mediatic, of Pacification, these lunches came to take on an origin-myth air that some find overblown. But for Vianna, the "tightness" of the lunch group was itself important to the early success of the reform effort. "We were all on board, nobody undermined it. It was clear to all of us that we wanted this, and that it was straightforward, and so it would be easy to win over [other key actors like the Governor]."

The CISEN working group in Mexico had a similar flattened-hierarchy structure that fostered brainstorming and creativity. "We were all free to bring things to the table," said one member. "Very open, a stimulating place for dialogue," said another. The group was not tasked with creating an actual policy proposal however. "We would discuss things a lot, Valdés would listen, figure out what he would say in the Gabinete de Seguridad. He didn't tell us what he was proposing. But [another working group member] told me [Valdés] was defending a focus on dissuasion, more strategic, focalization, be more selective with the targets."[13]

The fact that similarly nonhierarchical fora for discussion and brainstorming were present in all cases, and in particular the importance attributed to these structures by participants themselves, suggests that they may be important to getting reform processes started. Given the failure of the CISEN working group's reform efforts, though, such structures are clearly no guarantee of success. One critical difference in the Mexican case was the fact that the working group was essentially limited to CISEN officials and consultants; as noted above, CISEN lacked its own operational capacity, and the working group never grew to include actors from other agencies with authority to put policy ideas into practice. In contrast, all the other working groups considered here involved actors with operational authority. This points back to the capacity for trial and error and "layering" as a decisive factor.

9.2.5 Delegation

One factor that reformers in Rio cited as important in the success of Pacification was the autonomy that Cabral gave Beltrame to develop and implement security policy in general. Cabral publicly deferred to Beltrame on issues related to public security; though he naturally retained a veto over Pacification and other police efforts, he rarely if ever exercised it, particularly once the policy showed signs of success. This arrangement gave Beltrame freedom to experiment, and to get credit for any successes, while also protecting Cabral—if Pacification had been a failure, he could have simply shunted the

---

[12] Interview, March 13, 2014.
[13] Interview, February 7, 2014.

blame onto Beltrame and appointed a new secretary. Indeed, at the height of Pacification's success, and prior to the 2013 street protests that severely tarnished Cabral's public approval, he was able to essentially share in the warm glow of Pacification's success, while always crediting Beltrame as its author.

Delegation had a second effect in Rio: Cabral, by deferring to Beltrame, put the decision to increase conditionality in the hands of an operational commander, and a particularly apolitical one at that. Numerous interviewees stressed Beltrame's lack of political ambitions, in contrast to most previous public security secretaries of Rio who have stayed little time in the post and quickly gone on to, or resumed, political careers. When decisions to implement conditional repression are made by "men in boots," it probably depoliticizes the issue, further relaxing acceptability constraints. This dynamic can be seen in the decision of US Marines in Marjah, Afghanistan, to back off a policy of poppy eradication, realizing that destroying the fields would push economically desperate locals into the hands of the Taliban (Nissenbaum 2010). Framing this decision as operational, apolitical, and key to primary mission goals helped overcome the objections of the pro-eradication State Department.[14]

Given the appeal of delegation, with its "heads-I-win, tails-I-don't-lose" arrangement for the delegator and the possibility of depoliticizing the move to conditionality, it is reasonable to think it aided the reform process in Rio. However, delegation was not a relevant factor in Colombia or Mexico. In Colombia, Gaviria took personal responsibility for dealing with narco-terrorism in his inaugural address, and never stepped back. Indeed, for Pardo, the fact that *Sometimiento* was seen as a "presidential policy" was critical to its success (Pardo Rueda 1996, 266). In Mexico, many of the operational decisions were in effect delegated to the various agencies, and in many ways the direction of the overall campaign was increasingly decided by Public Security Secretary Genaro García Luna. Nonetheless, President Calderón retained intellectual authorship of, and hence responsibility for, the battle against the cartels.

9.2.6 Sino-Nixonian Effects

A final potentially important factor is the extent to which the decision-makers responsible for pro-conditionality reforms had established a prior reputation as hardliners. Just as "it took a Nixon to go to China," perhaps it took a Gaviria to offer a plea bargain to Escobar. As Rafael Pardo put it, "Nobody else but the president chosen as Galán's successor, the most severe in his opposition to the cartels ... could be the one to offer a way out of the war" (Pardo Rueda 1996, 266).

---

14   Interview, US government official, October 4, 2011.

Similarly, it may have taken a Cabral/Beltrame team to implement a project like Pacification. By beginning his term with a massive traditional crackdown, Cabral cemented a public image as a hardliner who was, if anything, all too brutal. Beltrame, as a former Federal Police officer with a history of solid anti-corruption work and a non-native of Rio de Janeiro, had great credibility as a law-and-order type. If the bloody 2007 mega-operation in Alemão and the record level of civilians killed by police that year led to widespread criticism of Cabral and Beltrame as overly eager to use repressive force, it also inoculated the duo from being outflanked as "soft on crime" after pivoting to the Pacification strategy in 2008. If this inoculation was indeed critical to the implementation of Pacification, then we might say that Sino-Nixonian effects played a decisive role.

However, Sino-Nixonian effects were as strong in Mexico as anywhere, yet reform efforts still failed. Calderón had certainly established himself as a hardliner by the time the selective-enforcement reform effort began in 2010: state capacity had been vastly increased, dozens of top capos arrested or killed, and enormous quantities of drugs and arms seized. Calderón's embrace of military language and even dress (he appeared in numerous photos wearing military garb) may have drawn criticism from liberal circles, but it only reinforced his reputation as a committed drug warrior. Nobody, in short, could accuse Calderón of being "soft on crime." Had he publicly pivoted toward conditionality with a Gaviria-like pronouncement, astute observers might very well have invoked a similar Nixon-goes-to-China explanation: "only someone who had demonstrated his bona fides like that could have credibly put in place selective enforcement."

A related aspect of Sino-Nixonian effects concerns corruption: perhaps only leaders with reputations for honesty can weather the common critique that conditional repression amounts to a corrupt pact with cartels. Here, the case is less clear: Calderón was haunted by, and frequently found himself vociferously rebutting, accusations of collusion with the Sinaloa cartel (the government PR video shown in Figure 7.5 offers a graphic example of one such rebuttal). Yet Calderón's preoccupation was due, in part, to his and his party's reputation for being less corrupt than their PRI predecessors: by most accounts, Calderón was personally scrupulous, and saw himself as heir and defender of the PAN's reputation for (relative) honesty.[15] A turn toward conditional repression could certainly have intensified accusations of collusion with Sinaloa, particularly because, as noted, Sinaloa was not the most violent cartel and would have received less repression than Los Zetas. Yet Calderón *already* faced such accusations, and by the period of reform efforts must surely have realized that they could not be permanently dispelled even without a turn toward conditionality. In any case, he would have faced far less criticism than a PRI president. Indeed, the mere suggestion by Calderón's successor,

[15] Interviews with Calderón officials, multiple dates.

Enrique Peña Nieto of the PRI, that he would focus on violence reduction brought immediate accusations—including by US officials—of seeking to return to the thoroughly corrupt "state-sponsored protection racket" that prevailed during the period of PRI hegemony. Such allegations would surely have had far less traction with Calderón. These counterfactual considerations suggest that Sino-Nixonian effects are not decisive.

10

The Challenge of Sustaining Conditionality

In both Colombia and Rio, conditional approaches were surprisingly successful in quickly reducing cartel–state conflict; ironically, this success contributes to the difficulty of sustaining conditionality over time. Rapid expansion of conditional programs, often into dissimilar and more challenging settings, can outstrip logistical and institutional capacity, leading to an erosion of program principles and the conditionality of repression in practice. Politically, the very same reframing of objectives that favors policy reform in the first place can create self-undermining dynamics later. Once leaders adopt violence reduction as the primary objective of anti-narcotics policy, thus "owning peace," the political optics of cartel violence change. Under an unconditional crackdown policy of "frontal combat," even extreme cartel violence can be interpreted as a positive sign that cartels are desperate or "in their last throes." In contrast, even sporadic violence calls into question the raison d'être of a conditional approach. Episodes of corruption can be similarly detrimental, particularly if leaders have suggested that a conditional approach will reduce corruption.

The previous chapter argued that political cohesion, room for trial-and-error policy experimentation, and effective reframing of the problem were important factors in overcoming logistical and acceptability constraints, ultimately helping pro-conditional reform efforts to succeed. Unfortunately, neither logistical nor acceptability constraints disappear once conditional repression is implemented, even when it proves effective at reducing violence. Indeed, conditional approaches appear to generate self-undermining dynamics that can lead to their erosion over time. For one thing, they can be—ironically—victims of their own success: precisely because conditionality produces sharp decreases in violence, conditional pilot programs can come to be seen as silver bullets, and hence are hastily replicated and deployed to problem areas. Three problems arise: first, the replicated versions of the original program may be imperfect copies, lacking key elements such as proper training, committed leadership, or buy-in and participation from civil society. Second, whereas pilot programs are generally developed in smaller, relatively controlled environments, replications can frequently get deployed in crisis areas whose characteristics make them far more challenging. Finally, conditional repression is generally more resource-intensive than unconditional repression, and expanding conditional programs from pilot areas to crisis areas further raises this cost differential.

In an ideal world, these logistical challenges would be seen as useful opportunities for improving and adapting conditional approaches that proved successful at smaller, experimental scales, eliciting broad-based social and financial investment; in the real world, an unfortunate political dynamic can take hold, undermining the sustainability of conditional policies. Beyond their cost and, in some cases, accumulating resistance from law-enforcement agencies bristling at restraints on their actions, conditional programs can be victims of their own success in another, more subtle way. If implementing conditional approaches in the first place involves convincing leaders, the media, and the public to accept reduced repression of non-violent trafficking in exchange for reduced violence, then sustaining conditionality requires a continuing perception that violence has actually been reduced. A few incidents of cartel violence, particularly anti-state violence, can thus severely undermine confidence in a conditional approach. If reformers have also suggested that corruption will be reduced under conditional crackdowns, then bribery scandals can have a similarly debilitating effect.

This chapter illustrates these dynamics at work in the cases of Rio de Janeiro and Colombia, where reform efforts were successful and conditional approaches were actually implemented. The case of Rio's GPAE[1] program—a precursor of Pacification—is particularly illustrative, since it was initially very effective, then degraded through hasty and inappropriate expansion, and ultimately abandoned. Mexico is not included, since conditional reform efforts never succeeded there.

10.1 LOGISTICAL CONSTRAINTS: OVEREXTENSION AND EROSION

Rio's policing experiments—though often successful at first—have provided hard lessons in the difficulty of implementing and sustaining conditional approaches. For a time, Pacification seemed to have avoided the mistakes made with GPAE, achieving widespread public approval and thoroughgoing institutional support. Yet, over time, it has come to suffer from many of the exact same ills that plagued GPAE.

In some sense, both GPAE and Pacification were victims of their own success. After decades of escalation, both proved effective at quickly reducing

---

1   GPAE stands for Grupamento de Policiamento em Áreas Especiais, or Policing in Special Areas Unit.

violence and sowing the seeds of a more positive and humane relationship between favela residents and police in the communities where they were piloted. This led, however, to their rapid replication in additional favelas, usually in response to momentary crises. Faced with outbreaks of inter-cartel turf war or resident protests in response to extreme police violence, leaders deployed new GPAEs and Pacifying Police Units (Unidades de Polícia Pacificadora, UPPs) at a brisk pace that outstripped institutional capacity. To function correctly, both programs required specially trained police forces, carefully vetted and led by local commanders committed not only to ideals of non-abusive, preventive policing but also to the core idea of conditional repression toward the drug trade, as well as support from civil society actors and residents. As the programs expanded, newer units invariably lacked for all of these.

This dynamic was particularly acute in the case of GPAE. The program's formulators lobbied for its slow, careful expansion to similarly sized communities; instead crises in large and extremely violent favelas like the CV stronghold Vila Cruzeiro led to hasty and underfunded deployments. As Rubem César Fernandes, head of the NGO Viva Rio that helped implement it, explained:

> GPAE came to be seen as a solution for problems. So, wherever there was a problem, "call GPAE." It's totally absurd because the idea of GPAE presupposes a certain isolated situation ... of small or medium size, a situation reasonably under control. In Vila Cruzeiro, in the middle of that enormous space, to have one little area with GPAE and the rest in chaos, this didn't have the slightest chance of success ... there were immediately shootouts, [GPAE] was totally debased.
>
> (Fernandes 2003, 99)

Leadership is also critical. The original GPAE unit was initially commanded by the program's intellectual author, Major Antônio Carballo Blanco. He played a central role, personally mediating relationships between residents and police (his cell phone number was handed out to residents), and maintaining tight control over the behavior of GPAE officers (he fired more than half his troops in the first year for bad behavior). Carballo Blanco was generally liked and trusted by residents, contributing to GPAE's incredible track record of zero murders during its first two years. His replacement with a traditional hardline police commander in 2002 brought a return of both cartel and police killings, and the rapid erosion of support for the program. The only truly successful follow-on GPAE unit, in the Cavalão favela of neighboring Niterói, was led by a young commander who deliberately copied Carballo Blanco's original directives. One portentous ongoing assessment of the program noted that while the presence of a charismatic, human, trustworthy commanding officer was a welcome and positive change, it was also "the locus of [GPAE]'s fragility: susceptible to personnel changes, the transfer of a commander can put at risk the continuity of the project" (Albernaz et al. 2007, 45–46).

The architects of Pacification sought to learn from the mistakes of GPAE. In particular, they understood the importance of institutional support for differentiated policing. Fearing that police institutions would be intransigent, Security Secretary José Beltrame deliberately created the UPP program as a kind of "silo" within the Military Police that could be directly controlled by him and his staff. UPP commanders in Pacified favelas reported directly to Beltrame, and he made frequent personal visits to their favela headquarters. At the same time, the program from its very outset had an integrated marketing component to win support from opinion-makers, the media, and the public at large, as I have described in detail in previous chapters. This too was critical. In the words of former UPP Commander-General Robson Rodrigues, "Without the support of the media and the business class, this would have become a GPAE a long time ago."[2]

Still, many factors lay beyond Beltrame's control. Many of the social programs that were supposed to complement UPPs were never deployed, leading to Beltrame's frequent public complaints that the police alone could not solve the favelas' problems. An economic downtown in 2013 further exacerbated both the financial constraints of the government and the conditions within many favelas. But the most important factor was certainly the rapid expansion of the Pacification strategy, beyond the state's capacity to recruit and train UPP officers and commanders. Beltrame's "silo" approach worked well when there were only a handful of UPPs; by 2014, however, UPP officers made up at least 20 percent of the overall number of military police officers in active street duty.[3] Yet most police, and, importantly, many high-ranking officers within the police command structure, remained highly dismissive of the Pacification approach and in particular of the notion of community policing in regions they saw as dominated by criminals. The original dictum that UPP battalions be composed of only newly recruited and specially trained cadets had to be abandoned, further degrading the differentiated nature of UPP policing.

In Colombia, the *Sometimiento* policy also faced a rapid expansion of sorts: to its formulators' surprise, it brought in not just low-level traffickers but first the three leaders of the Ochoa clan of prominent Medellín traffickers, and eventually Pablo Escobar himself. The nature of the policy, however, did not present nearly the kind of logistical challenges that Pacification's success did. After all, *Sometimiento* did not require massive training and recruitment efforts, nor establishing state territorial control in hundreds of urban regions where it had been absent for generations. On the contrary, *Sometimiento* required little more than some judicial acrobatics: finding appropriate crimes for traffickers to confess to and establishing guarantees that they would not be held accountable for any others. While this took some time and effort, it was hardly a major challenge.

What did turn out to be deeply challenging was *Sometimiento*'s other logistical requirement: a prison to hold traffickers in. Once *Sometimiento* was

---

extended to accommodate Escobar's surrender, the state faced the problem of where to keep him. Escobar manipulated this issue to his own advantage in spectacular fashion, but the underlying problem was very real: the state needed to simultaneously imprison Escobar and protect him from attack by murderous rivals and potentially vindictive state agents. Lacking sufficient control over its own police, the state was forced to concede to Escobar's demands that La Catedral be guarded by army troops, who he knew to be more corruptible. This allowed Escobar to slowly erode state control over the prison, culminating in the absurd conditions of near-total freedom he enjoyed for much of his time there. These, in turn, triggered the government's bungled attempt to move him to more secure facilities, and permitted his escape. Why this led to the complete collapse of the *Sometimiento* policy, however, had nothing to do with logistics and everything to do with politics.

10.2 POLITICAL CONSTRAINTS: THE CHALLENGE OF "OWNING PEACE"

Once Escobar escaped from La Catedral, President César Gaviria rescinded all offers of leniency under *Sometimiento*. Escobar repeatedly made overtures to the government for a second surrender, and surely would have accepted far less advantageous terms—there is even evidence that police forces deliberately blocked any attempt at unconditional surrender (Strong 1995, 282)—but Gaviria rebuffed these offers out of hand. This sudden collapse of conditionality was driven entirely by political concerns. For Gaviria, Escobar's escape was deeply and personally humiliating. Critics of his original policy, though outnumbered at the time by those happy to see Escobar contained, had been proven right: his imprisonment was a farce. Once this perception took hold, negotiating a second surrender simply became too costly in political terms to even consider.

That is saying something: Gaviria's choice to hold fast until Escobar was eventually located and killed may look good in hindsight, but at the time was extremely risky. The manhunt for Escobar lasted almost a year and a half, during which time he once again unleashed a barrage of killings and terror tactics. Gaviria could not know how long it would take to finally destroy Escobar, and with elections looming in 1994, faced the prospect of having to leave office with Escobar still on the loose.

To ensure that did not happen, Gaviria was willing to expend serious political capital. Perhaps it is not terribly surprising that he let the Bloque de Búsqueda police force run amok in the poor neighborhoods that Escobar recruited foot soldiers from, or that he gave DEA and CIA operatives unprecedented access to state intelligence and operational influence (Bowden 2001). More shocking was the government turning a blind eye to, if not encouraging and facilitating, the terrorist actions of Escobar rivals Los Pepes and the Cali cartel. Indeed, the potential collusion, or impression of collusion, between Los Pepes and the Bloque de Búsqueda was worrying enough to US Ambassador Morris Busby that he personally intervened, pressuring Gaviria to have its commander sacked and all ties to Los Pepes definitively cut (Bowden 2001, 198–220). Yet even then, Gaviria stood firm, perhaps wisely: as I have argued, it is not at all clear whether Gaviria's manhunt would have succeeded without the pressure that Los Pepes put on Escobar.

Rio's Pacification strategy is, as of this writing, in a state of severe retrenchment, but not collapse. While the government has suspended the Pacification of new territories, and in some cases has had to withdraw UPP units and reoccupy with special forces (Magalhães et al. 2015), the majority of UPP units remain intact. This state of retrenchment is reflected in public opinion: a 2014 poll found that while 70 percent of Rio residents thought reforms to the Pacification strategy were needed, only 9 percent thought it should be terminated (Brito et al. 2014). Nonetheless, the golden age of Pacification has ended; where Beltrame and his team once spoke proudly of the program, they now sound defensive. What once was heralded as a policing policy to be emulated throughout Brazil became, by the 2014 election, a subject of active debate, with some candidates suggesting they would terminate the program. Whereas the successes of 2008–12 brought a rare tinge of hope to discussions of Rio's security problems, skepticism, never dormant for long in Brazilian politics, has become the dominant tone once again.

There is a common thread in these two stories, relevant to a broader assessment of the sustainability of conditional policies. Conditional policies came about after reformers and leaders reframed the policy question, adopting violence reduction rather than drug eradication as their primary objective. While this reframing appears to be critical in the process of policy reform, it also leads to an unavoidable shift in optics: leaders who publicly adopt conditional policies, I argue, come to "own peace." That is, conditional policies ask the public to tolerate (to some extent) non-violent trafficking in exchange for reduced violence; they thus stand or fall on their ability to keep violence low. Under an unconditional, "frontal combat" policy, even extreme cartel violence can be interpreted positively, as a metric of progress: cartels, defenders of such policies argue, must be desperate or "in their last throes." In contrast, even sporadic cartel violence calls into question the effectiveness of a conditional approach.

The dynamics of owning peace interact with the logistical constraints mentioned above in deleterious ways. Objectively, it may be perfectly understandable that Rio's state government was not able to immediately deploy fully fledged, high-quality UPP units to vast favela regions where it had not held territorial control for generations. Yet in terms of public optics, if UPP stations are being machine-gunned and burned down, and UPP cadets are afraid to patrol at night, then how could officials say a favela had been "Pacified" and keep a straight face? Similarly, allowing Escobar such leeway in designing the La Catedral prison, however laughable in retrospect, was a sincere attempt by the Colombian state to square a circle, and it certainly led to a vast reduction in armed violence while Escobar was there. Moreover, from a strategic point of view, it is not surprising that Escobar actually enjoyed his time there, since he freely surrendered in the first place. Yet his embarrassingly easy escape made a mockery of the underlying notion of *Sometimiento*: if Escobar could take a minister hostage and then simply walk into the jungle with his band of armed lieutenants, then in what sense had he ever really surrendered?

A similar dynamic exists with regard to corruption, as the case of La Catedral suggests. The formulators of both Pacification and *Sometimiento* avoided reframing their policy goals around reducing corruption per se—probably a wise move since reducing cartel violence in no way guarantees reduced bribery, and may even involve *more* bribery. Yet neither did leaders declare that reducing corruption would *not* be a goal; indeed they often hinted that conditional approaches would curb corruption. For example, in Rio, one reason Beltrame insisted that UPP units be made up entirely of fresh recruits trained separately from the main body of police was in order to keep out officers already contaminated by a culture of corruption. However admirable the motives, associating the goal of reduced corruption with conditional policies is dangerous, because it creates an expectation that is difficult to meet in practice. Thus, the arrest of several UPP commanders for bribe-taking severely undercut the credibility of the program, even though there is nothing about bribe-taking in and of itself that goes against the core goal of reducing cartel violence.

These are not easy political knots to cut through. It is difficult enough to generate support for policies that "go easy" on traffickers who eschew violence, much less openly acknowledge that such policies may not reduce, and may even increase, the amount of bribery going on. Even where bribery is not an issue, conditional approaches, like ceasefires, are easily undermined by spoilers. No conditional approach is likely to end all cartel-related violence, or even all cartel–state violence. This means that if episodic violence is taken as evidence of the failure of conditional approaches, these approaches are unlikely to be sustainable in the long run. There is, perhaps, no easy solution; one must hope that awareness and public discussion of these difficulties can help reduce their deleterious political impact on programs whose overall record remains strong.

11

Conclusion

In much of the world, human development and democratic consolidation are threatened by the presence of armed, non-state groups. Important progress has been made in the study of armed conflict, especially civil war, but as our understanding has advanced, the phenomenon itself has receded (Blattman and Miguel 2010, 18). The end of the Cold War thankfully brought a sharp decline in the prevalence of civil war (Kalyvas and Balcells 2010), but it also saw the rise of a new security threat: militarized drug war.

Over the last thirty years, sustained armed conflict involving large and well-equipped drug cartels has ravaged Latin America's three largest countries, spilled into Central America, and even threatened US border towns. Especially puzzling is that in Colombia, Mexico, and Brazil, cartels attacked not only one another but the state itself. In fact, in Colombia cartel–state conflict erupted while cartels were at peace with one another, and overshadowed not only subsequent inter-cartel warfare but ongoing guerrilla insurgencies as well. In Mexico, turf war accounts for the numerical bulk of violent events, leading a flurry of recent scholarship to focus almost exclusively on the causes and consequence of violence among cartels. But cartel–state conflict has an outsized impact on society, directly challenging state authority and the rule of law. It can begin as an unexpected response to state crackdowns intended to *restore* state authority, and its duration can make a mockery of leaders' original state-building ambitions.

As our understanding of inter-cartel turf war slowly advances, cartel–state conflict remains a puzzle. This study represents a first analytic cut at the problem, and an attempt to systematize our broader thinking about militarized drug wars as a class of conflict. It suffers from many of the weaknesses endemic to the study of violence in general: poor and overly aggregated data (Kalyvas 2008), too few cases, and too many critical variables—including the prevalence of corruption and the extent of successful extortion—that are difficult or impossible to observe.[1] In addition, Mexico and Brazil are ongoing affairs, with major developments of both substantive and analytic importance happening over the course of this study. Conclusions and conjectures based on extrapolation of trends at mid-conflict can prove wildly offbase: Francis Fukuyama once compared studying Mexico in 2011 to analyzing the future of Europe from the vantage point of 1943.[2]

By the same token, the sheer magnitude of cartel violence—and at times its almost exponential growth—compels us to at least try to understand its causes. When the stakes are so high, even small and tentative steps forward are worth taking. This is particularly so in the case of cartel–state violence, since the timing and degree of shifts in its intensity point to a causal role for state policy. Cartel–state violence may prove largely avoidable, or at a minimum subject to better management by the state.

Why do cartels attack the state, if not to overthrow it? I argue that cartel–state conflict is a war of constraint: that anti-state violence by cartels is fundamentally coercive, aimed not at destroying or seceding from the state but at inducing changes in its behavior. If, in one sense, it is "no surprise" that traffickers fight back when governments interfere with their profit-generating activities, neither is it a foregone conclusion: cartel–state conflict is rare globally, and varies over time in the cases studied here. To explain this variation, I advance a rationalist, strategic framework: cartels employ anti-state violence when the benefits of doing so outweigh the (sometimes) hefty costs. Unconditional, blanket crackdowns, particularly in contexts of rampant corruption, increase cartels' incentives for anti-state violence, through several distinct logics of violence. Conditional crackdowns, by hinging the amount of state repression cartels face on their use of anti-state (or other targeted forms of) violence, can induce cartels to adopt less violent strategies and produce periods of significant abatement. These findings, and the theory underlying them, have important implications for several strands of scholarship within comparative politics and international relations. The following section explores these at length.

The real mystery may be why *states* fight militarized drug wars, or at least fight them the way they do. The core findings of this book—that state repressive policy can both fuel or deter cartels' use of violence—pose a puzzle, since leaders could apparently curb cartel–state violence by adopting more conditional repression. Why then have conditional approaches been rare and short-lived in practice? Part III offered a narrow answer, focusing on factors that aided the efforts of actors within the state security apparatus to implement conditional reforms and sustain them over time. These findings inform the discussion of the book's implications for policy in this chapter's

---

[1] We generally only observe bribery and blackmail when they are unsuccessful.

[2] Comments at the Violence, Drugs and Governance: Mexican Security in Comparative Perspective Conference, Stanford University, Palo Alto, October 4, 2011.

third section. They leave open, however, the question of leaders' true incentives and preferences. These, as I discuss in the concluding section, will ultimately determine the future of drug war.

11.1   THEORETICAL IMPLICATIONS

In developing a theory of cartel–state conflict, this book has drawn on a number of important bodies of scholarship in comparative politics, conflict studies, and bargaining theory. At the same time, the book's findings contribute to long-standing theoretical debates across these literatures. These contributions tend to raise more questions than they answer—a result of the relatively novel nature of drug war and the approach to studying it taken here. This section surveys the relevant literature and the avenues for future research this study points to.

11.1.1   State Formation: Do Drug Wars Make States?

Charles Tilly's seminal paper "State-Making and War-Making as Organized Crime" (1985) made two distinct points that are equally relevant to this study. The first, and best remembered, is summed up in the adage "states make war and war makes states." Tilly's claim—made with reference to early territorial wars in medieval Europe—spawned a rich "bellicist" literature dedicated to testing its external validity to other regions, time periods, and types of armed conflict. Several authors in this tradition have attributed endemic state weakness in Latin America to the prevalence of internal over interstate wars (Centeno 2002; Thies 2005); yet as Slater (2010a) demonstrates, internal conflict can lead to effective state-formation. The obvious question, then, is: do drug wars make states?

Drug wars, and particularly the unconditional crackdowns that usually mark their onset, are often cast by leaders as state-building endeavors. Many of the stated goals of their campaigns—eliminating armed opposition, establishing the monopoly on the use of force, consolidating the rule of law, and protecting civilians—are largely coterminous with Weberian and Tillyian conceptions of state-making.[3] Felipe Calderón, for example, first indicated his intentions to declare war on Mexico's cartels with the argument that "we cannot allow powers to exist that attack our society and challenge the authority of the state" (Jiménez 2015). Once underway, he characterized the crackdown thus: "to make of Mexico a nation of laws ... today we wage a frontal war for the rule of law and public safety, against organized crime" (Bravo 2011). In Rio de Janeiro, Moreira Franco, taking office as governor in 1987 and launching a campaign of repression that he had promised would "eliminate violence and

---

3   One important exception is revenue extraction; I discuss this aspect of state formation with respect to drug war momentarily.

the drug trade within six months" (Ramos 2016, 21), declared that henceforth the state would "restore the principle of [state] authority" and "guarantee [the population's] right to life" (quoted in Silva 2009, 114).

These crackdowns failed to achieve their lofty state-building goals, to put it mildly. In some places, rule of law, state authority, and certainly citizen safety have worsened. Of course, war only builds those states that *win*, and since the conflicts in Mexico and Rio are ongoing, it may be premature to judge. Crackdowns, I have argued, can provoke cartels to violently challenge the state's monopoly on the use of force, but drug warriors would claim this only reflects a preexisting lack of state control, which their crackdowns will eventually restore. They often point to Colombia, which can be said to have won its war against Pablo Escobar, and to have shored up the rule of law in the process. Yet Colombia still struggles with drug cartels, criminal governance in its urban peripheries, and a civil war whose belligerents are deeply involved in the drug trade. Indeed, decisive victories in drug wars—and campaigns against organized crime in general (Skaperdas 2001)—are hard to come by, complicating any evaluation of drug war's efficacy in building states. If none of the states studied here have succeeded in reclaiming a monopoly on the use of force throughout their territories, neither are they at risk of being overrun or hollowed out by the cartels. In sum, since the cases studied here involve neither the birth (Slater 2010a) nor failure (e.g., Bates 2008; Reno 1998) of states common to contemporary postcolonial periods, and since drug wars tend to stretch on for years if not decades, perhaps the most pertinent question is whether and in what sense the *process* of fighting them builds states.

In a superficial sense, the answer would seem to be yes. Drug wars generally involve expansion of the coercive apparatus, intelligence services, and the judiciary. In Colombia there is a broad consensus that the state—and particularly its justice institutions—emerged from its struggle against the Medellín cartel stronger than it went in. Mexico's Federal Police grew from 6,000 to 36,000 members during the Calderón administration. In both countries, growth came in part through US technical and financial assistance, but the Rio case shows that foreign aid is not necessary to expand police headcounts, equipment, and budgets. In Mexico too, US aid was small relative to the overall increase in spending on security. Meanwhile, the US war on drugs has produced not only consistent growth in policing capacities, but has played a key role in our radical experiment with mass incarceration and the advent of the "carceral state" (Gottschalk 2008; Lerman and Weaver 2016; Simon 2007).

Upon closer inspection, though, drug wars raise a host of thorny problems for state consolidation. First and foremost, a century of global drug prohibition and repression has neither eliminated drug trafficking nor made it rare; instead, it has created perhaps the largest illicit economy in world history. This is problematic in at least three interrelated ways. First, it often leaves states committed to goals, like eradication of drug trafficking and elimination of cartels, that are simply not achievable. Second, black markets are by nature stateless areas, prone to violent competition among criminal groups; inter-cartel turf war even in the absence of cartel–state conflict, as we saw in the Mexican case, can strain and blunt state capacity. Finally, and most importantly, repression of profitable illegal activities creates endless opportunities for corruption of state enforcers. As I have argued, crackdowns increase cartels' incentives not only to bribe state agents but to use anti-state violence in the process of bribe negotiation. States may accompany expansions of repressive capacity with anti-corruption efforts, but the former works against the latter. More often, states simply replace more corrupt forces with initially less corrupt ones; in practice, this has led to the contamination of elite forces like Rio's BOPE Special Forces Battalion[4] (e.g., *O Globo* 2015). In short, drug wars generally lead to a larger coercive apparatus, but not necessarily a less corrupt one. The implications of corruption for state-building are a topic unto themselves, which I explore in the following section.

A second pathology of state-building through drug war is the tendency of states to tolerate or cooperate with illegal armed groups willing to take on targeted drug cartels. Los Pepes in Colombia, the police-linked *milícias* in Rio, and *autodefensas* in Mexico all arose to challenge drug cartels, and all enjoyed significant freedom from state repression and sometimes active (if covert) support. As Paul Staniland has argued, states adopt a wide range of strategies toward armed groups, from active collusion to standoffishness to military aggression (Staniland 2012, 2015), with long-term consequences for state-building. For example, the Colombian state's complicity with Los Pepes helped bring down Pablo Escobar, but also produced the AUC paramilitaries in the 1990s, to whom the state ceded its monopoly on violence in many regions (Acemoglu et al. 2013).

How states choose whether to combat or collude with different armed groups constitutes a critical research agenda, to which the study of drug war can make a key contribution. Pro-government militias and paramilitaries are usually studied in a context of civil war, where their defining trait is their lack of revolutionary or secessionist goals. Cartels, however, also lack such goals; perhaps because of this, Rio's *milícias* and Mexico's *autodefensas* present themselves as defending the country not against revolution but from the scourge of drug trafficking. This suggests a more general theoretical understanding of paramilitaries, not as counterinsurgents per se, but as the lesser of two evils (Hidalgo and Lessing 2014). Whether partnering with such groups to defeat or roll back specific cartels is, on balance, state-strengthening or state-weakening is a difficult but crucial question for scholars to grapple with.

Setting aside these unintended consequences for a moment, and assuming that drugs wars lead to some form of state-building, we must ask "What kind of states do drug wars build?" One danger is that drug wars may

---

[4] BOPE stands for Batalhão de Opereções Especiais.

lead to an over-strengthening of certain state actors, creating entrenched stakeholders with excessive authority and discretion, who are resistant to necessary adjustments of policy once drug violence has abated. A parallel political dynamic can emerge, in which escalating hardline positions yield electoral advantage, while reform efforts are toxically painted as "soft on crime" (Holland 2013). Former Colombian defense minister Rafael Pardo echoed this sentiment when I asked him about the state-building effects of the drug war he helped lead. "The growth [of state capacity] can be disproportionate, or generate distortions. The penalties for drug trafficking are more severe than for multiple homicide, or for stealing public money. It distorts society's priorities."[5]

These concerns relate back to Tilly's second, and often overlooked, point. States are like organized crime not just because they provide protection for a fee, but because they often create the very threats they offer protection from. When Tilly wrote "To the extent that the threats against which a given government protects its citizens are imaginary or *are consequences of its own activities*, the government has organized a protection racket" (1985, 171; emphasis added), he had in mind traditional war-mongering and saber-rattling. But the statement seems even more relevant to drug war, since without the state activity of prohibition, there would be no illicit drugs in the first place. States don't create demand for drugs, of course, but by directing repression at suppliers, states create the very barriers to entry that make trafficking so profitable for those firms willing to take the risk. These profits, in turn, fuel the growth of cartel firepower and sophistication that is a necessary condition for cartel–state conflict and militarized drug war in general.

My hypothesis that state crackdowns can exacerbate anti-state violence bears directly on this point. If true, it implies that cartel–state conflict is Tillyian in this second sense: a consequence of the state's own actions. At a minimum, state repressive policy clearly shapes the market for drugs. Demonizing traffickers favors traffickers willing to be demonized, and unleashing murderous police against the drug trade favors cartels willing to fight back. Cartel violence in turn can justify the building out of extensive anti-narcotics agencies (Nadelmann 1993) or, as we have seen, the essentially permanent deployment of the armed forces, as protective measures. A policy of legalization, on the other hand, might increase the threat from drug *use*, but would almost certainly eliminate cartel–state violence. The common stance among law-enforcement agencies against legalization, on the grounds that the threat posed by rampant drug use is worse than that of militarized drug war, is entirely consistent with a Tillyian racketeering story.

In an added twist, some of the revenue extraction that drug-war hysteria permits comes from drug profits themselves. In my cases, such extraction occurred mostly illicitly, via systematic and sometimes state-sanctioned bribery;

---

[5] Interview, Bogotá, December 14, 2010.

I examine these in the following section. But state-building revenue can also be extracted legally: increasingly permissive US civil forfeiture laws allowed law enforcement to seize $4.5 billion dollars in assets in 2014 alone (Carpenter et al. 2015). A large proportion of these funds return to federal, state, and local law-enforcement agencies, who often use them to purchase equipment and pay salaries. Although the potential moral hazard is obvious, legislation to prevent "policing for profit" is often circumvented in practice (Carpenter et al. 2015, 28), and there is empirical evidence that county and municipal agencies that receive forfeiture funds tend to become dependent on them as a necessary budgetary supplement (Worrall 2001). Ultimately, the costs of this expansion in policing capacity are paid by a mix of drug consumers (who pay higher prices in the wake of drug busts) and an alarming number of innocent victims of overzealous seizures (Stillman 2013). Given the centrality of revenue to state power (Levi 1989), and the sheer amount of money involved, this troublingly Tillyian mechanism of extraction and state-building deserves to be explored both theoretically and empirically.

The line between state extraction and state extortion, like so many central issues in state formation (Slater 2008, 2010b), takes us beyond positive research into a larger normative debate. This is a good thing. Whether drug wars make *healthy* states is a question to which political science can and should contribute, not least because it relates to additional, critical bodies of theory in comparative politics. Let us now consider some of these.

11.1.2 "Stateness" and Corruption

The foregoing concerns over what kind of states drug wars make speak to another major strand of literature, which analyzes state strength, power, and cohesion by breaking it up into various dimensions. In this tradition, scholars typically distinguish state capacity from some other aspect of "stateness." For the foundational "Bringing the State Back In" movement (Evans et al. 1985), the foil was usually state autonomy—roughly speaking, an ability of leaders and state agencies to carry out projects without the approval of powerful social classes or interest groups. Mann's (1986) distinction between infrastructural power and despotic power is broadly similar. One straightforward way that drug war touches on this body of literature is the common concern in Latin America that accepting US aid to combat trafficking will reduce a government's freedom to set drug policy in the national interest. An intriguing question is whether this tying of leaders' hands might, under certain circumstances, increase the state's autonomy vis-à-vis domestic power groups.

The more central issue, however, concerns the complicated relationship between corruption—especially police corruption—and "stateness," which can include capacity, autonomy, and in a more recent tradition, state "quality" (e.g., Rothstein and Teorell 2008; Taylor 2011). As I have argued, increasing the state's capacity to repress drug trafficking increases cartels' incentives to bribe enforcers. On its face, increased police corruption would seem to weaken the state. After all, a captured state is hardly autonomous or high quality, and corruption can be seen as a means of capturing the state through informal and illicit channels. More broadly, the Weberian conception of rational-bureaucratic authority—often treated as a sine qua non of strong states—precludes personalistic practices like patronage, graft, and bribery. Much of the economics literature on corruption takes this idea as a starting point, casting bribery as a failure of institutions to solve the principal–agent problem between leaders and bureaucrats (Rose-Ackerman 1975).

Nonetheless, systematic corruption may be compatible with, and even help build, strong states. Yahya Sadowski (1987), for example, argues that only by embracing systematic corruption was Syria's Ba'ath Party able to seize and consolidate power. Graft, bribery, smuggling, and other illegal activities were not only tolerated but unofficially sanctioned, because they "establish a relationship of political subordination by a[n] ... act of exchange" (Sadowski 1985). Similarly, Keith Darden draws on the case of Ukraine to argue that informal control and sanctioning of graft can reinforce rather than undermine the administrative hierarchy. He proposes a tripartite conceptualization of graft: state-weakening, state-benign, and state-strengthening, and suggests that the latter has produced states that are Weberian ("monopolistic, hierarchical, impersonal, and effective") while lacking Weberian (i.e., rational rather than patrimonial) bureaucracy (Darden 2008, 43).

The cases studied here are directly relevant to this discussion, particularly Mexico. Corruption was an integral part of the PRI's hegemony, reaching into every corner of society. As per Darden's characterization of state-strengthening graft, bribes were "part of the bargain struck between leaders and their subordinates to sustain the administrative hierarchy" (Darden 2008, 43), and thus likely to have been state-strengthening. In the state-sponsored protection racket engineered by the PRI to manage and tax Mexico's drug trade, bribery was not only unofficially tolerated, but encouraged. Given that repression against drug cartels was highly conditional, designed not to prevent trafficking per se but deter cartel violence and political interference, it seems likely that anti-corruption internal enforcement was also conditional, "limited," as in the case of Ukraine, "to cases of disobedience or political disloyalty" (Darden 2008, 47). The system of illicit rent extraction described in the case study of Rio was less thoroughgoing and more bottom-up than the PRI's, but nonetheless has proven extremely stable, outlasting Brazil's military dictatorship and persisting through decades of lethal cartel–state conflict. Whether it should ultimately be characterized as state-strengthening, state-benign, or state-weakening is an interesting question for further research.

Cases like these provide two important sources of empirical variation for the study of corruption and state strength. First, as a source of illicit or divertable revenue—the fuel on which the engine of systematic corruption runs—the illicit drug trade is simply enormous, probably second only to the state's coffers in size. Unlike diversion of public funds, however, systems of illicit rent extraction bring money *in*. Of course, this money generally remains off the books, but if state agents' salaries are set with the widespread expectation that they will earn a supplement from bribes (as was the case, for example, with Mexico's police), the overall effect is still state-enriching. This suggests twin mechanisms through which state-sponsored protection rackets can be state-strengthening: by simply increasing state revenue *à la* Levi (1989), and by providing raw material for the corrupt reinforcement of bureaucratic hierarchies *à la* Darden (2008). Comparing the dynamics of inward and outward flows of illicit revenue could provide important new insights.

A second source of variation is temporal: the evolution of Mexico's drug war may offer an illustrative example of widespread corruption shifting from state-strengthening to state-weakening. With the end of the PRI's hegemony in the 1990s, the informal institutions regulating corruption withered. Important recent work attributes the onset of inter-cartel turf war to this breakdown of state-sponsored protection, by giving cartels incentives to build private armies (Trejo and Ley 2016) and use violence to settle business disputes (Snyder and Durán-Martínez 2009a). But this same process may have also reduced state capacity. Where rampant bribery once gave PRI leaders an important mechanism of control over subordinates, it now simply meant that subordinates could not be counted on to carry out directives. Without thoroughgoing informal institutions to regulate it, corruption takes on the familiar cast of a principal–agent problem (Darden 2008, 43). Paradoxically, democratization may have both made it harder to strike bribe agreements and ensured that what agreements were struck (and many were still struck) would leave the state weaker.

11.1.3 Corruption (and Violence) as Influence

Another body of theory for which my findings have implications comes from the comparative study of political development, and specifically its view of corruption as a form of political influence. My theory of cartel–state conflict draws heavily on this literature, as noted in Chapters 1 and 3; at the same time, it calls into question this tradition's tendency to treat violence and corruption as distinct alternatives. My analysis of the logics of violence in cartel–state conflict shows how violence can be used coercively as a complement to strategies of influence like lobbying and corruption. This section considers the implications of my findings for the corruption-as-influence view.

In his classic *Political Order in Changing Societies*, Samuel Huntington took a counterintuitive view of corruption as a useful mode of influence, particularly during modernization. He defined corruption in terms of norms rather than laws, and warned that overzealous technocrats pushing "unreasonable puritanical standards" might lead to a "rejection of the bargaining and compromise essential to politics" (1968, 59–71). Most relevantly, he argued that modernization breeds corruption not only by normatively or legally ruling out previously tolerated practices, but by putting newfound wealth in the hands of groups lacking formal channels of political influence. In this nuanced view, corruption can play a positive, system-reinforcing role, taking up the slack between economic development and outdated political institutions. "The new millionaires buy themselves seats in the Senate or the House of Lords and thereby become participants in the political system rather than alienated opponents of it" (Huntington 1968, 61). Unfortunately, this approach proved fraught in practice for drug kingpins. As we saw in Chapter 5, Pablo Escobar bought himself a seat in Congress only to be quickly expelled for his trafficking ties, leaving him a deeply alienated and extremely dangerous opponent of the Colombian state.

James Scott (1972), building on Huntington's analysis, argues that corruption can be fruitfully understood as a means of influencing *policy outcomes*. Scott distinguishes attempts to influence de jure policy from attempts to influence enforcement, and adds an important theoretical prediction: since the benefits of lobbying are universal, while those of corruption are particularistic, the latter is likely to be preferred by actors lacking the means for effective collective action. Scott's theoretical framework is a major building block of the theory of violent lobbying and corruption I lay out in Chapter 3, and his theoretical prediction carries over into my explanation of why violent lobbying was more prevalent in Colombia than elsewhere.

One limitation of this literature with respect to drug war, however, is a tendency to see violence as an alternative to, or substitute for, corruption. This is somewhat surprising, because both Huntington and Scott see corruption and violence in similar terms, as extra-systemic means of winning influence, and hence likely to occur in similar situations. As Huntington puts it, "Both are encouraged by modernization; both are symptomatic of the weakness of political institutions ... Hence the society which has a high capacity for corruption also has a high capacity for violence" (Huntington 1968, 63). Yet, for Huntington, the two forms of influence are unlikely to be used together, because "Violence is more often a symbolic gesture of protest which goes unrequited and is not designed to be requited." The forms of violence Huntington has in mind seem, almost by definition, not coercive.

Scott's work goes further by recognizing the potentially coercive role violence can play, but ultimately follows Huntington in treating violence as an alternative to, and hence analytically separable from, corruption. At the macro level, he echoes Huntington in arguing that corruption can be a "stabilizing or conservative force" for wealthy groups "that might otherwise ... even assist in violent attempts to overthrow the existing regime," citing the PRI's early reliance on systematic corruption to pacify Mexico as an example (Scott 1972, 35). At the micro level, while admitting that those looking to strike a bribe agreement can offer sticks as well as carrots, he nonetheless draws a sharp conceptual distinction between corruption and coercion. Describing a prototypical corrupt negotiation, he notes that "Negative inducements (e.g., the threat to withdraw a benefit, to impose a penalty) are often involved too, but, beyond a certain point, negative inducements must be considered coercion rather than corruption. Corruption thus frequently represents an alternative to coercion as a means of influence" (Scott 1969b, 322).[6] Even Susan Rose-Ackerman, in her game-theoretic study of corruption, follows Scott both in categorizing threats of violence among "forms of influence similar to bribery," and in treating threats as a distinct alternative to bribes to which her study "does not attempt to do justice" (Rose-Ackerman 1978, 4).

The study of cartel–state conflict contributes to this literature by showing how systematic anti-state violence can be used coercively, to shift state policy outcomes in cartels' favor, without seeking to upend the regime or the political system. At the de jure level, violent lobbying generally involves explicit and concrete policy demands that are, quite unlike the "gestures of protest" Huntington describes, very much designed to be requited. At the level of de facto enforcement, the distinction between corruption and coercion drawn by Scott and Rose-Ackerman, however useful in the contexts they study, becomes downright misleading when *plata o plomo* threats are part of cartels' modi operandi. In these settings, violence, by giving enforcers incentives to disobey orders and take (smaller) bribes, complements rather than substitutes for corruption. As the model of Chapter 4 shows, although individual bribe negotiations present a dichotomous choice between bribery and a violent confrontation upon enforcement, in equilibrium, the occasional violence that occurs if no agreement is reached reduces the size of bribes when they are paid. Moreover, the use of coercive violence slackens the conditions for bribery to take place at all (Dal Bó et al. 2006).

An interesting question arises concerning the long-term effects of *violent* corruption on political development and state-building. For Huntington, violence is clearly more detrimental than corruption, expressing more extreme alienation from the political system and hence a greater threat to it. As he says, "He who corrupts a system's police officers is more likely to identify with the system than he who storms the system's police stations" (Huntington 1968, 64). What then can we say of a group that does both? This study has sought to explain the drivers of violent corruption; future work could fruitfully explore its effects.

---

6   That said, Scott is correct when he goes on to say that non-coercive corruption is "likely to be employed where each party to the transaction is powerful enough to make coercion very costly." This may frequently be the case in transactions between, say, bureaucrats and legal firm owners, both with much to lose from resorting to physical violence. But anti-narcotics agents by definition have coercive power over traffickers; indeed, the use of *plata o plomo* threats by traffickers is precisely a way to make state coercion costly to enforcers. The remaining question is, how can police make coercion costly enough for cartels to switch to hide-and-bribe strategies? The answer, I have argued throughout, is by making repression conditional.

11.1.4 Drug War as a Form of Armed Conflict

My theory of cartel–state conflict is firmly situated within in the rationalist approach to conflict studies, drawing on two important bodies of work. First, starting with Fearon's seminal paper (1995b), a line of thought has analyzed conflict as "bargaining breakdown." Since fighting inevitably destroys *something*, there is less to be divided up in its wake; this implies that prior to the outbreak of war, there were allocations that would have made both parties at least as well off and one better off than they could expect from war. For Fearon (1995b, 383–4), "The central question, then, is what prevents states in a dispute from reaching an *ex ante* agreement that avoids the costs they know will be paid *ex post* if they go to war? Giving a rationalist explanation for war amounts to answering this question." The second is Kalyvas' "logics of violence" approach. Equally rationalist in nature, Kalyvas focuses not on the decision to go to war, but rather, once in a state of war, the shifting strategic considerations that lead belligerents to employ different types of violence. While both traditions are applicable to "classic" interstate war, both have focused their empirical attention on civil war and insurgency, in part because it was the dominant form of armed conflict in the second half of the twentieth century.

In Part I, I argue that cartel–state conflict is fundamentally different from civil war. Chapters 2 and 4 discuss some of these differences, and the consequent need to develop new models and logics of violence. Three key points are worth highlighting here. First, the canonical models of war as bargaining breakdown developed by Fearon, Powell, and others follow the general approach of international relations scholars by assuming that the state is a unitary actor. As I note in Chapter 4, this is a workable assumption for modeling violent lobbying, where cartels directly engage leaders with direct control over de jure policy, but not for violent corruption, in which cartels use violence to drive a wedge between de jure policy and the willingness of enforcers to carry it out. Second, canonical models of war generally assume that belligerents are negotiating, and possibly fighting, over a mutually desired "pie" that has a zero-sum quality. In these settings, one side's loss is the other's gain. In drug war, states and cartels impose losses on one another that are purely punitive: a kilo of cocaine seized is worth nothing (presumably) to the state that seizes it. Finally, in canonical models, fighting generally "locks in" a division of the pie or a flow of benefits; it has a decisive quality that makes it a solution to commitment problems. In drug war, it is not clear that fighting has this decisive quality: even when the state successfully destroys a cartel, the very act creates unmet market demand, encouraging new cartels to enter.

Although the literature on armed conflict has little to say about corruption per se, it has long understood violence as part of a bargaining process, and thus is better positioned than the corruption-as-influence literature to understand its complementarity with bribery. As Thomas Schelling, a pioneer in identifying conflict as a form of bargaining, put it: "a strike or a price war or a racketeer's stink bomb in a restaurant is *part* of the bargaining and not a separate activity." Indeed, part of Fearon's accomplishment was to formalize Schelling's insight by translating economics research on inefficient strikes, slowdowns, and price wars into the context of war. In this way, Fearon's central question—why do parties to a conflict fail to reach Pareto-superior bargained solutions—applies to the question of violent corruption two times over. Since enforcers do not keep the drugs, guns, and money they seize during busts, interdiction is, like war, inefficient (from the perspective of police and traffickers). Since cartels do not directly gain from the pain they impose on enforcers, opting for fight-and-bribe over hide-and-bribe strategies constitutes a second inefficiency to be explained. Leaders presumably want to avoid the latter, which I have argued requires increasing the conditionality of repression, while *inducing* the former, so that bribe negotiations fail. As enforcers' interdiction capacity grows, so too does the "inefficiency" associated with non-corrupt enforcement, one reason that keeping even elite state forces clean has been so challenging.

Stepping down from the abstract heights of formal models, Schelling's discursive explorations of conflict as bargaining, particularly his work on limited war, yield additional insights. Where initial unconditional crackdowns on cartels sought to simply destroy them through brute force, conditional repression mirrors efforts to fight a war while limiting the extent of violence employed in it. As Schelling puts it, "In limited warfare, two things are being bargained over, the outcome of the war, and the mode of conducting the war itself." The key to limited war is using some amount of available force (to weaken the enemy) while holding something in reserve (to deter the opponent from escalating). Conditional repression does just this, using some state repressive capacity to interdict and arrest—both physically reducing the supply of drugs and presumably pushing cartels closer to "surrender," bankruptcy, or simply market exit—while keeping repressive capacity in reserve, to deter cartels from resorting to anti-state violence.

The art of limiting warfare is thus relevant to cartel–state conflict, particularly the challenges of implementing and sustaining conditionality. One of Schelling's crowning insights is that effectively limiting warfare requires clear and easily recognized limits—what came to be called focal points in the context of multiple-equilibrium games (Myerson 2009). It must be clear to both sides what it means to go too far. In territorial struggles, rivers, mountain ranges, and coastlines all make good focal points; drawing credible lines in the sand is harder. In terms of tactics, whole classes must generally be ruled out. "'No nuclears' is simple and unambiguous. 'Some nuclears' would be more complicated. Ten nuclears? Why not eleven or twenty or a hundred?" (Schelling 1966, 132).

Focal points can be particularly elusive in drug war. For conditional repression to work, the state must clearly communicate a limit on cartel violence beyond which additional repression will kick in. Anti-state and anti-civilian violence hold out some promise as focal points. In practice, though, both can be highly problematic. In settings of rampant corruption, murders of officials often raise legitimate suspicion that the victims were already involved in corruption and that the violence was mere score-settling. This can make following through on the threat of increased repression operationally difficult. At the micro level, a fallen officer's colleagues are far more likely to rally around an effort to avenge her death if they can be fairly certain she was "clean." At the macro level, garnering political support for a conditional approach is harder when the reduced repression on non-violent cartels it requires could, from the public's point of view, be the result of successful bribe negotiations.

Similarly, it can be difficult to distinguish legitimate civilian victims of cartel violence. Traffickers do not wear uniforms; they will always claim to be innocent civilians if at all possible, and they also actively recruit from and at times coercively pressure the civilian populations they dominate. Not only that, officials have incentives to categorize the victims of cartel violence as traffickers. My cases provide ample evidence of this. Felipe Calderón once dismissed a massacre as inter-cartel violence until a public backlash forced him to publicly apologize. In Rio de Janeiro, police regularly characterize virtually all victims of armed violence as criminals unless incontrovertible evidence and/or community protest force them to recant.

11.1.5 Avenues for Empirical Research: Additional Cases

Wars and revolutions are classically small-*n* phenomena, which makes them both fascinating and difficult to study. Full-blown cartel–state conflict is even rarer still. If the cases I have studied here do not exhaust the universe of cartel–state conflict, they are certainly the most salient. A natural extension, then, would be to consider negative cases, places with large, profitable markets for production and transshipment of cocaine and heroin, corrupt enforcers, and perhaps even inter-cartel or other forms of armed conflict, that nonetheless have not suffered cartel–state conflict. What, for example, has prevented cartel–state violence from erupting in Bolivia, Afghanistan, and Burma? The latter cases in particular might provide useful leverage on a question this study cannot answer: how does regime type affect the dynamics of cartel–state conflict?

Future research might also fruitfully focus on positive cases (if they can be found) that go against the predictions of my theory, or present a radically different trajectory from those observed here. These "theoretical outliers" could help identify additional variables and scope conditions.[7] To see how, consider the conventional wisdom that coalesced around the Colombia case: the crackdown that eventually eliminated Escobar was thought to have curbed cartel–state conflict by fragmenting his Medellín cartel into pieces too small to attack the state. The Mexican experience, in this light, constitutes a theoretical outlier, since a crackdown there produced fragmentation, but not

---

[7] I thank one of my anonymous reviewers for this insightful suggestion.

abatement. The deliberately unconditional nature of Calderón's crackdown in turn suggested that conditionality of repression might be a key variable. Looking forward, cases where unconditional crackdowns did in fact lead to the abatement of cartel–state conflict, or cases of truly conditional repression that aggravated cartel–state conflict, would be of particular interest.

One potential out-of-sample, positive case worth exploring is the Sicilian Mafia's "war" on the Italian state in the early 1990s. This episode recalls Escobar's contemporaneous attacks on officials; in response to a Mafia crackdown, the Cosa Nostra launched a series of spectacular bombings that eliminated the tenacious anti-Mafia investigators Giovanni Falcone and Paolo Borsellino. However, unlike Escobar's campaign, the Cosa Nostra's violence quickly abated (Stille 1996), and anti-state violence by the Mafia has been rare ever since. This case may constitute a theoretical outlier: if repression was unconditional (perhaps because anti-Mafia efforts were already maxed out) and yet deterred further Mafia attacks, then other variables related to the Mafia and the Italian state merit consideration as explanatory factors. Conversely, it could be the case that repression was already sufficiently conditional, and that Cosa Nostra leaders quickly learned that further anti-state violence would only bring stronger state repression. A third possibility exists: an emerging body of journalistic and judicial evidence[8] suggests that the attacks produced a new state–Mafia pact with Silvio Berlusconi's ascendant Forza Italia party that effectively weakened state repression. Such an outcome suggests interesting extensions of the theory of violent lobbying developed here.

Finally, one of the contributions of this study is to show how violent corruption can fester at low levels before exploding in response to sudden, unconditional crackdowns. Part of its lesson is thus that cartel–state violence can be latent, off the equilibrium path, or at low, hard-to-detect levels. This suggests that there may be more positive cases than is immediately apparent: places where a "coerced peace" prevails, with enforcers coerced into essentially universal bribe-taking, and little or no equilibrium violence. I have conjectured that such scenarios are often gateways to full-blown cartel–state conflict, because cartels have already adopted violent strategies, and are prepared, as it were, to pull the trigger. Identifying cases of coerced peace and more thoroughly studying them could provide insight into how cartel–state violence begins. In this respect, Central America could be an important site for further research. The Northern Triangle—El Salvador, Honduras, and Guatemala—is now the most violent region in the world (World Bank 2011), and seems poised to be overrun by Mexican cartels and homegrown *mara* gangs whose prison-based structure mirrors that of Rio's syndicates. Meanwhile, the southern countries of the region have remained surprisingly peaceful, particularly Nicaragua, which

---

8   The most accessible source for non-Italian speakers is the 2014 film *La Trattativa*, translated as *The State-Mafia Pact*, by journalist Sabina Guzzanti.

has suffered many of the same historical setbacks as its Northern Triangle neighbors.

11.2 POLICY IMPLICATIONS

Thomas Schelling's insights into limited war carry over to his analysis of crime, and the design of appropriate policies to deal with it.

> There are issues of policy in identifying what it is we dislike about criminal activity, especially in deciding where and how to compromise ... there is some incompatibility between a campaign to eradicate venereal disease and a campaign to eradicate prostitution, and one may prefer to legislate a public health service for prostitutes and their customers *even at the expense of "diplomatic recognition" of the enemy*. The point is that a hard choice can arise ... If two of the primary evils connected with a criminal activity are negatively correlated, one has to distinguish them, separately evaluate them, and then make up one's mind.
>
> (1967, 71–72; emphasis added)

In the case of drug trafficking, the three primary evils are trafficking itself, police corruption, and violence. A central implication of my findings is that simultaneously deterring all three is likely an impossible challenge. As policy goals, they represent an "unholy trinity," because the pursuit of one can undermine the others. Giving enforcers the repressive capacity to deter trafficking necessarily hands them extortionary power over traffickers, potentially increasing corruption. Anti-corruption efforts, even if effective, can give traffickers incentives to resort to anti-state violence, both as brute-force defense and as a coercive counterweight to increased official sanctions for bribe-taking. Conditional repression creates incentives for cartels to eschew anti-state violence, but requires applying less than maximum repression against non-violent traffickers, possibly increasing the flow of drugs. States thus face difficult trade-offs, further complicated by the politics of drug war. Policy recommendations necessarily involve weighing these trade-offs, but also assessing what is politically possible.

My view is that violence reduction should be the orienting goal of anti-narcotics policy, and public security more generally. Violence, I would argue, is not only more destructive and normatively objectionable than drug consumption and police corruption, but can be more effectively deterred. Moreover, an effective conditional approach can improve overall anti-corruption efforts and potentially reduce the total social harms from drug consumption, though probably not the flow of drugs itself. Conditional repression, however, faces important political obstacles; widespread adoption will likely require a significant reframing of the problem of drug trafficking and the sort of "diplomatic recognition" Schelling describes. In the remainder of this section, I elaborate on each of these points.

First, it has proven extremely difficult to deter, and impossible to eliminate, drug trafficking and consumption. Today we take this for granted, but it is

worth recalling that a successful global prohibition regime like the abolition
of slavery, though it required a phase of intense active repression, ultimately
reached a stage where the prohibited activity became very rare and subject to
near-universal moral reprobation (Nadelmann 1990). Rarity is not only normatively desirable—the whole point of prohibition—but efficient: repression
lies "off the equilibrium path," effectively deterring would-be slave traders
without having to physically engage in large-scale interdiction efforts.[9] The
global drug prohibition regime, in contrast, remains "stuck" at the prior
stage, in which despite intense, ongoing, and costly repression, trafficking
and consumption continue to be widespread. Indeed, defenders of prohibition
recognize that a drug-free world is implausible, but advocate permanent
equilibrium repression as part of a necessary "containment" strategy (e.g.,
Costa 2007), even if it produces "unprecedented violence and corruption" as
"unintended consequences" (UNODC 2009, 3). Drug warriors insist that drug
flows and criminal violence can and must be simultaneously minimized. Yet
while we know little about the actual causal effect of repression on drug use
and trafficking, there is ample evidence that repression can generate violence.

Moreover, even if drug violence were an acceptable price to pay for reducing
drug flows, there is little evidence that such a potential trade-off exists.
Figure 11.1 offers a broad view of the relationship between militarized drug
war and drug markets; it shows US street prices and world cocaine production,
with Colombia's contribution highlighted, over the past three decades. Periods
of intense cartel–state violence in Colombia and Mexico, through which a huge
proportion of the US cocaine supply flows, seem to have done little more than
introduce noise into the relentless downward trend of prices over the past thirty
years.

One can't help but notice an upward blip in prices toward the end of this
time series. Figure 11.2 offers a closer look, and includes Mexican cartel-related
homicide data from both government and media sources. During the period
from 2007 to 2009, the correlation between armed violence in Mexico and
cocaine prices in the United States seems undeniably strong. In some ways,
such a result is a drug warrior's dream, at least if the arrow of causality runs
from violence to higher prices. After all, the overriding goal of US anti-narcotics
efforts in Latin America is supply reduction, which it is assumed will raise prices
and thus, via another assumption, reduce consumption.

However, from 2009 onward, this correlation all but disappears. One
plausible explanation for this stark shift is that in the short run, the Mexican
crackdown and attendant violence created uncertainty, shortages, and perhaps

---

[9]   Slavery, of course, abides, and efforts to combat human trafficking are thankfully on the rise.
      That worldwide policing capacity is so disproportionately focused on stopping drug flows rather
      than the enslavement and exploitation of human beings is one more normatively perverse
      consequence of the global war on drugs. That said, the end of chattel slavery in most of the
      world stands as one of the great moral accomplishments of the modern era.

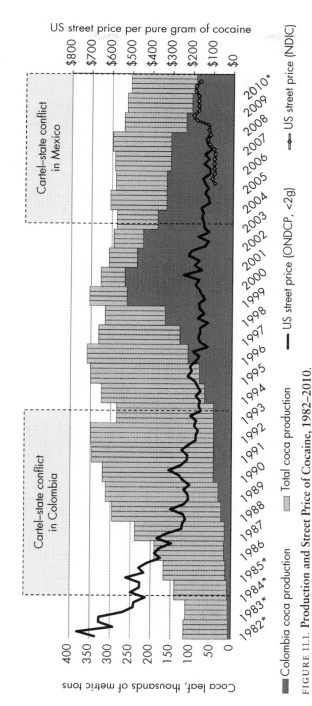

FIGURE 11.1. **Production and Street Price of Cocaine, 1982–2010.**

Sources: Prices: Fries et al. (2008); NDIC (2009); NDIC (2010); NDIC (2011); Production. UNODC (2003); UNODC (2010b); ODCCP (1999); ODCCP (2000a); ODCCP (2000b). *Production values for 1982–1985 and 2010 are estimates.

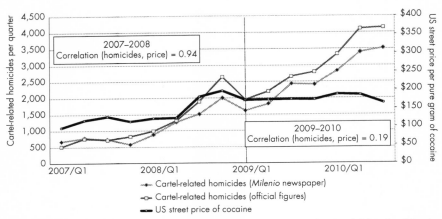

FIGURE 11.2. **US Cocaine Street Prices and Cartel-Related Homicides in Mexico, 2007–2010.**
Sources: Prices: NDIC (2011). Homicides: *Milenio* (2010a); *Milenio* (2010b); *Milenio* (2011); Shirk et al. (2013).

even hoarding or speculation in US retail drug markets, but that as traffickers adapted by building more fluid and redundant supply chains, prices leveled off. Whatever the case, the fact remains that 25,000 homicides between 2009 and 2010 seem to have had virtually no effect on the US street price, suggesting that generating drug violence in supplier countries is a horrifically inefficient way to address a consumption problem in the United States.

A second common goal of cartel crackdowns, reducing police corruption, is an eminently worthy one, and the US experience since the 1970s suggests that even thoroughly corrupt corps can eventually be cleaned up. However, in the context of anti-cartel operations, as opposed to routine policing, reducing corruption is likely to be more difficult, risky, and, arguably, of less social value. It is more difficult for the simple reason that drug cartels can pay enormous bribes. Summarizing the model of Chapter 4, enforcers are dissuaded from taking bribes by a combination of "moral pain" and expected official punishment; call the total λ. If cartels opt for peaceful, hiding strategies, then the eliminating corruption requires $\lambda \geq l$, where l is the maximum loss that enforcers can inflict on the cartel through enforcement. Anti-drug crackdowns seek precisely to increase the size of such losses, thus fomenting corruption. Building a larger anti-narcotics police force (capable of imposing larger costs, l, on cartels, and thus making the inequality above less likely to hold) is not the same thing as ensuring that the agents of that force are more likely to be punished for bribe-taking (raising λ, making the inequality more likely to hold). The fact that λ and l lie on opposite sides of the inequality reflects a profound trade-off for state builders. Increasing the state's capacity to physically prevent illicit economic activity simultaneously aggravates the principal–agent problem between state enforcers and decision-makers.

For this reason, seemingly savvy leaders often deploy special forces known to be less corrupt when fighting cartels. This is doubly risky: first, it risks contaminating "clean" forces through contact with traffickers, as occurred with Rio's elite BOPE force; second, it can give traffickers incentives to use coercive *plata o plomo* threats to push honest cops into bribery. When cartels make credible *plata o plomo* threats, the no-bribery condition becomes $\lambda - \pi \geq l$, where π is the amount of pain cartels inflict if no bribe agreement is reached. The larger cartels' "power to hurt" police, the more difficult it is to eliminate corruption. Indeed, this is one reason cartels adopt fight-and-bribe strategies in the first place.

Finally, in contexts like Mexico or Rio, law-abiding citizens are regularly extorted by police for minor infractions (Fried et al. 2008); ending such practices would probably have greater social benefit than reducing high-level bribery by international drug traffickers. Eliminating cartel–state conflict, by contrast, would have society-wide beneficial impacts. The reductions in cartel–state conflict documented in the cases studied here, as well as the preponderance of negative cases—in which DTOs never engage in systematic anti-state violence to begin with—suggest that this is an achievable goal. Moreover, adopting a violence-reducing conditional approach does not necessarily imply increased corruption; dissuading cartels from making coercive threats against enforcers can actually reduce the frequency of bribes. Conditional approaches do, however, require holding considerable repressive capacity in reserve to punish traffickers that resort to violence, and credibly communicating this deterrent threat ahead of time. This raises a host of logistical and political problems; in the cases studied here, as well as in some US policing projects, conditionality has proven difficult to implement and sustain.

Two tentative recommendations arise from my analysis of efforts to reform repressive policy (Part III). First, it is important for policymakers to have the resources and political breathing room to experiment, to learn from trial and error. Second, it is critical to reframe the policy problem, from eradicating drugs or crushing the cartels or punishing dastardly traffickers, to minimizing the harms produced by the drug trade. Unfortunately, these two factors can work against each other: once policymakers redefine their goal from maximum interdiction to violence reduction, then any eruption of violence, even if a useful learning moment, can be interpreted by critics as evidence of the conditional approach's failure. Moreover, reframing the problem ultimately implies "diplomatic recognition:" accepting that as long as there is demand for drugs, there will be traffickers, and orienting repressive policy to favor the sorts of traffickers we would like to have. At present, the opposite dynamic obtains. Public demonization of drug traffickers goes hand-in-hand with repressive policies that ensure that only the most demonic drug traffickers will prevail in a violent market. This contributes to a strong social taboo on anything resembling negotiation with trafficking groups, and lends toxicity to characterizations of conditional approaches as "pacts."

What about legalization? Much depends on what is meant by the term. If drugs were completely legalized, from production to retail, then the markets for cocaine and heroin might plausibly come to resemble those for alcohol and tobacco, for better and for worse. Consumption, addiction, and adverse health and social effects would probably rise (by how much is an active and contentious debate), possibly stoked by now-licit drug corporations. Illicit production and consumption would become rarer but not extinct, and states' capacity to regulate and tax would be limited by consumers' propensity to substitute into black markets (as with moonshine and illegal, tax-free cigarettes). Effective regulation could also be distorted by drug firms' political power and, possibly, their capacity to bribe regulators. If the behavior of Big Alcohol, Tobacco, and Pharma is any guide, "Big Cocaine and Heroin" would aggressively engage in all manner of influence politics—from high-power lobbying to subtle corruption of medical research and practice—quite probably to the detriment of society as a whole. They would, however, be very unlikely to resort to violence. By essentially eliminating repression against non-violent trafficking, legalization necessarily maximizes conditionality; if any policy can deter drug-firm violence, legalization surely would.

However preferable or not such a scenario may be to the status quo, full repeal of global drug prohibition is not realistic politically. A far more likely scenario is the piecemeal extension of marijuana decriminalization experiments to other drugs. This suggests that while possession and consumption of small quantities, and perhaps even limited retail operations, might become decriminalized in the near future, large-scale international transshipment of cocaine and heroin—precisely the market segment dominated by large and powerful cartels—will remain illegal. Indeed, the prominent Latin American and Global Commissions on Drug Policy, important political forces for policy reform that include former presidents of Mexico, Colombia, and Brazil, advocate decriminalizing consumption precisely in order to fight *harder* against cartels (Cardoso et al. 2009). Since these are the groups most likely to engage in militarized violence, including cartel–state conflict, the question remains: in a context of prohibition, how do we design repressive policy so as to minimize violence? Building the logistical capacity and political support to implement and sustain conditional repression, this book argues, is our best hope.

11.3   WHITHER DRUG WAR?

If full legalization is a political non-starter, and shifting the goal of repression from eradication to violence-minimization politically fraught, it is worth asking why. What do leaders get out of seemingly interminable drug wars?

The truth is that the global war on drugs—including its episodes of intense militarized drug war—has been about as effective in eradicating the illicit drug trade as violent religious persecution was in eradicating targeted religions. If states fight drug wars principally to reduce drug trafficking and use, the apparently meager impact of crackdowns would imply an enormous deadweight loss. Yet both leaders and enforcers remain deeply committed to the abstract goals of eradication and prohibition after decades of abject and expensive failure to make concrete steps toward those goals. Cynical careerism and even outright corruption are compelling explanations up to a point; but both the global war on drugs in general and the decades-long armed conflicts studied here seem too complex, coordinated, and sustained to be entirely due to such motives.

With respect to unconditional crackdowns, the justification most leaders give is that they *must* smash the cartels, lest the nation, hemisphere, or world be overrun by criminals and the dangerous drugs they peddle. This speaks to a common view of wars as zero-sum games, and it is indeed tempting to think that the losses drug wars impose on cartels are the state's gain and vice versa. But such a frame of analysis deeply distorts the underlying problem, which, I have argued, is not really zero-sum at all. The costliness of drug wars and their resilience over time make the question of leaders' incentives all the more puzzling.

One possibility is that leaders simply make mistakes. In general, scholars should start from the assumption that the actors they study understand their situation at least as well as we do. However, in all three cases studied here, leaders were genuinely surprised, both pleasantly and tragically, by cartel responses to changes in repressive policy. This suggests that they may have misunderstood, initially at least, the driving logics of cartel–state violence. Former president of Colombia César Gaviria, architect of both the conditional *Sometimiento* policy that induced Escobar's surrender and the unconditional crackdown that finally killed him, now warns other leaders bent on launching militarized drug wars not to "repeat my mistakes" (Gaviria 2017). As noted in Chapter 9, room for trial-and-error experimentation and a rich pool of policy ideas and past experiments both seem to favor the adoption of conditional approaches. All of this suggests that ideas and knowledge-accumulation matter. To the extent that this and related studies improve our understanding, perhaps some future mistakes can be avoided.

Of course, there is another possibility: leaders know exactly what they are doing, but there is some mismatch between their true and stated objectives. For Fearon (1995b, 379), the possibility that "the leaders who order war enjoy its benefits but do not pay its costs", though not a rationalist explanation by his definition, is nonetheless "very important empirically". Perhaps the best explanation of endless drug wars is that the mere process of fighting them produces a consistent flow of benefits to leaders, generating "victories" in the form of arrests and seizures, attracting foreign aid and winning diplomatic favor, and affording a pretext for expansions in coercive capacity that range from democracy-enhancing to quasi-authoritarian.

Whatever the true calculus of leaders, it is beyond dispute that cartel–state conflict creates tragic losses for entire populations unlucky enough to get caught in the crossfire, such as Rio's favela residents, Andean coca growers, and Mexican residents of border regions. It is also of dubious value to the rank-and-file police officers and soldiers who fight it (beyond any bribe money the corrupt among them might collect), and to the taxpayers who foot the bill. Indeed, it is hard to imagine any calculus in which society as a whole is better off having such conflict.

This suggests that the path forward involves changing *leaders'* incentives. Despite salient public outcry over the violence in Mexico and criticism of Calderón's policies from many quarters, he left office with an approval rating only slightly lower than when he began—less variation than any of his three predecessors. Careful empirical work reveals a kind of rally-around-the-flag effect: citizens supported Calderón merely for fighting organized crime, and did not personally blame him for the results of his crackdown (Romero et al. 2014). Calderón's wife Margarita Zavala is the PAN's candidate for the 2018 presidential election, and was leading the polls as of November 2016 (Gallegos 2016); her victory would certainly qualify as a political vindication for Calderón and his policies. The example suggests that leaders could quite plausibly prefer to leave office with some 60,000 civilian deaths on their watch than to be perceived as having gone easy on cartels. Unfortunately, as long as *that* calculus holds, we have probably not seen the last episode of cartel–state conflict.

Appendix A

Violent-Event Data

Figures 3.4, 5.2, 6.2, and 6.3 present descriptive statistics from the NRI/OBIVAN dataset of coded newspaper reports of cartel-related violent events in Colombia, Mexico, and Rio de Janeiro, Brazil, produced by the author.[1] This appendix offers a brief summary of the dataset and the coding methodology employed.

For each case, the universe of cartel-related violent events was collected from newspaper reports over the relevant period, manually in Colombia (1984–1993), and using digital search algorithms in Mexico and Brazil (2002–2012). Relevant reports were then manually coded by native-speaker research assistants working at partner NGOs in each country. Reports were collected from multiple newspapers, but coding was only completed for the leading national newspaper in each case: *El Tiempo* in Colombia, *Reforma* in Mexico, and *O Globo* in Brazil. Some 30,000 events have been coded to date.

A single coding methodology was adopted for all three countries: the unit of analysis is the violent event, which in turn is composed of one or more actions contiguous in time and place. Actions are coded by type, protagonists, affected groups, outcomes (death tolls, drug and arms seizures, arrests, etc.); the event as a whole is coded for date and location. Some actions are not considered violent, such as police patrols, seizures, arrests, etc., but are coded as sequential components of events that contained other violent actions.

A long list of action types (such as "assassination," "kidnapping," "arson," and so on) and corresponding criteria was developed to accommodate the particularities of the three cases.[2] However, a single action type, "clash," was

---

[1] The dataset-coding project received critical financial support from numerous outside sources, especially the National Science Foundation, the Open Society Institute and the Centro Andino de Fomento (CAF).

[2] Available (in Spanish and Portuguese) from the author upon request.

used across cases to code *any* situation in which two or more groups exchange lethal force. All other violent actions are considered "unilateral actions." All clashes have at least two protagonists, though one or more may be unidentified.

Figure 6.3 examines the universe of *event reports* that included one or more clashes for Rio de Janeiro, regardless of the protagonists involved. In the left-hand chart, all clashes between organized criminal groups and state forces are categorized as "Cartel vs. State." Only clashes in which both protagonist could be identified as organized criminal groups were categorized as "Cartel vs. Cartel." Clashes involving individuals as at least one of the protagonists were excluded.

The right-hand chart exploits two unique features of the dataset. First, all events are coded for "type of locality"; in Rio, this distinguishes between *favela* (slum) areas and formal, non-favela city areas (known as *asfalto*—asphalt—in Portuguese). Second, by breaking violent events into sequential component actions, the dataset sheds light on what types of (often non-violent) actions immediately precede armed clashes. While many clashes were the first or only component action of their respective events, more than half were preceded by some type of police action, usually an incursion into a favela. As noted in the article, police incursions that were themselves in response to a violent action are counted as cartel-initiated.

The data reported here represent individual *reports of events*. Since events can be reported on multiple times, this is a better measure of the public impact of violence than a precise count of discrete events. While this surely biases the results toward high-impact types of violence like bombings, this bias should be similar over time, particularly given that in these charts restrict attention to a single type of violent action.

Appendix B

List of Interview Subjects

B.1 COLOMBIA

Policymakers and Enforcers:
Afonso Salazar, Former Mayor of Medellín
Jay Bergman, Regional Director of Bogotá DEA Office
Gustavo De Greiff Restrepo, First Attorney General of Colombia
César Gaviría Trujillo, Former President of Colombia
Manuel Segundo Hoyos Benítez, Lawyer, Investigation Unit of the Medellín Police
Hugo Martínez Poveda, Former Head of the *Bloque de Búsqueda* ("Search Block") police unit that killed Pablo Escobar
Rafael Pardo Rueda, Former Minister of Defense
Enrique Peñalosa, Former Mayor of Bogotá
Rosso José Serrano Cadena, Former Head of the Colombian National Police
Francisco José Sintura Varela, Former Vice Attorney General of Colombia

Anonymous Interview Subjects:
Former M-19 Regional Commander
Police officers wounded during the narco-violence period
Former Judge and *fiscal sin rostro* (anonymous public prosecutor) during the narco-violence period

Journalists and Academics:
Alvaro Camacho Guizado, Sociologist
Fidel Cano Correa, Journalist and great-grandson of the founder of the newspaper *El Espectador*
Jorge Cardona, Editor-in-Chief, *El Espectador*
Daniel Coronell, Editor-in-Chief, *Noticias Uno*
Francisco (Pacho) Leal Buitrago, Sociologist
Andrés López Restrepo, Sociologist

B.2 RIO DE JANEIRO

Policymakers and Enforcers:
Bete Albernaz, UPP Police Academy Instructor
Antônio Carballo Blanco, Founder and First Commandor of GPAE
Tania Dâhmer, Director of Social Services for Penitentiary System of Rio
Antônio Roberto Cesário De Sá, Federal Police Commissioner and
    Vice-Secretary of Public Security for Rio
Marcelo Freixo, State Legislator
Vinícius George, Former Civil Police Detective, Member of Marcelo Freixo's
    Cabinet
Julita Lemgruber, Former Director of the Penitentiary System of Rio de
    Janeiro
Leonardo Mazzurana, Director of UPP Instruction and Research
Guaracy Minguardi, Former National Vice Secretary of Public Safety
Joana Monteiro, Director, Institute for Public Security (ISP)
Luciane Patrício, Director of Education and Prevention in Public Security
    Secretariat
Robson Rodrigues Da Silva, Founding Commander of the UPP Program
Pedro Strozenberg, Chair, Human Rights Commission of Rio de Janeiro
Dirceu Vianna, Consultant to Public Security Secretariat
Orlando Zaccone, Civil Police Officer, Former Director of Jails

Anonymous Interview Subjects:
Mid-Level Comando Vermelho Manager
Mid-Level Terceiro Comando Manager
Non-Trafficking Former Comando Vermelho Member and Prison Capo
Former Comando Vermelho Drug Boss and Prison Inmate
Former Comando Vermelho Arms Specialist
Former Comando Vermelho Member
Former Terceiro Comando Drug Boss
Former Terceiro Comando Member
Former Terceiro Comando Member

Civil Society Actors and Scholars:
Luke Dowdney, Director, Luta Pela Paz
Rubem César Fernandes, Director, Viva Rio
Ilona Szvabó de Carvalho, Director, Instituto Igarapé
Damian Platt, Brazil Specialist for Amnesty International

B.3 MEXICO

Policymakers and Enforcers:
Jessica Duque Roquero, Former Director of the Consejo de Seguridad
    Nacional Technical Secretariat

Eduardo Guerrero Gutierrez, Member of CISEN Working Group and
  Security Consultant
Manlio Gutiérrez, Former Vice Director-General of Speeches for President
  Calderón
Alejandro Hope, High-Ranking Officer of the Center for Intelligence and
  National Security (CISEN)
Jaime Domingo López Buitrón, Former Director of the Center for
  Intelligence and National Security (CISEN)
Miguel Ángel Mancera, Former Attorney General of Mexico City
Pino Oliver Sánchez, District Head of Public Security in Mexico City
Polo Oteiza, Former Advisor-in-Chief to the Secretary of Public Security
  Garcia Luna
Gabriela Pérez, Former Vice-Secretary of the Penitentiary System
Alejandro Poiré, Former Chief of Staff and Other Positions in Calderón's
  Cabinet
Leticia Ramírez, Advisor in the Secretariat of Public Security (SSP)
Sofía Ramírez, Former Director of the Consejo de Seguridad Nacional
  Technical Secretariat
Wilfrido Robledo, Former Director of the Agencia Federal de Investigación
  (AFI)
Christel Rosales, Former Associate Director of Systems and Indicators in
  the Office of President Calderón
Rubén Rosas, Security Advisor for District Police Mexico City
Facundo Rosas, Federal Police Commissioner in Charge of 2011 Ciudad
  Juárez Operation
Alejandro Rubido García, Former General Secretary of the Center for
  Intelligence and National Security (CISEN)
Jaime Trewartha, Member of CISEN Working Group, Security Consultant
Jaime Uchunda, Former Director of the Consejo de Seguridad Nacional
  Technical Secretariat
Guillermo Valdés Castellanos, Former Director of the Center for
  Intelligence and National Security (CISEN)
José Arturo Yáñez Romero, Consultant and Instructor, Mexico City Police
  Academy

Anonymous Interview Subjects:
CISEN Operative
CISEN Operative
Police Officer, Mexico City
Police Officer, Mexico City

Bibliography

Acemoglu, Daron, and Alexander Wolitzky. 2011. "The Economics of Labor Coercion." *Econometrica* 79 (2): 555–600.

Acemoglu, Daron, James A. Robinson, and Rafael J. Santos. 2013. "The Monopoly of Violence: Evidence From Colombia." *Journal of the European Economic Association* 11 (January): 5–44.

Adorno, Sérgio, and Fernando Salla. 2007. "Criminalidade Organizada nas Prisões e os Ataques do PCC." *Estudos Avançados* 21 (61): 7–29.

Aguayo, Sergio. 2001. *La Charola: Una historia de los servicios de inteligencia en México*. Mexico City: Grijalbo.

Aguayo, Sergio, Delia Sánchez del Angel, Manuel Pérez Aguirre, and Jacobo Dayán Askenazi. 2016. *En el Desamparo*. Mexico City: El Colegio de México.

Ahnen, Ronald E. 2007. "The Politics of Police Violence in Democratic Brazil." *Latin American Politics and Society* 49 (1): 141–164.

Albarrán, Ernesto Núñez. 2012. *Crónica de un Sexenio Fallido*. Mexico City: Grijalbo.

Albernaz, Elizabete R., Haydée Caruso, and Luciane Patrício. 2007. "Tensões e desafios de um policiamento comunitário em favelas do rio de janeiro." *São Paulo em Perspectiva* 21 (2): 39–52.

Alston, Philip. 2007. "Press Statement by the Special Rapporteur of the UN Human Rights Council on Extrajudicial, Summary or Arbitrary Executions." Brasília. November 14.

Amnesty International. 2005. "Brazil: 'They come in shooting': Policing Socially Excluded Communities."

Amorim, Carlos. 1993. *Comando Vermelho: a História Secreta do Crime Organizado*. Rio de Janeiro: Record.

Amorim, Carlos. 2003. *CV-PCC: a Irmandade do Crime*. São Paulo: Record.

Andreas, Peter. 1998. "The Political Economy of Narco-corruption in Mexico." *Current History* 97: 160–165.

Andreas, Peter, and Joel Wallman. 2009. "Illicit Markets and Violence: What is the Relationship?" *Crime, Law and Social Change* 52 (3): 225–229.

Aranda, Jesús. 2011. "Ataques al Ejército cobran la vida de 253 soldados desde 2006." *La Jornada*, August 1.

Araújo, Vera. 2010. "Feira de drogas resiste à UPP da Cidade de Deus." *O Globo*, July 2.

Archibold, Randal C. 2012. "Mexico Holds 4 High-Ranking Army Officers." *New York Times*, May 18.

Arias, Enrique Desmond. 2006. "The Dynamics of Criminal Governance: Networks and Social Order in Rio de Janeiro." *Journal of Latin American Studies* 38 (2): 293–325.

Arias, Enrique Desmond. 2013. "The Impacts of Differential Armed Dominance of Politics in Rio de Janeiro, Brazil." *Studies in Comparative International Development* 48 (3): 263–284.

Arjona, Ana. 2016. *Rebelocracy: Social Order in the Colombian Civil War*. New York: Cambridge University Press.

Astorga, Luis. 1999. "Drug Trafficking in Mexico: A First General Assessment." *UNESCO Discussion Paper No. 36*.

Astorga, Luis. 2001. "The Limits of Anti-Drug Policy in Mexico." *International Social Science Journal* 53 (169): 427–434.

Astorga, Luis A. 2004. "Mexico: Drugs and Politics." In *The Political Economy of the Drug Industry*, ed. Menno Vellinga. Gainesville: University Press of Florida. 85–102.

Bailey, John. 2011. "Prepared Statement for the House Committee on Homeland Security, Subcommittee on Oversight, Investigations, and Management." Hearing on US Homeland Security Role in the Mexican War against Drug Cartels, Washington, DC, March 31.

Bailey, John, and Matthew M. Taylor. 2009. "Evade, Corrupt, or Confront? Organized Crime and the State in Brazil and Mexico." *Journal of Politics in Latin America* 1 (2): 3–29.

Bailly, Nestor. 2011. "WikiLeaks: US on 2009 Favela Violence." *The Rio Times*, January 4.

Barbosa, Antonio Rafael. 1998. *Um Abraço para Todos os Amigos: algumas considerações sobre o tráfico de drogas no Rio de Janeiro*. Niterói: EDUFF.

Barcellos, Caco. 2003. *Abusado: o Dono do Morro Dona Marta*. Rio de Janeiro: Livraria Tempo Real Inform.

Barragán, Sebastián. 2013a. "Ejército mató 248 presuntos agresores en 5 meses." *Unión Jalisco*, July 3.

Barragán, Sebastián. 2013b. "Los soldados desertores del Ejército en 12 años." *Unión Jalisco*, June 8.

Bastos, Marcelo. 2011. "Secretário de Segurança admite temer que policiais das UPPs atuem como milicianos." *R7*, May 12.

Bates, Robert H. 2008. *When Things Fell Apart: State Failure in Late-Century Africa*. New York: Cambridge University Press.

Batista, Vera Malaguti. 2003. *Difíceis ganhos fáceis: drogas e juventude pobre no Rio de Janeiro*. Vol. 2 Instituto Carioca de Criminologia.

Beltrame, José Mariano. 2014. *Todo Dia É Segunda Feira*. Rio de Janeiro: Sextante.

Bergal, Carina. 2011. "Mexican Drug War: The Case for Non-International Armed Conflict Classification." *Fordham International Law Journal* 34: 1042–1088.

Bicudo, Hélio. 2000. "A Unificação das Polícias no Brasil." *Estudos Avançados* 14: 91–106.

Blattman, Christopher, and Edward Miguel. 2010. "Civil War." *Journal of Economic Literature* 48 (1): 3–57.

Bonner, Robert C. 2010. "The New Cocaine Cowboys: How to Defeat Mexico's Drug Cartels." *Foreign Affairs* 89 (4): 35–47.

Borjón Nieto, José J. 2010. "Lucha contra el crimen organizado: fracaso de la militarización." *Letras Jurídicas* 21: 2–21.

Bottari, Elenlice, and Sérgio Ramalho. 2006. "Milícias avançam pelo corredor do Pan 2007." *O Globo*, December 9.

Bowden, Mark. 2001. *Killing Pablo*. New York: Atlantic Monthly Press.

Bradford Hill, Austin. 1965. "The Environment and Disease: Association or Causation?" *Proceedings of the Royal Society of Medicine* 58 (5): 295.

Bravo, Carlos. 2011. "Una ayudadita de memoria para Felipe Calderón." *Nexos*, Blog de la redacción, January 22.

Brito, Diana, Italo Nogueira, and Marco Antônio Martins. 2014. "No Rio, 70% dos moradores querem mudanças nas UPPs." *Folha de S. Paulo*, August 25.

Britto, Lina. 2010. "A Trafficker's Paradise: The 'War on Drugs' and the New Cold War in Colombia." *Contemporánea: Historia y Problemas del Siglo XX* 1 (1): 159–177.

Buarque de Hollanda, Cristina. 2005. *Polícia e Direitos Humanos*. Rio de Janeiro: Revan.

Burgoyne, Michael L. 2012. "The Right Tool for the Job: An Evaluation of the Effectiveness of Counterinsurgency Principles Against Criminal Insurgency." *Small Wars Journal*, February.

Burnett, John, Marisa Peñaloza, and Robert Benincasa. 2010. "Mexico Seems to Favor Sinaloa Cartel in Drug War." *NPR*.

Caldeira, Teresa P. R. 2002. "The Paradox of Police Violence in Democratic Brazil." *Ethnography* 3 (3): 235–263.

Calderón, Gabriela, Beatriz Magaloni, Gustavo Robles, and Alberto Diaz-Cayeros. 2015. "The Beheading of Criminal Organizations and the Dynamics of Violence in Mexico." *Journal of Conflict Resolution* 59 (8): 1455–1485.

Câmara, Breno P. 2009. "Segurança Pública carioca: conflitos urbanos revelam violências desiguais." Paper presented at the 28th Latin American Studies Association Congress, Rio de Janeiro.

Cano, Ignacio. 1997. *Letalidade da Ação Policial no Rio de Janeiro*. Rio de Janeiro: ISER.

Cano, Ignacio. 2010. "Racial Bias in Police Use of Lethal Force in Brazil." *Police Practice and Research: An International Journal* 11 (1): 31–43.

Cano, Ignacio. 2012. *"Os Donos do Morro": Uma Avaliação Exploratória do Impacto das Unidades de Polícia Pacificadora (UPPs) no Rio de Janeiro*. Rio de Janeiro: LAV/UERJ.

Cano, Ignacio, and Thais Duarte. 2012. *No Sapatinho: A Evolução das Milícias no Rio de Janeiro (2008–2011)*. Rio de Janeiro: Fundação Heinrich Boll/LAV.

Cano, Ignacio, and Carolina Iooty. 2008. "Seis por Meia Dúzia?: Um Estudo Exploratório do Fenômeno das Chamadas Milícias no Rio de Janeiro." In *Segurança, Tráfico, e Milícias no Rio de Janeiro*. Rio de Janeiro: Justiça Global/Fundação Heinrich Boll. 48–103.

Cano, Luís Carlos. 2008. "Figuraba Román García en narco lista de policías *ejecutables*" *El Universal*, May 10.

Cañón, Luis M. 1994. *El patrón: vida y muerte de Pablo Escobar*. Bogotá: Planeta.

Carballo Blanco, Antônio Carlos. 2003. "GPAE, uma experiência de Policiamento Comunitária." *Comunicações do ISER* 22 (58): 101–110.

Cardona, Jorge. 2009. *Dias de memoria: del holocausto del Palacio de Justicia al falso sometimiento de Pablo Escobar.* Bogotá: Aguilar.

Cardoso, Fernando Henrique, César Gaviria, and Ernesto Zedillo. 2009. "Drugs and Democracy: Toward a Paradigm Shift." Latin American Commission on Drugs and Democracy.

Carneiro, Júlia Dias. 2010. "Operação acaba com crença em 'invencibilidade' do Alemão, diz Beltrame." *BBC Brasil*, November 2.

Carpenter, Dick M., Lisa Knepper, Angela C. Erickson, and Jennifer Mcdonald. 2015. *Policing for Profit.* Arlington: Institute of Justice.

Castañeda, Jorge G. 2013. "Pongan fin a la guerra que nadie quiere librar." *Reforma*, August 8.

Castillo, Fabio. 1987. *Los jinetes de la cocaína.* Bogotá: Documentos Periodísticos.

Castillo, Juan Camilo, Daniel Mejía, and Pascual Restrepo. 2014. "Scarcity without Leviathan: The Violent Effects of Cocaine Supply Shortages in the Mexican Drug War." Working Paper 356. Washington, DC: Center for Global Development.

Centeno, Miguel Angel. 2002. *Blood and Debt: War and the Nation-State in Latin America.* University Park: The Pennsylvania State University Press.

Cerqueira, Carlos Magno Nazareth. 1996. "Remilitarização da Segurança Pública: a Operação Rio." *Discursos Sediciosos: Crime, Direito e Sociedade* 1 (1): 141–168.

Cerqueira, Carlos Magno Nazareth. 2001. "As políticas de segurança pública do Governo Leonel Brizola." In *O Futuro de Uma Ilusão: O Sonho de Uma Nova Polícia.* Rio de Janeiro: Freitas Bastos. 165–194.

Cerqueira, Daniel. 2011. "Mortes Violentas Não Esclarecidas e Impunidade no Rio de Janeiro." Mimeograph. Instituto de Pesquisa Econômica Aplicada.

Chazkel, Amy. 2011. *Laws of Chance: Brazil's Clandestine Lottery and the Making of Urban Public Life.* Durham, NC: Duke University Press.

Chepesiuk, Ron. 2003. *The Bullet or the Bribe: Taking Down Colombia's Cali Drug Cartel.* Westport: Praeger.

Chinelli, Filippina, and Luiz Antônio Machado da Silva. 1993. "O vazio da ordem: relações políticas e organizacionais entre as escolas de samba e o jogo do bicho." *Revista do Rio de Janeiro* 1 (5): 42–52.

Chwe, Michael Suk-Young. 1990. "Why Were Workers Whipped? Pain in a Principal-Agent Model." *The Economic Journal* 100 (403): 1109–1121.

CIJ. 1992. *Justicia Para La Justicia: Violencia contra jueves y abogodaos en Colombia 1979–1991.* Bogotá: Comisión Internacional de Juristas.

CIJL. 1990. "Attacks on Justice, July 1989–June 1990." Mimeograph. Centre for the Independence of Judges and Lawyers.

CNNMéxico. 2011. "El 'Triángulo Dorado', resguarda la droga entre el frío clima y la pobreza." February 1.

Coelho, Edmundo Campos. 1988. "Da Falange Vermelha a Escadinha: o Poder nas Prisões." *Presença* 11: 106–114.

Coimbra, Cecilia M. B. 2001. *Operação Rio: o mito das classes perigosas: um estudo sobre a violência urbana, a mídia impressa e os discursos de segurança pública.* Rio de Janeiro: Oficina do Autor.

Collier, David. 2011. "Understanding Process Tracing." PS *Political Science and Politics* 44 (4): 823.

Collier, Ruth Berins. 1993. "Combining Alternative Perspectives: Internal Trajectories versus External Influences as Explanations of Latin American Politics in the 1940s." *Comparative Politics* 26 (1): 1–29.

Collier, Ruth Berins, and David Collier. 1991. *Shaping the Political Arena*. Princeton: Princeton University Press.

Corchado, Alfredo. 2009. "Mexico's Drug Violence to Escalate in 2009." *Dallas Morning News*, January 4.

Corchado, Alfredo. 2011. "Arrest Signals Targeting of Zetas." *Dallas Morning News*, July 5.

Corcoran, Patrick. 2011. "Zetas: We Are Not Terrorists, Nor Guerrillas." *InSight Crime*, December 1.

Cornell, Svante E. 2005. "The Interaction of Narcotics and Conflict." *Journal of Peace Research* 42 (6): 751.

Costa, Ana Cláudia, Athos Moura, and Rogério Daflon. 2011. "Polícia ocupa Complexo de São Carlos para instalação de Unidades de Polícia Pacificadora (UPPs)." *O Globo*, February 6.

Costa, Ana Cláudia, Cristiane de Cássia, Marcelo Gomes, and Carlos Brito. 2007. "Megaoperação no Alemão deixa 19 mortos." *O Globo*, June 27.

Costa, Antonio Maria. 2007. "Free Drugs or Drug Free?" Speech delivered at the International Drug Policy Reform Conference, December 7.

Costa, Arthur T. M. 2011. "Police Brutality in Brazil: Authoritarian Legacy or Institutional Weakness?" *Latin American Perspectives* 38 (5): 19–32.

Dal Bó, Ernesto, and Rafael Di Tella. 2003. "Capture by Threat." *Journal of Political Economy* 111 (5): 1123–1154.

Dal Bó, Ernesto, and Robert Powell. 2009. "A Model of Spoils Politics." *American Journal of Political Science* 53 (1): 207–222.

Dal Bó, Ernesto, Pedro Dal Bó, and Raphael Di Tella. 2006. "'Plata o Plomo?': Bribe and Punishment in a Theory of Political Influence." *American Political Science Review* 100 (1): 41–53.

Darden, Keith. 2008. "The Integrity of Corrupt States: Graft as an Informal State Institution." *Politics & Society* 36 (1): 35–59.

Davis, Diane E. 2006. "Undermining the Rule of Law: Democratization and the Dark Side of Police Reform in Mexico." *Latin American Politics and Society* 48 (1): 55–86.

de Carvalho, Olavo. 1994. "As Esquerdas e o Crime Organizado." In *A Nova Era e a Revolução Cultural: Fritjof Capra e Antonio Gramsci*. Instituto de Artes Liberais e Stella Caymmi Editora.

Dell, Melissa. 2015. "Trafficking Networks and the Mexican Drug War." *American Economic Review* 105 (6): 1738–1779.

Diaz-Cayeros, Alberto, Beatriz Magaloni, and Barry R. Weingast. 2003. "Tragic Brilliance: Equilibrium Hegemony and Democratization in Mexico." Available at SSRN: http://ssrn.com/abstract=1153510 or http://dx.doi.org/10.2139/ssrn.1153510. Accessed July 31, 2017.

Denyer Willis, Graham. 2015. *The Killing Consensus*. Berkeley: University of California Press.

Dorn, Nicholas, Karim Murji, and Nigel South. 1992. *Traffickers: Drug Markets and Law Enforcement*. New York: Routledge.

Dowdney, Luke. 2003. *Children of the Drug Trade*. Rio de Janeiro: 7 Letras.

Dowdney, Luke. 2005. *Neither War nor Peace: International Comparisons of Children and Youth in Organised Armed Violence*. Rio de Janeiro: ISER/IANSA/Viva Rio.

Dube, Arindrajit, Oeindrila Dube, and Omar García-Ponce. 2013. "Cross Border Spillover: U.S. Gun Laws and Violence in Mexico." *American Political Science Review* 107 (3): 397–417.

Dugas, John. 2001. "Drugs, Lies, and Audiotape: The Samper Crisis in Colombia." *Latin American Research Review* 36 (2): 157–174.

Durán-Martínez, Angelica. 2012. "State Power, Criminal Competition, and Drug Violence." Paper prepared for NPSA 44th Conference, Boston, November 15–17.

Durán-Martínez, Angelica. 2015. "To Kill and Tell? State Power, Criminal Competition, and Drug Violence." *Journal of Conflict Resolution* 59 (8): 1377–1402.

El Tiempo. 1990. "Libre Camarógrafo Orlando Acevedo." December 1.

El Tiempo. 1991. "Gabo: Es un triunfo de la inteligencia." June 20.

El Tiempo. 1993. "Atacan refugion de la familia de Pablo Escobar." October 5.

El Universal. 2009. "Presunto líder de La Familia llama al diálogo." July 15.

English, Richard. 2005. *Armed Struggle: The History of the IRA*. New York: Oxford University Press.

Escalante, Fernando. 2009. *El homicidio en México entre 1990 y 2007*. Mexico City: El Colegio de México.

Escobar Gaviria, Roberto. 2000. *Mi Hermano Pablo*. Bogotá: Quintero Editores.

Evans, Peter B., Dietrich Rueschemeyer, and Theda Skocpol. 1985. *Bringing the State Back In*. Cambridge and New York: Cambridge University Press.

Ezequiel, Flores Contreras. 2012. "En narcomantas, Caballeros Templarios dan la bienvenida a Peña." *Proceso*, December 19.

Fausset, Richard, and Cecilia Sanchez. 2013. "Mexico Prosecutors Say Evidence Lacking Against Military Officers." *Los Angeles Times*, January 23.

FBI. 1990. "Pablo Emilio Escobar-Gaviria: Racketeering Enterprise Investigation." Miami: Federal Bureau of Investigation. File No. 12H-MM-50238.

Fearon, James D. 1994. "Domestic Political Audiences and the Escalation of International Disputes." *American Political Science Review* 88 (3): 577–592.

Fearon, James D. 1995a. "Ethnic War as a Commitment Problem." Paper presented at the American Political Science Association, New York, August 30.

Fearon, James D. 1995b. "Rationalist Explanations for War." *International Organization* 49 (3): 379–414.

Fearon, James D., and David D. Laitin. 2003. "Ethnicity, Insurgency, and Civil War." *American Political Science Review* 97 (1): 75–90.

Fearon, James D., and David D. Laitin. 2005. "Civil War Narratives." *Center for Advanced Studies Working Paper* 218: 1.

Fearon, James D., and David D. Laitin. 2007. "Civil War Termination." Paper presented at the Annual Meeting of the American Political Science Association, Chicago, IL, August 30.

Felbab-Brown, Vanda. 2009. *The Violent Drug Market in Mexico and Lessons from Colombia*. Washington, DC: Brookings.

Fernandes, Nelito. 2007. "Os bandidos já viram que não estamos de brincadeira." *Epoca*, July 7.

Fernandes, Rubem César. 2003. "GPAE, uma experiência de Policiamento Comunitária: Polícia sozinha não produz segurança." *Comunicações do ISER* 22 (58): 93–101.

Figueiredo, Talita. 2005. "Polícia mata garotos de 11 e de 12 anos no Rio." *Folha de S. Paulo*, December 6.

Fiorentini, Gianluca, and Sam Peltzman. 1997. *The Economics of Organised Crime*. New York: Cambridge University Press.

Fisman, Ray, and Edward Miguel. 2007. "Corruption, Norms, and Legal Enforcement: Evidence from Diplomatic Parking Tickets." *Journal of Political Economy* 115 (6): 1020–1048.

Fraga, Plínio. 2010. "Aos EUA, Rio previu ação 'traumática' no Alemão." *Folha de S. Paulo*, December 7.

Freixo, Marcelo. 2008. *Relatório da CPI das Milícias*. Rio de Janeiro: Asembléia Legislativa do Estado do Rio de Janeiro (ALERJ).

Fried, Brian J., Paul Lagunes, and Atheendar Venkataramani. 2008. "Corruption and Inequality at the Crossroad: A Multimethod Study of Bribery and Discrimination in Latin America." *Latin American Research Review* 45 (1): 76–97.

Fries, Arthur, Robert Anthony, Andrew Cseko, Carl Gaither, and Eric Shulman. 2008 *The Price and Purity of Illicit Drugs: 1981–2007*. Alexandria: Institute for Defense Analysis.

Friman, Richard H. 2009. "Drug Markets and the Selective Use of Violence." *Crime, Law and Social Change* 52 (3): 285–295.

Fuentes, Carlos. 1994. "Chiapas: Latin America's First Post-Communist Rebellion." *New Perspectives Quarterly* 11 (2): 54–58.

Gallegos, Zarayda. 2016. "No Title." *El País*, November 8.

Gambetta, Diego. 1993. *The Sicilian Mafia: The Business of Private Protection*. Cambridge, MA: Harvard University Press.

García, Gustavo Castillo. 2008. "Confesos de atentados en Morelia, tres presuntos zetas, según la PGR." *La Jornada*, September 27.

García, Gustavo Castillo. 2014. "Investiga la PGR a Morales y García Luna, afirma Javier Herrera Valles." *La Jornada*, April 19.

García, Gustavo Castillo, Armando Torres Barbosa, and Martín Sanchez Treviño. 2003. "Bajo fuego, la captura del capo Osiel Cárdenas." *La Jornada*, March 15.

García, Maria Isabel. 1993. "Alemania impide a la familia de Pablo Escobar la entrada en el país." *El País*, November 29.

García Márquez, Gabriel. 1997. *News of a Kidnapping*. New York: Knopf.

Garotinho, Anthony, and Luiz Eduardo Soares. 1998. *Violência e criminalidade no Estado do Rio de Janeiro: diagnóstico e propostas para uma política democrática de segurança pública*. Rio de Janeiro: Hama.

Gaviria, César. 2017. "President Duterte Is Repeating My Mistakes." *New York Times*, February 7.

Gaviria, César. 1990. "Inaugural Address." Bogotá, August 7.

Glasziou, Paul, I. Chalmers, M. Rawlins, and P. McCulloch. 2007. "When are Randomised Trials Unnecessary? Picking Signal from Noise." *BMJ* 334 (7589): 349–351.

Gleditsch, Nils Petter, Peter Wallensteen, Mikael Eriksson, Margareta Sollenberg, and Havard Strand. 2002. "Armed Conflict 1946–2001: A New Dataset." *Journal of Peace Research* 39 (5): 615–637.

Gloudemans, Mathijs J. 2010. "A Community's Devil's Deal: The Dynamics of the Struggle for Hearts and Minds in Rio de Janeiro's Favelas." Ph.D. thesis, Utrecht University.

Goldstein, Paul J. 1985. "The Drugs/Violence Nexus: A Tripartite Conceptual Framework." *Journal of Drug Issues* 39: 143–174.

Gomide, Raphael, and Sergio Torres. 2006. "Cupula do governo diverge sobre causas dos ataques." *Folha de S. Paulo*, December 29.

Gómora, Doris. 2011. "'Lince Norte' daña estructura 'zeta'." *El Universal*, August 5.

Gootenberg, Paul. 2012. "Cocaine's Long March North, 1900–2010." *Latin American Politics and Society* 54 (1): 159–180.

Gottschalk, Marie. 2008. "Hiding in Plain Sight: American Politics and the Carceral State." *Annual Review of Political Science* 11: 235–260.

Grayson, George W. 2010. *Mexico: Narco-violence and a Failed State?* New Brunswick: Transaction.

Grillo, Carolina C. 2013. "Coisas da Vida no Crime: Tráfico e roubo em favelas cariocas." Ph.D. dissertation, Universidade Federal do Rio de Janeiro.

Grillo, Ioan. 2011. *El Narco: Inside Mexico's Criminal Insurgency.* New York: Bloomsbury Press.

Guerrero, Eduardo. 2010. "Como Reducir la Violencia en México." *Nexos*, November 1.

Guerrero, Eduardo. 2011a. "La Raiz de la Violencia." *Nexos*, June 1.

Guerrero, Eduardo. 2011b. "Security, Drugs, and Violence in Mexico: A Survey." Mexico City: Lantia Consultores.

Gugliotta, Guy, and Jeff Leen. 2011. *Kings of Cocaine: Inside the Medellín Cartel.* New York: Simon & Schuster.

Guillermoprieto, Alma. 1994. "The Only Way to Win?" *The New Yorker*, August 15, 32–33.

Hacker, Jacob S. 2004. "Privatizing Risk without Privatizing the Welfare State: The Hidden Politics of Social Policy Retrenchment in the United States." *American Political Science Review* 98 (2): 243–260.

Hagedorn, John M. 1994. "Neighborhoods, Markets, and Gang Drug Organization." *Journal of Research in Crime and Delinquency* 31 (3): 264–294.

Hawley, Chris. 2008. "Mexico Cartels Post 'Help Wanted' Ads." *USA Today*, April 24.

Hernández, Anabel. 2010. *Los señores del Narco.* Mexico City: Grijalbo.

Hidalgo, F. Daniel, and Benjamin Lessing. 2014. "Endogenous State Weakness: Paramilitaries and Electoral Politics." Paper presented at the American Political Science Association, Washington, DC, August 25.

Holland, Alisha C. 2013. "Right on Crime? Conservative Party Politics and *Mano Dura* Policies in El Salvador." *Latin American Research Review* 48 (1): 44–67.

Hope, Alejandro. 2011. "Los Zetas son disuadibles." *Animal Político*, December 16.

Hope, Alejandro. 2015. "*Plus Ça Change*: Structural Continuities in Mexican Counternarcotics Policy." Washington, DC: Brookings, Latin America Initiative.

Huntington, Samuel P. 1968. *Political Order in Changing Societies.* New Haven: Yale University Press.

International Crisis Group. 2013. "Peña Nieto's Challenge: Criminal Cartels and Rule of Law in Mexico." Brussels, March 19.

ISP-RJ. 2016. "Dados Oficiais." Monthly reports. Rio de Janeiro: Instituto de Segurança Pública.

Jiménez, Sergio Javier. 2015. "Retomará Calderón modelo colombiano contra narco." *El Universal*, October 4.

Kalyvas, Stathis N. 1999. "Wanton and Senseless?" *Rationality and Society* 11 (October): 243–285.

Kalyvas, Stathis N. 2006. *The Logic of Violence in Civil War*. Cambridge: Cambridge University Press.

Kalyvas, Stathis N. 2008. "Promises and Pitfalls of an Emerging Research Program: The Microdynamics of Civil War." In *Order, Conflict, and Violence*, ed. Stathis N. Kalyvas, Ian Shapiro, and Tarek Masoud. New York: Cambridge University Press. 397–421.

Kalyvas, Stathis N. 2015. "How Civil Wars Help Explain Organized Crime–and How They Do Not." *Journal of Conflict Resolution* 59 (8): 1517–1540.

Kalyvas, Stathis N., and Laia Balcells. 2010. "International System and Technologies of Rebellion: How the End of the Cold War Shaped Internal Conflict." *American Political Science Review* 104 (3): 415–429.

Kavieff, Paul R. 2000. *The Purple Gang: Organized Crime in Detroit*. New York: Barricade Books.

Keen, David. 1998. "The Economic Functions of Violence in Civil Wars." *The Adelphi Papers* 38 (320): 1–89.

Kennedy, David M., Anthony A. Braga, Anne M. Piehl, and Elin J. Waring. 2001. "Reducing Gun Violence: The Boston Gun Project's Operation Ceasefire." *National Institute of Justice Research Report*.

Killebrew, Robert. 2011. "Criminal Insurgency in the Americas and Beyond." *Prism* 2 (3): 33–52.

Kingdon, John. 1984. *Agendas, Alternatives, and Public Policies*. Boston: Little, Brown and Company.

Kirk, Robin. 2003. *More Terrible than Death: Massacres, Drugs, and America's War in Colombia*. New York: PublicAffairs.

Kleiman, Mark. 2009. *When Brute Force Fails: How to Have Less Crime and Less Punishment*. Princeton: Princeton University Press.

Kleiman, Mark. 2011. "Surgical Strikes in the Drug Wars." *Foreign Affairs* September: 89–101.

Konrad, Kai A., and Stergios Skaperdas. 1997. "Credible Threats in Extortion." *Journal of Economic Behavior & Organization* 33 (1): 23–39.

Labrousse, Alain. 2005. "The FARC and the Taliban's Connection to Drugs." *Journal of Drug Issues* 35: 169–184.

Lacey, Marc. 2008. "Grenade Attack in Mexico Breaks From Deadly Script." *New York Times*, September 24.

Leal Buitrago, Francisco. 2006. *La inseguridad de la seguridad: Colombia 1958–2005*. Bogotá: Planeta.

Lee, Rensselaer W. 1994. "Global Reach: The Threat of International Drug Trafficking." *Current History* 592 (May): 207–211.

Leeds, Elizabeth. 1996. "Cocaine and Parallel Polities in the Brazilian Urban Periphery: Constraints on Local-Level Democratization." *Latin American Research Review* 31 (3): 47–83.

Lerman, Amy E., and Vesla M. Weaver. 2016. "The Carceral State and American Political Development." In *The Oxford Handbook of American Political Development*, ed. Richard Valelly, Suzanne Mettler, and Robert Lieberman. New York: Oxford University Press. 642–661.

Lessing, Benjamin. 2008. "As Facções Cariocas em Perspectiva Comparativa [Rio's Drug Syndicates in Comparative Perspective]." *Novos Estudos – CEBRAP* 80: 43–62.

Lessing, Benjamin. 2013. "A Hole at the Center of the State: Prison Gangs and the Limits to Punitive Power." CDDRL Working Paper No. 143, Stanford University.

Lessing, Benjamin. 2015. "Logics of Violence in Criminal War." *Journal of Conflict Resolution* 59 (8): 1486–1516.

Levi, Margaret. 1989. *Of Rule and Revenue*. Berkeley: University of California Press.

Levitt, Steven D., and Sudhir A. Venkatesh. 2000. "An Economic Analysis of a Drug-Selling Gang's Finances." *The Quarterly Journal of Economics* 115 (3): 755–789.

Lima, William da Silva. 1991. *Quatrocentos Contra Um: Uma História do Comando Vermelho*. Rio de Janeiro: ISER.

Lins, Paulo. 1997. *Cidade de Deus*. Rio de Janeiro: Companhia das Letras.

Long, William R. 1989. "Unlike Their Medellin Brethren, They Shun Open Violence." *Los Angeles Times*, August 17.

López Restrepo, Andrés. 2005. "Conflicto interno y narcotráfico entre 1970 y 2005." In *Narcotráfico en Colombia Economía y Violencia*. Bogotá: Fundación Seguridad y Democracia. 183–226.

López Restrepo, Andrés. 2006. "Narcotráfico, ilegalidad y conflicto en Colombia." In *Nuestra guerra sin nombre: transformaciones del conflicto en Colombia*, ed. W. Gutiérrez and S. Gómez. Bogotá: IEPRI. 405–440.

Lupsha, Peter A. 1991. "Drug Lords and Narco-Corruption: The Players Change But the Game Continues." *Crime, Law and Social Change* 16: 41–58.

Machado da Silva, Luiz Antônio, Márcia Pereira Leite, and Luis Carlos Fridman. 2005. *Matar, morrer, "civilizar": o "problema da segurança pública."* Rio de Janeiro: IBASE, Action Aid, Ford Foundation.

Magalhães, Maria Inez, Valdevino Diego, and Nicolás Satriano. 2015. "Policiais do Bope e do Choque entram e PMs de UPP deixam o Jacarezinho." *O Dia*, July 12.

Magaloni, Beatriz. 2005. "The Demise of Mexico's One-Party Dominant Regime." In *The Third Wave of Democratization in Latin America: Advances and Setbacks*, ed. Frances Hagopian and Scott P. Mainwaring. New York: Cambridge University Press. 121–148.

Mahoney, James. 2001. *The Legacies of Liberalism: Path Dependence and Political Regimes in Central America*. Baltimore: Johns Hopkins University Press.

Mahoney, James. 2006. "Path Dependence in Historical Sociology." *Theory and Society* 29 (4): 507–548.

Mampilly, Zachariah Cherian. 2011. *Rebel Rulers: Insurgent Governance and Civilian Life during War*. Ithaca: Cornell University Press.

Mann, Michael. 1986. "The Autonomous Power of the State: Its Origins, Mechanisms and Results." In *States in History*, ed. John A. Hall. Cambridge: Basil Blackwell. 109–136.

March, James G., and Johan P. Olsen. 1984. "The New Institutionalism: Organizational Factors in Political Life." *American Political Science Review* 78 (3): 734–749.

March, James G., and Johan P. Olsen. 2004. "The Logic of Appropriateness." *ARENA Working Papers* WP 04/09.

McCann, Bryan. 2013. *Hard Times in the Marvelous City: From Dictatorship to Democracy in the Favelas of Rio de Janeiro*. Durham, NC: Duke University Press.

Meiner, Stephen. 2009. *Central America: An Emerging Role in the Drug Trade*. Stratfor.

Mejía, Daniel, Juan Camilo Castillo, and Pascual Restrepo. 2013. "Illegal Drug Markets and Violence in Mexico: The Causes Beyond Calderón." Unpublished manusciapt, Universidad de los Andes.

Merino, José. 2011. "Los operativos conjuntos y la tasa de homicidios: Una medición." *Nexos*, June 1.

Milenio. 2010a. "Noviembre, el mes con menos muertes diarias." December 1.

Milenio. 2010b. "Un ejecutado cada hora durante 2009." January 2.

Milenio. 2011. "Declina en agosto número de ejecuciones ligadas al 'narco'." September 1.

Misse, Michel. 1997. "As ligações perigosas: mercado informal ilegal, narcotráfico e violência criminal no Rio." *Educação e Contemporaneidade* 1 (2): 93–116.

Misse, Michel. 1999. "O Movimento." Ph.D. Dissertation, Universidade Federal do Rio de Janeiro.

Misse, Michel. 2003. "O Movimento: A constituição e reprodução das redes do mercado informal ilegal de drogas a varejo no Rio de Janeiro e seus efeitos de violência." In *Drogas e Pós-modernidade*, ed. Marcos Baptista, M. S. Cruz, and R. Matias. Rio de Janeiro: UERJ. 147–156.

Misse, Michel. 2007. "Illegal Markets, Protection Rackets and Organized Crime in Rio de Janeiro." *Estudos Avançados* 21 (61): 139–157.

Mollison, James, and Rainbow Nelson. 2007. *The Memory of Pablo Escobar*. London: Chris Boot Ltd.

Morales, Natalia, and Santiago La Rotta. 2009. *Los Pepes: Desde Pablo Escobar hasta Don Berna, Macaco, y Don Mario*. Bogotá: Planeta.

Munck, Ronaldo, and Pumaka L. De Silva, eds. 2000. *Postmodern Insurgencies: Political Violence, Identity Formation, and Peacemaking in Comparative Perspective*. New York: Macmillan.

Muro, José. 2014. "SEDENA resiste 2 mil 935 ataques en 4 años." *Unión Jalisco*, March 18.

Myerson, Roger B. 2005. "Justice, Institutions, and Multiple Equilibria." *Chicago Journal of International Law* 5 (1): 91–108.

Myerson, Roger B. 2009. "Learning from Schelling's Strategy of Conflict." *Journal of Economic Literature* 47 (4): 1109–1125.

Nadelmann, Ethan A. 1990. "Global Prohibition Regimes: The Evolution of Norms in International Society." *International Organization* 44 (4): 479–526.

Nadelmann, Ethan A. 1993. *Cops Across Borders: The Internationalization of U.S. Criminal Law Enforcement*. University Park: Pennsylvania State University Press.

Navarro, Luis Hernández. 2010. "Joaquín Villalobos, el intelectual del calderonismo." *La Jornada*, January 26.

NDIC. 2009. *National Drug Threat Assessment 2009*. Washington, DC: US Department of Justice.

NDIC. 2010. *National Drug Threat Assessment 2010*. Washington, DC: US Department of Justice.

NDIC. 2011. *National Drug Threat Assessment 2011*. Washington, DC: US Department of Justice.

Needler, Martin C. 1961. "The Political Development of Mexico." *The American Political Science Review* 55 (2): 308–312.

Nissenbaum, Dion. 2010. "Afghan Poppy Harvest is Next Challenge for U.S. Marines." *McClatchy Newspapers*, March 21.

Notícias EFE. 2010. "El Gobierno mexicano condena el ataque contra jefa de la policía de Michoacán." April 24.

Novaes, Regina. 2003. "Polícia, polícias: as percepções dos jovens." *Comunicações do ISER2* 22 (58): 111–119.

ODCCP. 1999. *Global Illicit Drug Trends 1999*. New York: United Nations Office for Drug Control and Crime Prevention.

ODCCP. 2000a. *Global Illicit Drug Trends 2000*. New York: United Nations Office for Drug Control and Crime Prevention.

ODCCP. 2000b. *World Drug Report*. New York: United Nations Office for Drug Control and Crime Prevention.

O'Donnell, Guillermo A. 1993. "On the State, Democratization and Some Conceptual Problems: A Latin American View with Glances at Some Postcommunist Countries." *World Development* 21 (8): 1355–1369.

O Globo. 2005. "Testemunhas contestam versão da PM." December 6.

O Globo. 2015. "Policiais do Bope vazavam operações e vendiam armas para traficantes." December 1.

Olson, Mancur. 1965. *The Logic of Collective Action: Public Goods and the Theory of Groups*. Cambridge, MA: Harvard University Press.

Osorno, Diego Enrique. 2009. *El Cartel de Sinaloa: Una historia del uso político del narco*. Mexico City: Random House.

Pape, Robert A. 2003. "The Strategic Logic of Suicide Terrorism." *American Political Science Review* 97 (3): 343–361.

Pardo Rueda, Rafael. 1996. *De primera mano: Colombia 1986–1994, entre conflictos y esperanzas*. Bogotá: CEREC.

Pécaut, Daniel. 2006. *Crónica de cuatro décadas de politica colombiana*. Bogotá: Editorial Norma.

Penglase, Ben. 2005. "The Shutdown of Rio de Janeiro: The Poetics of Drug Trafficker Violence." *Anthropology Today* 21 (5): 3–6.

Penteado, Gilmar, André Caramante, and Cristiano Machado. 2006. "Cúpula do PCC Ordena Fim dos Ataques em SP." *Folha de S. Paulo*, May 16.

Pérez-Plá, María. 2007. "México usará experiencia de Colombia en lucha antinarco." *El Universal*, January 26.

Phillips, Tom. 2010. "Rio de Janeiro Police Occupy Slums as City Fights Back Against Drug Gangs." *Guardian*, April 4.

Pinheiro, Alvaro de Souza. 2009. *Irregular Warfare: Brazil's Fight Against Criminal Urban Guerrillas.* Hurlburt Field: Joint Special Operations University.

Pinheiro, Paulo Sérgio. 1997. "Violência, Crime e Sistemas Policiais em Países de Novas Democracias." *Tempo Social* 9 (1): 43–52.

Pinheiro, Paulo Sérgio. 2000. "Democratic Governance, Violence, and the (Un) Rule of Law." *Daedalus* 129 (2): 119–143.

Poiré, Alejandro, and María Teresa Martínez. 2011. "La caída de los capos no multiplica la violencia: El caso de Nacho Coronel." *Nexos*, May 1.

Poiré Romero, Alejandro. 2011. "El quinto mito." *Blog de la Presidencia*, July 4.

Poppa, Terrence E. 2010. *Drug Lord: The Life and Death of a Mexican Kingpin.* El Paso: Cinco Puntos Press.

Powell, Robert. 2002. "Bargaining Theory and International Conflict." *Annual Reviews in Political Science* 5 (1): 1–30.

Powell, Robert. 2004. "The Inefficient Use of Power: Costly Conflict with Complete Information." *American Political Science Review* 98 (2): 231–241.

Powell, Robert. 2006. "War as a Commitment Problem." *International Organization* 60 (1): 169–203.

Powell, Robert. 2012. "Persistent Fighting and Shifting Power." *American Journal of Political Science* 56 (3): 620–637.

Proceso. 2011. "Por cada narco detenido, 1.1 policías pierden la vida: SSP." July 11.

Rafael, Tony. 2007. *The Mexican Mafia.* New York: Encounter Books.

Rama, Anahí. 2010. "Ola violencia narco México podría durar años." *Reuters*, May 5.

Ramos, Silvia. 2016. "Violência e Polícia: Três Décadas de Políticas de Segurança no Rio de Janeiro." *Boletim Segurança e Cidadania*, March.

Reforma. 2009. "Arma 'La Familia' protesta antimilitar." April 21.

Reforma. 2013. "Crece en Veracruz el cártel de Los Zetas." May 20.

Reno, William. 1998. *Warlord Politics and African States.* Boulder: Lynne Rienner.

Reuter, Peter. 1995. "The Decline of the American Mafia." *Public Interest* 120: 89.

Reuter, Peter. 2009. "Systemic Violence in Drug Markets." *Crime, Law and Social Change* 52 (3): 275–284.

Reuter, Peter. 2013. "Drug Markets and Organized Crime." August: 1–15.

Reuter, Peter, and Victoria Greenfield. 2001. "Measuring Global Drug Markets: How Good Are the Numbers and Why Should We Care About Them?" *World Economics* 2 (4): 159–174.

Ribeiro, Camila, Rafael Dias, and Sandra S. Carvalho. 2008. *Discursos e práticas na construção de uma política de segurança: o caso do governo Sérgio Cabral Filho (2007–2008).* Rio de Janeiro: Justiça Global/Fundação Heinrich Böll.

Rodrik, Dani. 2013. "The Tyranny of Political Economy." *Project Syndicate*, February 8.

Romero, Vidal, Beatriz Magaloni, and Alberto Diaz-Cayeros. 2014. "Presidential Approval in Hard Times: Mexico's War on Crime." Paper presented at the American Political Science Association National Conference, Washington, DC, August 25.

Rose-Ackerman, Susan. 1975. "The Economics of Corruption." *Journal of Public Economics* 4 (2): 187–203.

Rose-Ackerman, Susan. 1978. *Corruption: A Study in Political Economy.* New York: Academic Press.

Rose-Ackerman, Susan. 2008. "Corruption." In *Readings in Public Choice and Constitutional Political Economy*, ed. Charles K. Rowley and Friedrich Schneider. New York: Springer. 551–556.

Rothstein, Bo, and Jan Teorell. 2008. "What is Quality of Government? A Theory of Impartial Government Institutions." *Governance* 21 (2): 165–190.

Saab, Bilal Y., and Alexandra W. Taylor. 2009. "Criminality and Armed Groups: A Comparative Study of FARC and Paramilitary Groups in Colombia." *Studies in Conflict and Terrorism* 32 (6): 455–475.

Sadowski, Yahya M. 1985. "Cadres, Guns and Money." *Middle East Research and Information Project Reports* 134 (July–August): 3–8.

Sadowski, Yahya M. 1987. "Patronage and the Ba'th: Corruption and Control in Contemporary Syria." *Arab Studies Quarterly* 9 (4): 442–461.

Salamanca, Alejandra Balcazar, and Fernando Gomez Garzon. 2003. *La Horrible Noche: La Fuga de Pablo Escobar*. Bogotá: Ediciones B.

Salazar, Alfonso. 2001. *La parábola de Pablo: auge y caída de un gran capo del narcotráfico*. Bogotá: Planeta Columbiana.

Sanín, F. G. and R. Stoller. 2001. "The Courtroom and the Bivouac: Reflections on Law and Violence in Colombia." *Latin American Perspectives* 28 (1): 56–72.

Sartori, Giovanni. 1970. "Concept Misformation in Comparative Politics." *American Political Science Review* 64 (4): 1033–1053.

Schedler, Andreas. 2013. "Mexico's Civil War Democracy." Paper prepared for presentation at the 109th Annual Meeting of the American Political Science Association, Chicago, August 30.

Schelling, Thomas C. 1960. *The Strategy of Conflict*. Cambridge, MA: Harvard University Press.

Schelling, Thomas C. 1966. *Arms and Influence*. New Haven: Yale University Press.

Schelling, Thomas C. 1967. "Economics and Criminal Enterprise." *The Public Interest* 7: 61–78.

Schickler, Eric. 2001. *Disjointed Pluralism: Institutional Innovation and the Development of the U.S. Congress*. Princeton: Princeton University Press.

Scott, James C. 1969a. "Corruption, Machine Politics, and Political Change." *American Political Science Review* 63 (4): 1142–1158.

Scott, James C. 1969b. "The Analysis of Corruption in Developing Nations." *Comparative Studies in Society and History* 11 (3): 315–341.

Scott, James C. 1972. *Comparative Political Corruption*. Englewood Cliffs: Prentice-Hall.

Semana. 1983. "Un Robin Hood Paisa." May 16.

Semana. 1986. "La Guerra es a Muerte." December 22.

Semana. 1987. "¿Quién mató al Coronel Ramírez?" April 13.

Semana. 1990. "Cumplirá Pablo Escobar?" February 19.

Serrano Cadena, Rosso José. 1999. *Jaque mate: de cómo la policía le ganó la partida a "El Ajedrecista" ya los carteles del narcotráfico*. Bogotá: Grupo Editorial Norma.

Shirk, David, and Viridiana Ríos. 2011. *Drug Violence in Mexico*. San Diego: Trans-Border Institute.

Shirk, David A., Kimberly Heinle, and Octavio R. Ferreira. 2014. *Drug Violence in Mexico: Data and Analysis Through 2013*. San Diego: Justice in Mexico.

Shirk, David A., Cory Molzahn, and Octavio R. Ferreira. 2013. *Drug Violence in Mexico: Data and Analysis Through 2012*. San Diego: Trans-Border Institute.

Silva, Eliana Sousa. 2009. "O contexto das práticas policiais nas favelas da Maré: a busca de novos caminhos a partir de seus protagonistas." Ph.D. dissertation, Pontifícia Universidade Católica do Rio de Janeiro.

Silva, Jailson de S. 2006. *Caminhada de crianças, adolescentes e jovens na rede do tráfico de drogas no varejo do Rio de Janeiro, 2004–2006*. Rio de Janeiro: Observatório das Favelas.

Simon, Jonathon. 2007. "Rise of the Carceral State." *Social Research* 74 (2): 471–508.

Skaperdas, Stergios. 2001. "The Political Economy of Organized Crime: Providing Protection When the State Does Not." *Economics of Governance* 2 (3): 173–202.

Slater, Dan. 2008. "Can Leviathan be Democratic? Competitive Elections, Robust Mass Politics, and State Infrastructural Power." *Studies in Comparative International Development* 43 (3–4): 252–272.

Slater, Dan. 2010a. *Ordering Power: Contentious Politics and Authoritarian Leviathans in Southeast Asia*. Cambridge: Cambridge University Press.

Slater, Dan. 2010b. "Review Article: The Art of Not Being Governed: An Anarchist History of Upland Southeast Asia, by James C. Scott." *Comparative Political Studies* 43 (11): 1527–1531.

SNSP. 2011. "Base de datos de fallecimentos." Sistema Nacional de Seguridad Pública.

Snyder, Richard, and Angelica Durán-Martínez. 2009a. "Does Illegality Breed Violence? Drug Trafficking and State-Sponsored Protection Rackets." *Crime, Law and Social Change* 52: 253–273.

Snyder, Richard, and Angelica Durán-Martínez. 2009b. "Drugs, Violence, and State-Sponsored Protection Rackets in Mexico and Colombia." *Colombia Internacional* 70 (July–December): 61–91.

Soares, Luiz Eduardo. 2000. *Meu casaco de general : 500 dias no front da segurança pública do Rio de Janerio*. Rio de Janeiro: Companhias das Letras.

Soares, Luiz Eduardo. 2011. "Além do bem e do mal na cidade sitiada." *Estado de S. Paulo*, November 2.

Soares, Luiz Eduardo, and João Trajano Sento-Sé. 2000. "Estado e segurança pública no Rio de Janeiro." Rio de Janeiro: UFRJ – Instituto de Economia.

Soares, Luiz Eduardo, M. V. Bill, and Celso Athayde. 2005. *Cabeça de porco*. Rio de Janeiro: Objetiva.

Soares, Ronaldo. 2007. "Sem hipocrisia." *Veja*, October 31.

Souza, Taiguara Libano e. 2010. "Constituição, Segurança Pública e Estado de Exceção Permanente: A Biopolítica dos Autos de Resistência." Ph.D. thesis, Pontífica Universidade Católica do Rio de Janeiro.

Spence, Michael. 2002. "Signaling in Retrospect and the Informational Structure of Markets." *The American Economic Review* 92 (3): 434–459.

SSP-RJ. 2003. "Anuário Estatístico do Núcleo de Pesquisa e Análise Criminal." Secretaria de Segurança Pública do Rio de Janeiro.

Stahlberg, Stephanie Gimenez. 2011. "The Pacification of Favelas in Rio de Janeiro." Paper presented at Mexican Security in Comparative Perspective Conference, Stanford University, February 22.

Staniland, Paul. 2012. "States, Insurgents, and Wartime Political Orders." *Perspectives on Politics* 10 (2): 243–264.

Staniland, Paul. 2015. "Militias, Ideology, and the State." *Journal of Conflict Resolution* 59 (7): 770–793.

Stille, Alexander. 1996. *Excellent Cadavers: The Mafia and the Death of the First Italian Republic.* New York: Random House.

Stillman, Sarah. 2013. "Taken." *New Yorker*, August 12.

Strong, Simon. 1995. *Whitewash: Pablo Escobar and the Cocaine Wars.* London: Macmillan.

Sullivan, John P. 2000. "Urban Gangs Evolving as Criminal Netwar Actors." *Small Wars & Insurgencies* 11 (1): 82–96.

Sullivan, John P., and Adam Elkus. 2008. "State of Siege: Mexico's Criminal Insurgency." *Small Wars Journal* 12.

Taylor, Brian D. 2011. *State Building in Putin's Russia: Policing and Coercion after Communism.* New York: Cambridge University Press.

Themnér, Lotta, and Peter Wallensteen. 2013. "Armed Conflicts, 1946–2012." *Journal of Peace Research* 50 (4): 509–521.

Thies, Cameron G. 2005. "War, Rivalry, and State Building in Latin America." *American Journal of Political Science* 49 (3): 451–465.

Thompson, Ginger. 2005. "Rival Drug Gangs Turn the Streets of Nuevo Laredo into a War Zone." *New York Times*, December 4.

Thoumi, Francisco E. 1995. *Political Economy and Illegal Drugs in Colombia.* Boulder: Lynne Rienner.

Thoumi, Francisco E. 2005. "The Numbers Game: Let's All Guess the Size of the Illegal Drug Industry." *Journal of Drug Issues* 35 (1): 185–200.

Tilly, Charles. 1985. "War Making and State Making as Organized Crime." In *Bringing the State Back In*, ed. Peter B. Evans, Dietrich Rueschemeyer, and Theda Skocpol. Cambridge: Cambridge University Press. 169–187.

Tiro, Roberto Jahaziel Reyes, and José Antonio O'Quinn Parrales. 2013. "La comunicación gubernamental de la guerra contra el narcotráfico en México." *Espacios Públicos* 16 (36): 55–75.

Tirole, Jean. 1996. "A Theory of Collective Reputations (With Applications to the Persistence of Corruption and to Firm Quality)." *The Review of Economic Studies* 63 (1): 1–22.

Tokatlián, Juan Gabriel. 2000. "La polemica sobre la legalizacion de drogas en Colombia, el Presidente Samper y los Estados Unidos." *Latin American Research Review* 35 (1): 37–83.

Trejo, Guillermo, and Sandra Ley. 2013. "Votes, Drugs, and Violence: Why Subnational Democratization Triggered Mexico's Inter-Cartel Wars." Unpublished manuscript.

Trejo, Guillermo, and Sandra Ley. 2016. "Why Did Drug Cartels Go to War in Mexico? Subnational Democratization, the Breakdown of Criminal Protection, and the Onset of Large-Scale Violence." Unpublished manuscript, University of Notre Dame-CIDE.

Turbiville, Graham H. 2010. "Firefights, Raids, and Assassinations: Tactical Forms of Cartel Violence and Their Underpinnings." *Small Wars & Insurgencies* 21 (1): 123–144.

UCDP. 2011. "UCDP/PRIO Armed Conflict Dataset Codebook Version 4-2011." Uppsala Conflict Data Program.

Ungar, Mark, and Enrique Desmond Arias. 2009. "Community Policing and Latin America's Citizen Security Crisis." *Comparative Politics* 41 (4): 409–429.

UNODC. 2003. *Global Illicit Drug Trends 2003*. New York: United Nations Office on Drugs and Crime.

UNODC. 2009. *Organized Crime and its Threat to Security: Tackling a Disturbing Consequence of Drug Control*. Vienna: United Nations Office on Drugs and Crime.

UNODC. 2010a. *The Globalization of Crime*. Vienna: United Nations Office on Drugs and Crime.

UNODC. 2010b. *World Drug Report 2010*. New York: United Nations Office on Drugs and Crime.

UNODC. 2014. *Global Study on Homicide 2013*. Vienna: United Nations Office on Drugs and Crime.

US Department of Justice. 2010. *National Drug Threat Assessment*. Washington, DC: National Drug Intelligence Center.

Valdés, Guillermo. 2013. *Historia del Narcotráfico en México*. Mexico City: Aguilar.

Valdés, Guillermo, and Alejandro Hope. 2013. "Significado de la Detención de 'El Zeta 40'." *Milenio*, July 19.

Verani, S. 1996. *Assassinatos em Nome da Lei: Uma Prática Ideológica do Direito Penal*. Rio de Janeiro: Aldebarã.

Villalobos, Joaquín. 2008. "México en guerra." *El Pais*, June 3.

Villalobos, Joaquín. 2010. "Doce mitos de la guerra contra el narco." *Nexos*, January 1.

Wacquant, Loic. 2003. "Toward a Dictatorship Over the Poor? Notes on the Penalization of Poverty in Brazil." *Punishment & Society* 5 (2): 197–205.

Wagner, R. Harrison. 1994. "Peace, War, and the Balance of Power." *American Political Science Review* 88 (3): 593–607.

Walter, Barbara F. 2009. "Bargaining Failures and Civil War." *Annual Review of Political Science* 12: 243–261.

Weinstein, Jeremy M. 2006. *Inside Rebellion: The Politics of Insurgent Violence*. New York: Cambridge University Press.

Werneck, Antônio. 2011. "Traficante Nem diz que metade do seu faturamento ia para policiais." *O Globo*, November 1.

Wood, Elizabeth J. 2001. "An Insurgent Path to Democracy: Popular Mobilization, Economic Interests, and Regime Transition in South Africa and El Salvador." *Comparative Political Studies* 34 (8): 862.

World Bank. 2011. *Crime and Violence in Central America: A Development Challenge*. Washington, DC: The World Bank.

Worrall, John L. 2001. "Addicted to the Drug War: The Role of Civil Asset Forfeiture as a Budgetary Necessity in Contemporary Law Enforcement." *Journal of Criminal Justice* 29 (3): 171–187.

Yashar, Deborah J. 1997. *Demanding Democracy: Reform and Reaction in Costa Rica and Guatemala, 1870s–1950s*. Presentation at UC Berkeley, May 14.

Zaluar, Alba. 1985. *A Máquina e a Revolta*. São Paulo: Brasiliense.

Zaluar, Alba. 1994. *Condomínio do Diabo*. Rio de Janeiro: Revan/UFRJ.

Index

Other Books in the Series *(continued from page ii)*

Herbert Kitschelt, *The Transformation of European Social Democracy*

Herbert Kitschelt, Kirk A. Hawkins, Juan Pablo Luna, Guillermo Rosas, and Elizabeth J. Zechmeister, *Latin American Party Systems*

Herbert Kitschelt, Peter Lange, Gary Marks, and John D. Stephens, eds., *Continuity and Change in Contemporary Capitalism*

Herbert Kitschelt, Zdenka Mansfeldova, Radek Markowski, and Gabor Toka, *Post-Communist Party Systems*

David Knoke, Franz Urban Pappi, Jeffrey Broadbent, and Yutaka Tsujinaka, eds., *Comparing Policy Networks*

Ken Kollman, *Perils of Centralization: Lessons from Church, State, and Corporation*

Allan Kornberg and Harold D. Clarke, *Citizens and Community: Political Support in a Representative Democracy*

Amie Kreppel, *The European Parliament and the Supranational Party System*

David D. Laitin, *Language Repertoires and State Construction in Africa*

Fabrice E. Lehoucq and Ivan Molina, *Stuffing the Ballot Box: Fraud, Electoral Reform, and Democratization in Costa Rica*

Mark Irving Lichbach and Alan S. Zuckerman, eds., *Comparative Politics: Rationality, Culture, and Structure, 2nd edition*

Evan Lieberman, *Race and Regionalism in the Politics of Taxation in Brazil and South Africa*

Richard M. Locke, *The Promise and Limits of Private Power: Promoting Labor Standards in a Global Economy*

Julia Lynch, *Age in the Welfare State: The Origins of Social Spending on Pensioner's Workers and Children*

Pauline Jones Luong, *Institutional Change and Political Continuity in Post-Soviet Central Asia*

Pauline Jones Luong and Erika Weinthal, *Oil is Not a Curse: Ownership Structure and Institutions in Soviet Successor States*

Doug McAdam, John McCarthy, and Mayer Zald, eds., *Comparative Perspectives on Social Movements*

Lauren M. MacLean, *Informal Institutions and Citizenship in Rural Africa: Risk and Reciprocity in Ghana and Côte d'Ivoire*

Beatriz Magaloni, *Voting for Autocracy: Hegemonic Party Survival and its Demise in Mexico*

James Mahoney, *Colonialism and Postcolonial Development: Spanish America in Comparative Perspective*

James Mahoney and Dietrich Rueschemeyer, eds., *Historical Analysis and the Social Sciences*

Scott Mainwaring and Matthew Soberg Shugart, eds., *Presidentialism and Democracy in Latin America*

Melanie Manion, *Information for Autocrats: Representation in Chinese Local Congresses*

Marc Howard Ross, *Cultural Contestation in Ethnic Conflict*

Roger Schoenman, *Networks and Institutions in Europe's Emerging Markets*

Ben Ross Schneider, *Hierarchical Capitalism in Latin America: Business, Labor, and the Challenges of Equitable Development*

Lyle Scruggs, *Sustaining Abundance: Environmental Performance in Industrial Democracies*

Jefferey M. Sellers, *Governing from Below: Urban Regions and the Global Economy*

Yossi Shain and Juan Linz, eds., *Interim Governments and Democratic Transitions*

Beverly Silver, *Forces of Labor: Workers' Movements and Globalization since 1870*

Theda Skocpol, *Social Revolutions in the Modern World*

Prerna Singh, *How Solidarity Works for Welfare: Subnationalism and Social Development in India*

Austin Smith et al, *Selected Works of Michael Wallerstein*

Regina Smyth, *Candidate Strategies and Electoral Competition in the Russian Federation: Democracy Without Foundation*

Richard Snyder, *Politics after Neoliberalism: Reregulation in Mexico*

David Stark and László Bruszt, *Postsocialist Pathways: Transforming Politics and Property in East Central Europe*

Sven Steinmo, *The Evolution of Modern States: Sweden, Japan, and the United States*

Sven Steinmo, Kathleen Thelen, and Frank Longstreth, eds., *Structuring Politics: Historical Institutionalism in Comparative Analysis*

Susan C. Stokes, *Mandates and Democracy: Neoliberalism by Surprise in Latin America*

Susan C. Stokes, ed., *Public Support for Market Reforms in New Democracies*

Susan C. Stokes , Thad Dunning , Marcelo Nazareno , and Valeria Brusco, *Brokers, Voters, and Clientelism: The Puzzle of Distributive Politics*

Milan W. Svolik, *The Politics of Authoritarian Rule*

Duane Swank, *Global Capital, Political Institutions, and Policy Change in Developed Welfare States*

Sidney Tarrow, *Power in Movement: Social Movements and Contentious Politics*

Sidney Tarrow, *Power in Movement: Social Movements and Contentious Politics, Revised and Updated Third Edition*

Tariq Thachil, *Elite Parties, Poor Voters: How Social Services Win Votes in India*

Kathleen Thelen, *How Institutions Evolve: The Political Economy of Skills in Germany, Britain, the United States, and Japan*